Principles of
Catholic Theology

BOOK 2

Principles of Catholic Theology

Book 2, *On the Rational Credibility of Christianity*

THOMAS JOSEPH WHITE, OP

The Catholic University of America Press
Washington, D.C.

Cataloging-in-Publication Data is available
from the Library of Congress
ISBN: 978-0-8132-3761-9
eISBN: 978-0-8132-3762-6

Contents

Preface

————:————

This second work, *Principles of Catholic Theology: Book Two: On the Rational Credibility of Christianity*, is a companion volume to the previously published *Book One: On the Nature of Theology*. While that volume considered the inner contours of Catholic theological reflection on divine revelation, this volume considers the natural rationality of Christian belief in divine revelation. This book, then, is composed of four interrelated parts pertaining to the reasonableness of Christianity. The first considers the problem of religious explanations of reality. Should one be open to the very idea of a religious understanding of the world we experience around us, and if so, what should we make of the claims of contemporary naturalistic atheism? Can one prefer one religious vision of reality over another reasonably, and should one take revelation seriously as a potential source for knowledge about reality? Does doing so lead necessarily to the compromise of one's intellectual integrity as a reasonable person?

The second part examines the related question of rational, demonstrative arguments for the existence of God and for the immaterial subsistence of the spiritual soul of the human person.

The third part examines the historical scriptural and patristic unfolding of the Church's basic Trinitarian claims. It argues that the very idea of the Trinity is contained historically in New Testament revelation, rightly understood by the early Catholic Church, and is logically coherent, as well as intrinsically interesting to natural philosophical reason, insofar as it claims to tell us something about the inner identity of God in himself that we could not otherwise know by natural reason but that is profoundly naturally desirable for us to know.

The fourth part considers the witness of Catholic saints philosophically, as a reason for natural motivation to treat Christian revelation with intellectual seriousness, so as to engage with it as a possibly true revelation. This last part also examines the philosophical grounds for our natural desire to see God, a desire that is met in a certain way by the Christian revelation of the beatific vision—the vision of God in his essence, which is made possible to human beings by grace.

A final coda in this work considers the challenge of Friedrich Nietzsche's criticism of Christianity and the question of a ground for truth, whether stated in philosophical or theological terms, in a supposedly postmodern epoch.

Principles of
Catholic Theology

---:---

A Brief Note on the Nature of Apologetics
Catholic Philosophical Argument as *Apologia*

The Latin term *apologia* signifies "defense," and it is used in a Christian theological context to denote an intellectual account of the Catholic faith in confrontation with cultured despisers. Prominent examples appear through Christian history, from Justin Martyr's two second-century letters of apologetics, to Augustine's *City of God*, to Aquinas's *Summa contra Gentiles*, to John Henry Newman's *Apologia pro Vita Sua*.

Nevertheless, it remains to be determined in the context of our considerations what precisely one is doing when one seeks to "defend" the Catholic faith by means of rational arguments. To be sure, one cannot seek to demonstrate the first principles or starting points of Christian belief merely by appeal to arguments from natural reason, for the articles of faith are received by way of divine revelation through the medium of scripture, tradition, and the living magisterium of the Catholic Church. One can only see into the truth of revelation and consent to its truth by means of grace, especially the grace of faith, informed by charitable love of God. A concerted defense of the Catholic faith that sought to demonstrate revealed first principles by direct appeal to prior starting points attained merely from natural reason would understandably soon fall under immediate

suspicion of crass rationalism. At the same time, if one cannot in any
way effectively demonstrate the reality indicated in mystery by the
symbol of faith (because intellectual contact with it is a gift), then
what is the point of proceeding to explain or defend the givens of
faith by means of rational argumentation?

As a prelude to the four sections of argument that follow, we can
respond to these queries succinctly in the form of three main points.

First, it is true that the content of divine revelation denoted
by the creed as a symbol of faith is supernatural in character and
thus intrinsically mysterious. "Mere" rational arguments, whether of a philosophical, scientific, or historical kind, are not sufficient
to demonstrate its reality, truth, or inner intelligibility. Knowledge
of the Trinity, for example, is acquired by the gift of grace, and it is
typically requested and received in prayer. It is not given to us as a
mere privilege of nature, like the capacity to learn mathematics or
gradually intuit the emotions of another person. Nevertheless, once
the mystery of God has been revealed, it is possible to orient natural reason toward a series of questions that pertain to truths *formally distinct* from those that are revealed, but logically compatible
with them. For example, one may rightly ask if natural reason is in
any way capable of coming to the knowledge, however indirect, of
the existence of God the Creator, who is the hidden mystery ontologically antecedent to the realities we perceive more immediately.
Likewise, one might ask if there is a way to argue philosophically toward the conclusion that the human soul is a subsistent immaterial
principle, one that by its nature cannot be subject to physical corruption in death in the way that the human body is. Can the philosopher speak to the question of whether the human soul continues
to exist after bodily death? Such questions emerge from within the
provenance of human nature. They press us to uncover certain and
secure premises of natural reason and to pass from these by means
of arguments through attempted demonstrations, so as to arrive at
sound and valid conclusions. Again, philosophical reflection of this
kind is natural, wholly native to the human intellect. However, these

same reasonings might be undertaken and sustained in the lives of particular individuals or cultures because of an antecedent spiritual sympathy for the Catholic religion, one that affects the native habits of the intellects and hearts of human persons due to their higher conformity to supernatural life, inspired inwardly by the theological virtues of faith, hope, and charity.

Second, we should also note that however great the influence of grace may be upon the inclinations of nature to consider the proper objects of rational knowledge allegedly in harmony with the truths of divine revelation, the natural reason of the human person still maintains its own specific autonomy with regard to its proper objects, initial starting points, modes of argument, and attitudes of prejudice, certitude, and doubt. A poor argument is a poor argument, even when it is dressed up in Christian regalia and imprudently promoted onto the field of argumentative battle, where it is sure soon to fall. But the generosity we accord reason in respecting its sharp contours when they doubt and probe at Christian teachings must also for consistency's sake be granted when reason is used in insightful and well-structured ways in philosophical modes that are of eventual service to the Catholic faith. There are not only highly intelligent ways of doubting the veracity of Christianity as divine revelation but highly intelligent ways of defending its rationality and veracity as well. The latter form of argumentation has to accomplish far less than the former, since it does not presume to demonstrate the supernatural truth of a divine revelation. Rather, it has merely to show that the claims of divine revelation in question need not stand in any settled and profound opposition to natural human reason. The atheist or religious skeptic, meanwhile, can set his or her sights at various levels of ambition, but typically to be effective, he or she must seek to refute the very possibility of rational religious belief, which is a much starker and ambitious, as well as less plausible, intellectual stance to take, when peering out honestly at the universe with the naivety that is requisite for anyone seeking to undertake an honest intellectual investigation of such a challenging subject.

Third and finally, then, the practice of apologetic reasoning has its own object or subject matter: it studies philosophical and historical truths that align closely with those of the Catholic faith, insofar as these former objects indicate the possibility of rational consent—that is, consent without harm to natural reason—to the supernatural faith. This "apologetic" form of reasoning does not procure the grace of faith in its practitioners or auditors but merely presupposes it either prior to, during, or after the time of the consideration of the arguments in question. This form of argument seeks, then, on the one hand, to demonstrate or argue reasonably for various things that can be observed or known according to nature and, on the other hand, merely to remove objections to the faith. It can do so by explicitly taking into account the claims of the Catholic faith so as to consider the inner intelligibility of the theological claims as such insofar as these are seen to be compatible or incompatible with natural human reason. This is distinct from the effort to demonstrate the truth of the faith, which natural reason cannot do, since it is only a prolongation of the effort to discern whether and how it is potentially permissible to embrace the Catholic faith without prejudice to human reason and in a way that stands in concord with the highest aspirations of human rationality in its search for truth in the domain of ultimate explanations.

Effectively, this is what we are seeking to explore in the four main parts of this book. The first considers the possibility of rational religious belief and concludes with a consideration of criteria for a genuinely reasonable form of religious belief in divine revelation. The second part considers various arguments for the existence of God and of the human soul as a spiritual principle bearing an immaterial likeness to God, particularly by means of the activities of intellect and volitional love. The third part considers the historical unfolding of the revelation of God as Trinity in the Old and New Testaments and the ways this idea was received and understood in the early Church. Is the notion of the Trinity one that is historically and conceptually coherent? That is to say, does it have a foundation in the ancient historical teachings of Christianity, or is it a later creation of the Church invented artificially and imposed on earlier texts that cannot in truth bear the weight of this subsequent dogmatic pronouncement? Likewise, is the very idea of God as a communion of persons who are one in being and essence an incoherent one, or is the revelation of the Trinity, if it is something genuine, of great profundity, such that it could have major implications for interpreting and explaining the meaning of human existence? In the fourth part, the last of these questions will be considered in greater precision. Why should we wish to understand the mystery of the Trinity? Can the human person naturally desire to see God? If so, does the revelation of the mystery of the Trinity speak, potentially, to the deepest aspirations of the human being insofar as he is a rational animal animated by the desire for the truth and the desire for happiness?

These four parts of our study on rational credibility serve primarily to demonstrate the possibility of rational consent to the Christian revelation of the mystery of God as Trinity. That is to say, our Christian consent to belief in the God of revelation—which is made possible only by way of supernatural grace—is not conducted in contradiction with natural reason. In addition, one may argue, as I will especially in part four, that the consent of faith is conducted in keeping with the ultimate and highest aims of natural reason. There is a certain degree of reasonable fittingness to the acceptance of the grace of faith, since the grace of faith—and the grace of the beatific vision to which it leads—answers to an innate desire in the human person for the fullness of the knowledge of the truth about God and for the fullness of happiness or beatitude. Even if arguments presenting the natural reasonableness and fittingness of consent to the grace of faith do not procure that grace as such, they do manifest, typically after the fact of consent, the profound harmony of grace and nature, of faith and reason, a harmony that grace itself helps to procure, structure, and fortify.

It is for this reason that I have arranged these arguments regarding the rational credibility of Christianity after those pertaining to the nature of theology made in book 1 of this series. The arguments made in this second book presuppose that there is a true revelation of God in prophetic and apostolic doctrine by which a nexus of mysteries is unveiled, and thus an intelligible truth about God as Trinity given to us to know by grace. This all occurs historically prior to our consideration of the rational warrant of the Christian religion or of ontological truth claims where natural reason and supernatural revelation come into deepest concord and alignment if not pure identity. Nevertheless, as I have noted above, natural reason has its own inherent starting points, ways of proceeding, and eventual destinations. Its own organic unfolding cannot be forced from without by violence, and even the sunlight of faith and the waters of inward grace must allow—and indeed stimulate—the life of natural reason to germinate, develop, and flower organically in its own ways. Consequently, in what follows, I seek to begin from an appropriately naïve and honest viewpoint of human natural reasoning, one that is attainable even from within the life of faith. In a certain sense, it is surprisingly easier to attain this stance of natural reasoning the longer one has studied theology, since theological study makes a person increasingly sensitive to the supernaturality of the object of faith as transcending natural understanding and so also augments a sense of the integrity of natural forms of reasoning as distinct from those based in the consideration of divine revelation. This does not mean my own aspirations to reason "merely naturally" are necessarily of universal value. They rightly aspire to be, and some should be, since human beings inevitably aim towards the knowledge of the universally true. However, we also do so in community with others, aided by one another through our mutual insights, despite our inevitable limitations and blindspots. As Newman famously said that "heart speaks to heart," so we might also add that "mind speaks to mind." In fact, all human beings who seek overtly to acquire existential orientation by means of human reasoning, despite its frailties, do speak to one another, especially when we collaborate in the pursuit of common insights, but also even when we reach distinct conclusions or reach the same conclusions in distinct ways. All who seek light are fellow travelers, pilgrims across the narrow bridge of time, staring above at the abyss of eternity, seeking to discern the inscape of the heavens. In that sense, our common efforts are mutually supportive and salutary, and it is in keeping with the latter sentiment that I undertake what follows.

1

Why Not Be an Atheist?

The Enigma of Human Existence and the Question of Reasonable Religious Belief

Everyone faces questions of ultimate explanation at some point in life. Why do human beings exist? Can there be a religious meaning to our lives in this world? Does an atheistic outlook constitute the more or the less reasonable stance when it comes to religious questions? Does God exist, and is God personal? Can we know God personally? Can we reasonably trust religious traditions or purported revelations to give us guidance in these matters? Do human persons have a destiny in the life to come?

These are classical questions in the European intellectual tradition. However, in the contemporary world there are distinct challenges and collective hesitations when these questions are raised in a serious way, especially within the academy. The natural sciences have given rise to an explosion of new learning in the last few centuries, spurring new forms of technological and medical advancement. Still, many also now wonder if the human race has evolved merely as a result of chance. Have we achieved scientific enlightenment only to discover that we are a mere cosmic accident that exists in vain? Prominent agnostic philosophies promote religious skepticism under the auspices of intellectual humility. "The wise person retreats from ultimate questions." Technology has fueled a globalized, more economically united society, but our knowledge of various cultures and religions has also raised serious questions about pluralism: are there simply many incompatible religions, worldviews, and ethical systems? Are all appeals to the truth arbitrary opinions promoted by various interest groups, whether political, cultural, or religious? Is every perspective on truth merely relative to every other, without any abiding transcendent or external criteria by which to judge them?

In this new context we rightly can appeal to the Christian intellectual tradition, which claims that the revelation of the Trinity affords the ultimate light on human creatures. In the beginning there is God, who is a mystery of *Logos* (truth) and *Agape* (divine love), an eternal communion of persons: the Father, his eternally emanating Word, and his eternally proceeding Spirit, who is Love. In light of this revelation and its claims, then, reality is personal from top to bottom. Human beings are persons made in the image of God, beings of truth and love, created to flourish in communion with God and one another. How can this traditional vision of ultimate reality—God as Trinity and human beings as persons destined for communion with God—be put in constructive engagement with the modern queries of our contemporaries, who are affected by materialistic intuitions, skeptical trends of thinking, and the quandaries of cultural pluralism?

The first half of this book is about the reasonableness of belief in God. Here "belief" can refer to both philosophical conviction and consent to divine revelation. In what sense can God be known reasonably by means of natural philosophical understanding, and in what sense is God a mystery known only by means of divine revelation? I will argue that we can know of God by both philosophical reason and faith in revelation. These two ways of knowing God are compatible and complementary, since revelation takes us further than philosophy, while philosophy keeps our appeals to revelation and religious practice grounded in something reasonable and intellectually responsible. After, all, we can rightly ask, "Is it reasonable to believe in divine revelation, and if so, in what sense?" This question is acutely important, especially if God is precisely a mystery unveiled to us by a form of knowledge given freely by grace. Are all religious traditions deserving of equal respect—or indeed should we even respect religious claims, philosophically speaking? How might we adjudicate between the diverse metaphysical and religious visions of the world so as to make a humane and ethically well-founded discernment of these issues? In this opening chapter, I begin by thinking constructively about points of departure and the nature of reality as it presents itself to us in ordinary experience. Is the world around us susceptible to a religious explanation, and if so, in what sense?

POSING QUESTIONS ABOUT ULTIMATE EXPLANATIONS

The human condition is enigmatic and mysterious. Most of the time, we give little reflection to this fundamental truth. Instead, we commute, work, enjoy friendships, and rejoice in or suffer from the events that make up our lives. Rarely do we acknowledge the simple gratuity and strangeness of our existence. We have being, we exist, in a strange and numinous world. Why is that the case? And why are we alone among all the other living things—microorganisms, plants, animals—so clearly aware of our existence, as cognitive, volitional creatures? Should we do something with this responsibility? What could we do? Does reflection on the question of why we exist have any real practical bearing on our life, and does our thinking about this question really affect the development of our character? Have human beings come to exist by mere chance or for a reason? Or are all our theories on the matter only intellectual postures concealing from us the (potentially devastating or liberating) truth that we exist for no reason at all? Can we expect only modest goods and aims out of life? Can any real explanation be obtained?

We largely ignore these questions about the enigmatic character of our existence, and even innocently so. Most days we have many meaningful or at least desirable things to do that stand well within the horizon of our understanding and touch directly upon our practical well-being and happiness. The mystery of our ultimate origins seems to lie at a far horizon, like the darkness at the edge of a lighted space. It exists for us more as a kind of absence than a presence, but it is one that beckons us all the same, like a contrast of obscurity in comparison to what is before us clearly at hand. One might complain with annoyance: if there is an *ultimate* reason for our being alive—for our seeking the truth, desiring happiness, and wanting to love—shouldn't it be more manifest? There should be unassailable evidence of it. God should speak directly to us, in a human voice, or even come down and manifest himself openly. But here we come back to the question of divine revelation: does God speak and has God even become human? If he has, why would such questions as those we have just posed even remain open questions?

One can just shut down the questions and declare them unanswerable. Nevertheless, this simple kind of resignation seems like an impoverishing option. The human being, after all, is able to seek the truth and is in a sense characterized by being a truth-seeker, a questioner, as children continually demonstrate to their parents. Human beings investigate causes in the world, in science, history, and political life. Can we not do so metaphysically as well, by speaking about the causes of the world? In that sense, resignation seems like a capitulation to intellectual despair or *acedia*, that is, a resignation that comes from sadness and lack of desire. Or perhaps there is in us all a deep temptation to overt anti-intellectualism. Some might say that instead of questioning everything, we should simply find the truth of our own lives within ourselves, perhaps in a way that is different from and ultimately unassailable by anyone else. In this way, it is hoped, we can avoid the danger of alienation, of being told what we are by others who do not really know us.

Yet, we have to observe how easily this culture of individual

12Why Not Be an Atheist?

authenticity, summarized by the phrase "you can decide the meaning of your own life," fits in fact into a consumerist model that would have us choose our meanings from a culturally prescribed menu— not only of food or clothing, but our very philosophy of life. How often does this metaphysical individualism really mean having the truth of our lives dictated to us by the fashions of the day and otherwise drowning our sorrows in the life of the senses? However, this is not what is best in us. The search for the truth, the life of the mind, is what is most vital to the human person, a being able to find answers, to be inventive, to come to deeper understanding, and to resolve crises and make good judgments. When we distinguish what is real from what is false, we become more ourselves and especially ourselves. We come into the truth, not our own private, personal "truth," but a truth that in principle can be shared with and appreciated by all. We contemplate the truth, and we become loving agents of the truth in our life with others. Hence, coming to right judgments about what is ultimately real affects in turn who we are or who we become. Making judgments about the truth is central to the dignity of the human person, and it is key to what makes a person an intellectual being. The human being is inevitably distinct from all the other animals because it is the truth-seeking animal.

In addition, making a judgment about ultimate things is, in fact, eminently practical. We do basically live instinctively in light of what we take to be most ultimately real. The person who suspects that atheism is true, perhaps because he presupposes that all of reality is merely material and that biological life arose principally by chance processes of cosmic history, will also be affected by this judgment (in a variety of possible ways) in ethical decision making. A person who seeks to live according to the teachings of Islam enshrined in the Quran and Hadith will in turn act very differently from the atheist. This is also the case for the person who suspends judgment about such matters and accepts agnosticism, deciding to seek happiness in this world alone. Ideas have consequences in each case. We would be terribly naïve to think that our intuitions, our gut instincts about ultimate things, fail to affect our behavior. We all have such intuitions, and they inevitably affect at least some of the main choices we make in life or the key choices we choose not to make.

Searching for an Unknown First Principle

Nevertheless, coming to any sharp convictions is a daunting task. The road seems fraught, and many have trod it before us, returning only to paint vivid pictures of different and incompatible landscapes. If diverse metaphysical and religious visions of reality were each distinct books, there would be entire libraries available to us of considerable size. Still, in the midst of this diversity, we can make some broad distinctions. First, we can ask whether the ultimate explanation of reality is materialistic or immaterial? For example, is everything that exists merely physical and material in the end, or do we need to "explain" the world by reference to something that transcends the material world, which we can call God? If the latter is a real source of explanation, is God the form or first immanent cause of the material world (in virtue of a kind of pantheism), or is God distinct from the corporeal and visible world, and if so, in what way? In the latter case, is what we call "God" a mystery that is personal or non-personal? Do we become more personal as we grow closer to God, or do we instead understand our human temporal personality as by and large a kind of illusion, one we need to shed if we are to live truthfully in light of what is ultimately real? Is personal identity something that comes from God and is stable in us, or is it ontologically superficial, an illusion and a practical hindrance that keeps us from recognizing God? And so, if God is non-personal, or transcends human personal identity, what are we to make of human personhood, and how do we explain it in light of the transcendent non-anthropomorphic first cause of all things? If we claim, by contrast, that God is somehow "personal," by analogy or similitude with created persons, how do we avoid the notion that our understanding of God is anthropomorphic? And if God is a personal Creator, how is God distinct from the world yet present to the world?

Or is God personal and present but indifferent to us, in which case God seems morally ambivalent to human suffering? This idea of God as omnipresent but indifferent seems particularly absurd, so it sends us back to the possibility of atheism. After all, a God who is present everywhere but who is basically unable or unwilling to confront the suffering and evil that all human beings experience may seem like no God at all. But perhaps God is the cause of all things and is unfathomably good and is present in all we experience as the source of all things. In this case, can we arrive at such a conviction about God exclusively by means of natural human reason—by approaching God uniquely as the God of the philosophers, so to speak—or can we also know God by means of human religious traditions that teach us spiritual disciplines for encountering God, or can we know God by means of authentic divine revelation, and if so, which claimant to divine revelation should we entrust ourselves to? Or do we know God by some combination of these? Let us consider some of these questions briefly, not so as to immediately resolve the questions superficially in a few pages, but merely so as to get a better sense of what is at stake.

Materialistic First Principles: In the Beginning Was a Material Plurality

Upon reflection, it can seem most reasonable, simplest, and most intellectually elegant to posit that all that exists is in some way "merely" material. Indeed, there is no transcendent reality, whether the *Brahman* deity of the Hindu Upanishads (God who is in some way one with the world) or the transcendent primal emptiness of Buddhist metaphysics (all things emerge from and return to the state of *Nirvana* which transcends all personality and desire) or the mysterious and unknown Creator of traditional Christianity (John 1:1: "In the beginning was the Word, and the Word was with God, and the Word was God."). On this view, in the beginning and in the end, there are only material entities and the cosmic processes that they give rise to or emerge from. Informed by the advances of modern physics and biology, proponents of this view tend to tell a story of material change and development from the Big Bang some 14 billion years ago to the emergence of organic matter on earth to the formulation of DNA in single cell bacteria some 4 billion years ago, marked by the processes we conventionally call life and reproduction. The drive toward reproduction inevitably produced genetic variation in living beings—initially single-celled organisms—and this process set up the conditions for the process of genetic recombination to take place, through which traits emerged in living things that were more advantageous to the survival of some individuals than others, which in turn eventually gave rise to new species. Some species possessed traits that were more advantageous than others, and various species also became symbiotic in the sense that they possessed traits that helped them survive either in dependence on or in opposition to others. The survival of the fittest individuals, and the species to which they gave rise over time, took place through the incorporation of genetically advantageous mutations (through chance alterations) and the adaptational attributes they helped produce. In the course of billions of years this process gave rise to more sophisticated (multi-celled and organically diversified) creatures with new capacities, including multiple sense organs and memory powers, capable of learning.[1] In time there came into being what scientists call *homo sapiens,* the first human beings, who have capacities of self-awareness, cognitive reflection, and deliberate choice-making. These features of the human personality can be hypothesized to emerge from our more sophisticated biological capabilities—the evolutionary development of human neurological processes. The emergence of human life can be explained, then, without reference to any transcendent or immaterial cause or workings of divine providence. There is no ultimate religious or immaterial "meaning" as to why the cosmos has developed or life

1. For a concise and clear overview of contemporary cosmology and evolutionary theory, see Robert N. Bellah, *Religion in Human Evolution: From the Paleolithic to the Axial Age* (Cambridge, MA: Belknap Harvard Press, 2011), 44–74.

has evolved the way it has, either as regards our first metaphysical origins or our ultimate final purposes, no "whence" or "why" beyond the mere brute fact of our existence.[2] We can explore the meaning, value, and appreciation of human life in a genuine way, but we should seek to do so within the framework of our immanent biological life and the human community in history to which it gives rise. Human existence understood in this sense is truly a "gift" precisely because it has the gratuity of having come about felicitously in an unintended way, and it can be enjoyed for a time (aesthetically, morally, and even in a very limited sense "religiously") and eventually relinquished without regret or resentment.[3]

There is undoubtedly a theoretical coherence to this viewpoint, first and foremost because it seeks to explain everything by reference to the material substructures of the physical world as they are manifest to the senses and studied by the gradual progress of the modern sciences. The claim that everything we experience is reducible to material particles and forces, chemical compounds and cells, and

2. The idea arguably finds its first forceful articulation in western philosophy in the works of Spinoza. See the argument to this effect by Jonathan Israel, *Radical Enlightenment: Philosophy and the Making of Modernity 1650-1750* (Oxford: Oxford University Press, 2002). In a 1948 BBC radio debate with Copleston, Bertrand Russell famously affirmed that, as an atheist materialist, he accepted as a principal presupposition that the material universe must just exist and that it needs no causal explanation. Kant develops a more systematically agnostic line of thinking in the *Critique of Pure Reason* (A592/B620–A625/B651) [trans. N. K. Smith (New York: St. Martin's Press, 1965)] by arguing that attempts to demonstrate immaterial causes of physical states are impossible, given the natural constraints of our metaphysical reasoning, which cannot transpose notions of causality beyond material states. Consequently, any such form of argument ends in irresolution, characterized by inherently incoherent conceptual antinomies. One finds parallels in the thought of some modern physicists. Stephen Hawking in *A Brief History of Time* (New York: Bantam, 1998) seeks to depict cosmic history in such a way that the historical development of the universe—Big Bang cosmology—stems from a given mere fact of material existence and its "initial" laws, which in turn are generative of the universe.

3. Materialistic philosophical interpretations of evolutionary history and of the emergence of human knowledge are presented by a variety of thinkers such as Ernst Mayer in *What Evolution Is* (New York: Basic Books, 2002); Daniel C. Dennett, *Darwin's Dangerous Idea: Evolution and the Meanings of Life* (New York: Simon & Schuster, 1996); Peter Godfrey-Smith, *Other Minds: The Octopus and the Evolution of Intelligent Life* (New York: Harper Collins, 2017).

organic living bodies and the interactions between species of living things certainly does have something simple about it. Indeed, one might go further than what has been suggested above and claim that all biological organic and cellular processes are ultimately explained by chemical and molecular processes, and that these in turn are explained by physical material component parts and physical forces. In this case, modern physics is a kind of "first philosophy" that seeks to explain all else. Once we understand the laws of physics and the most basic particles and forces of matter, we can explain all else that is. Nor is the attempt to find simple primary explanations of reality a mere hobgoblin of lesser minds (as Nietzsche claimed but which he also sought to undertake himself in the field of ethics). On the contrary, when we encounter complex realities that are interrelated and mutually determined by one another, often within a complex history, we naturally desire to explain them or understand them more adequately by finding the unity and causation that underlies their complexity. This is true whether one speaks of complex interrelated processes in matter, in living things, or in human interactions in history and politics. When we seek to figure out why a thing or process occurs regularly or has occurred singularly, we seek to find its causal origins and wish to explain the overarching or undergirding source of the complexity in question.

However, we might also observe that the seeming simplicity-of-explanation of the kind of modern materialism we have been considering is also more illusory than real. Yes, the materialistic hypothesis does exhibit a certain degree of metaphysical parsimony that bodes well for the candidature of a simple, overarching explanation of all things: there is only matter and no other principle. However, when we begin to think about the contours of this theory—its logical conditions, its metaphysical presuppositions and entailments—more complex and unresolved questions emerge. We should note some of them, not so as to dismiss the thesis of contemporary scientistic materialism superficially but in order to consider more deeply what implicit commitments it entails as an intellectual option.

A first problem arises from the notion of the one and the many. It is true that the view we have been considering seeks to explain many physical things and their vast cosmic history by reference to a numerically small set of realities and a most narrow set of processes and "laws" that obtain between them: DNA can be used to explain living things, atomic particles and forces can be used to explain material things (including living ones), forces and their histories can be used to explain the "pre-history" of atoms, etc. Thus, a great multitude of diverse things is seemingly understood by reducing them to simpler constituent parts. Nevertheless, this still leaves us with an irreducible multiplicity of entities and forces, such as the diverse atomic particles and the forces that move them. The order that is exhibited within and among these most primeval elements is considered properly basic: it must be presupposed on some level as something complex that is irreducible and not explained by reference to something further. There just is a universe of initial forces and particles that gives rise to subsequent degrees of complexity, and that itself is a primeval given. Some difficulties follow from this, however, since legitimate questions inevitably remain. What is the reason that such a complex set of beings exists in the first place? Why is there intelligible order within these primeval given realities that is properly basic, such as the atomic structures of physical reality, the laws of their interaction, or the forces that give rise to their inter-relations? And why is there such an order between these realities that there can emerge from them over time other realities with greater degrees of complexity? Why does the universe evolve instead of remaining simpler and more static? Why did atomic structures come about after the Big Bang? Is such a question about ultimate causal reasons for cosmic development even legitimate if the cosmos is all that exists without reference to anything beyond itself? And if there is a legitimate question of why such evolving degrees of complexity exist, is it possible that the most basic things will further develop and that we have not yet reached an ultimate omega point of evolution? The facticity of such complexity, as well as its complex order and intelligibility,[4] raises the question of whether there is something yet more primary in the universe giving rise to the physical cosmos or existing in transcendence behind the veil of matter.[5] Is it possible

4. On essence and identity in non-living material entities, including atoms and chemical compounds, see David S. Oderberg, *Real Essentialism* (London and New York: Routledge, 2007), 86–120; William A. Wallace, *The Modeling of Nature: Philosophy of Science and Philosophy of Nature in Synthesis* (Washington, DC: The Catholic University of America Press, 1996), 35–75.

5. Thorough-going materialism entails necessarily that there is some form of ontological pluralism that is absolutely primary and irreducible in reality. In the beginning, there were many material things of differing kinds and of differing number. This is true, for example, of the atomic structures discovered by modern physics or the particles and forces that gave rise to them. Or if we move up a level, it is true of the chemical compounds represented by the periodic table or of the genetic structures of DNA studied in modern biology. We can attempt to reduce all of these realities to the atomic particles as basic, but in the end, we have to posit that there "just are" diverse atomic structures as a basis for the history of the universe and that they "just fell together" in complex forms of order so as to permit chemical and ultimately biological realities to emerge that are more complex. The material diversity is properly basic. Even if we posit that complex atomic properties in matter arose from a more primordial state at the Big Bang and in the ensuing cosmos of the early period, there is some kind of composition at work in that epoch that gave rise to our own more proximate one, and we cannot entirely discount the hypothesis of a previous epoch before that of the Big Bang, in which case there is also a chronological composition of era, in which the material cosmos undergoes successive waves of expansion and contraction, a process that is metaphysically complex to be sure. This means there are various first principles (whether one considers what is first to be merely at the atomic level or one adds the "higher" orders to them), and they simply exist as something properly given. The order between physical beings and physical forces and the "laws" or patterns that govern their interaction "just are." This claim is not metaphysically parsimonious or simple. It does not explain anything as to why this original multiplicity exists in the form it does but just states it as a fact (or starting hypothesis) so as to explain everything else in light of these diverse first principles. Furthermore, in any account of pure materialism, no matter what cosmic history we allude to, we must simply presuppose the existence of material things. They are always already there and always already capable of some kind of mutual engagement and interaction that produces change. No explanation of their being is forthcoming, nor is it considered warranted. Histories of things "coming into being spontaneously from nothing" do very little to help the case for this kind of philosophy, because if one really means by "nothingness" the sheer absence of being, then there is nothing "there" to exert causality in the first place and consequently no sufficient explanation of existent things can be obtained. See in this regard Lawrence M. Krauss, *A Universe from Nothing: Why There Is Something Rather Than Nothing* (New York: Free Press, 2012). Krauss is a scientist and a kind of philosophical positivist whose argument is characterized by a problematic equivocation in the use of the term "nothingness." In using this term in equivocal senses, he confuses a distinctively metaphysical notion of "nothingness" (as the sheer absence of being) with physical theories

that we have not yet reached a simpler and most ultimate explanation for why we inhabit the kind of physical universe we do?

Second, the presence and developmental emergence of various forms of order in the natural and material world does not seem to be explained uniquely or sufficiently by appeal to chance.[6] Chance, as Aristotle noted, is not a proper cause found in natural realities— one of their essential features, typical properties, or proportionate effects they produce. Aristotle famously speaks of four explanatory causes in things: those pertaining to form, matter, origin, and teleology. If we think of a modern artifact like an automobile, the form is the whole dynamic automobile that is constituted by a wealth of material parts (the matter) and their composite natural substances. The origin of the car is the designer team, engineers, industrial producers, and artisans. The end or purpose is the function of the automobile, the safe and humane conduit of persons from one place to another in accord with their intentions. These various causes can explain a great deal about a car, in what it is and does, and in what ways it can fail. But none of them per se can explain various forms of traffic accidents, if and when one vehicle collides with another due to

___

in which there is posited no quantifiable data prior to the emergence of quantifiable data (the absence of measurable quantity internal to a scientific theory). The former idea denotes something that in reality does not and could not exist—a state of affairs in which nothing existed, from which, necessarily, nothing could come to be. The latter denotes an epistemological marker within a scientific framework for interpreting data, in which the presence of quantifiable data can arise temporally subsequent to a state in which there previously was none. Basically, this is the idea of nothingness as a "placeholder" in a theory of modern particle physics, and if physics can discuss it at all (which evidently Krauss believes), then it is related to quantifiable matter. Since the natural sciences are conducted by intrinsic dependency upon mathematics and the measurable and therefore by reference to quantifiable data derived from material reality, they cannot by definition attain to any knowledge of "nothingness" properly denoted. However, anything that does not fall within the realm of positivistic notions of science can mistakenly be taken to be "nothing" by the positivist.

6. Metaphysical accounts of evolution that stress strongly the significant role of "chance" or random selection as the source of evolutionary development and distinctively human traits are found in works like Jacques Monod, *Chance and Necessity: An Essay on the Natural Philosophy of Modern Biology*, trans. A. Wainhouse (New York: Vintage, 1992); Richard Dawkins, *The Blind Watchmaker: Why the Evidence of Evolution Reveals a Universe Without Design* (New York: W.W. Norton & Co., 1996).

two drivers navigating the same space at the same time in a parking lot or road, perhaps even without fault on either side. The collision of two vehicles by chance can have major effects on persons and objects in the universe, so the effects of car accidents are very real, but the effects still happen randomly when seen from the perspective of the typical natural causes and designated purposes of the car.

We could use a similar example for natural entities. Strands of DNA combine in novel ways each time a new mammal is conceived from two parent ancestors, male and female, which contribute the genetic material of sperm and egg respectively. That the DNA should recombine in new ways and as a result produce diverse natural traits is to some extent a matter of chance, since the natural dispositions of various strands of DNA to produce this or that proper effect in combination with another variable strand can produce a huge variety of outcomes. These outcomes depend upon the matching genetic material of the various individuals a given parent mates with and thus the diverse eggs or sperm that come together to produce a new individual, as well as numerous factors in the genetic recombination process. That this individual with this DNA or that individual with that DNA should come to be in each instance from such reproductive processes and that these or those traits should emerge is not determined only by the consideration of any individual mammal or its individual genetic material but occurs in virtue of a larger process of transmission of life in which chance encounters of male and female progenitors and chance recombinations of DNA produce new individuals and sometimes significantly novel outcomes.

We can also give an example from the rationally deliberate, free decisions of persons. One human being might go to university with the intention of studying for a higher degree, while another goes there for the same reason, and the two have never met nor intend to meet, but their particular meeting might be fateful and lead, for example, to marriage, or a religious vocation, or a fateful business venture, or homicide, or some combination of the above. Many significant historical events arise by chance in this way.

Chance is, then, precisely that form of occasional event that occurs between realities and falls outside the spectrum of their essential natures, properties, and naturally ordered processes—the inalienable characteristic traits and effects they typically produce in accord with their nature. Let us define chance events, then, as unintended, accidental effects produced from natural (ordered and predictable) lines of interaction between distinct causal agents.[7] Chance events among natural, human, and artifactual entities lead to unpredictable interactions and alternations, ones that can even alter the natures of things, especially if one considers the evolution of natural species. On this view, chance events are indeed something real, but they also only make sense (and indeed are only even intelligible to us as chance events) against the backdrop of a prior existent order of recurrent natural kinds, properties, actions, and outcomes. The deer naturally tends to nourish and protect itself, while the wolf naturally preys on the deer. The encounter between the two—in which one dies and the other lives, or one evades the other due to superior speed—is a matter of chance, not because there are not natural explanations for the outcomes but because the encounter of this one here with that one there leads to outcomes that could not be predicted by simple consideration of one or the other individually or of their respective kinds considered essentially. We can understand, then, the mutations of DNA and their outcomes either before or

7. Aristotle, *Physics* II, c. 4–6 (195b31–198a13). In chapter 4, Aristotle considers opinions of philosophers regarding chance, including those who think chance events are the primary causes of the universe. He goes on in chapters 5–6 to distinguish chance, which he defines as something proper to unforeseen outcomes of human free agents, from "spontaneity," which he defines as accidental outcomes produced from the interactions of natural, non-voluntary agents. In both cases—natural free agents and natural non-rational agents—activity presupposes natural forms of behavior that produce predictable outcomes and happen by nature always or for the most part. This kind of natural intelligibility is the presupposition of all our predictions about ordinary outcomes and thus also provides the condition for our identification of accidental causes. Chance or spontaneous outcomes occur as the result of "accidental causes," as when a man randomly meets a friend at the store unexpectedly (that is not why he intended to go to the store) or a dog avoids a house fire because it went outside hours before to chase a bird (it did not intend to avoid the fire).

after the fact, but we cannot predict or know comprehensively when and how DNA will undergo mutations in new individuals, even as we cannot predict comprehensively how larger population groups of a given species will survive, thrive, or perish under the pressures of larger ecosystems within reality.

So if chance events do occur and are consequential, this is a reminder that the causal order found in any given natural entity or set of entities is more fundamental in reality. Before there is chance, there is natural order, and chance events, which are real, presuppose the deeper natural order in the realities that are subject to chance events. At the same time, naturally ordered realities must interact with and be affected by other natural realities, sometimes at random or by chance. Seen in this light, every chance event comes to pass only ever within a deeper order of nature that precedes such an event and is a prior metaphysical condition for its possibility.[8] Without order there is no chance.

This fact suggests that no reality subject to random alteration by others is perfectly explained ontologically by reference to itself. Why is this the case? Chance events do presuppose some more fundamental pattern of order, and by that very fact they point us back to

8. That is to say, chance events happen to natural agents but presuppose the existence of natural order (as proper causality) as a prior condition for their emergence (by what Aristotle terms "accidental causality"). Aristotle draws the logical conclusion:

> Spontaneity and chance are causes of effects which, though they might result from intelligence or nature, have in fact been caused by something accidentally. Now since nothing which is accidental is prior to what is *per se*, it is clear that no accidental cause can be prior to a cause *per se*. Spontaneity and chance, therefore, are posterior to intelligence and nature. Hence, however true it may be that the heavens are due to spontaneity, it will still be true that intelligence and nature will be prior causes of this universe and of many things in it besides. (*Physics II*, 198a5-13.)

The "intelligence" in question denotes the rational agency of man that is at the heart of human history even as chance events occur to free agents, but it also denotes the immanent intelligibility of natural form that is found in non-rational realities and is the basis for the philosophical intelligibility of the world. [All citations from Aristotle are taken from *The Complete Works of Aristotle*, ed. J. Barnes (Princeton, NJ: Princeton University Press, 1984).]

a natural order that precedes chance, as we have already noted. But they also invite us to note simultaneously *certain limits of natural order*. After all, when ordered realities (human, natural, or artificial) are subject to random or chance events that can deeply alter their properties or perhaps even their natures, then these various realities and the orders embodied in them cannot be said to be entirely ontologically necessary or immutable. If they possess order within themselves, that order is nonetheless not so stable as to be perennially, ahistorically stable or somehow self-caused or self-maintaining. This raises the question of whether the order in question and the history of random occurrences that unfolds within the ordered pattern of the natural world are in fact derived from a higher source of understanding from which the order of nature and its history of random or chance events are utterly derivative.

Even if this is the case, however, we can and must say that chance events between realities we observe occur "outside the spectrum" of predictable natural order, inclination, or intention in any creature, and so chance events are real. Natural entities "collide" in ways that produce outcomes they are not normally ordered by their intrinsic natures to produce, as when a deer runs in front of a car on the highway and both the deer and the driver are killed, something neither of them is oriented toward by intrinsic principles of their respective natures. Yet these events also can only occur precisely because there are natural orders, inclinations, and intentions within natural realities that give rise to intelligible lines of causation and engage with one another, sometimes by chance.

One can thus reasonably raise the question of an overarching transcendent governance that is not identical with the natural order but that works within the order of nature *and* in chance events in a cosmic, biological, and human history of developmental evolution. Nevertheless, chance events also illustrate the limitations and provisionality of natural forms of order and natural causes. When one points to natural causal order in realities as a sign of intellectually derived reality—God as the source of natural order—one also runs the risk of thinking superficially insofar as there are chance events that give rise to new and other natural configurations. Indeed, some chance events imply serious natural evils, as in our example of the driver killed by the collision with the deer on the highway. However, chance events also raise the question of whether there is any deeper order to reality or whether such order is only ever provisional, one that is ontologically effervescent and ephemeral.

Those who seek to argue from chance occurrences in cosmic and evolutionary history to the truth of modern scientistic materialism—there is no transcendent Creator or providence guiding things—always are subject to a metaphysical paradox arising from their philosophical strategy. The more they appeal to the reality of chance to suggest that the universe is non-intellectually originated through a kind of primal indeterminism, the more they delimit the intelligibility of the natural order. Simultaneously, however, they must appeal to that same natural order consistently to try to indicate that the world is intelligible uniquely in virtue of material causes and the chance occurrences that occur between them. The basic givenness of an intelligible order in material causes that we can understand progressively by scientific means is thus inevitably reasserted. Furthermore, such argumentation must also appeal to an intelligible order of nature precisely so as to make chance intelligible, as something that emerges or happens against the backdrop of that primal order and gives rise to new and previously unforeseen and unintended forms of nature. In underscoring the intelligibility of material nature, then, one also revisits the topic of proper causality that is explanatory, as distinct from chance occurrence, and in doing so revises the question of ultimate causal explanation "beyond" the realm of chance. After all, where there is order, there is the question of a transcendent source of the intrinsic intelligibility of that order. Furthermore, precisely because chance occurrences illustrate the finite and limited character of all natural causes, they also raise the question of a Creator and point to the metaphysical possibility of a primary explanation, one pertaining to some other form of transcendent metaphysical agency that sustains natural realities in existence and is governing all things, even in and through the chance events that occur between natural, created causes. Paradoxically, the more atheistic visionaries appeal to chance to explain the current state of our existing universe, the more they rely implicitly on an appeal to intelligible natural order, and by that fact they implicitly raise again the specter of the possibility of God.[9]

A third difficulty with the "simplicity of atheism claim" has to do with the problem of the hierarchy of perfections in nature. It is not simply that the picture of the world we have been discussing posits a long history of material natural events that modern scientists help us to discover. It also tends to presume that there are diverse natural kinds of things that arise within that history. Broadly speaking, one can distinguish between non-living and living things. Living beings are self-movers—self-organizing entities with organic bodies (that is, bodies with diverse organs or living functions) that by various internal actions and organic operations (1) maintain their bodily integrity and defend themselves against outside realities, (2) nourish themselves by assimilating nutrients, (3) grow, (4) repair themselves or naturally heal, and (5) reproduce. Non-living things do not do any of these things. The five properties I have noted pertain in some way to all living things. There are diverse powers and degrees of perfection that emerge in them in such a way as to pursue these various ends.

However, there are also some living things that have sense knowl-

9. This argument suggests, however, that as long as atheist materialists appeal to chance as a proper explanation of the emergence of "higher" things, such as living things, from "lower" things, such as non-living things, there will be religionists who will appeal in turn to a transcendent cosmic order or karma or providence, and as long as those religionists argue by appeal to chance that God or a more ultimate transcendent principle must be governing all things, those who wish to appeal to material causes alone will be able to indicate reasonably genuine material, natural causes that allow one to explain (in part at least) the supposedly "random" events that religionists may seek to attribute to divine governance. Nature and chance are both appealed to in sometimes inconsistent ways by religionists and materialists so as to contest one another and often in ways that lead to interminable disputes and irresolvable difficulties.

edge. Animals, as distinct from plants, have the external knowledge of the senses of touch, smell, taste, hearing, or sight, and some animals also have internal sense powers of imagination and memory, passions (animal emotions), sensate appetites, and common sensible power (that is, the power to synthesize complex internal and external sensible experiences with memory so as to acquire a kind of animal prudence, like the dog learning to play with the tennis ball).

Human beings are animals animated by distinct powers of intelligence and volition. By intelligence, I mean the human power of natural apprehension of the natures and causes of things in a conceptual mode and the intentional forms of judgment and reasoning about the world to which this apprehension gives rise. Human beings contemplate and understand the world around them, and they seek to develop that understanding by explaining the world in causal fashion. Their understanding in turn gives rise to external practices and products that are typically human: language, tools, art, and technology, as well as philosophical and religious behaviors, such as contemplation, worship, and meditation. Volition refers to the human being's free power to love rightly and well, a power that is the seat of moral responsibility. Each human being loves others whom he or she knows and each desires to be loved by others. Each human being acts in view of the pursuit of happiness, love, and just concord by way of free decisions. In doing so, he or she forms moral intentions to pursue spiritual or material goods, like friendship, learning, honor, wealth, and pleasure. Through this process persons make ethical discernments and choices and undertake a variety of morally charged actions that form their characters over time. Plants and other animals do not seem to do any of these things.

A problem of explanatory power arises, then, with the kind of material explanation from below we have been considering, which seeks to explain reality comprehensively and most simply by the reduction of all things to their most basic material parts as fundamental and total causes. This kind of approach to *comprehensive* explanation does not readily explain the kind of hierarchy or diversification of characteristics that has emerged in the universe, from non-living things to the emergence of living things, and from simple (for example, single-celled) organisms to more complex vegetative life, to animal life and the eventual emergence of rational and free animals. One can argue, of course, that all of this arises gradually from nature through chance processes and thus the seemingly diverse and complex realities we call living things and knowledgeable living things—animals and human beings—are all ultimately reducible to impersonal non-living physical forces. Physics explains all. In this case, it must be assumed that non-living things must have some kind of virtual power (residual ontological potency) to give rise to living, sentient, and intelligent, deliberating realities if they are placed in the right conditions and that those conditions have arisen more or less accidentally or haphazardly rather than as a result of an intellectually guided process. So the godless universe is potentially capable of becoming aware of itself for no particular reason at all. In such a case, however, new questions arise. Why are the primary material realities—let us say atoms, for the sake of argument—potentially capable of generating living things, and why are non-rational living things capable of generating free and reasonable beings that have self-awareness? Can life be explained merely by recourse to the consideration of atomic structures? Can deliberation and freedom in human persons be explained merely by recourse to physical forces? Even if one answers these questions affirmatively, by way of hypothesis, we can still ask: where does this residual potency in the physical world come from in the first place, such that it can give rise eventually to living beings and agents of knowledge and volitional love? Why have a remarkable series of chance encounters taken place so as to produce living and sentient and rationally free creatures, so that a universe that eternally self-perpetuates has "learned" to reproduce itself by propagation and to become aware of itself? Does this mean the universe is alive and in fact a kind of entity or living god that is eternal and progressively self-aware?

Finally, and perhaps most significantly, can this hypothetical explanation of all things by way of micro- and macro-material causes really account sufficiently for the diversity of natural kinds of things, that is to say, of living as distinct from non-living things and of rational and free animals as distinct from non-rational living things? This question seems most acute when one considers human reason and freedom, which seem to presuppose abstract forms of knowledge, and the free decision-making that stems from it and that is not determined as such or even constituted formally by material processes. Or so one may argue. (I treat this topic in the next chapter.) In this case the gradual emergence of "higher" forms of living beings in the midst of lower living things and of living things in the midst of non-living things may require explanation "from above" by appeal to God the Creator and his intervention rather than explanation merely by appeal to material causes and their interactions. This may be true even if one accepts every jot and tittle of contemporary evidence for the 14-billion-year-old development of the physical cosmos and for the evolution of living things over the past 4 billion years.

As an addendum to these reflections, we should also raise the question of the good. It seems reasonable to affirm in some basic way that it is good to exist and good to be alive. We can also speak of various goods or of the goodness of various realities and activities, such as the acquisition of right understanding, friendship and mutual love, the life of the human family, the pursuit of justice, fairness, and peace in society. Some forms of goodness are more aesthetic in kind, as when we speak of something as beautiful and splendid. So then, what is goodness and what is beauty? Our experiences of them confront us with the gratuity of our existence in its fullness and with our gratitude for and enjoyment of being. They also confront us with the problem of rival options: the goodness of some things rather than others, including the good of other persons and societies that we can prefer to one another. And there is the major problem of evil and of ugliness, of actions or events that deprive us of the good and the beautiful or that are deprived of goodness and nobility. Can all of this be explained comprehensively simply by the concentrated attentiveness to material particles and physical forces? Can justice be found under a microscope? Can the beauty of human life, of noble actions, learning, art, or music be understood simply by appeal to material particles and forces? Some natural materialists claim that once we really understand our material origins, our moral and aesthetic values are exposed as something illusory or meaningless. And yet this seems counter-intuitive, if not self-contradictory.

For these various reasons, it is reasonable to consider alternative explanations of reality, perhaps ones that are not as narrowly aligned with the scientistic materialist intellectual project. Despite the significant advances made by the modern sciences, any philosophical stance that seeks to make use of them to explain reality comprehensively seems reductively narrow and overly simplistic in some respects, while still too complex and inconclusive in others.

PRIMARY REALITY AS IMMATERIAL AND IMPERSONAL: NAGARJUNA'S MAHAYANA BUDDHISM AND SHANKARA'S VEDANTIC MONISM[10]

Let us consider another option. The philosophical traditions of both Hinduism and Buddhism are complex. Both of these religious traditions contains within themselves diverse schools of thought, and each has also developed in reaction to the other as a philosophical rival.[11] Nevertheless, in the midst of this complexity and richness, both religions contain a prominent strand of thought that claims that

10. In the section below, I am greatly indebted to recommendations and phraseology suggested to me by Philip and Carol Zaleski.

11. On the development of Vedic traditions in ancient India and the emergence of Buddhism in response to ancient Hindu tradition, see Romila Thapar, *The Penguin History of Early India: From the Origins to AD 1300* (New York: Penguin, 2015). On the formation of the Upanishads, see the work of Patrick Olivelle, *Upanishads* (Oxford: Oxford University Press, 1996). On Theravada Buddhism, see Steven Collins, *Selfless Persons: Imagery and Thought in Theravada Buddhism* (Cambridge: Cambridge University Press, 1982). On Mahayana Buddhism, see the work of Paul Williams, *Mahayana Buddhism: The Doctrinal Foundations*, 2nd ed. (London: Routledge, 2008), and on the formation of Buddhist philosophy, see Amber D. Carpenter, *Indian Buddhist Philosophy: Metaphysics as Ethics* (London and New York: Routledge, 2014).

the ultimate principle of reality is *both non-personal and immaterial.*
Consider for example the third-century AD Buddhist philosophy
of Nagarjuna, a prominent representative of mainstream Mahayana
("greater vehicle") Buddhism.[12] For Nagarjuna the material world
is characterized by ontological contingency, impermanence, and
flux.[13] An epistemological truth is paired with this metaphysical one:
precisely due to the impermanence of things, we cannot grasp stable structures in the world that remain and are the source of enduring intelligibility.[14] Consequently, our primary perceptions of reality
are illusory, and to the extent we can grasp something of the world
through them, we should acknowledge only a world of change that is
passing away. This idea leads to the conclusion that only the emptiness standing behind and undergirding all things truly endures or exists perennially. By "emptiness" (*Sunyata*) Nagarjuna denotes the reality that is the primal foundation and deepest truth about our being,
the uncaused reality (*Nirvana*).[15] In one sense, this absolute principle is an absence of being, but in another sense, it is the absence of
anything contingent. Unoriginate emptiness is the reality behind
all things that all apparent realities-in-flux arise from and fall back
into. In this second sense, it is the abiding transcendent truth about

12. See the translation and commentary on Nagarjuna's influential work *Madhya-
maka* ("middle way"), by Mark Siderits and Shoryu Katsura in *Nagarjuna's Middle Way:
Mulamadhyamakakarika* (Somerville, MA: Wisdom Publications, 2013), and Carpenter,
Indian Buddhist Philosophy, ch. 4.

13. His own ontology is distinguished from that of the Abhidharma Buddhists whom
he writes against, in that he argues that even the *Dharmas* (foundational non-personal
ontological principles) that they hold to be real are themselves lacking in intrinsic nature
or ultimate reality. As Siderits and Katsura note, "Realization [in classical Buddhism] of
the emptiness of the person was thought to be crucial to liberation from *samsara* [the
cycle of suffering, death and rebirth]. The earliest Mahayana texts go considerably beyond this claim, asserting that not just the person (and other aggregate entities like the
chariot) but everything is devoid of intrinsic nature. While they assert that all things are
empty, however, they do not defend the assertion. Nagarjuna's task in MMK is to supply
its philosophical defense." "*Nagarjuna's Middle Way*, 1."

14. Consider the radical epistemological skepticism concerning causality, identity,
and nature exhibited in *Madhyamaka*, chs. 1, 8, 9, 11, and 15.

15. *Madhyamaka*, ch. 25. Nagarjuna actually goes as far as to identify *Nirvana* with
Samsara, insofar as the latter—the cycle of life, suffering, death and rebirth—is illusory
at base and characterized by the primal emptiness that undergirds all things.

reality, which provides an ultimate explanation for all that is and can give stability and purpose to our existence. The enlightened person can come to recognize that all things pass through being temporally, against the backdrop of an eternal stillness, one that establishes the ultimate truth about the human condition. By philosophical reflection and meditation, the human being can come to a profound and abiding realism about the truth of the human condition and can rest in selflessness, free from illusions. Through this process of enlightenment, human beings are able to free themselves from the illusion of selfhood and the delusional desires that stem from it, which are a principal cause of suffering in ourselves and others. The enlightened individual can accept and find rest in the ultimate reality of emptiness, a primal reality that is impersonal. The realism this engenders is meant to allow the Buddhist practitioner to enter into a life of freedom from false attachment, one characterized by selfless ethical compassion. From the realization of selflessness, a new moral power arises.

A very different and in some ways directly contrasting view is found in the philosophical reflection of the Hindu school of Advaita Vedanta, as characterized by Shankara (early eighth century AD) who conceived and gave voice to his vision of reality over and against Buddhist philosophy in distinctive ways.[16] Shankara develops his school of Vedantic philosophy in response to Buddhism by insisting on the reality and primacy of self (*atman*), rather than selflessness. However, he also identifies the unique true principle of self in all things with the primary principle from which all things emanate—God or ultimate reality.[17] In this way he offers a qualified monistic (and "non-dualistic") interpretation of reality, one he sees reflected in the classical writing of the Upanishads. On this view, there is no fundamental duality of God on the one hand and all other reality created by God, including human persons, on the other. There is

16. On Shankara and his interpretation of Advaita Vedantism, in response to various schools of Buddhism in particular, see Natalia Isayeva, *Shankara and Indian Philosophy* (Albany, NY: SUNY Press, 1993).

17. See Isayeva, *Shankara and Indian Philosophy*, 38–39, 172–98.

only God expressed in and through all of reality. For Shankara, all ordinary realities we experience, including human persons, are a kind
of emanation from the one first principle, who is in all things as the
ground of all things. In this line of thinking, God is at once the ultimate transcendent reality and the deepest dimension of the physical
world and of human self-hood or personal identity. Within all things
is a monistic, unifying principle that is divine and that gives being
and order to all things.[18] Each human being seems to us in our common experience to have a distinct substantial unity, a personal identity or "self," but at a deeper level, the human being has its identity
essentially in God and with God. God is the true ground of the self.
Consequently, the realization of the presence of God within one's
self and in a certain sense as identical with one's deepest self leads
to a different kind of selflessness, an enlightenment that comes from
discovering the divinity that lies within. On this view, our illusions of
individual personhood can fall away as the inner reality of the deity
shines forth. Shankara therefore depicts the world of distinct things
as a veil of illusion (*maya*[19]) that both conceals and manifests its hidden ground, namely, God.[20] God is understood in quasi-impersonal
terms as Brahman—the unifying order within all things—and at the
same time as the fundamental agent that gives rise to the world and
undergirds all things.[21] In this sense, there is an ambiguity about the
personal character of God in Shankara's vision, something his interpreters in turn debate. Some see in his thinking a mirror image of
Buddhism. In contradiction to the Buddhist claim of a primal emptiness, Shankara affirms that there is a positive reality undergirding
all things, but this principle is the only thing real that subsists under-
neath the veil of illusion and change that we typically take for reality.
Consequently, as in Buddhism, the enlightened person undergoes

18. Isayeva, *Shankara and Indian Philosophy*, 38–39.
19. Isayeva, *Shankara and Indian Philosophy*, 3.
20. Isayeva, *Shankara and Indian Philosophy*, 118–19. Some commentators on Shankara qualify the "veil of illusion" and insist that for Shankara the world is rather a contingent aspect or provisional image of God—as the sun's reflection in water is not the sun
but neither is it an illusion; it is a real image.
21. Isayeva, *Shankara and Indian Philosophy*, 165–72.

a progressive realization of selflessness. Furthermore, this ultimate principle, God, is in some sense impersonal, and we gain contact with God, or the divine within, by realizing that much of what we take to be our "selves" is in fact a contingent illusion.[22]

Both of these traditions—Nagarjuna's Buddhism and Shankara's Vedantism—are invested in questions of the metaphysics of "karma," albeit in differing ways. Why does the world of human affairs unfold as it does, and what are our moral responsibilities? How do our moral actions have effects on the world, and what consequences flow from them? One might wonder why such questions arise in this context. After all, the forms of *impersonalist* transcendence these philosophies propose (in different ways) imply that human personhood is ephemeral. In our deepest self we are either the plenitude of God (the *Atman*) or emptiness (*Sunyata*). Why then should our moral actions really matter? However, these traditions are not ethically nihilistic. They each teach that human decisions and actions are metaphysically meaningful in this life and consequential for the larger cosmos. Human decisions have an intrinsically ethical quality and a metaphysically irreducible significance. There is a deeper moral order in the world that pre-exists us, and that we are all a part of. Furthermore, our human activity affects the status of this order depending on whether we conform to it or not. This idea is exemplified by the fact that human actions have enduring consequences beyond one's own individual life in subsequent lives by way of the process of a transmigration of the soul at death leading to subsequent rebirth (reincarnation).[23] Human acts of selfishness or selflessness, of delusional attachment or realistic detachment, affect the larger state of

22. One finds an alternative view in Ramanuja, the eleventh-century Hindu philosopher, with his "qualified non-dualism," in which he affirms the personal character of both God and the soul and relatedly provides a theological and metaphysical rationale for devotional Hinduism (the *Vaishnava* tradition). On Ramanuja, see Martin Ganeri, *Indian Thought and Western Theism: The Vedanta of Ramanuja* (New York: Routledge, 2015).

23. Although some western commentators attempt to present Buddhism divorced from the doctrine of reincarnation and karmic effects from one life to another, the teaching of ontological reincarnation is axiomatic to Buddhism and is of course central to Vedic Hinduism as well as the metaphysical-religious justification of the caste system.

the human race in its collective life and even the cosmic (spiritual and physical) harmony of the world.[24] Actions have rippling effects on the lives of subsequent generations, especially due to the reincarnation of the soul (or life principle of each individual) after the time of his or her death in a life to come. In this sense, there is a form of non-personalistic "eschatology" present in such traditions, which seek to promote the ideal of universal enlightenment, a state of being in which all things will be governed rightly by their highest principle and in light of it. Political programs become possible on the basis of such non-personalist ontologies of transcendence, ideals for regimes designed to help us live in light of what is most ultimate.[25] Buddhist and Hindu religious traditions can thus animate historical social orders and give rise to organized political systems.

Of course, we have alluded to the traditions in question only very superficially and topically. Even so, we can see how the ideas just mentioned seek to address fundamental questions about human existence, but nevertheless also lead to genuine perplexities. Some of the problems raised above regarding materialism are still present when one considers the Buddhist philosophy of Nagarjuna. If emptiness is the ultimate principle that transcends all other realities, does it cause all other realities to exist? If so, how can something come from this non-personal transcendent principle of absence of being? If it does not exert causation, why does the world of impermanent beings exist?[26] If the emptiness in question does not cast

24. Isayeva, *Shankara and Indian Philosophy*, 158.
25. Buddhism, with its strong sense of cyclical degeneration and renewal, need not promote a notion of final universal enlightenment. The bodhisattva Maitreya has this role in some traditions of Buddhism, and there are esoteric and political eschatologies that prophesy final enlightenment. There are also Pure Lands beyond this space-time universe, created and presided over by celestial Buddhas, in which the conditions are conducive to universal enlightenment.
26. Nagarjuna seeks in his own way merely to *eradicate* this question rather than answer it. He denies that the emptiness that undergirds all things is an *absence* of being and instead argues that any "absence" of a thing must presuppose a prior "existence" of something. But on the contrary, nothing fundamentally exists of itself (thus the denial of individual natures) or in causal dependence upon others (thus the denial of ontologically antecedent causes). Rather, one is taught by Buddhist practice and metaphysics

light upon the enigma of existence, have we yet uncovered the whole truth about being, or have we only identified an important aspect of being: the truth of the temporal contingency of all material things? All that we experience is passing away, and this raises the question of what stands behind the contingency of the world we know. However, is this contingent material world not something rather than nothing?

In regard to the theory of *Atman* elaborated by Shankara, there seems to be a serious question about the relationship between the one God and the many creatures. If there is one unifying principle that is present as the ground of all things and that *is all things* in some real sense, does this mean that the apparent multiplicity of things we experience daily (including ourselves) is merely illusory?[27] That seems counter-intuitive to say the least, but even if one were to take the claim very seriously, there is a problem of epistemology, since we only come to the resolution that there exists one really subsisting principle (*Atman*) through the prior examination of the world as we experience it, which is a world we perceive and normally first judge as consisting of many distinct existing things and not as a mere illusion. It would seem that we need to acknowledge the reality of the very things we deny if we are to come to affirm the principle (God) by which we in turn explain the realities in question. Would it not be more sensible simply to affirm that there is some kind of real distinction between creatures and God? But in that case, how would one go about understanding the relation between the two in any kind of intelligible way?[28]

Many questions occur on the ethical side as well. These philosophies have the advantage of taking seriously our daily ethical life and responsibilities. In one sense, they may appear to trivialize it, since

---

to see through to the fundamental emptiness underlying all things. See *Madhyamaka*, chs. 1, 20, and 25.

27. Isayeva, *Shankara and Indian Philosophy*, 161–62.

28. As noted above, Ramanuja provides an alternative form of reflection in the Hindu metaphysical tradition, one that acknowledges the reality and dependence of all things upon God.

they announce the contingency and sheer relativity of so much temporal and bodily existence and the social life that goes with it. However, on a deeper level they promise a pathway toward salvation, one of enlightenment and compassion, which opens up to a cosmic religious horizon. Here, however, paradoxes emerge. On the one side, the self seems basically illusory, a kind of superficial aspect of our being, which meditation and right reflection can deliver us from. On the other side, there is some kind of ontological core in each of us, one that "survives" death and reincarnates, for if not, then nothing that these traditions affirm about karma or rebirth would make any sense. But if there is no core of our personal being that reincarnates, then how do we identify in truth "what" it is in each of us that is the source of good or bad agency (that is, a deliberative, free human agent)?[29] Typically we only ascribe moral responsibility to a free subject who discerns the truth and takes responsibility for his or her actions. Purposeful action and moral praise thus imply some kind of personal selfhood.[30] So too does the belief in moral justice: if someone incurs just punishment or reward in the life to come (by the status of his next reincarnation) due to actions he performed in this life, then this would seem to denote a subject of justice, an agent who can be enlightened by moral truth and blessed by the benefits of just deliberation. In this sense, reincarnation would seem to entail some minimal notion of selfhood. However, at the same time, it is not clear that reincarnation can really assure any form of justice,

---

29. The classical Indian Buddhist way of dealing with this is to say that one's actions in this life plant seeds that bear fruit in future lives; it is the actions that survive (through their consequences) rather than an ontological core that reincarnates. Buddhist philosophers are convinced that we do not need assurance of personal identity or continuity in order to ground moral agency and accountability. Later forms of Buddhism complicate this idea considerably with elaborate theories of consciousness transference between lives, but they all insist (in theory at least) that there is no ontological core to the soul or self. They claim that this is good news, a message of liberation, a motive for compassion, and an index of one's interdependent communion with all other sentient beings. (I am grateful to Carol Zaleski for her help in framing this observation.)

30. Aquinas offers a sustained philosophical argument to this effect in *Summa contra Gentiles* II (*SCG*), cc. 58–73, in response to Plato's notion of the transmigration of the soul, as well as Averroes, who posited one possible intellect present in all human beings.

even if we assume there is such a thing as selfhood, since the "person" who is to be rightly rewarded or punished ceases to be at death, and the soul of the person after reincarnation is instantiated as another conscious entity (or personal agent) in the life to come.[31] Can one have a continuity of the moral agent who acquires progressive praise or blame across a span of successive lives if there is no continuity of personal subject who has an enduring self-knowledge and ethical love of self and others across biological life states? Moreover, the cosmic justice of karma that reasserts laws of justice through time (by means of reincarnation) would seem to require a larger personal intentionality, a universal balance of wisdom or an intentional principle of order, that acts upon or within the cosmos, something akin to the divine providence ascribed to the transcendent God of classical monotheism. And yet the non-personalism of such ontologies seems to forbid such a possibility. Why, then, is there a karmic order of balance and moral weight within the universe?[32]

When we consider this ontology, we encounter problems very different from but somewhat analogous to those found in materialism. Why are there simply particles and physical forces given in a particular order capable of producing the universe as it now exists? Why is there forever and always simply a complex order of karmic consequences that is deeply affected by human moral actions but has no monotheistic origin? One can of course assert: this state of affairs simply is the case and ever was so. But again, we confront a complexity: a material universe governed by an immanent order of karma (we know not why), itself expressed in and through seemingly personal agents (considered as subjects of ethical enlightenment, capable of compassionate or morally problematic actions), and yet

31. This is the early Christian critique articulated in response to the Platonic theory of the transmigration of souls by Justin Martyr in his *Dialogue with Trypho the Jew*, Book I, ch. 4. [*Ante-Nicene Fathers*, vol. 1, ed. A. Roberts, J. Donaldson, and A. C. Coxe; trans. M. Dods and G. Reith (Buffalo, NY: Christian Literature Publishing Co., 1885).]

32. It is worth noting that most Hindu religious philosophers and the vast majority of practicing Hindus believe in a personal God; devotional theism is the dominant tradition, with one God at the center and others in subordinate positions. In this respect, Advaita Vendata is not representative of mainstream trends in classical Hinduism.

their personhood is ultimately a kind of illusion or epiphenomenon, something that temporarily seems to exist but in fact covers over the deeper principle that alone is primal and imbues everything (*Atman*, or by contrast, emptiness).

Such ontologies seem to provide more explanation than that of the naturalist materialism considered above—at least in some respects, since they admit that contingent reality is not self-explanatory—and go on to acknowledge the existence of transcendent reality. They are also less reductive, because they take seriously the ontological complexity of the material and immaterial, and they recognize the intellectual and ethical role of the human being who is responsible for making religious discernments about reality as a distinctively intellectual and moral agent. But due to the appeal to a transcendent principle that is ultimately non-personal, and due to their denial of the personal identity of the human agent, such approaches raise many enigmatic questions, even as they seek to resolve the philosophical mystery of our existence.

THE METAPHYSICS OF TRANSCENDENT PERSONALISM: VARIOUS FORMS OF MONOTHEISM

The appeal to some form of personalistic monotheism might seem to present a simpler and more comprehensive explanatory thesis. Monotheism seeks to account for the very existence or being of the world, and it can be appealed to in order to explain the deep multiplicity and order one finds in things, their various intelligible causalities, and the processes that emerge from and through them over time. On this view, the natural order of the world and its history emerge from the wisdom of God. They are created and so they indicate to us, however obliquely, a transcendent principle that remains unknown and mysterious. If the first principle and cause of all things is in some way personal, implying something like wisdom and volition, this would also have implications for how we think about human persons as intelligent and free creatures, being both like and unlike their transcendent source. The Biblical tradition speaks of human persons being made in the "image and likeness" of God.[33]

This book will argue that this vision of things is reasonable and true. Nevertheless, we should also recognize that many intellectual conundrums arise from such a way of thinking. First of all, and this is a serious point, if any particular form of monotheism is intelligible and true, then it follows necessarily that many affirmations made about God or the gods in various religious traditions must also be false. The reason for this claim is obvious. There are many historical claims about the divine, about gods or about "the one God," that are mutually incompatible, so that if there is a basic truth to the claim that "God exists," then this also means that many gods do not exist, that many theistic religious traditions are false, that not all revelations are true (or perhaps none is), and that many philosophical and theological visions of God are misleading or partially erroneous at best, if not projective and delusional, misleading products of sheer human invention. In this sense, to be a theist and an atheist are in reality not necessarily mutually opposed stances, but rather, in some cases, are mutually consistent stances and even necessarily reciprocally related options. To believe in God in one way is to disbelieve in God or the gods in other ways. For to believe certain things about God requires that one deny the existence of many gods and take issue with various erroneous philosophical conceptions of God or various supposed revelations about God. We can say this even before we have advanced far into the investigation of the matter simply by recognizing as a simple fact the great disparity of mutually incompatible opinions about God or the divine that are common among men. Monotheism appears in part, then, as a problematic idea, one that leads to intellectual, religious, and political divisions.

Second, and in a sense this is a contrary point, one might ask whether the widespread affirmation of a personal source of reality (God) is not the attestation of a commonly held truth in humanity. After all, belief in God is not rare in human culture. We might

---

33. Gen. 1:26. See the analysis of Aquinas in *Summa theologiae* (*ST*) I, q. 93.

ask, then, whether belief in monotheism is natural to all human beings. However, we have access to this natural knowledge of God only
through a vast web of complex human traditions. Many are incompatible with one another in some of their main details, but perhaps
this complexity exists on a secondary level while referring to a primary simplicity that lies behind them: widespread acknowledgement of an unknown God. In other words, perhaps we find God in
and through human religious traditions, which precisely because
they are "all too human" both testify to but also obscure the possibility of any real knowledge of God, his presence, and his mystery.
In this case, God is hidden behind human traditions as an ultimately
inaccessible enigma. A kind of religious agnosticism ensues. Interpreted in this way, the religious traditions may be seen to hide God
in darkness, concealing him as much or as more than they might reveal him. Modernist theologians of the early twentieth century proposed this kind of idea in order to emphasize what they took to be
the fatal limitations of dogmatic forms of religion. The dogmas are
seen as ideological superstructures or scaffolding covering over the
unknown mystery of God.[34] Epistemic humility requires that we un-
learn what we think we know of God.

It is worth nothing that there are also alternative versions of
this view in classical Hinduism that contrast with those of the early twentieth-century modernist movement. Consider, for example,
what one finds in certain sophisticated versions of Vedantic theology, in which the absolute divine principle is understood to be one
by way of a kind of philosophical monotheism. The God of Ven-
danta is one. However, this understanding of God is not juxtaposed
to the seeming polytheism of ancient Indian culture. Rather, the
Hindu practitioners who embrace post-Vedic traditions and worship various Hindu gods are said here to worship in truth the one
God presented to them under the various visages or apparitions of

---

34. I am thinking here of the work of early twentieth-century figures such as Paul
Sabatier, Alfred Loisy, George Tyrell, Wilhelm Herrmann, and Rudolph Otto. This is
said without prejudice to their differing accounts of dogmatic truth claims.

distinct entities, such as Brahma, Vishnu, and Shiva. Here monotheism and polytheism merge but not without some kind of deeper synthetic principle.[35] Being devoted to a particular deity in the pantheon of gods is a way of entering into a closer relationship with the hidden ground of being that lies behind all the deities of the tradition. The many faces of God, the avatars of the divinity, all have their own reality but also are understood to be simultaneously partial, non-comprehensive manifestations of the one divinity as voices of the godhead, who is beyond these diverse finite expressions.[36]

One may wonder about the wisdom of this approach. Is God really one, or is God really many? If he is truly one, does the multiplicity of deities truly permit a diversity of pathways to the one God, or does it thwart and obscure realism about the transcendence of God? Human idolatry is dangerous because it obscures or trivializes the divine and is often linked to problematic forms of human political power and the erroneous projection of anthropomorphic properties onto God. The intellectually arbitrary imposition of man-made religious traditions should remain a real fear, since human beings can become religiously self-deceived. This in turn can lead to a just reaction: skepticism, intellectual derision, and the rejection of religion. What sort of critical apparatus exists in classical Hinduism to appease our rational fears in this regard?[37]

Of course, other traditions are purely monotheistic. One may naturally think of Judaism and Christianity, as well as their famous rival Islam. But there are less widespread monotheistic traditions, which are also quite significant, such as Hindu Vaishnavism,

35. See the reflections on Hindu monotheism by the Jesuit scholar of Hinduism, Richard De Smet in *Brahman & Person: Essays by Richard De Smet,* ed. Ivo Coelho (Delhi: Motilal Banarsidass, 2010).

36. See in this respect the western popularization of this idea by John Hick in *An Interpretation of Religion: Human Responses to the Transcendent,* 2nd ed. (New Haven, CT: Yale, 2005) and Paul Knitter, *No Other Name? A Critical Survey of Christian Attitudes toward the World Religions* (Maryknoll, NY: Orbis, 1985).

37. For a defense in this regard of some Hindu traditions, see Julius J. Lipner, *Hindu Images and Their Worship with Special Reference to Vaisnavism: A Philosophical-Theological Inquiry* (New York: Routledge, 2017).

Sikhism, and Persian Zoroastrianism. These traditions and their diversity raise several significant questions. Should any one religious tradition really be allowed to tell us something final and conclusive about God, or should we rely uniquely or primarily upon philosophy in order to think about such questions? Perhaps philosophical reason can be used to protect us from the "myths of the poets" and the religious delusions of men, even while steering us toward God. This was the claim of several prominent modern Enlightenment philosophers.[38]

At the same time, we should ask whether philosophy alone suffices to give us conclusive knowledge of who God is and, if not, whether we should trust appeals to revelation?[39] If we do open ourselves up rationally to the possibility of divine revelation, under what circumstances or conditions should we do so? Likewise, if we do appeal to divine revelation to think about God, must we then abandon the philosophical attempt to attain knowledge of God?[40] Do we have to choose between divine revelation and human philosophy? And should we be forced into a situation where we are obliged to choose "the one true religion" against all other forms of religiosity

38. See, for example, the moderate version of this idea in John Locke, "The Reasonableness of Christianity," in *Writings on Religion*, ed. V. Nuovo (Oxford: Oxford University Press, 2002), as compared with the more aggressive version found in Immanuel Kant's *Religion within the Boundaries of Mere Reason*, ed. A. Wood and G. di Giovanni (Cambridge: Cambridge University Press, 1998).

39. The thirteenth-century Latin Averroists were characterized as holding such a position by their contemporaries. See Fernand Van Steenberghen, *La philosophie au XIIIe siècle*, 2nd ed. (Leuven: Peeters Publishers, 1991).

40. See in this respect the Vatican's reasonable condemnations of theses attributed to the nineteenth-century French thinker Louis-Eugène Bautain, who refused the possibility of a philosophical treatment of the topic of monotheism, apart from revelation. Among the condemned theses is included the idea that "by the sole light of natural reason, leaving aside divine revelation, one could not provide a genuine demonstration of the existence of God." Other topics of rational discovery or demonstration that are affirmed include "the spirituality and the immortality of the soul," "principles ... of metaphysics," and the "grounds of credibility [for the rationality of Catholic belief]," due to the reality of miracles or the historical resurrection of Christ, and so forth. See Denzinger, §§ 2765–69. [Heinrich Denzinger, *Compendium of Creeds, Definitions, and Declarations on Matters of Faith and Morals*, 43rd edition, ed. P. Hünermann, R. Fastiggi, and A. E. Nash (San Francisco: Ignatius Press, 2012).]

distinct from it? Can one believe in an absolute revelation and still learn from other religious traditions? In other words, how should we navigate claims of the different religious traditions, their truth foundation or absence thereof, and the questions of their compatibility with one another and with philosophical reason?

These topics can seem vast and even overwhelming or at least seriously challenging. Presumably, if there is a true "revealed religion," then we need that religious tradition itself to help us resolve these thorny issues. If we were to find such intellectual competence in Christianity, for example, that would be precisely one sign of its unique truthfulness, and it could in turn help us come to terms with these legitimate questions. Furthermore, on this view, shouldn't the revealed religion in question also provide us with a living tradition of *philosophical* resources by which we can think through these complicated issues? For if a "revealed religion" presents us with a theological form of thinking about God we are meant to take seriously, it must also make competent use of natural human reason in the service of and in harmony with its religious teachings. This is an issue we will return to below.

MAKING DISCERNMENTS: THE CRITERIA OF THE TRANSCENDENTALS

Where ought one to begin when making discernments about ultimate truth, or what ought we to presuppose as we start out? Arguably we should not leap immediately to the question of ultimate reality, but we should start instead with the topic of ordinary reality as we perceive it all the time. What is indisputably real? Interestingly, Christian, Jewish, and Muslim philosophers in the high Middle Ages who were inspired by Aristotle started their philosophical investigations typically not with reflections on God but with reflections on what they called "common being," the kinds of things we experience all around us, and moved from these to the consideration of

God.[41] How then can we think non-controversially about the multiplicity of realities that we typically experience? What properties do they all have in common? To address this question, medieval philosophers developed the concept of the transcendentals: being, unity, truth, goodness, and beauty.[42] These are basic notions of reality that we inevitably make use of when we think about ordinary reality as we encounter it each day. They emerge in us naturally and inevitably as we begin to think about realities around us, in their natures and properties. Since these notions are very basic, they are something all persons inevitably employ, including those who hold to any of the distinctive worldviews we noted above (or any others for that matter). Such notions stem from consideration in ordinary experience of what exists and does not really exist, the multiplicity and unity of beings, their truth and falsehood, their goodness and the reality of evil, and the beauty in things and their potential ugliness. Everyone inevitably thinks about these things, no matter how basic their reflection may be. Transcendental notions are so general that everyone makes use of them in some way, even if they never reflect on this usage self-consciously.[43] We should consider each of them briefly, then, as it concerns our investigations. Why? If we can identify a general form of metaphysical realism that is natural to all

41. Aquinas distinguishes between a philosophical *via inventionis*, or way of inquiry, by which the intellect proceeds from initial, self-evident principles to scientific conclusions, and the *via judicii*, by which the intellect judges in the light of its more ultimate discoveries the initial principles from which it began. The first *via* concerns the genetic order of discovery of things as known for us, while the second concerns the order of nature, or perfection, concerning things as they are in themselves. See *ST* I, q. 79, a. 8. [All quotations are taken from *Summa Theologica*, 1920 translation of the English Dominican Province (New York: Benziger, 1947).]

42. See the standard work on this subject by Jan A. Aertsen in *Medieval Philosophy as Transcendental Thought: From Philip the Chancellor (c.a. 1225) to Francisco Suárez* (Leiden: Brill, 2012). Transcendental notions denote features of being that "transcend" any particular categorial mode of being (any genus or species-kind of thing) and therefore enter into every form of being universally. All that is, insofar as it exists, implies being, unity, truth, goodness, and, on my reading of Aquinas's implicit teaching, beauty as well.

43. See the argument to this effect by Aquinas in *De ver.*, q. 1, a. 1 and the analysis by Lawrence Dewan, "The Seeds of Being," in *Form and Being: Studies in Thomistic Metaphysics* (Washington, DC: The Catholic University of America Press, 2006).

human beings in virtue of their intellectual activity, we can in turn identify the foundations in reality from which these notions derive. Subsequently we can consider how those foundations (structures of being themselves) provide an indication to us of what is ultimately real. This will allow us progressively to think in a constructive and focused way about the controverted question of the truth of Christianity.

Being and Non-Being

The things in the world around us and we ourselves truly exist. This is in a sense a trivial observation, but it also is an enigmatic one, as we have noted. The notion of being or existence is natural to our thinking insofar as it allows us to refer to the distinctiveness of the existence of each singular thing and the gratuity and reality of its being in act, its actuality of being.[44] "Does this thing really exist in its singular unity?" "Did it always exist?" "Will it come to be or go out of being?" Our thinking about existence is deeply interrelated to our thinking about truth and time. What is real or true about a thing in

---

44. Aristotle notes this relationship between our understanding of the singular reality of each thing and the grasp of its existence in *Post. Analytics* II, 7, 92b5–12:

> Again, how will you prove what a thing is [*ti esti*]? For it is necessary for anyone who knows what a man is, or anything else is, to know too *that* it is [*ei esti*] (for of that which is not, no one knows what it is—you may know what the account or the name signifies when I say goat-stag, but it is impossible to know what a goat-stag is). But if you are to prove what it is and that it is, how will you prove them by the same argument? *For both the definition and the demonstration make one thing clear; but what a man is and that a man is are different.* Next, we say it is necessary that everything that a thing is [*einai*] should be proved through demonstration, unless it is its substance. But existence [*to einai*] is not the substance of anything, for being [*to on*] is not in any genus (translation slightly modified, emphasis added).

Aristotle is saying that we grasp essences (what things are) and existence (that things exist) as something properly basic, even before we begin to analyze the essences and existences of things in greater detail. To argue that a given thing exists is different from demonstrating what it is essentially. We cannot demonstrate the existence of everything, but have to begin with knowledge of what exists evidently, and from this argue to what the realities in question are essentially, and also consider what their existence and their essential natures might logically entail about the ultimate causes of existence. See the commentary of Aquinas in *In Post. Analyt.* II, lec. 6.

the world as it exists currently or existed in the past? When is something said to be true, and how long will it be true, since things are constantly changing?

Four principles are enunciated by modern Thomists that help us identify reflexively the principles of metaphysical realism that everyone makes use of daily, virtually at every moment, in thinking about being.

1. *Non-contradiction.* The principle of non-contradiction, famously elaborated by Aristotle in *Metaphysics* IV, can be stated in two ways. The first is the ontological version—concerned with things in themselves: "One and the same thing cannot both be and not be under the same aspect, at the same time."[45] The second is semantic in form, and it presents us with a corollary idea: "opposite assertions cannot be true at the same time."[46] When we attempt to speak about things, if we wish to speak truthfully and intelligibly, we cannot say that a thing both is and is not under the same aspect at the same time.

This principle may seem quite modest or even banal in its applications to real life, since it simply underscores the fact that we constantly try to talk about reality in non-contradictory ways. Nevertheless, the implications of the principle are far-reaching. The principle is concerned with far more than laws of speech or logical thinking and even with more than our sensate experiences of the world as a world consisting of distinct sensible things. In fact, the principle touches upon the very laws of being: there are in the world things that are real and have enough intelligibility in them to be *both* distinguished from one another *and* compared with one another according to something fundamental they all share in common, namely, existence. That is to say, being is *both* what distinguishes or separates realities from one another (since each individual being is not

45. "Evidently then such a principle is the most certain of all; which principle this is, we proceed to say. It is, that the same attribute cannot at the same time belong and not belong to the same subject in the same respect" (*Metaphysics* IV, 3, 1005b19–20).

46. I am paraphrasing the text from *Metaphysics* IV, 6, 1011b13–20.

identical with or reducible to another) *and* what unites them (since they all really do *exist* and by that same measure, are related to one another *qua* existing as part and parcel of a larger reality in which each of them participates in existence). Our act of simply noting this does not resolve the enigma of existence but, on the contrary, establishes the reality of that enigma. The world is not an illusion or a mere dream but is a complex web of existing entities, all related to one another in intelligible ways as being. There just are many things, irreducible to one another in being, and yet at the same time, what they all have in common is that they exist, that they have being. Being is what unites them most fundamentally, and being is also what separates them from one another most fundamentally.

2. *Identity.* The positive corollary of the principle of non-contradiction is the principle of identity. If distinct realities really are *not* identical with one another, that is because each one has a positive identity in itself, an identity that is determinate, that is to say, concrete, real, and intelligible.[47] We might put this in terms of *both* existence *and* essence by speaking in this way: each reality we experience has an *existence* that is unique. Whether it is a blade of grass, a household pet, or a star, it is truly something uniquely existent, wholly distinct from all other things. It is a reality actually existing, that is to say, one which has come into being and which will eventually undergo radical alteration and cease to exist. Also, each reality has a concrete *essence*, an interior determination of a natural kind characterized by specific properties. There are distinct kinds of things—such as human beings, deer, oak trees, stars, lakes, water molecules, and

---

47. The Aristotelian roots of this principle are found in the idea that the human being encounters and begins to understand (prior to reasoning) the fundamental categorial modes of being in things. We simply apprehend the existence of substances, their quantities, qualities, relations, actions, passions, habits, time, place, and position, even if we initially understand these "folds" of reality imperfectly. See *Metaphysics* IV, 2, 1003b23–35, and Aquinas's commentary in *In IV Meta.*, lec. 2, § 561. [*In duodecim libros Metaphysicorum Aristotelis expositio*, ed. M. R. Cathala and R. M. Spiazzi (Turin and Rome: Marietti, 1964); all citations refer to *Commentary on Aristotle's Metaphysics*, trans. J. P. Rowan (Notre Dame, IN: Dumb Ox Books, 1995).]

atoms—marked by particular natural distinctions of genus and species, which we can call essences.[48]

If we consider the identity of each given thing both in terms of its singular existence and its essential kind simultaneously, we can speak of the various "substances" of things around us. Each thing (or, substance) is a singular existent. It not only has an essence or nature, but it is a singular individual whose existence is unique. ("This man *exists*.") It not only exists in a singular way but has a given kind of essence or nature. ("This particular thing is a *man*.")[49] Existence and essence are thus present in all things we experience, and they are really distinguishable but also inseparable. We navigate our way through reality by taking account of the distinct realities around us—diverse existents—and by apprehending the kinds of things they are, learning about their natures and making progress in understanding their essential characteristics. This kind of fundamental metaphysical realism is presupposed in the practice of all the modern sciences, which seek to study diverse truly existent things and attempt to identify their physical properties within generalized taxonomies.[50]

48. In *De ver.*, q. 1, a. 1, Aquinas speaks of *res* and *aliquid* as transcendental notions that follow closely upon *ens* and *unum*. In other words, where there is a being, it has some kind of unity but also some kind of essence (*res*) or intelligible content, and a kind of actuality by which it is differentiated as "something" (*aliquid*) distinct from other things. [*De veritate*, In *Sancti Thomae de Aquino opera omnia*, vol. 22, Leonine Edition (Rome: Editori di San Tommaso, 1975–76); *Truth*, in 3 vols., trans. J. V. McGlenn, R. W. Mulligan, and R. W. Schmidt (Indianapolis, IN: Hackett, 1994).]

49. *ST* I, q. 3, a. 7, ad 1: "It is of the intelligibility of a created thing that it is in some sense composite [in being], for at the very least its existence [*esse*] is other than what it is [its essence]." [Trans. by the author.] Aquinas argues from Aristotle's treatment of the existence/essence distinction in semantics presented in the *On Interpretation* that this basic conceptual distinction is not only founded in the very structure of things (ontologically) but also enters imperfectly into our first apprehensions of reality, insofar as we are always already able to distinguish the "what" of a thing from the being or existence of the reality (existence being common to realities that are not of the same kind). See *Expositio libri Peryermeneias*, I, lec. 5, § 20. "But the word "being" [*ens*] does not principally signify the composition that is implied in saying "is" [*est*]; rather, it signifies with composition inasmuch as it signifies *the thing* having existence." [*Expositio libri Posteriorum*, in *Sancti Thomae de Aquino opera omnia*, vol. 1, Leonine Edition (Rome: Editori di San Tommaso, 1882); Translation from *Aristotle on Interpretation*, trans. J. Oesterle (Milwaukee: Marquette University Press, 1962).]

50. See the helpful study on this subject by Oderberg, *Real Essentialism*.

3. *Causality*. Not only do we come to know that there are various kinds of realities around us. We also come to understand them better precisely by understanding their causes. The principle of causality states that each reality is intelligible in light of its causes: formal, final, material, and efficient.[51] The principle is pre-demonstrative, not the result of a proof or argument. In other words, we cannot prove to one who seeks to be omni-skeptical that there are *any* known causes whatsoever in the realities we experience. To do so, we would have to have explanatory recourse to causes known prior to these causes, and that cannot be possible if we have to begin our explanations precisely from *some* causes that are already known. Instead, we simply grasp that it is the case that there are at least some causes in things, and we then make progress in understanding these and other causes throughout the duration of our lives. Otherwise stated, some knowledge of causes must precede knowledge by demonstrative argument as the necessary condition for demonstration.[52] From imperfect knowledge of causes we seek to gain more perfect knowledge, through recourse to our causal knowledge. Indeed, argument is precisely about causal definitions and explanations. "Was that a lie that he told?" "Where does this ancient artifact come from?" "Who is responsible for this task?" "What is that chemical compound composed of?" "What is organic life and how did it originate?" "What are the functions of the frontal lobe?" In short, it is because we begin to grasp the reality of causes in the world that we can have any kind of argument at all about the nature of things or about what reality truly consists of.

Aristotle, in *Metaphysics* books I and II, rightly identified four causes we necessarily make use of in almost all our definitions and arguments, albeit in different ways. Formal causality pertains to the

---

51. The basic text on this subject is found in Aristotle, *Metaphysics* II. Aquinas often articulates the principle especially in terms of the efficient cause: an effect is only explicable ontologically in light of its cause. See *De pot.*, q. 5, a. 1. [Ed. P. M. Pession in *Quaestiones disputatae*, vol. 2, ed. R. Spiazzi (Turin and Rome: Marietti, 1965); *The Power of God*, trans. R. J. Regan (Oxford: Oxford University Press, 2012).]

52. See the analysis of Lawrence Dewan in "St. Thomas and the Principle of Causality," in *Form and Being*, 61–80.

essence or nature of a given thing, which as noted above denotes the core of its identity, what kind of thing it is specifically, and what properties emerge from it necessarily based on the kind of nature that it possesses. Material causality has to do with what a thing is made of, its component parts and material elements. Forms are more than the sum of their parts, at least in the sense that the unifying natural form of a thing "explains" or gives intelligibility to the order and relationship of all the parts, their dynamic unity within a larger whole.[53] A tree, for example, has elementary particles, chemical compounds, and organic parts, but all these material elements only exist and are organized within the large whole, namely, the organic living tree.

Efficient causality has to do with where a thing originates from or with its activities, what it effectuates. This is true whether the reality is an artifact (like a wooden table crafted by a carpenter) or a natural reality (like a young colt being born from a mare, or a mountain chain produced by titanic shifts in the earth's plates hundreds of millions of years ago). Not only do things originate from one another. They also act upon one another in virtue of their natural or artifactual properties and capacities.

Final causality has to do with intrinsic inclinations or predictable outcomes of natural entities: what does a reality tend toward doing or producing based on the kind of thing it is? Chemical bonds tend to produce predictable outcomes and results, such as when particular ratios of hydrogen and oxygen inevitably bond in such a way as to form water, or when water as a fluid substance tends to act as a solvent upon solid substances. Plants tend to nourish themselves through photosynthesis and to produce offspring by seeds. Animals tend to use sense knowledge for their own advancement in individual nourishment, reproduction, and survival. Human beings tend to seek the truth about reality, and they desire naturally to find personal happiness.[54]

53. See Aquinas, *In* II *Meta.*, lec. 4.
54. On human agency and its natural and inevitable pursuits, see for example *ST* I-II, q. 94, a. 2.

4. *Sufficient reason.* The principle of sufficient reason states that for every effect that stems from a cause, there must be a proportionate cause that serves as the source of and explanation for that effect. To give examples, if a certain body of water comes to a boil, there must be a sufficient degree of heat present that is active upon the water and explains why it is boiling. If a person dies from stomach cancer, there must be a sufficient degree of damage done by the cancer to the internal organs of the body to explain why the person's body was subject to death. If a child is born, there must be a sufficient cause of explanation for how the child came to be conceived and how it gestated to maturity in the womb of its mother. The "principle of sufficient reason" is typically associated in the modern era with the philosophy of Leibniz.[55] There are modern disputes about whether it has any foundation in classical philosophy generally or in Aquinas's philosophy specifically.[56] However, if one interprets the principle as something pertaining to the truth about the nature of being, it can be seen to have clear foundations in the thought of Aristotle and Aquinas, as well as other classical philosophers.[57] There is

55. See the study by Vincent Carraud, *Causa sive ratio. La raison de la cause, de Suarez à Leibniz* (Paris: Presse Universitaires de France, 2002), esp. 391–496.

56. Reginald Garrigou-Lagrange emphasized the centrality of this principle in his presentations of Aquinas, and this was subject to criticism from Marie-Dominique Chenu on the presupposition that the principle is alien to Aquinas's thought and derives from the epoch of modern rationalism. See Garrigou-Lagrange, *La Synthèse Thomiste* (Paris: Desclée de Brouwer, 1946) and Marie-Dominique Chenu, "Vérité évangélique et métaphysique wolfienne à Vatican II," *Revue des Sciences Philosophiques et Théologiques* 57 (1973): 632–40. This criticism is problematic on Chenu's part. It is true that both Garrigou-Lagrange and Bernard Lonergan [*Insight: A Study in Human Understanding* (New York: Longmans, 1957), 657–69] psychologize the principle as one of internal reference of the human mind in its effort at explanation, undertaken as a logically coherent intellectual act. Without the principle of sufficient reason (PSR), the life of the mind erodes. But the PSR has a basis in metaphysical realism, particularly with regard to this issue: that for every effect there must be a sufficiently proportionate cause. This idea is clearly found in Aristotle and Aquinas, as noted below.

57. See in particular, Plato, *Timaeus* (28a4–5 and 51d): "Now everything that comes to be must of necessity come to be by the agency of some cause, for it is impossible for anything to come to be without a cause." [Trans. D. J. Zeyl in *Plato Complete Works*, ed. J. M. Cooper (Indianapolis: Hackett, 1997).] Aristotle articulates the principle in a series of claims regarding the metaphysical primacy of actuality to potency in *Metaphysics* IX, 8, 1049b17–29; 1050a4–8; and 1050b6–16. See Vasilis Politis, *Aristotle and the Metaphysics*

nothing particularly obscure or mysterious about the principle, since
it simply claims that when lines of causation are detected that allow
us to discover chains of interdependency, we progressively uncover
an intelligible order that exists between causes and their proportionate effects or effects and their proportionate causes. Therefore, the
principle is first and foremost metaphysical (concerned with things
in themselves) not epistemological (a principle applied in our search
for explanations). In a commonsense way, all human beings advert
to this principle regarding the natures of things in their practical lives
when they take note that if they fall from a high place, the fall will kill
them, or that if they put their hand in boiling water, it will burn their
skin. More positively, they realize that if they apologize to a friend
they have offended, the friend will likely forgive them, or if they tell
a person they care about them, this can cause the affection to be re-
ciprocated. The principle of sufficient reason stems organically from
the principle of causality.

In fact, the presentation of these aforementioned principles suggests that in a certain sense each one unfolds organically from the
former. When we first grasp by simple apprehension that, for example, one being is not another being (the metaphysical truth of the
principle of non-contradiction), we also simultaneously grasp that

---

(London: Routledge, 2004), 272–74, who shows that this principle is in turn deployed
by Aristotle in *Metaphysics* XII, 7, 1072b1–31 to argue for the existence of the first mover,
God. Aquinas gives a very clear statement of the principle in *ST* I, q. 3, a. 4, in the context of his discussion of the real distinction of existence and essence in creatures: "[F]or
nothing can be the sufficient cause of its own existence, if its existence is caused. Therefore, that thing, whose existence differs from its essence, must have its existence caused
by another." ["Impossibile est autem quod esse sit causatum tantum ex principiis essen-
tialibus rei, quia nulla res sufficit quod sit sibi causa essendi, si habeat esse causatum."]
The principle appears again in *ST* I, q. 44, a. 1, characterized in terms of the metaphysics
of participation, and in *ST* I, q. 4, a. 2: "Whatever perfection exists in an effect must be
found in the effective cause." Norman Kretzmann provides arguments that the principle
is clearly found in Aquinas in *The Metaphysics of Theism: Aquinas's Natural Theology in
Summa Contra Gentiles I* (Oxford: Clarendon Press, 1997), 106–9. See also the evidence
mounted in the pertinent study of John Wippel, "Thomas Aquinas on Our Knowledge
of God and the Axiom That Every Agent Produces Something Like Itself," in *Metaphysical Themes in Thomas Aquinas II* (Washington, DC: The Catholic University of America
Press, 2007), 152–71.

there is an inward ontological content to the distinct beings in question (the principle of identity), which is characterized by the diverse categorial modes of being (that is, all things have given natures, qualities, quantities, relations, etc.). This in turn gives rise to the understanding that there are causes of the diverse beings in question, characterized in terms of the four causes (the principle of causality). From thinking about the causal order, we begin to think about the wider set of causes and explanations for the existence and nature of a given kind of reality (the principle of sufficient reason). In other words, each reality we experience, including ourselves, is present in a world of interdependency and causal interaction. Thus, there are webs of causal explanation that emerge, and we must analyze them in order to explain why various things exist, and why various events occur as they do, in a sufficiently exhaustive way. As I am characterizing them, these principles are grounded in our pre-critical, pre-demonstrative grasp of beings in the world around us, and they come to us by way of simple apprehension or intuition through common experience. They are inevitably present in the mind of each person in some degree of intensity, whether they are recognized reflexively or not.

Unity and Multiplicity

The second transcendental property is unity. Aquinas, following Aristotle, notes that unity tracks onto being and, in a sense, reveals being.[58] We said above that each reality we encounter (each substance), no matter how modest, has a certain singularity of existence and a certain kind of essence or nature. The insect or the leaf on the ground, the stone or the glass of water: we perceive in each of these not only a *singular* thing but also a *kind* of individual thing. But by that same measure, we also find in each such thing a given *unity*, since it is one being and has one nature, and also a kind of *multiplicity*, since it is

---

58. Aquinas, *In Meta.* IV, lec. 2, commenting on *Metaphysics* IV, 2, 1003b22–1004a9. The idea has imperfect foreshadowings in Plato's *Sophist*, 245c–255e.

composed of parts and has diverse characteristics.[59] This means that knowledge of the unity and multiplicity of things enters into our thinking in an initial, inevitable, and commonsense sort of way, as does the knowledge of being. However, unity (and multiplicity) can be characterized in importantly distinct ways. Let us consider four such ways so as to make this transcendental notion more intelligible.

1. *Form and Matter.* The idea of a basic form-matter distinction present in all physical beings is grounded in common sense. Each individual we perceive has a unified form of a given kind, be it that of a plant, a stone, or an artifact, such as a piece of furniture. The form is the nature considered as something that provides for the determination of species, essential properties, and unity of parts. One may speak, for example, of the form of the kangaroo as its animal nature by which it falls into a given genus (as an organic living thing characterized by sensate powers) that has a distinct species (being characterized by distinctive properties of the kangaroo, such as being a mammal, hopping on two legs, and bearing its young in a pouch). This nature informs all the material parts of the kangaroo and provides for an organic unity from within. To say that a given substance is a unified thing of a given kind, then, is to say that it has a given "form." However, such a being also has component parts, and they can exist at subjacent levels. In a human being, for example, there are organs of a living body, but there are also the cells of the organs, the chemicals in the cells, and the atoms in the chemicals. At each "level" of formal determination, there are material parts: organs, cells, chemical compounds, and atoms. Indeed, there are material parts within all the things we experience, which contribute to the constitution of those realities as their material parts.[60]

59. I am not treating here the question of artifactual unity versus natural unity but presupposing a broader concept that encompasses both.

60. On the whole and the part, with regard to the form and the matter of the human body, see *ST* I, q. 76, a. 8. On natural form and matter more generally see *In* II *Phys.*, lec. 1–2, on Aristotle's *Physics* II, 1, 12b8–193b21. For an application of this analysis to contemporary natural science, see Wallace, *The Modeling of Nature.*

Following what he takes to be Aristotle's view, Aquinas also posits something more fundamental within the material parts we find
in things: a basic potency that is present in all physical realities
that makes them capable of further transformation, divisibility, or
re-determination.[61] Even the most determined material particle can
be split or re-determined so as to be changed into something else.
(This idea seems to hold true in modern physics, since the elementary particles, such as the atom, have the potency to be split into smaller configurations or forces). That is to say, for Aquinas, there is a deep
plasticity or potentiality within all things that he calls "prime matter" and that makes all things subject to potential change and alteration. Aquinas's analysis of this principle shows that its affirmation is
well-founded and based in reality.[62] However, for our purposes here,
we can simply note a less controversial and more evident sense of the
terms "matter and form": there are distinct realities around us that

61. See Aquinas, *De principiis naturae*, §§ 3 and 14–17, and the extended discussion
of this topic in Aquinas in John F. Wippel, *The Metaphysical Thought of Thomas Aquinas: From Finite Being to Uncreated Being* (Washington, DC: The Catholic University of
America Press, 2000), 396–475.

62. Prime matter is not a "thing" but a co-constitutive principle of every formally
determined reality. All that is physical and material, insofar as it is material, contains a
fundamental potency that allows it to undergo further transformation and redefinition.
This explains why, for example, further material change and division are possible even
in the supposedly "smallest" of material particles and why quantitative dimensions of
reality (signified by mathematical numbers) are always divisible. There is no smallest
number. Furthermore, the affirmation of prime matter as a co-constitutive principle of
substantial form is required if one is to make sense of substantial corruption and generation, that is to say, of one distinct individual thing coming to be from another distinct
individual thing, while retaining some of the matter of the former substance. Otherwise,
all material change would have to be characterized only in terms of the reassembling of
material particles. But material particles truly become part of the larger reality they are
assimilated into, as when a man eats a piece of bread, first breaking it down into parts and
then assimilating it biologically into his own substance. This process would be metaphysically unintelligible if there were only particle change without a change of one substance
to another. Furthermore, even on the presupposition that "only atoms really exist" and
that they alone are the "simple" material particles that constitute all other things, it would
seem necessary to affirm that various kinds of atoms naturally join to one another to take
on new atomic forms, and so atoms themselves seemingly undergo substantial change,
which is only possible if there is some basic source of indeterminacy and potency present
in each material particle.

consist of material parts. All of modern biology, chemistry, and physics presupposes this basic fact in some way, since these disciplines presuppose that living organisms, organic and inorganic compounds, and atomic particles are all explicable in part at least by reference to their component material elements. There is, then, a multiplicity of material parts within the formal unity of each individual thing.[63] This is something basic that every person experiences prior to any attempt to provide deep philosophical explanations about the structure of reality. Consequently, any account of reality (whether materialistic, Buddhist, Vedantic, or monotheistic) needs to take such dimensions of reality into account in some way.

2. *Substance and Properties.* The distinction between a substance and its properties denotes another kind of unity and multiplicity we find in things. This is a composition of reality that arises in material things consisting of form and matter, of the aforementioned kind noted above. Aquinas develops a line of thinking he finds in Aristotle to argue that there are nine properties (categorial modes of being) basic to all realities around us: quantity, qualities, relations, actions, passions, habits, time, place, and position.[64] There are traditional debates about this list among metaphysicians. Do all the categories denote truly distinct modes of being found in material things that are not reducible to one another? Or are some categories like time and place basically special forms of relations and therefore ontologically reducible to relations? The first of these positions seems the most reasonable to me. However, to simplify matters here, we can consider only the first three of these properties: quantity, qualities,

63. Here, without entering into the question of prime matter, I am only claiming that animals and plants have biological parts (organs), that physical objects have chemical compositions, that chemical elements have atomic compositions, and that atoms have parts or charges.

64. I have argued above that the categorial modes of being are apprehended by the human intellect naturally and give rise to what I have termed the principle of identity. See Aquinas's profound analysis of the roots of the distinction of categories in *In* VII *Meta.*, lec. 9, §§ 891–92.

and relations. Every reality we encounter possesses such properties. For example, every physical thing, whether living or non-living,
natural or artifactual, has a given quantity—dimensional size and
extension. Each has various qualities, such as being warm or cold,
white or black, kind or cruel, capable of sensation, or capable of
mathematical reasoning. And from these quantities and qualities
there derive relations: one thing is relatively larger or smaller than
another, situated in this place or relative to that place, active upon
others—such as by playing music for them—or dependent upon
others—such as depending upon the activity of the sun for one's
continuance in being, and so forth.[65]

These various "properties" of quantity, quality, and relation are
not *identical with a nature as such* but *manifest that nature*. For example, the mere quantity of a hydrogen molecule cannot be identical
with the molecule as such, simply because there are also qualities of
the molecule that are key properties and distinguish it from molecules of other kinds. The quality of being able to solve mathematical
problems, no matter how noble, is not identical with the quantity of
the mathematician, nor is that quality simply "what" a given thing is
(a human animal, for example). Rather, it is a property and quality *of*
that being. The scientist is not his capacity for scientific exploration
but possesses this capacity as a qualifying property.

This kind of composition of substance and properties is properly
basic to all the realities we experience and constitutes a kind of multiplicity (of properties) inherent in unified subjects (the substances
themselves that possess these properties). The multiplicity of properties is contained within the unity of the substance and manifests
that unity in a myriad of ways, since the properties in question are
properties *of* the substances in question, which stem from its nature.

65. In his commentary of *In* VII *Meta.*, lec. 9, §§ 891–92, Aquinas argues that quantity derives principally from the material individuality of a given physical form, while quality derives principally from the formal nature and its operations, so that distinct natural
kinds of things have distinct natural kinds of *qualities* that are expressive of their nature.
The other categories: relations, actions, passions, habits, time, place, position, and so on,
are ontologically distinct expressions of the substantial nature, qualities, and quantity of
the reality in question.

3. *Distinction of Individuals.* A third form of unity and multiplicity we encounter in things stems from their existence as individuals. Here the multiplicity is more evident than the unity. Clearly there is a vast multitude of individual beings in the world. The sun is distinct from the oak tree, which is distinct from the man who peers upon both of them together. Our common experience is one of multiple things that all exist in actuality. Aquinas speaks here of the *actus essendi*, the "act of being" of each distinctive thing that makes it a kind of irreducible singular existent.[66] Each reality, from the blade of grass to the mouse in the field to the plastic artifact to the human child, is in its own way ontologically singular. It has its own particular grainy reality. In this sense, it is right to say that "being separates" or that "being divides," because the being of each thing is always singular and individual, the being of this thing or that thing which is not another thing.[67] However, upon reflection, we can also see that being *unites* as well, in the sense that all the things we experience truly do *exist*. In fact, existence is common to everything that is real. If we seek to think realistically about the world, we must take account of what really exists as distinct from what does not, and this means taking note of the great multitude and diversity of existent things. But by this same measure, we must also acknowledge the underlying commonality of existence present within all things and seek to identify the ultimate cause of this totality and unity of all that exists. Aquinas speaks here of *ens commune* or *esse commune*: common being or common existence.[68] Everything that is real truly exists. So there is a kind of inevitable unity to reality: *all that exists has something in common, something that unites it,* namely, the fact that it is real, that it exists.

4. *Distinction of Natural Kinds.* A final kind of multiplicity and unity derives from the diverse kinds of things that exist. Here again,

---

66. See *De hebdom.* I, lec. 2; *De ver.*, q. 1, a. 1, ad s.c. 3; *De ente*, ch. 1 and *De pot.*, q. 7, a. 2, ad 1 and ad 9.

67. "For, just as a being is said to be *one* in so far as it is without division in itself, so it is said to be *something* in so far as it is divided from others." *De ver.*, q. 1, a. 1. [Trans. R. W. Mulligan, *Truth* (Chicago: Henry Regnery Company, 1952)].

68. See *De pot.*, q. 7, a. 2, ad 4; *ST* I, q. 3, a. 4, ad 1 and *In div. nom.* V, lec. 2.

we discover multiplicity and unity. There is a multiplicity of things in the world: hydrogen atoms, planets, suns, lakes, trees, eukaryotic bacteria, cars, clay, diamonds, snowflakes, chimpanzees, human beings. We have the capacity to place things in our rough taxonomies—to name them by their natural kinds—because there is a multiplicity of natures (of substances having diverse properties) that we discover in the world around us and submit to study and analysis. At the same time, this implies that there are unities of kind as well: each snowflake truly is a snowflake, and therefore, although each one of them is in some way singular, they are also the same essential kind of thing. They can be distinguished from deer, each of which is also singular but also has something in common with other deer, that is to say, all are the same essential kind of thing. This latter distinction of unity and multiplicity (of natural kinds) is grounded in the first distinction given above of form and matter. There are distinct "forms" or natures present in the material world. The lamb is distinct from the rose, and this one lamb is distinct from that other lamb. The distinction between the lamb and the rose is formal or natural. It stems from a distinction of natural kind. The distinction between this lamb and that one or this rose and that one is primarily material. It stems from the material individuality of this lamb, which has a distinct material body, organic constitution, cellular, and atomic composition, as compared with another of the same kind.[69]

Truth and Falsehood

The third transcendental is truth. Technically speaking, truth is primarily in the mind or the intelligence of a perceiver and is not something in external reality itself.[70] What a person thinks is true when it

69. See Aquinas, *De ente*, ch. 2. Although matter is a principle of individuation in physical bodies, existence and essence also factor into individuation and metaphysical singularity, since a given individual nature is "singular" in being due to its unique act of existing. On this complex topic see Lawrence Dewan, *Form and Being*, 229–47. [*De ente et essentia*, in *Opuscula philosophica*, vol. 1, ed. R. Spiazzi (Turin and Rome: Marietti, 1950). Translations below are taken from "On Being and Essence," in *Medieval Philosophy: Essential Readings with Commentary*, ed. G. Klima (Blackwell Publishers, 2007).]

70. As Lawrence Dewan notes in "Is Truth a Transcendental for St. Thomas Aquinas?," *Nova et Vetera* (English edition) Vol. 2, no. 1 (2004): 1–20.

corresponds adequately or realistically to the nature of reality itself. "Is what you say really true?" "Do unicorns truly exist?" "Do kangaroos exist?" "Was that truly an ethical action?" "Are human beings truly purely material beings?" "Does the world originate from a Creator or is it true to say that God does not exist?" "Is the New Testament truly an inspired book, or is it merely an artifact of human culture?" "Is Jesus Christ truly raised bodily from the dead, or not?" "If he is, must I strive to surrender my life to him, or can I realistically live in indifference to him?" Truth is the correspondence of the mind to reality, so what we think and say is true when what we think and say corresponds to reality.[71]

On the other hand, falsehood is something that does not correspond to reality and appears only in the mind. When a person believes something that is in fact false, he believes something that has

71. *De ver.*, q. 1, a. 1:

The soul ... has both knowing and appetitive powers. "Good" expresses the correspondence of being to the appetitive power, for, and so we note in the *Nicomachean Ethics*, the good is "that which all desire." "True" expresses the correspondence of being to the knowing power, for all knowing is produced by an assimilation of the knower to the thing known, so that assimilation is said to be the cause of knowledge. Similarly, the sense of sight knows a color by being informed with a species of the color. The first reference of being to the intellect, therefore, consists in its agreement with the intellect. This agreement is called "the conformity of thing and intellect." In this conformity is fulfilled the formal constituent of the true, and this is what *the true* adds to being, namely, the conformity or equation of thing and intellect. As we said, the knowledge of a thing is a consequence of this conformity; therefore, it is an effect of truth, even though the fact that the thing is a being is prior to its truth. Consequently, truth or the true has been defined in three ways. First of all, it is defined according to that which precedes truth and is the basis of truth. This is why Augustine writes: "The true is that which is"; and Avicenna: "The truth of each thing is a property of the act of being which has been established for it." ... Truth is also defined in another way—according to that in which its intelligible determination is formally completed. Thus, Isaac writes: "Truth is the conformity of thing and intellect"; and Anselm: "Truth is a rectitude perceptible only by the mind." This rectitude, of course, is said to be based on some conformity. The Philosopher says that in defining truth we say that truth is had when one affirms that "to be which is, and that not to be which is not." The third way of defining truth is according to the effect following upon it. Thus, Hilary says that the true is that which manifests and proclaims existence. And Augustine says: "Truth is that by which that which is, is shown"; and also: "Truth is that according to which we judge about inferior things."

no foundation in reality, that is, it does not correspond to reality.

Aquinas rightly notes that if this is the case, then a number of important truths follow. First, as he notes, the human intellect is perfected by the judgment of the truth.[72] Our activity of seeking the truth and trying to understand the world by reasoning about it comes to fruition or inward perfection when we make more and more realistic, penetrative, and sophisticated judgments about the world. The materialist naturalist who claims in light of natural science to detect the total explanatory principles of reality in material particles alone as the exclusive content of all that exists claims to have reached a perfection of judgment and truthfulness about reality, one that is perfective of the mind.[73] So does the Buddhist who claims there is no "self" in the human agent, as well as the monotheist who argues that the existence of the material world and the metaphysical features of reality we experience require us to posit a hidden, transcendent cause that has given being to the world, in wisdom and goodness. These are all truth claims (incompatible with one another) based on the goal of true judgment. Judgment is equally present in the agnostic or skeptic, who claims either that we cannot know the answers to ultimate metaphysical questions or that we should prudently suspend judgment.[74] The suspicion of a

---

72. See, for example, *Expos. de Trin.*, q. 1, a. 3.

73. Presumably, if he is consistently physicalist, he should also believe that he reaches that perfection only through a particular configuration of matter in his own physical body and brain. This raises the question of whether in principle one could rearrange the material parts of the brains of people so that they would arrive at the truth of materialism without doing any of the work of scientific and philosophical study and inference, so that they could make atheistic claims without having to carry out a succession of logical inferences to arrive at such views. But if this is possible even in principle, then it would seem that the logical processes of argument and inference, as well as free consent to the truth, are accidental to the essential content of a truth claim. Although it would take more time to spell out the argument here, one can begin to intuit a paradox: the materialist who insists on the "truth" of materialism also creates very great problems for himself in explaining what any logical consent to the truth looks like in the human mind, if that action has to be understood in purely material terms. The affirmation of the ontological truth of materialism thus begins to undercut any workable explanatory account of how we have epistemic access to the truth of materialism as merely material human subjects.

74. So, for example, David Hume's line of argument developed in the *Dialogues*

consequent judgment depends upon the firm commitment to an antecedent judgment—that is, "it is best to stay out of irresolvable intellectual controversies." In this sense, no one fails to make judgments and claim a horizon of perfecting truth for the realm of intellect. Differences occur only with regard to the scope and content of such judgments. No one's judgments are free from risk. Fallibility and error threaten all of us on all sides and burden each of us equally with the obligation to seek the truth carefully, honestly, and deliberately. When we seek to make significant judgments regarding reality, the truth is at stake, and this in turn touches directly upon the dignity of the human intellect and its perfection in relation to reality.

Of course one can object: "Isn't the truth primarily a construct of the human mind? Is it not principally the product of a given human culture? Is it not construed differently in diverse cultural-historical situations? Is it not produced by webs of language that are conventional and sociologically differentiated from one another, so that distinct forms of discourse produce irreducibly distinct notions of truth?" These are all important objections, but they are also all objections based on judgments about reality themselves. The truth is that our truth assertions are (1) conceptual products of human thought present in all cultures, which (2) develop in distinct modes in various times and places, (3) expressed in and through distinct languages with their idiosyncratic idioms. Nevertheless, these features of our truth-seeking are all *conditions* of that search. They are not the final source of the *determination* of the truth content. That ultimate determination of truth content comes from *reality itself*, since the search for the truth is precisely a search regarding the inner content of reality, not its mode of human linguistic expression or sociological conveyance. In and through the comparison of various socially particular and culturally conditioned conceptions of reality, we seek to discover the actual truth about reality.

It follows from the conception of truth we have been pursuing

---

Concerning Natural Religion seeks to terminate in a principled set of judgments even if (or especially because) these are skeptical in kind.

that truth has its metaphysical foundation in reality itself, while false-hood does not. Truth relates back to and is co-extensive with being. What do we mean by "co-extensive"? There where we find being, we find truth. What exists or is real determines the content of what is true. Correspondingly, this also means that reality is intrinsically intelligible. All that exists can potentially be understood, at least to some extent. This is why we can make progress in understanding the world around us, whether in the natural sciences, technological know-how, ethical discernments about just and unjust actions, determining whether someone else loves us, deciding what a human person is, or making decisions about the meaning of existence more generally. To the extent that we come to know what reality is or what it consists in, in its diverse dimensions, we acquire a realistic world-view, a true understanding of the intelligibility of reality.

This means, in turn, that the truth of the world exists prior to the truth explorations of the human mind, at least in the sense that the truth about reality is there prior to our discovery of it.[75] The earth revolved around the sun prior to the human scientific understanding of this fact that developed in modern culture due to the efforts of Copernicus and Galileo. Truths of classical geometry or modern biology have a foundation in reality prior to our deduction or discovery of them. If the mystery of God is real, this is true prior to our discovery of it. If the universe itself is ultimately one with God, or if there is no God, these are truths that hold independently of whether we accept them or not. Reality does not favor the delusional or the willfully ignorant. Consequently, it is the task of the human learner to conform his thinking to reality and not to seek the inverse, to conform reality to his thinking.[76] At the same time, we are able to engage

75. This is what some scholastic authors traditionally refer to as "ontological truth," and it corresponds to Aquinas's first definition of truth noted above in *De ver.*, q. 1, a. 1, in which he cites Augustine: "The true is that which is."

76. A kind of contrast exists in artistic creativity, where the human learner takes pre-existing materials from reality and refashions them artificially to conform them to a pre-existing idea he or she has of an artistic creation. This process is always of a "second-order" ontologically, however, insofar as it presupposes the "given" ontological natural structures of reality that precede the artistic creative process and that genuine

in the search for the truth freely and willingly, so as to grow to love the truth for its own sake, not because it has been imposed upon us by violence, extrinsically, but because we have come to discover it freely from within. This is in fact the only way we really come to an integral understanding of the truth, freely and personally, through desire, love, intellectual investigation, and rational consent.[77]

Perennial truths exist in a mind-independent way. This fact raises metaphysical questions of importance. For example, it would be "true" that there is a vast multitude of different stars and solar systems in our cosmos, even if there were no human beings to perceive it or think about it. This was true prior to our knowledge of the universe, indeed, prior to the time that the human race existed. It is a truth of mathematics that 7,439 times 23 equals 171,097. This truth has its ultimate foundation in the structures of material quantity, and the quantitative world we live in would contain this truth ontologically even if no one ever made the human calculation. Furthermore, it seems evident that there could not exist any possible material world in which that calculation was not true, since truths about mathematical quantity would apply in any such world.[78]

This raises the broader question of whether there are truths that hold always and everywhere, independently of the material facts present in our universe and to which we have access mentally through

---

artistic talent presupposes a familiarity with and a knowledge of. A genuine painter, for example, has to be realistically knowledgeable not only about the subjects of representation but also the material media (paint, canvas) and so on, through which the artistic idea for the work is realized. There is no realistic artistic creativity without an antecedent familiarity with and training in the materials of art that make the expression possible. Art thus presupposes nature and builds on nature. There is no human artistic creation of being in the strict sense, and we do not create ourselves or our natures through our art. Rather, we have creative, artistic natures precisely because we are rational animals who can reformulate natural realities in light of our rational apprehension of their qualities and other properties subject to recombination and reconfiguration.

77. As Aquinas analyzes in profoundly helpful ways in *De Malo*, q. 6.

78. This must be the case since the laws of quantity that give rise to this equation would obtain in the same way in any universe with quantity of either a discrete or dimensive kind. The laws do not derive, then, from ideal numbers but from the structure of quantitative being, in which being as such implies quantitative constants and a logic of mathematical truths that stems from these constants.

our encounter with reality as we experience it. What kind of truths might this idea refer to? Examples would include the metaphysical principles we noted above: the principles of non-contradiction, identity, causality, and sufficient reason. Is there a universe that could exist, whether material or immaterial, impersonal, or personal, in which the law of non-contradiction would be inapplicable? Or, is there a world in which there would be no law of identity—in which things would not have any inner ontological identity or intelligible definition based on their essence—or in which there would be no principle of sufficient reason? It seems not. Nothing of this kind is intelligible, and it seems like we depend on intelligibility to conceive of any kind of possible world. Accordingly, we can state a fundamental truth claim: in any case where there exists a set of realities, there exists a real distinction between them, an intelligible (causal) content within and between them, and a proportionate intelligibility present within their causal originations and mutual interactions. Similarly, laws of mathematics (laws of quantity) would and do apply in any material universe. (It is not logically possible to envisage a universe in which 2+2 would equal 5, which suggests that this truth is not derived primarily from our intellect but is a truth about the reality of quantitative entities that precedes our discovery and understanding of it.) Consequently, we can conclude at the very least that there are truths about reality that are always and everywhere true, which do not depend upon our minds for their existence and that contribute to the inner intelligibility of reality.

A final point we should make in this context is that falsehood stems from an absence of truth or, more precisely, a privation of truth in the mind, where it should exist. This occurs when the human mind affirms or judges to be true what is in fact not the case.[79] Falsehood is contrary to the good of the human intellect as such. Error, delusion, laziness, and anti-intellectualism are not virtuous.[80]

79. *ST* I, q. 17, aa. 1, 3, and 4. A. 4: "Falsity asserts something, for a thing is false, as the Philosopher says (*Metaphysics* IV, 7, 1012a26), inasmuch as something is said or seems to be something that it is not, or not to be what it really is."

80. *ST* I-II, q. 110.

They do not perfect the human mind. The more consequential the truth for human existence, the more serious the falsehood in question becomes. Consequently, religious delusion can do grave harm to the human person. Atheistic falsehoods and erroneous judgments that stem from anti-religious prejudice and philosophical error can do so as well, and perhaps even more so, as exhibited in the case of the violent atheistic political ideologies of the twentieth century. Everyone should seek the truth as rigorously as they are able. No one has a natural desire to be in error or to embrace falsehood, and naturally no one wishes to be lied to or deceived.[81] Rather, human beings have a natural love for and aspiration to the truth. Truthfulness in speech and thought and studiousness (zeal) in the search for the truth are virtues. They qualify the human person, giving perfection to human reason and human desire. The deliberate cultivation of falsehood and the culpable negligence of the truth (affected ignorance[82]) are vices that diminish the dignity of the human person.

Goodness as Metaphysical Perfection and "Evil" as Privation

A third basic notion that is co-extensive with being, along with unity and truth, is goodness.[83] All that exists is in some way good. This may seem like an unfounded religious claim. However, it can be understood as an epistemologically modest and uncontroversial, realistic claim, if we define goodness in a certain way. Furthermore, it can be shown that virtually any worldview depends upon some notion of goodness and its contrary—the privation of goodness—as a condition for thinking seriously about the nature of the world.

Consider Aquinas's definition of goodness as the mature, intrinsic perfection of a given thing.[84] Frequently, this is a perfection that

---

81. See on this matter ST I-II, q. 94, a. 2 and II-II, q. 109.

82. ST I-II, q. 76, aa. 2–4.

83. ST I, q. 5, a. 1. See the adumbrations of this idea in Plato, Republic VI, 507b, and Aristotle, Nicomachean Ethics I, 6, 1196a23–34; Metaphysics IX, 9, 1051a4–34.

84. ST I, q. 5, a. 1, ad 1: "But goodness signifies perfection which is desirable; and consequently, of ultimate perfection. Hence that which has ultimate perfection is said to be simply good; but that which has not the ultimate perfection it ought to have

the reality may achieve over time. This modest and universal definition is applicable to a wide range of realities, and it can be employed quite clearly in the case of non-human living things. Plants, for example, tend to flourish by putting down roots, putting out leaves and flowers, and by reproducing through the production of fruits or seedlings. Their growth, organic development, and successful reproduction are objectively detectable forms of biological perfection. A plant self-perfects through these processes. This means, however, that we can speak about what is "objectively good" for this or that type of plant, what soil and temperature it grows well in, what sunlight and water it needs, and whether it is free of disease or not. Judgments about these topics are measured by what is good for the plant, based on its own internal dynamics and particular form of perfection.[85] Botanists may speak rightly, then, about whether they are looking at a healthy ("good") specimen or not, based on objective factors. We can speak similarly about animals: what is the good of the animal as it tends to gain sense-knowledge of its environment, to adapt, to hunt prey or seek to survive against potential predators, and to nourish and protect its young? There are clear and uncontroversial signs of good states of being—of animal health, sense knowledge, and flourishing—that bring animal life to perfection.

Human beings also seek various kinds of goods that are distinctive. One of them is a distinctive grade of conceptual knowledge and understanding about the world. It is good and perfect for human beings to advance in the study of the truth and in a genuine knowledge of reality. Likewise, human beings freely seek happiness and stable

---

(although, in so far as it is at all actual, it has some perfection), is not said to be perfect simply nor good simply, but only relatively."

85. *ST* I, q. 5, a. 1, ad 2: "Goodness is a form so far as absolute goodness signifies complete actuality." *ST* I, q. 5, a. 5:

Everything is said to be good in so far as it is perfect; for in that way only is it desirable.... Now a thing is said to be perfect if it lacks nothing according to the mode of its perfection. But since everything is what it is by its form (and since the form presupposes certain things, and from the form certain things necessarily follow), in order for a thing to be perfect and good it must have a form, together with all that precedes and follows upon that form.

and just forms of life in society. The pursuit of happiness through deliberate free action constitutes a perfection for them, a form of life by which they acquire their genuine human good.[86] To be sure, what this "good" or "these goods" consist in is a vexing and controversial topic. Materialist naturalists may claim, for example, that humans are best served (best perfected) when they advance in realistic modern scientific knowledge, let go of the illusions of religious worldviews, build societies based on stable forms of health care and education, diminish religious violence, establish equality among persons, and advance the causes of neglected minorities. They consider these states of being objective forms of good for the human race and consequently make inevitable appeal to some metaphysical notion of goodness as a distinctive aspect of being: that which is perfective of a given kind of being. Mahayana Buddhist philosophers tailor the list of human goods very differently in many respects but similarly in others. Islamic religious authorities maintain a different set of criteria for what constitutes the best form of knowledge and ethical happiness. The point here is simply that even in order to debate the nature of the good and to think about it constructively (in and through controversy), there must be present in the mind of each interlocutor a "most basic" notion of goodness that is common to all and inevitable, whether it is adverted to overtly and grasped self-consciously or not.

What about non-living things? Do we find goodness in stars and stones and lakes? There are four distinct ways to respond to this question. First, on one level it is possible to say that they have a basic goodness (a perfection of being) just insofar as they exist. There is goodness and perfection in being itself.[87] That claim is subject to controversy, of course, because some may argue that the world's existence is not a good thing or that many particular things that exist are not good. This was the claim of ancient Manicheanism, which asserted that the sheer existence of material things is basically an evil

---

86. *ST* I-II, q. 3, a. 2.
87. *ST* I, q. 5, a. 3.

rather than a good.[88] The material world and its order are "regrettable." Others might say that the question is simply unintelligible or too anthropomorphic. After all, in asking this question, are we not merely asking about whether it is good for human beings to exist? However, it is intelligible to ask questions about the goodness of the existence of the physical world as such. Human beings are capable of doing so, and most would consent to the idea that it is better for things to exist than to not exist and that the existence of the material world in this sense constitutes a good in itself.[89]

Second, we can also speak about the "goodness" of the formal determinations of things in the sense of their inner perfection. We may think of a "perfect snowflake" as a well-formed snowflake with its own integrity and internal order. This is a "good" snowflake in that it has a completeness and internal harmony. This notion of goodness is quite modest, but it is intelligible, as when we speak of a good specimen of uranium or hydrogen, worthy of our study.[90]

---

88. Henry Chadwick, preface to Augustine, *Confessions*, trans. H. Chadwick (Oxford: Oxford University Press, 1992), xiv:

> Mani ... [was] ... a Mesopotamian gnostic of the third century [A.D.] whose religion was zealously propagated by underground missionary work, despite fierce prohibitions from the [Roman] imperial government. The religion of Mani's followers, called in Latin *Manichaei*, Manichees, expressed disgust at the physical world and especially at the human reproductive system. Procreation imprisoned divine souls in matter, which is inherently hostile to goodness and light. Manichees had a vegetarian diet, and forbade wine. There were two classes, Elect who were strictly obliged to be celibate, and Hearers allowed wives or concubines as long as they avoided procreating children, whether by contraceptives or by confining intercourse to the "safe" period of the monthly cycle. Manichean propaganda was combative against the orthodox Catholic Church, which granted married Christians to be in good standing.... Baptism and eucharist were held in contempt by Mani [as physical rites] ... Mani strongly denied the historical reality of the crucifixion of Jesus; for him the Cross was a symbol of the suffering of humanity.

89. This idea constitutes a major theme in Augustine's *Confessions*, book VII. See the prolongation of Augustine's argument by Aquinas in *ST* I, qq. 48 and 49, which cohere closely with the notion of goodness as a transcendental property of being in *ST* I, q. 5.

90. See *ST* I, q. 5, a. 4, where Aquinas notes that some idea of perfection stems from the basic notion of form and of the efficient causes that terminate in that form as well as the operations or properties that result from that form (final causality or characteristic

Third, a more complete form of goodness emerges in the physical world from the complex interactions of a multiplicity of beings. There is an integral order between the many distinct individuals and their natural kinds that allows systems to emerge—physical systems, like the solar system, and environmental systems, like those that exist on the surface of planets. The good or perfection of these systems is again modest; it is that of a given form of order that has come into being. We can think about what is good for the system in question and whether it may be sustained.[91] This is something akin to the preservation of order.

Fourth, such systems can be judged as objectively good in a relative sense, in that they provide an environment for living things and human beings.[92] The physical laws of the cosmos and the environment of the earth's surface are truly good insofar as they provide an environment where living things can come into existence and flourish. We can speak realistically, therefore, of objectively good environments for human and non-human life and of bad environments for the same. Environmentalism and the modern science that undergirds it presuppose this kind of objective realism about goodness in the natural order. What are the necessary and good conditions that must obtain within the environment in order to sustain thriving ecosystems from generation to generation? So too can we think of the physical world insofar as it is good for the flourishing of human beings in the operations proper to them. It is objectively good to seek knowledge of the physical world around us (whether theological, philosophical, or scientific), and the experience of this practice of knowledge acquisition permits us to appreciate the goodness of the world. It also provides the necessary conditions for artistic creativity and technological development. So too a human being can be

---

qualities and effects of the form). This broad definition applies to all species and modes of being, as he notes in turn in q. 5, a. 5.

91. On the idea of ontological common goods of this sort, see ST I-II, q. 109, a. 3; SCG III, cc. 17 and 22.

92. See in this respect, SCG III, c. 22.

thankful for the existence of the physical world insofar as it provides an environment where the human community can seek knowledge, communal happiness, moral freedom, and creative discovery.

Where one finds various forms of goodness, there is the possibility of an absence or privation of goodness, which is traditionally termed "evil."[93] Evil conceived in this way is a broad, general concept, beyond the distinction between natural evils (like blindness, as the privation of sight) and moral evils—unethical actions that human beings do freely, whether by weakness or in ignorance or by rationalized selfishness.[94] We can think briefly about these distinct forms of goodness and their corresponding natural privations. If living things flourish through their vital operations of nourishment, growth, reproduction, and sense knowledge (in animals), then natural evils for them consist in the privations of these vital functions. A plant or animal that ceases to be able to nourish itself or to function adroitly in its animal movements or sense operations is a wounded or naturally deficient being subject to natural evils. Of course all living things eventually undergo substantial corruption through death, by which they are subject to a privation of their living form, while their bodily matter passes over into a larger order of other living and non-living things that it helps to sustain. This process represents a natural evil for each individual living thing, even if its death contributes to the perpetuation of other realities. Similarly, in the non-living world, we can speak of the natural privation of being present in things when they cease to exist (substantial corruption) or in the cessation or privation of natural order (when a wider collective order of things undergoes disruption) or in the loss of an environmental equilibrium that provides sanctuary and protection for living things. The human being is subject to distinctive forms of internal evil in the twin forms of ignorance (privation of knowledge or presence of falsehood) and moral misery (weakness or vice, the privation of ethical rectitude,

93. *ST* I, q. 48, a. 1: "[B]y the name of evil is signified the absence of good. And this is what is meant by saying that 'evil is neither a being nor a good.' For since being, as such, is good, the absence of one implies the absence of the other."
94. *ST* I, q. 48, a. 5.

virtue, justice, and happiness).[95] Just as goodness and perfection are present in distinct ways and in differing modes, so privation is present also in distinctive ways.

Beauty as the Splendor of the Form

The final transcendental is beauty. Aquinas claims that everything that exists is in some way beautiful. Is this a realistic claim? That depends upon one's definition of beauty. Aquinas speaks about three properties present in all things from which their beauty arises: *integrity* or *perfection* of the form, *proportionality* or *harmony* of elements within the form, and the *splendor* or *clarity* of the form.[96] This definition is surprisingly nimble, since it is applicable to all kinds of diverse realities and allows one to analyze various kinds of beauty present within them. Let us briefly consider each of the three elements in turn and advert to the wide, analogical range of its applicability.

First, the integrity of a given form (a kind of thing) has to do with the wholeness of that form. A tree is whole when it has all its branches and each is healthy. A philosophical argument is integral when it has all the necessary elements and no significant part is missing. A mountain is integral when its figure is unified and takes on a coherent visible definition against the backdrop of the landscape.

Second, the proportionality or harmony of the elements has to do with the qualitative and quantitative relations that emerge between the parts of a given thing. A complex, massive tree may have many branches, leaves, and flowers that are all also spaced in balanced fashion, with qualities of color and texture whose combination of diversity and coherence appears as harmonious. An argument may have many elements that fit well together. A mountain may have a multi-faceted geometrical shape and diverse colors that

95. See *ST* I-II, qq. 75–78.
96. *ST* I, q. 39, a. 8: "For beauty includes three conditions, 'integrity' or 'perfection,' since those things which are impaired are by the very fact ugly; due 'proportion' or 'harmony'; and lastly, 'brightness' or 'clarity,' whence things are called beautiful which have a bright color."

form a striking unity and provide a fitting contrast with the shape and colors of the ambient landscape and background.

Third, splendor or clarity emerges when the integral form and the proportionate parts are present. The tree that has holistic integrity and a beautiful proportion of quantitative shape and qualities emits a natural splendor or radiance. We say an argument is beautiful when its integrity and proportionate elements are such that the conclusions emerge from it in splendid and excellent fashion. A mountain is splendid when its unitary figure in many integrated aspects of majestic quantity and varied qualities stands out against the backdrop of the landscape in proportionally splendid and clear ways.

As these examples suggest, then, beauty can be spiritual as well as physical, as when we say that this person possesses a beautiful mind or a beautiful humility. This means there is an integrity and proportionate, multi-sided balance to the intelligence or the humility of this person. Again, there is a distinction to the kinds of beauty in things, just as there is a distinction to the kinds of goodness; inorganic realities can all be said to be beautiful in various ways due to the order of their various physical perfections and qualities. Plants are beautiful in ways that differ from non-living things and according to various degrees. There is beauty in the diverse animals that is distinct from that of non-sentient creatures. And there is beauty in human beings, especially due to their moral qualities, their reasoning, and their artistic abilities.[97]

If this is the case, we may ask about the relationship between truth, goodness, and beauty. What is the difference between the goodness of things and their beauty? Goodness has to do with perfection of the form, the end toward which it tends: a given nature is good when it reaches its internal perfection. Beauty has to do with

97. *ST* II-II, q. 142, a. 2: "[I]n human affairs a thing is beautiful according as it harmonizes with reason." *ST* II-II, q. 145, a. 2: "[B]eauty ... results from the concurrence of clarity and due proportion.... Hence the beauty of the body consists in a man having his bodily limbs well proportioned, together with a certain clarity of color. In like manner spiritual beauty consists in a man's conduct or actions being well proportioned in respect of the spiritual clarity of reason."

the integrity of the form insofar as it draws admiration: a thing is beautiful when it has an internal order and harmonious proportions of qualities and quantity, so as to exude splendor and incite contemplative admiration.[98] To state things in this way is to characterize beauty in terms of intelligibility. Beauty is the splendor of the form. A given thing is beautiful when it has a richly intelligible nature, with harmonious proportionate aspects that relate to one another. However, we could also say that beauty is the intelligible determination of goodness. When we encounter something perfect, something that has achieved a certain goodness of perfection, there is an intelligible beauty to it. This way of speaking places emphasis on the goodness of beautiful things but in doing so notes that beauty implies a kind of formal determination in things (and thus a truth or intelligibility within them). In sum, we can say that beauty emerges from both truth and goodness together, and is the goodness or splendor of the truth. This is why beauty invites admiration, while goodness perfects. Goodness is grounded in final causality, while beauty is grounded in formal causality. Beauty has the power to hold our gaze. Goodness has the power to give our lives ultimate purpose or meaning. The two are not to be confused, even if they are often found together.

98. *ST* I, q. 5, a. 4, ad 1:

Beauty and goodness in a thing are identical fundamentally; for they are based upon the same thing, namely, the form; and consequently goodness is praised as beauty. But they differ logically, for goodness properly relates to the appetite (goodness being what all things desire); and therefore it has the aspect of an end (the appetite being a kind of movement towards a thing). On the other hand, beauty relates to the cognitive faculty; for beautiful things are those which please when seen. Hence beauty consists in due proportion; for the senses delight in things duly proportioned, as in what is after their own kind—because even sense is a sort of reason, just as is every cognitive faculty. Now since knowledge is by assimilation, and similarity relates to form, beauty properly belongs to the nature of a formal cause.

On beauty as a transcendental in Aquinas, see questions raised by Aertsen, *Medieval Philosophy and the Transcendentals*, 335–59 and the reflections of Pasquale Porro, *Thomas Aquinas: A Historical and Philosophical Profile*, trans. J. Trabbic and R. Nutt (Washington, DC: The Catholic University of America Press, 2016), 203–5.

THE ANTECEDENT PROBABILITY OF
MONOTHEISM AND THE RATIONAL POSSIBILITY OF
DIVINE REVELATION

A consideration of the transcendental features of reality gives focus to our consideration of ultimate explanations of reality. Our ordinary experience should be trusted at least to some extent, because the knowledge we derive from it is essential to any constitutive understanding of the world we form, whether philosophical or scientific. The world we experience, however, is one of multiple realities, marked by an orderly distinction of kinds (that is, other human beings, animals, plants, non-living things), existing in an order of interdependence and mutual simultaneous causal interaction. It is a world in which there are beings that come to be and pass away, in which change is real, but also in which there are stable features of reality that make it intelligible through time and subject to our understanding. Things possess natural structures. There is intelligibility within them as a result. We discover truth in being itself and falsehood in our mistaken conceptions of reality, which we try to correct over time. There is also goodness and beauty in things, and we can identify the privation of these features of being as evil and ugliness.

Classical monotheism proposes that underlying this world of changeable beings there is a Being unlike all other beings, in whom there is no shadow of change and with whom no evil or ugliness can be found. This Being is called God, the incomprehensible Creator of all things, whose attributes may be opposed to those of the gods of polytheism. It is not my intention here to construct formal arguments for the existence of God, monotheism, or a consideration of divine attributes. That will be the subject of the following chapter. However, we can note ways that the transcendental features of reality intuitively suggest to human reason the rational possibility and even the antecedent probability of monotheism as providing the best and (I will argue eventually) rationally demonstrable explanation of reality. Why is this the case?

First, from the existence of beings that are each ontological-ly contingent and causally dependent upon others, there arises the idea of a transcendent cause of existence that is not contingent. If all the things we experience come into being, pass out of being, and are themselves dependent upon others for their continued existence, is it reasonable to posit something that exists "necessarily" and perpet-ually, giving being to all things?

Second, from the multiplicity of beings existing within a com-mon framework of interaction that presupposes common natures, intelligible tendencies, and laws governing their engagements, there arises the idea of one reality that transcends all the multiple beings within the created order, which is the source of their being and of the order that unites and characterizes them amidst their multiplicity.

Third, from the diversity of kinds of reality and the grades of be-ing according to diverse orders of perfection (namely, being, life, intelligence), there arises the idea of a transcendent source of that hierarchy of perfections, of God who is the hidden and incompre-hensible author of the hierarchy of being.

Fourth, from the finite and diverse forms of goodness and beauty found in things, there arises the idea of one who is the author of all that exists insofar as it is good and beautiful.

Fifth, from the caused nature of all things that depend upon oth-ers for their existence, it would seem that if a first principle does ex-ist, one that explains all other things in an ultimate way, that prin-ciple must be utterly distinct from caused realities that come into being, even as it is the cause of their very existence. If this is the case, then God is not identical with the created world of things that depend upon him, and so pantheistic conceptions of the world are problematic in some fundamental way.

Finally, there is also the fact that human beings can think con-structively about the transcendental features of reality, and in so doing, they cultivate personal features of their existence (intelli-gence and will) through their reference to the properties of truth and goodness present in reality. If these most distinctively personal dimensions of man (knowledge and love) imply some form of immateriality, then they suggest a form of likeness to the first principle, God. That is to say, they correspond by analogy—they are both like and unlike—the transcendent principle and first cause of all things, the Creator, who is wise and good.

Here we are only suggesting that the idea of monotheism is intelligible and has a kind of intuitive plausibility that is realistic. However, the mere idea of monotheism, no matter how initially coherent it may be, does not give rise to certitude of the existence of God. The argument I am making is most certainly not that the rationality of monotheism or the knowledge of the existence of God can be immediately derived (intuitively or a priori) from the consideration of the transcendentals nor from the mere concept of deity itself. We cannot come to know that God exists merely from thinking about the notion of God. This claim was formulated by medieval expositors of the ontological argument (notably Anselm, Bonaventure, and John Duns Scotus, in various ways) but was one that Aquinas rejected. Kant did not read these medieval figures carefully, but he did formulate a sophisticated critique of the ontological argument as it is found in Descartes and Leibniz. Not only was he critical of it but he also took it to be at the base of all forms of philosophical argumentation for the existence of God. Although I agree that the argument is problematic (especially as formulated by Descartes), I decidedly disagree on both historical and conceptual grounds that it is emblematic of all forms of rational argument for the truth of monotheism.[99]

99. The "ontological argument" makes its first appearance in Anselm of Canterbury in his *Proslogion*, ch. II, which in turn influenced in different ways thinkers like Bonaventure, Scotus, Descartes, Leibniz, and Hegel, but also those who reacted against them, such as Kant and Heidegger. As is well known, then, Kant understands the ontological argument to be at the base of all theistic speculative argumentation, such as that found in the cosmological argument (taken from the contingency of creatures) or the physio-theological argument (based upon the presence of teleology in creatures). [*Critique of Pure Reason*, II, III, 5; II, III, 6, 507–24.] Meanwhile, Aquinas poses fundamental objections to Anselm's mode of argumentation in *ST* I, q. 2, a. 2, corp. and ad 2. This in turn suggests that Aquinas's whole approach to philosophical reasoning about the nature of God does not follow the specific pattern which is criticized and rejected by a thinker like Kant. Nor would Aquinas grant Kant's assertion that all forms of argumentation for

What I am suggesting at this point, however, is something quite modest: that the basic form of reality we experience in its transcendental ontological features does naturally give rise to the question of the existence of God as a potentially intelligible source of explanation for reality. This means, firstly, that one cannot "eliminate" the idea of God as an inherently unintelligible or irrational notion. Atheists may try to find psychological or sociological explanations for the genesis of the idea of God, but ultimately, they do so in vain.[100] It has a firm metaphysical rootedness in the very nature of things, since those things themselves interpolate the questioning mind in such a way as to raise legitimately the question of God and so as to suggest the very idea of God as Creator. Otherwise stated, monothe-

---

the existence of God are themselves "onto-theological," that is to say, based on the premises and conclusions of Anselm's ontological argument. *ST* I, q. 2, a. 2, ad 2:

> Perhaps not everyone who hears this word "God" understands it to signify something than which nothing greater can be thought, seeing that some have believed God to be a body. Yet, granted that everyone understands that by this word "God" is signified something than which nothing greater can be thought, nevertheless, it does not therefore follow that he understands that what the word signifies exists actually, but only that it exists mentally. Nor can it be argued that it actually exists, unless it be admitted that there actually exists something than which nothing greater can be thought; and this precisely is not admitted by those who hold that God does not exist.

Aquinas exhibits some genuine alignment here with Kant and Heidegger on the idea of the ontological argument as primarily an exercise of mental constructivism.

100. The most famous case is found in Sigmund Freud's *Civilization and its Discontents*, trans. J. Strachey (New York: W. W. Norton, 2010), where he characterizes religious impulses as a form of psychologically immature behavior by which human beings anthropomorphically and delusionally project personal attributes onto an impersonal universe. Marx's notion of religion as an opiate similarly considers religion as a system that promises deferred justice in the face of class alienation, and Nietzsche sees Judeo-Christianity in particular as a repressed expression of the will-to-power by which human beings seek to construct self-deluded forms of meaning and affirm moral claims over against one another, artificially. One problem with such forms of explanation is that they can easily be reversed, since the religionist can seek to explain the atheists of this kind in primarily psychological or ethical ways. The atheist can respond in turn like the accused religionist: what you present is merely a psychological or moral caricature, not the real spirit of atheism. The true resolution of such controversies requires a proper engagement with the metaphysical question of the ultimate principle of reality, an engagement that is not resolved without searching intellectual effort and that invites all who undertake it to genuine humility.

ism is not only not an inherently irrational hypothesis; it is in fact
always an inevitably realistic possibility for any thinking person or
culture once one begins to take seriously the transcendental features
of being. This is so very much the case that the real philosophical
disputes between monotheists and principled philosophical skeptics like Hume, Kant, or (in another way) Nietzsche are most typically disputes about the realistic foundations of prior principles
like those mentioned above, not the philosophical conclusions one
might rightly infer from them.[101]

Finally, we should add here that if God exists (which we are
treating still as a potentially reasonable way of interpreting reality),
then it seems at the very least possible, if not fitting, that God should
reveal himself to the human race. In other words, if God exists, then
appeals to divine revelation cannot be considered irrational out of
hand, a priori, due to fear of human superstition, sacerdotal manip-
ulation, or religiously motivated violence, however reasonable these
concerns are.[102] There are pathological and self-deluded features of

101. See for example this affirmation of Kant in *Critique of Pure Reason*, A 609/B
637, 511:

> We find [in the cosmological argument] the transcendental principle whereby
> from the contingent we infer a cause. This principle is applicable only in the
> sensible world; outside that world it has no meaning whatsoever. For the mere
> intellectual concept of the contingent cannot give rise to any synthetic propo-
> sition, such as that of causality. The principle of causality has no meaning and
> no criterion for its application save only in the sensible world.

The presupposition here is that the human being cannot attain knowledge of being, substance, or causality *in sensible realities we experience directly* in such a way that we could
in turn apply these notions *by analogy* to realities that are immaterial. The genetically
primary instance of skepticism pertains not to immaterial reality as such (God or the human spiritual soul) but to our knowledge of the metaphysical dimensions of the realities
we experience directly (material substances). It is based on this prior, basic skepticism
about knowledge of existence more generally that skepticism emerges regarding the possibility of demonstrating the existence of God more specifically. This is a strange mirror
image of the problematic thought-form one finds in some medieval and modern proponents of the ontological argument, where knowledge of any being whatsoever implies
the possibility of a concept of God as perfect being, from which in turn we can generate
philosophically certain knowledge of the existence of God. Kant denies there is genuine
knowledge of the conclusion (the existence of God) but also of the premise from which
the conclusion follows (the existence of material substances).

102. See David Hume's essay "Of Miracles," in Section X of *Enquiries Concerning*

human religiosity that exist, to be sure, and some are even present currently in modern culture, such that we could provide many historical and contemporary examples. But such human pathologies need not be endemic to any understanding of divine revelation as such or characteristic of divine revelation as such. Nor should they be if God is truly good and has truly revealed himself. If God exists as the author of the human race and its potential search for the truth, and if God is the author of the limited forms of being, truth, goodness, and beauty we find in reality, then God clearly possesses the power to manifest himself to the human race by way of his own self-communication (in the gift of divine revelation), and he has the capacity to give us the means of understanding who he is in ways that do no violence to human reason, human freedom, or the common good of political life.[103] Indeed, it is fitting to think that God would reveal himself, insofar as revelation would allow us a greater knowledge of God than human reason can attain by its own powers. But we will return to this subject in a subsequent chapter. Our conclusion at this juncture is that if God exists, it seems rationally fitting that we should be open to the possibility of divine revelation, under this condition: that the revelation should accord with human reason and be morally elevated and humane in kind. This argument, again, is not meant to demonstrate that God has revealed himself but only that there are antecedently rational motivations for philosophically motivated, truth-seeking human beings to remain open to this possibility.

Human Understanding and Concerning the Principles of Morals (Oxford: Clarendon Press, 1975).

103. For more on this notion, see Thomas Joseph White, "The Right to Religious Freedom: Thomistic Principles of Nature and Grace," *Nova et Vetera* (English edition) Vol. 13, no. 4 (2015): 1149–84.

TRUE AND FALSE FORMS OF TRANSCENDENCE:
RATIONALITY AND IRRATIONALITY IN SEEKING
RELIGIOUS EXPLANATIONS OF REALITY

What have we argued thus far? First, we noted that our human condition and the existence of the world more generally express a complex set of natural enigmas, and the diverse explanations of these
enigmas have noteworthy differences to one another. Second, we established some criteria of fundamental realism concerning the transcendental features of reality that need to be taken into account by
any realistic explanation of things, be it atheistic or theistic, metaphysically personalist or non-personalist. Third, we noted that, in
light of the transcendental features of reality we identified, there are
antecedent reasons we might be intellectually inclined to explain reality truthfully by recourse to monotheism and to be open to the
possibility of divine revelation, at least under certain conditions.

In the final section of this chapter, let us consider briefly some
conditions of rationality that need to obtain for any possible religious explanation of reality that can function as basic minimal criteria. In other words, if one is going to attempt to explain the world
rationally by recourse to monotheistic metaphysics, allied with an
appeal to divine revelation, what are basic minimal criteria that must
obtain if such attempts are to achieve rational plausibility? I propose
five criteria. Two caveats should be stated about them from the start.
First, these criteria are based on principles articulated by the Catholic Church at the First Vatican Council in the 1870 document *Dei
Filius* in response to objections of Enlightenment rationalists who
denied the rational plausibility of belief in both divine revelation
and Christianity and looked askance at human religious belief more
generally.[104] Consequently, these criteria stem from the Catholic tradition (especially Aquinas), but they might be applied to other religions critically (as accessing them for their rationality). I am employing them because I think they are true. Second, these criteria

104. For *Dei Filius*, see *Denzinger*, 3000–3045.

present what are only *necessary* conditions for a religious understanding of reality, not *sufficient* conditions of reason. In other words,
any rationally sound appeal to the transcendent mystery of God
must take account of these criteria, but the presence of the criteria in
question, which I take it are present authentically in Catholic Christianity, is not a sufficient condition for the recognition that Catholic Christianity is true. This must be the case due to the fact that the
meaning of human existence, from a Catholic Christian perspective,
is never identified merely as a matter of human rational investigation—philosophical, historical, or religious probing on our part—
but always *also* and even first and foremost as a matter of divine revelation, the gift of grace, and the acceptation of this revelation on our
part through the grace of supernatural faith.[105] Ultimately, if there is
a Catholic rationality of the human ascent toward God (the *analogia
entis*), it only ever makes its deepest and surest approach from within the already existing sphere of grace (the *analogia fidei*). Grace presupposes nature as a "structure" to which it is given, but grace incites
nature in the concrete exercise of its operation and comes to the help
of human rationality in its ascent toward God. These are topics we
will return to in subsequent chapters.

*Criterion 1: The Natural Openness of Human Reason to Divine Revelation and
the Openness of Divine Revelation to Contributions of Natural Reason*

The Catholic appeal to divine revelation presupposes a two-fold
thesis concerning the inherent compatibility of supernatural faith
and natural reason, of divine revelation regarding God the Holy
Trinity, and natural truth derived from knowledge of the created order. The first thesis is that human reason is inherently open to the
possibility of divine revelation. This may seem like a repetition of
what has been stated above, but here I am restating it in a distinct
context and different way. The point being made here is not simply
that the rational human being as a philosopher should be open to the

---

105. On both the supernatural *origin* and *motives for consent* to divine revelation, see
Aquinas, *ST* I-II, q. 62, aa. 13–; II-II, q. 1, a. 1; q. 2, aa. 3–4; q. 6, a. 1.

possibility of divine revelation but that the *theologian* who appeals to divine revelation must also affirm philosophically that human reason is open to divine revelation. Thus, any form of theological interpretation of divine revelation that does not hold itself accountable to natural reason in this respect, especially if it does not hold natural reason accountable to its philosophical capacities for God, cannot rightly articulate the intricate harmony of natural and supernatural knowledge. Appeals to revelation that fail to address this point inevitably also fail to address adequately how the natural life of human persons is open to the supernatural, so that the two orders are seen to be complementary and not in opposition.[106] The First Vatican Council accordingly states that God can be known by natural human reason as the first principle and final end of all things.[107] The human mind can attain philosophically to a genuinely universal science of being and seek naturally to understand all things light of its primary transcendent cause. Just because this is the case, however, the

---

106. Natural knowledge is that form of understanding that human beings can acquire by the use of their own natural powers and intellectual capacities. Supernatural knowledge is understanding attained in virtue of the particular assistance of God and by his gift of divine revelation. Catholic Christianity claims that this revelation unveils to us who God is (in his own mystery and identity), a truth that in itself transcends the realm of our natural understanding but that in no way stands in contradiction to it.

107. *Dei Filius*, ch. 2 (*Denzinger*, 3004–5):

The same Holy Mother Church holds and teaches that God, the beginning and end of all things, may be known with certainty from the things that were created through the natural light of human reason, for "ever since the creation of the world his invisible nature ... has been clearly perceived in the things that have been made" [Rom. 1:20]; but it pleased his wisdom and goodness to reveal himself, and the eternal decrees of his will in another and a supernatural way, as the apostle says, "In many and various ways God spoke of old to our fathers by the prophets; but in these last days he has spoken to us by a Son" [Heb. 1:1–2]. It is to be ascribed to this divine revelation that such truths among things divine that of themselves are not beyond human reason, can, even in the present condition of mankind, be known by everyone with facility, with firm certitude, and with no admixture of error. It is, however, not for this reason that revelation is to be called absolutely necessary, but because God of his infinite goodness has ordained man to a supernatural end, viz., to share in the good things of God that utterly exceed the intelligence of the human mind, for "no eye has seen, nor ear heard, nor the heart of man conceived, what God has prepared for those who love Him" [1 Cor. 2:9].

human mind also has the capacity within faith to interpret all of reality coherently in light of the mystery of God without finding this activity alien to or estranged from its natural philosophical knowledge. The sapiential perspective of faith that sees all things in light of God presupposes the human capacity for a sapiential metaphysics, which sees reality in light of its primary cause. The light of faith allows a higher interpretation of all things in light of the Trinity, which the light of reason can anticipate when we think philosophically about all of creation in reference to God. This epistemologically inclusive and holistic feature of Catholic theology, which avails itself of the universal knowledge of both divine revelation and philosophical knowledge of God, depends upon a right understanding of revelation in relationship to natural knowledge.

The second thesis included within this first criterion is that divine revelation and the content of Catholic theology that derives from it must be open to the genuine discoveries of natural human reason, be they philosophical, scientific, or historical. This does not mean that the truths of divine revelation are measured inwardly or determined inherently in their content by the truths of natural reason. On the contrary, the novelty of divine revelation is found precisely in the fact that it comes from outside the sphere of our ordinary human knowing. One can affirm this extrinsic and transcendent derivation of revelation even while also stating unequivocally that divine revelation addresses the desire for the truth that lies most "within" us naturally and indeed is located in our intellectual appetite for ultimate explanation, perspective, and intimate, personal knowledge of God. The two ideas are not mutually incompatible but mutually reinforcing. In divine revelation, God gratuitously and extrinsically initiates the fulfillment of what is most intrinsic to our human desire for the truth.[108] Divine revelation answers an eminently

108. On the gratuity of the divine revelation, see Aquinas in *ST* I-II, q. 62, aa. 1–3. On the natural desire to see God, see *ST* I, q. 12, a. 1. On this topic of the simultaneous gratuity and anthropological intrinsicism of the offer of the vision of God by grace, see Marie-Joseph Le Guillou, "Surnaturel," *Revue des sciences philosophiques et théologiques* 34 (1950): 226–43 and Thomas Joseph White, "Imperfect Happiness and the Final End of

human question, even if that question was often unasked prior to the encounter with revelation: who is God in himself, and what is the creation as understood in his light? Nevertheless, grace does not destroy nature, faith does not impede natural reason, and supernatural revelation does not do violence to human knowledge. Seemingly unresolvable conflicts between natural reason and divine revelation, then, are always only apparent and arise from either a mistaken notion of the revelation itself or a mistaken perspective of natural reason, which can and should be renegotiated in light of fairer reflections. Consequently, any sound understanding of revelation in the Catholic tradition needs to keep in mind these two fundamental theses in order to preserve from the start and throughout the intrinsic harmony of faith and reason, as a foundational principle for Catholic theology.

Criterion 2: The Internal Coherence of Revealed Religious Teaching.

The second criterion of rationality is concerned with what the nineteenth-century Catholic theologians termed the "analogy of faith": the internal coherence of the revelation with itself, as understood in all of its enigmatic and luminous elements.[109] The basic idea here is that any reasonable revelatory claim must be one that is logically and conceptually coherent with itself in its many elements, in terms of what is taught doctrinally, metaphysically, and historically about the mystery of God, creation, and human beings. For example, the Catholic Church teaches that the Old and New Testaments together form the inspired scriptures of Christian revelation. Therefore, the teachings of scripture bear within themselves teachings

---

Man: Thomas Aquinas and the Paradigm of Nature-Grace Orthodoxy," *The Thomist* 78, no. 2 (2014): 247–89. I return to these matters in chapter 4 of this book.

109. The *Catechism of the Catholic Church* (CCC), § 114, states in succinct fashion: "By 'analogy of faith' we mean the coherence of the truths of faith among themselves and within the whole plan of Revelation." *Dei Filius*, ch. 4 (*Denzinger*, 3016): "[I]f reason illumined by faith inquires in an earnest, pious, and sober manner, it attains by God's grace a certain understanding of the mysteries, which is most fruitful, *both from the analogy with the objects of its natural knowledge and from the connection of these mysteries with one another and with man's ultimate end.*" [Emphasis added.]

concerning God, creation, and human beings that can be seen to co-here with one another and in turn to cohere with the subsequent magisterial clarifications of the Catholic Church regarding the content of scripture. On this view, then, there is a deep internal consistency to the inner form and content of divine revelation, even if it may not immediately appear evident or likely. Indeed, Catholic theology must occupy itself in good measure with the task of uncovering the deeper coherent meaning and consistency in divine revelation as it emerges across ages in a variety of expressions, and as it is better understood and expressed by the Church down through time.[110] Moreover, the mysteries that the Church espouses—that of God the Holy Trinity, the creation of the human person in a state of grace, original sin and its consequences, the election of Israel, the Incarnation, the atonement, the resurrection, the Church, the life of grace in the Holy Spirit, the sacraments—cohere with one another as mutually illuminating and intelligible claims that cast light on the meaning of existence. The study of the Holy Trinity helps a person understand the mystery of the Incarnation and vice versa, just as the study of the Eucharist helps one understand the mystery of the Church as the mystical body of Christ, and vice versa.[111]

It should be noted that I am not claiming here that the mysteries of the faith are believable simply due to the fact that they are coherently explained in their doctrinal, metaphysical, or historical

---

110. See on this topic, Gottlieb Söhngen, "The Analogy of Faith: Likeness to God from Faith Alone?," *Pro Ecclesia* 21, no. 1 (2012): 56–76 and "The Analogy of Faith: Unity in the Science of Faith," *Pro Ecclesia* 21, no. 2 (2012): 169–94, trans. K. Oakes. The originals appeared in the German theology journal *Catholica* 3, no. 3 (1934). "The Analogy of Faith: Unity in the Science of Faith," 193:

> There are four relationships within this analogy of faith.... 1. Epistemologically there is the service of knowing in faith, whereby in and from faith we know more than we did before. 2. Ontologically there is the elevation of nature by grace, nature taken here according to its pure essence. 3. In terms of salvation history, there is the salvation of nature by grace, nature now seen in its historical circumstances. 4. For the order of knowing and language there is the reestablishment of the obscured Book of Nature in the Book of Scripture.

111. See the extended argument to this effect by Matthias Joseph Scheeben, *The Mysteries of Christianity*, trans. C. Vollert (New York: Crossroad, 2008).

content. On the contrary, such mysteries can only be believed, studied, and understood in virtue of the supernatural gift of faith and
under the aegis of the initiatives of divine grace. (So the Catholic
Church herself claims.) Nevertheless, one cannot believe things that
are inherently unintelligible or contrary to simple intelligence. In reality, one is led to believe in them to the extent that one perceives an
inner reality, unity, truth, goodness, and beauty to them. Though the
mysteries of the faith are enigmatic and perceived only in the light of
faith, which in this life entails a coexistent obscurity, they can manifest their own reality and beauty to the human mind over time, and
they contain nothing intrinsically repugnant to natural reason.[112] In
fact, the mysteries of Christianity illumine the mind in its pursuit of
the knowledge of the transcendental features of reality precisely by
introducing it to the highest register of the mystery of being in its ultimate hidden causes and primary explanatory principles.

Criterion 3: Revelation Can Enlighten External Natural Realities

The third criterion has to do with the way in which the mysteries of the faith are not only intrinsically intelligible and non-
contradictory (internally, as it were, in regard to one another) but
also illumine external realities, the world we "already" are capable of
knowing naturally, which remains naturally enigmatic or philosophically unclear in its meaning.[113] What is this criterion meant to indicate? We might consider as a primary example the human struggle
with moral evil. Human beings do lesser and greater evils to one another throughout history and struggle with moral weakness or mediocrity in a basic way in their day-to-day lives. One cannot infer
from this truth a mystery of original sin and a collective fallen state
of human nature affecting all of mankind. Nor can one infer from
the reality of human evil and the hope of human redemption that
there is a mystery of atonement and the forgiveness of sins, as well

---

112. See the discussion of this idea by Scheeben in *The Mysteries of Christianity*, 3–21.
113. Reginald Garrigou-Lagrange discusses this idea at some length in *De Revelatione: Per Ecclesiam Catholicam Proposita* (Paris: J. Gabalda, 1921), vol. II, ch. 8, 238–71.

as one of regenerative grace that progressively heals and sanctifies human nature. These truths must be revealed by God, and they are only known in the light of faith. Once they are revealed, however, they do cast a light upon common human experience and invite us to interpret our enigmatic, numinous experience of human mediocrity, evil, and hope in light of the mystery of the fall from grace of our first ancestors, the atonement of Christ, and the gift of grace and forgiveness.[114] Claims to Christian revelation must in some way illumine the world, whereas problematic religious claims must somehow inhibit our intellectual progress or make our understanding of the world more opaque.

This idea of insight into reality stemming from divine revelation also applies to historical claims about divine revelation. One cannot prove by the modern historical-critical study of ancient Israel, the prophets, Jesus of Nazareth, or the apostolic age of Christianity that Christianity is a revealed religion. (One cannot disprove such claims either.) However, through historical study, one can see sufficient evidences of reason to make several determinations: there was an ancient Israel; there was most likely (from the point of view of mere historical demonstration) an exodus event; there was a Davidic monarchy; persons such as Jeremiah and Ezekiel existed and claimed to be prophets; Jesus of Nazareth made high claims about himself

---

114. On original sin, for example, consider the teaching of the Second Vatican Council, *Gaudium et spes* (GS), § 13:

> What divine revelation makes known to us agrees with experience. Examining his heart, man finds that he has inclinations toward evil too, and is engulfed by manifold ills which cannot come from his good Creator. Often refusing to acknowledge God as his beginning, man has disrupted also his proper relationship to his own ultimate goal as well as his whole relationship toward himself and others and all created things. Therefore, man is split within himself. As a result, all of human life, whether individual or collective, shows itself to be a dramatic struggle between good and evil, between light and darkness.

See likewise, *GS*, §§ 37–38, 41. In a not dissimilar way, Aquinas claims that such arguments are (from a strictly rational point of view) only probable signs of a fallen human nature. See *SCG* IV, c. 52: "Certain signs of the original sin appear with greater probability in the human race." [Trans. C. O'Neil, *Summa contra Gentiles* IV (Garden City, NY: Doubleday, 1952).]

and was known for working public miracles; this Jesus' apostles carried on his ministry; these apostles claimed to encounter Jesus of Nazareth after his physical execution alive in his bodily resurrection, and they died for this teaching; the apostles transmitted rituals such as baptism and the Eucharist that they claimed Jesus himself had instituted; and the New Testament was composed within two or three generations of the death of Christ.[115]

All of this forms a point of contrast with claims to revelation that are "merely" symbolic or mythological in character (such as the appeals in ancient Hinduism to incarnations of Krishna, which are non-historical in nature) and with claims to historical revelation that are demonstrably false (as found in Mormonism, in regard to the Israelite origins of South American culture or the absurd claims of determination of skin pigment and racial diversification due to ancestral sins).[116]

This criterion also points one toward an important point of contrast between Christian and Islamic claims to rationality in matters of revelation. Muslims claim that the Quran is entirely derived directly from an uncreated source, without the mediation of human authorship. On this view, which is theologically normative in orthodox Islam, God is said to have provided humanity with the text of the Quran uniquely through the mediation of an archangel who revealed it to the prophet Mohammed. Indeed, it is a common teaching of orthodox Islam that the Arabic of the text is of pre-existent

115. On the historicity of Old Testament figures and events, see for example Roland De Vaux, *The Early History of Israel*, 2 vols., trans. D. Smith (London: Darton, Longman & Todd, 1978); John Bright, *A History of Israel*, 4th ed. (Louisville: Westminster John Knox, 2000); Walther Eichrodt, *Theology of the Old Testament*, 2 vols., trans. J. A. Baker (London, SCM, 1961). On the New Testament figure of Jesus and on the early Church, see for example Luke Timothy Johnson, *The Real Jesus* (New York: Harper Collins, 1996); N. T. Wright, *Jesus and the Victory of God* (Minneapolis: Fortress, 1997); Richard Bauckham, *Jesus and the Eyewitnesses: The Gospels as Eyewitness Testimony* (Grand Rapids, MI: Eerdmans, 2008); Larry Hurtado, *Lord Jesus Christ: Devotion to Jesus in Earliest Christianity* (Grand Rapids, MI: Eerdmans, 2005).

116. See Richard Abanes, *One Nation Under Gods: A History of the Mormon Church* (New York: Basic Books, 2003). On "historical" ancestral sins that supposedly created physical racial change in ancient Americans, and the curse of the dark skinned "Lamanites," see *The Book of Mormon*, 2 Nephi 5:20–24, Jacob 3:5, 8, and Alma 3:6–16.

origin, prior to the foundations of the world.[117] It has no human authorship whatsoever, and therefore no origin of composition in and through human traditions, those whereby it could be influenced from pre-Muslim texts or depend upon previous historical oral or written culture.[118] This claim, however, is demonstrably problematic when one considers the text of the Quran in its cultural context and human historical influences, a form of cultural analysis that mainstream Islam widely prohibits.[119] Furthermore the Quran presumes that elements of revealed truth are to be found in the Old and New Testament, while also claiming that those documents and their stories are inherently untrustworthy.[120] In practice this means that the Quran presupposes that elements of the Bible must be truly revealed

117. On the historical origins of the Quran as a text see Gabriel Said Reynolds, *The Emergence of Islam: Classical Traditions in Contemporary Perspective* (Minneapolis: Fortress, 2012).

118. For a helpful presentation of an Islamic understanding of the inspiration of the book, see Muhammad Mustafa al-Azami, "The Islamic View of the Quran," in *The Study Quran*, ed. S. H. Nasr (New York: Harper Collins, 2015), 1607–23.

119. For a wealth of examples, see Gabriel Said Reynolds, *The Qur'an and its Biblical Subtext* (New York: Routledge, 2010).

120. See for example the denial that Jesus of Nazareth was crucified historically, which is an axiomatic belief of Islam, in contrast to the affirmations of the New Testament. Sura 4:157: "[T]hey did not slay him; nor did they crucify him, but I appeared so unto them." The Quran speaks of a Samaritan existing at the time of Moses (Sura 20:83–97) which is an impossible anachronism, and it denotes Mary, the mother of Jesus, as "sister of Aaron" (Sura 19:23–28), which seemingly entails a historical confusion with Miriam, the sister of Moses, mentioned as his sibling in the Torah. Muslims have long disputed the nature of this textual affirmation and have strategies to explain away the fantastic historical error, but the manifest sense of the text does seem to indicate such a confusion. Furthermore, the origins of Islam are depicted anachronistically as stemming from Abraham's sacrifice of Ishmael rather than Isaac, conducted in Mecca rather than Jerusalem, in Sura 2:125–28, a claim standing in contradiction to any reasonable archeological or genealogical historical claim. Throughout the Quran, stories of Joseph, Moses, the Virgin Mary, and Jesus Christ are retold in fragmented partial ways, in accord with oral traditions from Mohammad and early Islamic tradition. These narrations are historically dependent upon oral Biblical traditions. (Mohammad had no access to any written source of the Old or New Testaments in his time and depended upon Arabic oral preaching and commentary). Nevertheless, the Quranic "retellings" systematically alter the original stories (knowingly or not, as the case may be). They do so while claiming to give final and definitive interpretations of the Biblical traditions, even as they also claim that the written Biblical texts are effectively untrustworthy (whether in part or in whole is not explained). See, for example, Sura 2:75, 4:46, 5:13, and 7:157.

(such as the divinely inspired role of Jesus of Nazareth in history),
while simultaneously denying others (such as the crucifixion of Jesus or his atonement) and inventing or introducing re-narrations of
others (for example, regarding the birth of Jesus), all in a form of
re-presentation of the events from the Old and New Testaments that
is arbitrarily partial, fragmented, and incompatible with modern historical study of the Bible. The latter fact can best be accounted for
rationally due to the fact that the original author(s) of the Quran
lacked access to the historical scriptures and had only oral traditions,
which (t)he(y) in turn re-narrated freely, but if this reasonable historical thesis is true, then the fundamental normative Islamic theory of Quranic inspiration is intellectually problematic and false. The
legends of the Quran, religiously profound though they may be, are
essentially derived from legends of the Arabian Peninsula prior to
the time of Mohammed or from his own reflections on oral traditions regarding the Bible or from the reflections of his early followers. Nevertheless, this reality is not acknowledged in any mainstream
orthodox interpretation of Islam, even though it is evidently a fact of
history. A difficulty of rational coherence emerges, since the responsible historical study of the Quran stands in fundamental conflict
with the immutable claims of Islam regarding the book's composition, non-historical derivation, and historical accuracy.

Of course, this latter criticism of Islamic views need not imply
that Christianity presents us with true authentic revelation. Christian tradition has always acknowledged human authorship of Biblical texts but it does not follow from this that any of the assertions of
that text about historical events, miracles, or mysteries of the faith
are indeed true. Furthermore, many Christians have been opposed
to modern historical-critical study of the Bible, and that study has
at times helped fuel the rise of atheism and religious indifference
in Europe. In addition, Christianity makes truth claims that some
might find more challenging to reason than those made by Islam,
such as the teaching that God has become human. One may therefore be skeptical of both Islam and Christianity for similar reasons

or for altogether different reasons. Nevertheless, noteworthy differences between the two religions persist, especially in respect of their understanding of textual history, its modern study, and due to the very different claims they make with regard to the human form of divine revelation. Catholic Christianity tends to acknowledge the reality of inspired Biblical human authors in a way that meets with criteria of rational plausibility and the possibility of historical truth that Islam has difficulty (or impossibility) attaining.[121] All this is noted not to engage in unwarranted polemic but in order to observe a singularly important point. Contradictory appeals to divine revelation by mutually incompatible sources readily lead many to religious despair, skepticism, or indifferentism. Such disputes must be adjudicated not merely by resignation (doctrinal skepticism or latitudinarianism) nor by mere struggles of the will to power (arbitrary religious

121. See, for example, the teaching of the Second Vatican Council, *Dei Verbum*, Constitution on Divine Revelation, §§ 11–12:

> Those divinely revealed realities which are contained and presented in Sacred Scripture have been committed to writing under the inspiration of the Holy Spirit.... In composing the sacred books, God chose men and while employed by Him they made use of their powers and abilities, so that with Him acting in them and through them, they, as true authors consigned to writing everything and only those things which he wanted. Therefore "all Scripture is divinely inspired and has its use for teaching the truth and refuting error, for reformation of manners and discipline in right living, so that the man who belongs to God may be efficient and equipped for good work of every kind" (2 Tim. 3:16–17). However, since God speaks in Sacred Scripture through men in human fashion, the interpreter of Sacred Scripture, in order to see clearly what God wanted to communicate to us, should carefully investigate what meaning the sacred writers really intended, and what God wanted to manifest by means of their words. To search out the intention of the sacred writers, attention should be given, among other things, to "literary forms." For truth is set forth and expressed differently in texts which are variously historical, prophetic, poetic, or of other forms of discourse.... For the correct understanding of what the sacred author wanted to assert, due attention must be paid to the customary and characteristic styles of feeling, speaking and narrating which prevailed at the time of the sacred writer, and to the patterns men normally employed at that period in their everyday dealings with one another.

My argument is not that this theory of inspiration renders the inspiration of the Old and New Testaments *evident* but only that it renders it theoretically plausible, with respect to the theological acknowledgment of the complex human historicity and composition of the text.

authoritarianism) but above all by responsible consideration of the divine revelation claims, which includes recourse to criteria of natural reason when considering both the claims and insights of respective revelation traditions and the historically realistic form of revelation itself that they themselves invoke.

Criterion 4: Signs of Credibility

The fourth criterion is concerned with signs of divine revelation given to natural human reason in manifest ways.[122] These signs may be miraculous or moral and thus pertain to the miracles of adherents of the religious tradition in question or the moral examples of its followers. They are manifest to public reason insofar as they are something one can learn about independently of the insight of faith and take note of as certain or probable truths, which indicate clearly but indirectly that God is somehow at the source of the religious tradition in question.

I have noted that mysteries of the Catholic faith, such as those of the Incarnation or the atonement, are inaccessible to unaided reason, but here I am suggesting that there are rational signs of the truths of the mysteries in question. Here, then, one must make an important distinction, according to Catholic theology. On the one hand, the mysteries of the faith concern truths that transcend the domain of natural human reason as such, in the sense that the human mind cannot discover them if left completely unaided by grace. The Holy Trinity, the Incarnation, the atonement—these are truths of faith that can be known only if they are unveiled to the human mind by the gift of grace. Consequently, we cannot understand their inner intelligibility or consent to their truth inwardly without the help of God and the distinctive gift of supernatural grace, which gives us both insight into their reality and inner structure and the power to consent volitionally to the truth in question.[123] On the other hand,

122. See on this point, the *CCC*, 811–12, and *Dei Filius*, ch. 3.
123. *Dei Filius*, ch. 4:

however, it pertains to the justice of God to give outward signs to human reason of the authenticity of his revelation and the truth of these mysteries, so that it is possible to detect indirectly but really the divine origins of the Christian religion, even naturally.[124] These signs are real but also discreet and for that reason *subject to being refused freely* even though also *freely discernible to natural reason*. For example, the miracles of Christ, of the apostles, and of many saints in the post-apostolic Church even until our own time serve as publicly detectable testimonies of the divine origin of God's activity in Christianity and the Church.[125] These signs are numerous for those who wish to investigate them, but they are not imposing or constraining and can be ignored or skeptically dismissed. Furthermore, even those who believe in or experience the miraculous cannot accede to the mysteries of the faith simply due to such experiences. One may ask, then, about the usefulness of such signs. They are not intrinsically efficacious. However, they do for those who already accede to faith grant rational evidence, not so as to motivate faith as such, but so as to show to reason the rational warrant and natural well-foundedness

---

The perpetual common belief of the Catholic Church has held and holds also this: that there is a two-fold order of knowledge, distinct not only in its principle, but also in its object; in its principle, because in the one we know by natural reason, in the other by divine faith; in its object, because apart from what natural reason can attain, there are proposed to our belief mysteries that are hidden in God that can never been known unless they are revealed by God.

124. See the discussion of the reasons of credibility by Guy Mansini in *Fundamental Theology* (Washington, DC: The Catholic University of America Press, 2017), 184–212 and by Mats Walberg, *Revelation as Testimony: A Philosophical-Theological Study* (Grand Rapids, MI: Eerdmans, 2014).

125. See Mansini in *Fundamental Theology*, 195–206. Aquinas mentions the effectiveness of these signs to convert the ancient Graeco-Roman world to Christianity (*SCG* I, c. 6):

This wonderful conversion of the world to the Christian faith is the clearest witness of the signs given in the past; so that it is not necessary that they should be further repeated, since they appear most clearly in their effect. For it would be truly more wonderful than all signs if the world had been led by simple and humble men to believe such lofty truths, to accomplish such difficult actions, and to have such high hopes. Yet it is also a fact that, even in our own time, God does not cease to work miracles through His saints for the confirmation of the faith.

of what is otherwise believed by supernatural faith.[126] This is a case of the famous Thomistic adage, "grace does not destroy nature but perfects it."[127]

Other signs of credibility include: the manifest holiness of the Catholic saints, the longevity of the persistence of the Church (and the Jewish people, as a sign of their election), the unity and stability of the Catholic Church down through time, the perennial and organically developing character of her teaching, and the universality of her growth toward all peoples and places.[128] One can of course point toward counterwitnesses: particular moral evils perpetuated by the clergy or other members of the Church, her great internal battles for doctrinal clarification, her setbacks and historical limitations, unedifying divisions among Christians, psychological rigidity and callous indifference among Christian believers, their mutual persecution of one another, and their violence toward non-Christians. One could multiply such examples. Signs of credibility co-exist with signs of contradiction.[129] Nevertheless, the reality of the holiness of

126. The key idea here is that the object of faith as such is supernatural and that grace is required in order to know and believe in this object, while the reality known by faith can also be otherwise understood by natural reason to be something indicating the presence, power and activity of God, as when for example, one might believe in the bodily resurrection of Christ by faith but simultaneously believe that there exist rational grounds for the affirmation of the historical bodily resurrection of Christ, which would in turn indicate to reason (in a limited but real sense) the rational warrant for the supernatural belief in Christianity. One might believe, for example, in the likely veracity of the historical testimony of the apostolic witnesses to the resurrection appearances based on a modern consideration of the origins of the early Christian movement. On the latter historical topic, see N.T. Wright, *The Resurrection of the Son of God* (Minneapolis: Fortress, 2003).

127. *ST* I, q. 1, a. 8, ad 2.

128. See the extensive discussion of traditional ecclesial reasons of credibility by Garrigou-Lagrange in *De Revelatione*, vol. II, 238–324.

129. See *GS*, § 19:

Undeniably, those who willfully shut out God from their hearts and try to dodge religious questions are not following the dictates of their consciences, and hence are not free of blame; yet believers themselves frequently bear some responsibility for this situation. For, taken as a whole, atheism is not a spontaneous development but stems from a variety of causes, including a critical reaction against religious beliefs, and in some places against the Christian religion in particular. Hence believers can have more than a little to do with the birth

the saints, the reality of the miraculous, and the perpetuity of the Church in spite of human limitations are all rationally discernible signs of the sacred mystery of the Catholic religion for those who are willing to advert themselves to the clear evidence and pray to God for assistance in making discernments in this domain. The words of Pascal are pertinent in this regard:

> He has wanted to make himself perfectly knowable by them [who sincerely seek him]. Thus wanting to appear openly to those who seek him with all their heart and hidden from those who fell him with all their heart, God has tempered the knowledge of himself by giving signs of himself that are visible to those who seek him, and not by those who do not seek him. There is enough light for those who desire only to see and enough darkness for those of a contrary disposition.[130]

Criterion 5: The Presence of the Praeambula Fidei

The final criterion has to do with significant rational truths that may be difficult to attain for many but which divine revelation makes readily available by divine promulgation. These are called "preambles of faith," or *praeambula fidei*, because they are metaphysical or moral truths that are harmonious with faith and presupposed by it logically.[131] Classic examples include: the existence and unity of God the Creator; the existence in each human being of a spiritual, immaterial soul; the fact that the human intellect is made for the discovery of truth and is capable of progressive insight into that truth; the moral teachings of the natural law (such as the fact that human life has intrinsic dignity and merits ethical protection from conception until natural death); or the fact that human life has a religious

---

of atheism. To the extent that they neglect their own training in the faith, or teach erroneous doctrine, or are deficient in their religious, moral or social life, they must be said to conceal rather than reveal the authentic face of God and religion.

130. Blaise Pascal, *Pensées*, S182/L149, trans. R. Ariew (Indianapolis: Hackett, 2004).

131. See on this topic Mansini, *Fundamental Theology*, 143–83, and Ralph McInerny, *Praeambula Fidei: Thomism and the God of the Philosophers* (Washington, DC: The Catholic University of America Press, 2006).

meaning and purpose.[132] These are all teachings that *in principle* human beings can come to discover *to some extent* imperfectly through the course of human existence. However, they are often difficult to ascertain and are discovered philosophically by a few, imperfectly, after a long time and often admixed with error.[133] The fact that they are presented to us in divine revelation makes them more readily accessible to all. The Church's promotion of the preambles of faith encourages rather than discourages the energetic use of philosophical reason, since their promulgation gives natural reason greater confidence and encourages human beings to seek the truth patiently, in collegiality, and in living contact with longstanding and trustworthy philosophical traditions.

Such truths are also logically implied by appeal to revelation in the Catholic religion. If God the Holy Trinity is revealed in Christ, then it is logically necessary to believe that God exists, and further, it is only because there is some natural capacity for knowledge and love of God that the divine revelation of the Holy Trinity appears as something of potentially real existential significance for all of humanity, rather than a simply unintelligible teaching, arbitrarily imposed by unnatural violence. Nevertheless, this does not presuppose that each person who comes to know God the Holy Trinity by recourse to divine revelation in Christ must first have thought about God philosophically or come to know God as a metaphysician would, that is, through the medium of natural reflection. On the contrary, the inverse is presupposed: in many cases human beings

132. Aquinas gives several examples of these in *Expos. de Trin.*, q. 2, a. 3.
133. *ST* I, q. 1, a. 1:

Even as regards those truths about God which human reason could have discovered, it was necessary that man should be taught by a divine revelation; because the truth about God such as reason could discover, would only be known by a few, and that after a long time, and with the admixture of many errors. Whereas man's whole salvation, which is in God, depends upon the knowledge of this truth. Therefore, in order that the salvation of men might be brought about more fitly and more surely, it was necessary that they should be taught divine truths by divine revelation. It was therefore necessary that besides philosophical science built up by reason, there should be a sacred science learned through revelation.

remain deeply religiously confused or skeptical prior to their encounter with the truth of divine revelation and stand in need of confirmation of the *praeambula fidei* of natural reason by the Church herself, who assures human beings of the genuine capabilities of natural reason. However, it is also true that grace does not destroy nature but heals and elevates it. Consequently, even from within the light of supernatural faith and after the reception of divine revelation, it is natural and typical for human beings to seek to better understand God, the soul, and the natural law even according to the lights of natural reason and always in harmony with faith.

Here our final criterion touches back upon the primary one noted above. The first criterion stated that authentic appeals to divine revelation and the theology they give rise to must promote an integral respect for the discoveries of natural human reason. The final criterion stipulates that divine revelation should also promulgate truths of natural reason itself that are themselves difficult to ascertain for natural reason.[134] The Catholic tradition underscores this notion however not in order to impose philosophical positions by authority but to invite the human mind into a deeper relationship with the truth, that which is represented by the second and third criteria especially. It is the mysteries of faith themselves, in their inner intelligibility and the light they cast on human existence, that form the inward core of Christian truth. The mysteries of the Holy Trinity, Jesus Christ, the Church, and the human person transformed by grace are the central mysteries that give intelligibility to the Catholic religion and cast ultimate light upon human existence.

TRINITY, EXPLANATIONS, AND PERSONHOOD

Any consideration of the rational credibility of Christianity must be concerned in some principal way with the revelation of the Holy Trinity, which is considered its highest mystery and also perhaps its most difficult to understand. In light of the criteria of rationality we

134. See Mansini, *Fundamental Theology*, 145–55.

have noted above, we may ask the following questions. Based on Criterion 2: What is the inward form or coherent character of Trinitarian theology as a way of understanding God? Based on Criterion 3: What light does the mystery of the Trinity cast upon reality as we otherwise know it in virtue of natural reason? How is Trinitarian revelation rooted in Christian claims about scripture and history (particularly in the writings of the New Testament and the purported teaching of Jesus of Nazareth himself ascribed to him there)? Based on Criteria 1 and 5: How and in what way is Trinitarian doctrine compatible with and indeed strengthened by engagement with philosophical reasoning regarding the one God, the Creator? Or otherwise stated: what role does philosophical discourse about God play in our understanding of the Holy Trinity as the God of the Bible? How does the teaching of the Holy Trinity help us understand the religious destiny of the human person? What may we reasonably hope for in light of the Trinitarian revelation of God? I will seek to address some of these questions in the following chapters of this book.

We should note what is at stake in treating these questions. If the revelation of the Holy Trinity is true, then the ultimate principle behind reality is personal, not impersonal. Moreover, it is a mystery of uncreated personal communion. Many other conclusions would follow from this truth or be logically coterminous with it. First, the created world is not all that exists, and it exists only ever in dependence upon God, who is immediately present to all that exists. Second, not all that exists in creation is material, since personhood in creatures entails immaterial operations of intellectual knowledge and volition, which originate from the immaterial soul. Third, the human person forms a special part of creation as made in the image of God the Holy Trinity, and created persons exist in view of interpersonal communion with God and with one another. Fourth, all I am stating here is compatible with, and in fact convergent with, truths of natural reason regarding God, creation, and human persons.

I will have more to say about each of these claims in ensuing

chapters. At the conclusion of this first one on reasonable credibility, we can simply note the following: the intelligibility of Trinitarian
faith and therefore of Christianity itself depends upon the coherence
and plausibility of these various theological and philosophical claims
about God, the creation, and human persons. To the extent that they
seem coherent, explanatory, warranted, or demonstrable, then the
alternative explanations of reality noted above seem increasingly implausible or unreasonable. Human beings typically do not reason to
momentous intellectual convictions in matters of religion by means
of one singular act of rational demonstration or intuition. They work
instead by what John Henry Newman denoted "the illative sense," a
series of intuitions, arguments, demonstrations, observations, and
tested desires by which a human person arrives at a global and coherent sense of the larger meaning of reality as understood in a complex and multilayered way.[135] This book undertakes that kind of approach to the truth of Trinitarian faith, first by examining the inner
intelligibility of the claims of revelation, and then by pursuing its
compatibility with philosophical reason, and the mutual inherence
of the two.

135. See John Henry Newman, *An Essay in Aid of a Grammar of Assent*, ch. 9 (Notre
Dame, IN: University of Notre Dame Press, 1992).

2

Is It Reasonable to Believe
in One God, the Creator of All Things?

Arguments for the Existence of God

In the first part of our argument regarding rational credibility, we considered the transcendentals, those features of reality present in all things, which obtain ineluctably in all ordinary experience of the world: being, unity, truth, goodness, and beauty. We concluded by arguing that monotheism has an antecedent probability as a form of explanation of the world around us, since we experience only dependent caused realities that do not "explain themselves" and seem to point toward a transcendent and unknown source of reality, a Creator, who gives being to all things.

In this chapter, we will follow up on that intuition by making use of structured forms of argumentation for the existence of God. These arguments are philosophical and metaphysical in kind. They are not based on the truths of modern natural science—though they are completely compatible with the findings of modern physics, chemistry, and biology. Instead, they take their starting point from fundamental features of reality that are indisputably present in ordinary experience, features of reality that the modern natural sciences themselves presuppose and inevitably depend upon in their own procedures. The aim of these arguments is not to compel or oblige epistemological consent to the affirmation that God exists—"proof" in the sense of vanquishing every conceivable objection. Rather, it is to show how it is possible and indeed demonstratively rational to believe in God as the Creator of all secondary reality, after which we can consider in chapters yet to come the hidden inner life of God in his transcendence, that mystery we call the Holy Trinity, revealed to us in the New Testament and above all in the life, death, and resurrection of Jesus of Nazareth.

ARGUMENTATION BASED ON REALISTIC CONSIDERATION OF CAUSALITY

Aquinas suggests that all human beings possess natural knowledge of God or the divine that is non-demonstrative, that is, minimally reflective, and based on core intuitions about reality as everyone experiences it.[1] The ideas of God or the gods or providence arise in human beings naturally from a variety of resources, including:

1. See Aquinas, *Collationes super Credo in Deum*, art. 1. See also *SCG* III, c. 38:

For there is a common and confused knowledge of God which is found in practically all men; this is due either to the fact that it is self-evident that God exists, just as other principles of demonstration are—a view held by some people, as we said in Book One—or, what seems indeed to be true, that man can immediately reach some sort of knowledge of God by natural reason. For, when men see that things in nature run according to a definite order, and that ordering does not occur without an orderer, they perceive in most cases that there is some orderer of the things that we see. But who or what kind of being, or whether there is but one orderer of nature, is not yet grasped immediately in this general consideration, just as, when we see that a man is moved and performs other works, we perceive that there is present in him some cause of these operations which is not present in other things, and we call this cause the soul; yet we do not know at that point what the soul is, whether it is a body, or how it produces these operations which have been mentioned. [Trans. V. J. Burke (Garden City, NY: Doubleday, 1956).]

See the study of this Thomistic notion of the pre-philosophical rational inference of the existence of God from experience by Lawrence Dewan in *Wisdom, Law, and Virtue: Essays in Thomistic Ethics* (New York: Fordham University Press, 2007), ch. 14: "Natural Law and the First Act of Freedom: Maritain Revisited."

- the consideration of the natural order in the world expressed through its ordinary movements;
- the question of the meaning of history;
- the singular dignity of the human person, who seems characterized by the drive for truth, explanation, and moral rectitude;
- the beauty of the world, which evokes wonder and admiration;
- and the sheer existence of the world itself, which exists in a seeming gratuity.

It is not particularly difficult, then, to arrive at the notion of God as a primary source of all that exists in the world, a transcendent origin of all the natural order, goodness, and beauty in the world, who is in some real sense "personal." Nor should we be too quick to characterize people's common intuitions about God as intellectually infantile, since they may well stem from something deep within our human nature. In fact, we can learn from children about our intellectual capacities for high intuitions of a religious kind that precede any formal training in philosophical reasoning. Children can readily believe in God the Creator of all things and in his divine providence, and they can freely pray to God in a rational and meaningful way. Just as they can learn sophisticated languages that adults from other cultures have trouble learning in adulthood, so they can learn to pray deeply to God and think realistically about God even if in a more primitive and intuitive way. Even if children typically do not discover their religious capacities alone and are taught about God from their parents who convey religious traditions to them, such children do think about God rationally and ask intelligible questions about God. So, knowledge of God seems to exist in all persons (at least potentially) in a more intuitive and conceptually embryonic state. This is the case even for those who can think about God and pray to him prior to the age of reason.

However, this does not mean such knowledge is innate if by that we mean that it precedes all experience or is given prior to our reflection on the world. Rather, it arises intuitively but in reaction or response to our engagement with the realities around us, often aided and induced by religious traditions and parental education, which can be more or less enlightened or misguided. This knowledge that most human beings have of God is not something that stands in contradiction to philosophical reasoning (or it need not be), but it is more intuitive and pre-philosophical, that is, only implicitly demonstrative or imperfectly reflective. Viable intellectual argument that is demonstrative in the strong sense can build on initial intuitions, but it must also challenge or purify these intuitions to see what stands up to scrutiny and what may only be erroneous intuition or sentiment or falsifying imagination, etc. That is to say, philosophical analysis can disillusion us helpfully even while bringing the quest for God in us to greater maturity.

The Thomist school follows Aquinas in affirming that all viable philosophical knowledge of God that is "demonstrative" in the strict sense has a set of basic stages.[2] First, it takes its initial starting points from ontological features of reality that we grasp intellectually in

2. Aquinas argues that demonstrative knowledge flows from *quia* argumentation from effects to causes rather than *propter quid* demonstrations from causes to effects. In the former, we can prove that a predicate pertains to a subject but cannot demonstrate why; with the latter we can show why. For example, a *propter quid* argument can demonstrate that man can laugh starting from the definition of human nature, taking account of the fact that the human animal is both rational and corporeal, and therefore has an intellectual sense of humor that can be expressed in physical gestures. Neither angels nor non-rational animals can laugh. The demonstration that human beings can laugh follows logically from the premise that a human being is a rational animal. The notion of humor follows from the notion of rational, which is included in the definition of man. A *quia* argument, by contrast, begins with an effect and seeks an unknown cause. I may see a friend laughing in a conversation, but not know the reason. However, one can infer that there is something humorous that is the source of the amusement. Likewise, observers can infer rightly that the smoke emanating from a forest comes from a fire or some other form of burning substance. They infer the existence of the cause, even though they do not know the cause in itself directly. The latter form of argument can be truly demonstrative, but it does not afford comprehensive understanding of the essence of the subject matter. Likewise, from the existence of things in this world that are derivative and thus are effects, we can infer indirectly the existence of a hidden cause of being. See, on these matters, Serge Thomas Bonino, *Dieu, "Celui Qui Est"; De Deo ut Uno* (Paris: Parole et Silence, 2016), 153–57, 160–63, and Lawrence Dewan, "The Existence of God: Can It Be Demonstrated?," *Nova et Vetera* (English edition) 10, no. 3 (2012): 731–56.

ordinary experience—basic metaphysical truths about the state of the world around us as we rightly understand it naturally. It then proceeds to identify how these principles denote to us that the realities of this world around us imply causal dependencies of one thing or activity upon another (such as the fact that change in one thing is exerted upon it by another) or participation within a larger order that each thing is part of and depends upon, but none of them causes to be. Next, it proceeds to argue that there cannot be an actual (non-temporal) infinite series of ontologically dependent causes, since such an actual chain of causes would not adequately and comprehensively explain the existence of the realities in question. It concludes from this that what we call "God" must exist, one who is the Creator (that is, the cause of all that exists), who exists by necessity and gives being to all things.

Rightly understood, the knowledge of God procured by this way of thinking, while real, is also deeply imperfect. It is inferential, as we infer the existence of God indirectly through the medium of creatures that are his effects rather than from some kind of immediate intuition of the divine essence, as if we could adequately define or perceive what God is. Furthermore, God is radically unlike the many dependent, limited realities from which we infer his existence as their transcendent and unknown cause. Consequently, we can only think about God by using negative comparisons. He must be known by analogy, in likeness and in contrast to the creaturely realities that depend upon him.[3] This means that the ultimate origin of the world is also something we fail to know well according to our natural powers. Philosophy in this respect finds a true explanation for the existence of the world by referring to God, but it also reaches its summit when it discovers an ultimate mystery about being, namely the incomprehensibility of the unknown Creator who gives being to all other things. This philosophical enigma is even deeper than the question that initiated it—namely, the mystery of the world around us—which seems to require a more ultimate explanation. In other words, we can come

3. *ST* I, q. 13.

to know progressively that God certainly exists, but in doing so, we also only come to know very imperfectly what God is, and we can say more safely what God is not by comparing him negatively to the created realities that depend upon him. Consequently, any natural or philosophical knowledge we have of God in a sense only intensifies the enigma of being, even as it casts some light on the unity and plurality of creatures that depend on God.[4]

In what follows I will present briefly seven distinct arguments for the existence of God, each of Thomistic provenance. The first is from the so-called "real distinction" in creatures of existence and essence. Aquinas developed this argument in his early work *De ente et essentia.*[5] The second through sixth arguments are taken from the famous "Five Ways" of the *Summa theologiae.*[6] The seventh argument is based on the spiritual operations of the human person, immaterial operations of conceptual understanding and free decision-making. Operations of understanding and free will in human persons, I will argue, have immaterial aspects that are not explicable only by recourse to the material body. Consequently, they point us toward the spiritual immateriality of the soul, the form of the body that is the fundamental principle of human identity in the rational animal. But the soul of the human person, while immaterial, is not a cause of itself, since it does not cause itself to be, nor is it caused by the material world, which cannot bring an immaterial reality into existence, so it points us toward a transcendent source, God the Creator, the immediate author of the immaterial human soul and its spiritual operations of intellect and volition.[7]

After the consideration of these arguments, I will also briefly examine the objection that one often hears, namely, that such arguments have no warrant in light of the discoveries and methods of the

4. This theme is strongly underlined by Aquinas in his prologue to *ST* I, q. 3, and some Thomists, like Denys Turner in his *Faith, Reason and the Existence of God* (Cambridge: Cambridge University Press, 2004).

5. See *De ente,* ch. 4.

6. *ST* I, q. 2, a. 3.

7. There are arguments very similar to those I will present in *ST* I, q. 75; q. 83; q. 118; *SCG* II, cc. 47, 50, 76, 79, 87.

modern natural sciences. I will argue that these classical arguments of the Thomistic tradition are not based upon the natural scientific method but are based rather on a direct form of experiential and philosophical realism that any modern natural scientific discipline necessarily presupposes and that its methodology therefore cannot suppress. To the extent that the modern sciences are presumed to yield realistic knowledge of the world (which they of course do), they presuppose metaphysical knowledge of the world of just the sort that inevitably also facilitates and invites demonstrative knowledge of the existence of God. Consequently, the exercise of modern scientific learning is dependent upon the kind of metaphysical realism that can and should lead us progressively to the acknowledgement of the existence of God. To the extent that the modern sciences flourish, then, they also always inevitably presuppose and implicitly promote the necessary conditions for the kind of metaphysical realism that leads to the acknowledgement of the existence of God.

ARGUMENT BASED ON THE REAL DISTINCTION
OF *ESSE* AND *ESSENTIA*

Thomas Aquinas argues that in each reality we experience (including ourselves), there is a real distinction between the act of existence of the reality and its nature or essence.[8] In other words, *what* a thing is essentially can be distinguished from *the existence of* a thing is. This is an ontological distinction we frequently take for granted and do not reflect upon overtly but that we also cannot avoid knowing something about. We can gain an initial understanding of this distinction by noting that all the individual things around

---

8. On the real distinction in Aquinas, see *De ente*, as well as *SCG* I, c. 22; II, c. 52; *De pot.*, q. 7, a. 2; *ST* I, q. 3, a. 4; *De spirit. creat.*, a. 1. Modern commentators include Wippel, *The Metaphysical Thought of Thomas Aquinas*, 132–76; Kretzmann, *The Metaphysics of Theism*, 121–29; Porro, *Thomas Aquinas*, 12–26; Steven Long, *Analogia Entis: On the Analogy of Being, Metaphysics, and the Act of Faith* (Notre Dame: University of Notre Dame University, 2011); Bonino, *Dieu, "Celui Qui Est"*, 260–70.

us—whether human beings, trees, cats, or stars—fall into groups of distinct kinds or essences. A star is not a human being or a tree, but there are many stars, many things of like kind. Some groupings of things are generic rather than specific, and so they are too broad to distinguish a thing's precise nature: stars are celestial objects, but so are planets, moons, nebulae, and so on. Cats are animals, but so are humans and sea anemones. Some classifications are merely accidental in kind, focusing on characteristics that do not really define a thing—"redheaded" human beings and "blonde" human beings can be grouped according to hair color, but the difference between them is not essential. However, it is not hard for us—even for children—to quickly reach a level of classification by which we identify the specific nature of what a thing is. Frequently we do this based on essential *properties* of the reality, meaning characteristics proper to the nature, not merely accidental, and that help distinguish this reality from other kinds of things. A star and a satellite may both shine in the night sky, but the star is a non-living natural body composed of elements like hydrogen and helium that emits a prodigious intensity of light and heat. A kangaroo and a cat are both mammals but the kangaroo is a two-legged marsupial. Human beings are rational animals characterized by powers of understanding and volition, distinct in this respect from the other animals. In a sense these specific definitions, while adequate, are only initial. We may learn more and more about the natures of things through time, by scientific examination and philosophical analysis. The term that Aquinas uses for this nature that adequately distinguishes a type of being is its essence (*essentia*).[9]

Yet the existence (*esse* or the act of existence) of each one of these individual things is unique—this human being here, that tree

---

9. Of course, later medieval thinkers (especially those labelled as "nominalists") and many modern philosophers call into question the notion that things have essences, and instead propose that what realists call essences are merely names imposed on individual realities by the human mind. This claim is false, for reasons that become clear when one considers the process of abstraction, which I will do later in this chapter in discussing the immateriality of the intellect.

there, this cat here, that star there—each exists as a singular reality, a real and not merely imaginary or past or future instance of the species. Reality is in fact a collection of distinctly existing things, each one being unique and singular in its existence or actual being. And reality is also constituted, as we have noted, by natural kinds wherein there are many things that each exist singularly but share a common nature.[10] Each human being is a distinct existent—his or her own person, in fact—but there are many such human beings.

It is important not to be misled into thinking that these *aspects* of a thing are *parts* of a thing: when Aquinas speaks of a real distinction of nature and the act of existence in each thing that exists, he does not mean to denote two entities in each reality, nor is he referring to a material structure of composition, like an arrangement of atoms and chemicals. Indeed, he means something like the opposite: each concrete singular existent is only ever understood both in terms of its nature (shared with others) and its singular existence (proper to itself alone). Furthermore, natures are common to multiple realities in a different way than existence is. I can share a common nature with others but not a common existence, as the latter would mean that I am the same being that the other is. Distinct human beings, like Jerome and Paula, are the same *kind* of thing but not the same *actual* thing. However, natures separate one kind of thing from another thing in ways that existence does not. I am an individual nature of one kind and not another (if I am a human being, and not an eagle or an oak tree), but both I and all other instances of a natural kind (like eagles or oak trees) truly all exist, and each of us also shares in existence as something fundamental characterizing all that we are. Existence is what divides or separates each thing from all others as

10. We should note briefly that this is true even on a reductively "atomist" account of physical matter. There are many kinds of molecules, each of the same nature, but each individual molecule exists in singularity, so that for a reductive materialism to be true (in which only atoms and their molecular structures are real and larger entities are mere bundles of relations of these smaller realities), there still must obtain this distinction of nature and singular existence, by which we understand the structure of reality around us. It is difficult, for example, to make sense of the periodic table without some notion of *essentially distinct kinds* of chemical elements that *exist* in individual singularity.

unique, since your existence is not my existence. However, it is also
what all things have in common on the most fundamental level, no
matter what their natures, since all the various kinds of things we
find in the universe exist and can thus be said to participate in being.[11] To recapitulate: essence is something that unites us to our like
kind but separates us from all other natural kinds. Existence is something that unites us to all things insofar as all things exist, no matter
what their natural kind, but it is also something that divides or separates us from all things, insofar as the existence of each thing is entirely singular and unique.

Why is this kind of distinction of essence and existence important? Now that we have introduced the distinction, consider three
arguments that show that it is not arbitrarily imposed by our minds
upon the beings around us, but is, on the contrary, grounded in the
very nature of things. From these arguments we can begin to see why
it is that the real distinction between essence and existence points us
toward the necessary existence of God.

Consider a first argument taken from the fact that existence is
not in any genus of being.[12] This argument takes its starting point
from the premise that every nature (every kind of thing) we know
fits into a larger genus and species of being, but existence does not.
For example, all lions are animals, that is to say, living beings with
sensate powers. But being is not reducible either to lions alone or
the genus of animals or even to the realm of living things in general, because if this were the case, then non-lions would not exist,
or plants would not exist, or non-living things would not exist. But
clearly there exist many things that are not living. Indeed, every kind
of thing exists, no matter what its genus or species. Consequently,
existence is not reducible to a given genus or species of being but

11. On the notion of "participation," in relation to the real distinction, see for example, Aquinas, *De hebdom.*, lec. 2. All that exists participates in being insofar as all things
share in being, and receive it from others in a common way.

12. See Aquinas, *In V Meta.*, lec. 9, 889–90 as well as *In III Meta.*, lec. 8, 433.; *In VI
Meta.*, lec. 1, 1147; *De ver.* q. 1, a 1. See also Dewan in "St. Thomas and the Distinction
between Form and Esse in Caused Things," in *Form and Being*, 188–204.

includes every genus of being. If existence were simply identical with nature in any given thing, then existence would be reducible to or identical with a given nature (and found only in a given genus and species), but we have just pointed out that this is not the case. Therefore, the Thomist claim is that there must exist in every reality we experience a real distinction of nature and existence. In short, existence is a more inclusive category than that of nature. It includes all genera of things, all natures. Therefore, existence is not in a nature or identical with any particular genus or nature.

This argument may sound abstract, but it is actually quite simple. Kangaroos exist, as do rose plants, stars, human beings, and artifacts (like chlorine or cars). But existence is not a particular kind of thing, like a kangaroo or a human being, because in this case only some kinds of things would exist (that is, only kangaroos or rose plants, etc.). Instead, being is common to all that exists, to every kind of thing that is. In fact, we must say that it is not only present in distinct *substances* (natural kinds, like rose plants) but also common to their properties or accidents (such as redness or a given quantity, such as two feet tall). After all, the red quality of the rose exists, as does its quantitative size, its real relations to its environment and soil, and so forth. Existence is never reducible to a given form or property of a form (to *either* substances *or* their properties) but is common to all that is.[13] Therefore, existence is really distinguishable and distinct (not separate however!) from natural form or essence in any given thing.

Secondly, existence is what allows us to understand the problem of the one and the many. There are many things that exist, and precisely because they each exist in distinction from one another, they are multiple, they are many.[14] The singular existence of a given

13. See the argument of Aristotle to this effect in *Nicomachean Ethics*, I, 6, 1196a23–29, concerning Plato's univocal notion of the good and why goodness cannot be reduced to a particular genus of being. He offers a parallel argument in *Metaphysics* IV, 003a32–b11, regarding being, which is known only analogically across every genera of being and is not reducible in essence or definition to any one "kind" of being. Aquinas follows these arguments himself in many texts, including those mentioned in the previous note.

14. For more on the notion of the one and the many in relation to Aquinas's analysis

individual being is what separates or distinguishes it from all others most fundamentally. Aquinas calls this the transcendental principle of "alterity" in all beings—*aliquid* in Latin. The act of being provides the alterity in being that separates and distinguishes one being from all others.[15] At the same time, as we have noted, it is also existence or being-in-act that is most common to all things and gives them their deepest "ecumenical unity" in the order of reality. Everything that is real, then, participates in existence. After all, we distinguish what is real from what is illusory by seeking to identify what really exists. Consequently (and somewhat paradoxically), being also unites or creates a common unity to all that is real in the world. Only existence allows us to conceive of what all things have in common (precisely in their irreducible singularity) that is more fundamental than their natures.[16] This kind of singularity and commonality is decidedly not what we find in a "common nature," as we have already noted. Therefore, there must be a real distinction between existence and nature in all the realities we encounter. Otherwise, we would be unable to understand how all the multiple singular realities truly exist as one collection of beings over and above their various groupings as natures, by which they are not united in common being.

Third and finally, we can note that it is only the acknowledgement of this distinction that allows us to make certain kinds of fundamental modal statements about what may possibly be or not be the case with regard to existence.[17] When we define a nature, we define what must be present for a thing to be a certain kind of reality. Thus, human beings are in essence animals capable of rationality and free deliberation. But certain kinds of modal statements pertain to the capacity of a thing to be or not to be, to exist in actuality or

of existence common to all things, see Wippel, *The Metaphysical Thought of Thomas Aquinas*, 65–73.

15. See *De ver.*, q. 1, a. 1, on *aliud* as a transcendental note of being.

16. In this sense, it is the basis for the principle of non-contradiction in its ontological dimensions, potentially extended to all that is, as explored in chapter 1.

17. Brian Leftow explores topics of this kind in *God and Necessity* (Oxford: Oxford University Press, 2012), 412–15. See also Gyula Klima, "Aquinas's Real Distinction and Its Role in a Causal Proof of God's Existence," *Roczniki Filozoficzne* 67, no. 4 (2019): 7–26.

to cease to exist in actuality. This is why we can define a thing essentially without necessarily knowing that it exists. The definition of the essence does not presume immediate experiential knowledge of the actuality of existence. We can study the nature of a kangaroo, then, without having ever experienced the singular existence of the kangaroo. Or we can study the essence of what has ceased altogether to exist, as is the case with various dinosaurs. Or we can postulate the essence of something that may never or indeed physically could never exist, such as the phoenix. This is also why we can note that a given natural essence that exists actually now could potentially not exist in the future, as with the danger of the extinction of species such as the panda or the bison. When we make such a claim, we are stating something true ontologically of the reality itself, not merely of our way of thinking. The statement "this man here could not exist" is true because the person in question does not exist "by nature." That is to say, existence is not identical with nature in him. His nature of being human—his essence—does not procure his existence nor preserve him in existence necessarily. Rather his human nature does exist currently but also could cease to exist in act. Indeed, our experience of most physical things is that they do not last, and modern science has shown us that even realities that seem most secure to us—such as the moon or the stars—will eventually cease to be. Modal statements about essential kinds of realities that may or may not come into existence or go out of existence have their ontological grounding in the real potency of each nature to exist or not exist in act. This potency/act distinction in all things that can be or not be indicates the reality of the distinction between essence and existence.[18]

18. Aquinas understands existence and essence in things by interpreting them in light of actuality and potency. (See, for example, *De ente*, ch. 4.) He understands the existence of a given thing as the actuality of an individual substance, the existence-in-act of a given human being for example. Meanwhile, he understands the essence of a given thing as the potency of its substance. So an individual substance such as a human being has an essential nature that can potentially exist or not exist, based on whether it has actual existence or not. Otherwise stated, the individual that has a given nature (a particular star, oak tree, horse, or human being) is in potency to being in act, it can come

I asserted above that demonstrative arguments for the existence of God of the kind Thomists favor begin by identifying metaphysical principles in the realities around us and then proceed to show how these principles indicate causal dependencies. The real distinction of existence (*esse*) and nature (*essentia*) in each reality we experience is something we can come to know once we reflect upon the principles discussed in the previous chapter of this book. That there is existence in each reality we encounter is a truth known in virtue of the principle of non-contradiction. This being here is not that being there, due to the singularity of the existence of each of these distinct realities. That there is a determinate nature or essence in each thing we know is a truth we apprehend intuitively, placed under the common title of the principle of identity. There is a nature or essence to each thing that is. From these basic, "pre-demonstrative" principles that each person knows, we can derive knowledge of the real distinction of existence and nature in all things we experience. As noted above, these two principles are not distinct things but are ontologically compositional and coextensive. Where there is an entity that exists (an "*ens*"), there is always a natural kind (an "*essentia*") having concrete existence ("*esse*"). Where there is an entity (*ens*) that has a nature (*essentia*), we always find something that really exists (*esse*).[19]

---

into existence and even while it is in existence it is capable of passing out of existence. Every reality we experience is capable of being or not being. Furthermore, its existence is not actually infinite, since each thing exists as only one kind of reality among others with an existence that is limited in its nature and potency. In this sense created essence always limits and contracts existence and each individual creature merely participates in existence and does not possess being in its plenitude.

19. Aquinas specifies that the "essence" of a material thing consists of both its form and matter and that a concrete being (*ens*) is the essence that exists, that is, has *esse*. *De ente*, ch. 2:

> [F]or the act of being [*esse*] of a composite substance is neither of the form alone, nor of matter alone, but of the composite itself; and the essence is that on account of which the thing is said to be. Therefore, the essence, on account of which the thing is denominated a "being," cannot be the form alone or the matter alone, but has to be both, although it is the form that causes this act of being in its own way.

The reason that this observation is not trivial for theological purposes is that it leads to a next metaphysical claim, which follows logically from the former arguments. In every being in which there is a real distinction of essence and existence, the being is not the cause of its own existence. Indeed, no being in which this distinction obtains can be the natural source of its own being. The reason for this can be stated simply: no such reality has a nature that gives itself existence. Instead, it has a nature that has come into being, that receives its existence. It is a reality that has been given existence. This "receiving of existence" can occur through complex physical processes of nature and can involve immensely complicated material changes, such as cosmological and physical forces, atomic alterations, chemical reactions, and biological functions. However, all this material complexity, while entirely real and worthy of study for its own sake, serves in this context only to illustrate a deeper metaphysical truth. When speaking about any singular reality that exists and that has a given nature, whether at the micro or macro level—an atom, a chemical element, a plant, a man, or a sun—we are speaking about a thing that is not the cause of its own being. It does truly exist, and it can exist or not exist, but it is not something that exists necessarily or that can assure its own continued existence uniquely in virtue of its nature or natural powers.

Furthermore, then, every such reality can only exist due to the activity of others, who in turn communicate existence to it and cause it to be or to come into existence. No reality we experience is the author of its own being. The reader will not be surprised that I am leading us towards the Christian claim that God is the ultimate author of our being, the giver of our existence. Such a claim could be pre-empted by the observation that things routinely receive their being from other beings or from physical forces, as noted above—the cat was born of other cats, the star from the compression of material (mainly hydrogen) by gravity until the point of fusion. The provenance of ordinary things—animals, artifacts—is obvious to us, and the provenance of grander things (the planet Earth, the moon, the stars) has been opened up to us by modern science. One may ask, then, is recourse to the notion of God really required to explain the existence of things?

Here then we come to the third stage of the argument mentioned above: the claim that there can be no recourse to the infinite when speaking about actual causes that are finite in kind. This point is central to many of the Thomistic arguments for the existence of God, so it is worth seeing in what way Aquinas makes this argument:

> Now, everything that a thing has is either caused in it by its own principles, as the ability to laugh in man, or it comes to the thing from an external source, as the light in the air is coming from the sun. But the existence of a thing cannot be caused by its form or quiddity itself (I mean, as by an efficient cause), for then a thing would be its own cause, and would bring itself into existence, which is impossible. Therefore, all such things, namely, those that have their existence as something distinct from their nature, have to have their existence from something else. However, since everything that is through something else [per aliud] is reduced to what is through itself [per se] as its first cause, there has to be something that is the cause of existence for everything, since it is existence only. For otherwise the series of causes would go to infinity, since everything that is not existence only has a cause for its existence, as has been said. It is clear, therefore, that an intelligence is both form and existence, and that it has its existence from the first being that is existence only; and this is the first cause, which is God.[20]

We should note some of the features of this argument. First of all, it is not a temporal argument. The claim is not that there had to be something first caused in time, before time, or prior to the history of physical processes—before the Big Bang, for example—which gave them existence. The claim is metaphysical, not chronological. Given the reality of many distinct things that are caused to be, are not self-derived in their very being, and cannot give themselves existence, there must be a transcendent cause of existence, one that gives existence to the whole chain of others. At this juncture the

20. Aquinas, *On Being and Essence*, ch. 5.

philosophical idea of creation begins to come into view. The First Cause does not merely give being to things in the past and then leave them to themselves. Rather, God gives being to all that is, in all times and places, like an eternal sun distributing the rays of being to all that is or that will ever exist. Creatures only exist in the given moment—in each moment in history—because God is communicating being to all that exists, and is doing so perpetually. This claim does not serve in any way to undermine the real history of causal interactions between creatures, such as the causal relationships we seek to delineate in the modern sciences. Rather, it would seek to explain the deepest foundation for this real history. It is because God is communicating existence to all that is in the universe that there is an ongoing history of the universe composed of beings acting upon one another in scientifically verifiable ways.

Second, this argument implies recourse to a version of the principle of sufficient reason we discussed in chapter 1. To explain an effect, we need to identify the proper cause that is proportionate to the effect. This commonsense, realistic metaphysical principle is applicable here, when we seek to consider "vertically," as it were, why all things are, given that nothing we experience is the cause of itself. We account for the existence of things by recourse to something that exists eternally "by nature," and that we call God.

Third, we should note that this form of argumentation is not open to the naive objection, "but if everything has a cause of its being, then God would need to have a cause as well." This objection is sometimes employed in an attempt to prolong the infinite regress of finite things, suggesting that (1) we cannot conceive of causes except as contingent material processes and that therefore (2) if "God" were to exist, then God would have to be reduced to another member in the series of such causes. The first premise in this argument is false, and so the second premise does not follow. In addition, those who make this kind of objection frequently presuppose that theistic argumentation must have logical recourse to the principle "everything has a cause for its existence," and they then seek to apply the principle to God as well, so as to show the absurdity of the use of the principle. However, theistic argumentation of the kind I have proposed above does not have any recourse to this principle. We do not know a priori nor should we presume that all things must have a cause of their existence. Some things clearly do, but it does not follow that everything does. Nor does it make sense to say that if God exists, then he must be caused by another or in some way be *causa sui*. (This latter claim is clearly problematic.) Based on the form of argumentation I have made above, one could apply the logical axiom that "nothing is a cause of itself" to both creatures and God in different ways, since God is not the cause of himself as one who just is eternally in virtue of his incomprehensible nature. But this use of a universal maxim that seeks to include God and creatures under one metaphysical law is potentially misleading, since it could give the impression that God and creatures are both subordinate together to systems of logic that transcend them both but that are adequately comprehended by the human mind. On the contrary, we should note that logical maxims of the kind under discussion are only mental rules of thumb derived from our mind's reflections on limited experiences and that they must be tested against reality. They are not a priori certitudes necessarily applicable in all cases.

The argument from the "real distinction" depends upon no such mental rules and is based on a genuine *quia* demonstration (in the scholastic Aristotelian sense of the term) that passes from effects to a demonstrable cause. The effect is existence, present in all things we experience but not accounted for by any reality we know and that is itself clearly caused in each reality. From this we can derive certitude of the existence of one who gives being to all things, in which the real distinction of essence and existence does not obtain. This means that for what we call "God," it is true to say that he "exists by nature": his nature is not limited or received from another. Rather, he possesses existence in its plenitude, by essence. And in him it is natural to exist, and he cannot not exist. Furthermore, he possesses all that is essential to existence, the very plenitude of being. If this is the case, God is literally unfathomable for us, as we are presented with the problem of God's transcendence, simplicity, and eternity. The ineffability of God is a topic we will return to in the next section of this book, but for now it suffices to say that if God is the author of our existence and is one in whom there is no origination of existence, then God is wholly unlike creatures and is deeply hidden from our ordinary understanding and our representational and conceptual powers.

THE FIRST WAY FROM MOTION

The famous Five Ways of argument for the existence of God found in Thomas Aquinas's *Summa theologiae* are not the only arguments he offers, nor are they always the most extensive form of the arguments in question, since they are merely summarized in *ST* I, q. 2, a. 3.[21] Nevertheless, they are presented there with clarity and brilliance. Each argument takes its point of departure from observable features of the world and argues from these to the necessity of a transcendent cause we call "God." The first takes its starting point from the existence of change in the world, the second from dependency of all things on efficient causes, the third from the ontological contingency of all physical realities, the fourth from the degrees of perfection found in things, and the fifth from the order and intelligibility of nature. Each in its own way shows that the God in whom Christians believe by grace may also be known imperfectly through the use of natural reason, and this knowledge is enriched progressively as the arguments are undertaken in cumulative fashion.

Aquinas calls the first argument from motion "the most manifest."

21. On the five ways see Wippel, *The Metaphysical Thought of Thomas Aquinas*, 442–500; Rudi Te Velde, *Aquinas on God: The 'Divine Science' of the* Summa Theologiae (Aldershot: Ashgate, 2006), 37–64; Edward Feser, *Aquinas* (Oxford: Oneworld, 2009); Porro, *Thomas Aquinas*, 222–28; Bonino, Dieu, *"Celui Qui Est"*, 159–219; Thomas Joseph White, *Wisdom in the Face of Modernity; A Study in Thomistic Natural Theology*, second edition (Naples, FL: Sapientia Press, 2016). On the longer arguments from the *Summa contra Gentiles*, see in particular Wippel, *The Metaphysical Thought of Thomas Aquinas*, 413–40; Kretzmann, *The Metaphysics of Theism*.

He does not mean that the argument is the most self-evident but that it begins from the observation of something that is most manifest: things in the world are subject to change. When Aquinas speaks of "motion" in his historical context, he is alluding to a set of philosophical observations regarding ontological change. Everything we experience is subject to one of four kinds of change: (1) substantial generation or corruption (a thing coming to be or ceasing to be as a whole), (2) qualitative change (change of color, temperature, temperament, moral aptitude, attitude, etc.), (3) quantitative change (of size, weight, or shape), or (4) change of location (or relative position). This argument is concerned primarily with the last three of these forms of ontological change. Everything we experience is subject to ontological change that is qualitative, quantitative, and positional, and typically everything we experience is subject to these three kinds of change all the time, in various ways.[22]

Second, then, all the realities that change around us are actually changing under the causal influence of other realities. The street grows light or dark under the influence of the presence or absence of the sunlight; the trees change shape due to the effects of wind, soil, and rain; the iron oxidizes and rusts over time due to the chemical accretion of water and oxygen; chemical emissions from cars affect the air and atmosphere as their chemical products change from one place to another.[23]

---

22. If we attempt to trace back the ontological roots of this kind of change to our principles from chapter 1, we can see that change of these kinds is grounded in the various properties or accidents of substances insofar as they can exist in potency or in actuality, under the causal influence of others. In other words, each substance we experience has a given quantity and material composition, a given set of qualities, and a given set of relations (including positions relative to other realities). The various quantities, qualities, and relations of position can exist in a diversity of ways and are subject to alteration under the causal influence of other realities acting upon them.

23. *ST* I, q. 2, a. 3:

It is certain, and evident to our senses, that in the world some things are in motion. Now whatever is in motion is put in motion by another, for nothing can be in motion except it is in potentiality to that towards which it is in motion; whereas a thing moves inasmuch as it is in act. For motion is nothing else than the reduction of something from potentiality to actuality. But nothing can be

Third, then, nothing that exists while undergoing change does so uniquely due to processes of self-alteration. All that we experience is subject to ontological change based on the activity of other agents that act upon the agent in question.[24] Note that this is not a claim about historical, chronological change from the past to the present to the future. It is a claim about actual chains of real interdependence at any given time. So, for example, it is the case now as a person reads this book that all the material things around us are moving or changing, and they in turn are being moved or changed by others, which are themselves in turn also being moved or changed by others. The causal line is actualistic and "vertical," not chronological or temporally "horizonal," going back in time.

Why can we not posit, then, the existence of an *actually existent* infinite series of finite causes of change? It is true after all that we have vast finite chains of dependent, changing agents that exist actually and require explanation by recourse to other agents so as to explain their ontological alteration.[25] However, to prolong such

---

reduced from potentiality to actuality, except by something in a state of actuality. Thus that which is actually hot, as fire, makes wood, which is potentially hot, to be actually hot, and thereby moves and changes it.

24. *ST* I, q. 2, a. 3:

Now it is not possible that the same thing should be at once in actuality and potentiality in the same respect, but only in different respects. For what is actually hot cannot simultaneously be potentially hot; but it is simultaneously potentially cold. It is therefore impossible that in the same respect and in the same way a thing should be both mover and moved, i.e. that it should move itself. Therefore, whatever is in motion must be put in motion by another.

Sometimes the objection is posited that this way of thinking does not consider the modern scientific question of movement in a void, marked by inertia, where concrete contact of motion is not accounted for. However, to this it may be said first that the "change" under consideration in the First Way concerns changes in quality and quantity, not merely changes in place. Second, the changes in place that occur in bodies undergoing inertial movement are themselves subject to larger physical forces, such as the constant gravitational attraction physical bodies exert upon one another. Third, no physical body undergoing inertial motion is ontologically explicable without reference to physical changes exerted upon it that have caused it to be what it is. See on these matters, Feser, *Aquinas*, 76–79; Wippel, *The Metaphysical Thought of Thomas Aquinas*, 453–56, which cites abundant secondary literature on this topic.

25. *ST* I, q. 2, a. 3:

explanations indefinitely by appealing always to a further dependent cause does not explain why such causal chains exist but only extends indefinitely the need for a further actual explanation. In doing so, one fails to explain in a sufficient way what is actually real now: a world of interdependent beings that are not the cause of themselves and that can each only be understood and explained realistically in light of other actual causes they depend upon. Why do they exist? To explain the chains of finite, dependent causes that exist, we must come to something that causes all physical beings to be and is not caused to be through processes of physical inter-dependence. In other words, there must be something absolutely primary, outside the sphere of dependence, that explains all the physically moved, materially dependent realities. To adequately explain the changing, dependent realities we experience around us, we must have recourse to something that is itself free from qualitative, quantitative, or positional change through the causal agency of others. This means that what we call "God" cannot be material or physical and is not subject to qualitative adaptation or improvement in light of the development of the world or by engagement with it. Rather, this mysterious Being transcends the world of finite change but is also the primary cause and author of this world of physically changing realities.

THE SECOND WAY FROM EFFICIENT CAUSES

Aquinas's "Second Way" takes its point of departure from our commonplace observance of efficient causes in the world around us. "In the world of sense, we find there is an order of efficient causes." Each thing that exists depends upon others for its being.

If that by which it is put in motion be itself put in motion, then this also must needs be put in motion by another, and that by another again. But this cannot go on to infinity, because then there would be no first mover, and, consequently, no other mover; seeing that subsequent movers move only inasmuch as they are put in motion by the first mover.... Therefore it is necessary to arrive at a first mover, put in motion by no other; and this everyone understands to be God.

There is no case known ... in which a thing is found to be the efficient cause of itself; for so it would be prior to itself, which is impossible. Now in efficient causes it is not possible to go on to infinity, because in all efficient causes following in order, the first is the cause of the intermediate cause, and the intermediate is the cause of the ultimate cause, whether the intermediate cause be several, or only one. Now to take away the cause is to take away the effect. Therefore, if there be no first cause among efficient causes there will be no ultimate, nor any intermediate cause. But if in efficient causes it is possible to go on to infinity, there will be no first efficient cause, neither will there be an ultimate effect, nor any intermediate efficient causes; all of which is plainly false. Therefore it is necessary to admit a first efficient cause, to which everyone gives the name of God.

Although this form of argumentation can seem similar to the First Way, the starting point of this Second Way is concerned with something different. The First Way concentrates on the causes of change or motion in all the realities we experience. It starts from the observation that all material things are in some way ontologically dependent upon other realities, and they point us toward a first immaterial reality that is not dependent upon others and not subject to redefinition due to the influence of an external physical agent. The Second Way, however, sets out to explain something else: not the change that occurs in things but their very existence as caused by others. The argument begins with the common observation that all things depend upon others for their very being. Everything we observe to exist actually exists only within an order of efficient causes. Furthermore, nothing is the cause of its own existence. Because the very being of things is under consideration in the Second Way, its scope of consideration is more extensive. It is concerned with the notion of creation, philosophically considered. Why do things exist? The question can apply not only to physical, material entities but also (in principle, if they exist) to the spiritual souls of human beings and to angels, which are pure spirits.[26] All that exists but depends upon others for its existence must in turn have a transcendent source for its existence.

Some commentators note that this argument is not concerned

26. As Bonino helpfully points out in *Dieu, "Celui Qui Est,"* 183–87.

with what Aquinas calls a *per accidens* series of efficient causes. An example of such a series would be the chronological begetting of one person from another, as in the example of parents who beget children, who in turn beget grandchildren. The grandchildren do not actually depend upon their grandparents for their existence now, nor the children upon their parents. Rather, the grandchildren depend actually upon a host of efficient causes around them, in the universe, that sustain them in being—oxygen, food, warmth, gravity, and so on. This is easiest to see in the case of children adopted by another family; the children could not have existed without their biological parents, but their parents provide no aid to their continued existence. They depend upon their parents and grandparents only chronologically and historically. It is not inconceivable to think that such accidental, chronological lines of dependence might go back forever, like a series of parent-child relationships of begetting that simply goes on perpetually. Likewise, consider the example of a primal atomic reaction that gives rise to the Big Bang, approximately 14 billion years ago, and this in turn has chronological consequences in the cosmos as time unfolds. This too would be an example of a *per accidens* series of causes that could in principle go on forever chronologically. (It is possible, for example, that there was a "history of matter" prior to the Big Bang.)

The Second Way does not argue for a finite chain of causes of the *per accidens* type. Instead, the argument is concerned with the fact that everything we experience has a derived existence. The point is not to explain reality chronologically but ontologically. We can use chronological examples to illustrate the force of the argument. The fact that children come into being due to their parents does illustrate the fact that they are dependent in the order of being and have an efficient cause (or causes). But the example is given not to discover a *chronological* first but an *ontological* first. Otherwise stated, the universe is only ever at any given moment a universe in which things exist in dependence upon a series of efficient causes and in which nothing is the cause of its own being.[27]

27. Immanuel Kant seeks to restrict the application of the principle of causality to the sensate world. However, Kant also makes clear that he wishes to argue against Hume

Once we begin from these premises, the argument is simple. Everything we experience is caused to be by others. However, nothing we experience that causes others to be is itself self-generated or self-caused. Consequently, each such cause requires an explanation for its being. However, there cannot exist only an infinite series of caused causes, whether in the actual or chronological order. For the purposes of this argument, it is immaterial whether we appeal to the per se causal series that is actual and non-chronological or to the accidental causal series that is historical and chronological. We can think "now" of all that exists around us and note that nothing we experience is the cause of its own existence, or we can think "back" historically to the unfolding of the cosmos, as best we understand it, and acknowledge that anything we can study in this context comes into being and is not the cause of its own being. Any appeal to an infinite series of caused causes would fail to explain adequately the real world we live in, since each new reality to which we would appeal to explain the continued existence of things would in turn require an additional cause to explain its existence. This would be true even if the universe we live in has always existed. Any entity that does not cause itself or account for its own existence points us toward something absolute or first that has a non-derived existence. Consequently, something has to exist that causes all the secondary, interdependent causes themselves to be and gives being to all others without receiving being from any of them.

We should note that this argument presupposes that in the world around us, the things we see are true efficient causes of real effects.

---

that the notion of God as a primary cause of the world is not unintelligible or literally inconceivable, and this capacity of the mind to orient itself toward God remains crucial to Kant's practical ethics, where one must be able to think of God as an intelligible idea that can motivate consent to the idea of a transcendent morality. Consequently, he also argues for the intelligibility in principle of a concept of God as a cause of the world analogically conceived (by analogy of proper proportionality). See *Prolegomena to Any Future Metaphysics*, trans. P. Carus (Indianapolis, IN: Bobbs-Merrill, 1950), §58 (357–61). The traditional Thomistic claims I am appealing to are stronger, of course, and arguably also more consistent and realistic.

One thing causes another thing to be, as when two parents beget a child or when a builder builds a house or the combination of various atoms gives rise to a chemical element. Such actions entail the causation of one thing by another (or others). But they are limited in effect. For example, a human being that causes another to be does not cause the *nature* of the human being to be. Rather, the parents transmit this nature, which they themselves received from others, to a new individual. Therefore, they are merely a kind of instrumental cause, disposed to giving being to another. Likewise, the parents give existence to their child in some real sense, but they do so only from the being of their own bodies that already exist and that they in turn have received from others. And this is true *mutatis mutandis* for all examples we devise by appeal to physical generation. Both our existence and our nature are received, even when we cause other things to be. A star (like the sun of our solar system) is not self-originating, even as its heat gives all living things on earth the possibility of continuing in existence. Rather, it has received its existence and nature from physical forces that preceded it and gave it definition—thus "explaining" it in some sense, which is why we can understand the sun better by studying its cosmological origins. Nevertheless, any such physical force or entity that produced stars (through physical interactions billions of years ago) is itself only explicable in dependency upon others, ontologically speaking. Whether we speak of living things or the most basic physical entities, none of these things is the unique source of its own being or nature, even when it is a real cause of other things "coming into being" with this or that nature. Consequently, Aquinas argues, there must exist something that is giving being to all things with their diverse natures, which we call "God." This primary reality must be ontologically uncaused and underived. God simply is, by nature, and gives being unilaterally to all else that exists. This means this mysterious Being is wholly unlike any of the realities we commonly experience and so in some way is truly incomprehensible to us. It follows from this line of argumentation that God subsists eternally without beginning or end. The

One who is the Creator of all things "has no history" but is wholly a-temporal, in contrast to all created natures.

The First Way denied that there is potency for change in God and therefore offers some notion of God as immaterial actuality. God has no material potency for change but also no immaterial potency for amelioration, since in that case he would depend upon another to develop spiritually. Consequently, God is a pure actuality of perfection, without any potential for change in view of amelioration. The Second Way provides the further notion that God is the hidden Creator of all being and therefore is in some numinous way Subsistent Being Itself, or as Aquinas says metaphorically and beautifully, an infinite sea of being.[28] The Second Way, then, brings us very close to the theological notions of God as Creator and divine providence, albeit from a philosophical perspective or vantage point. If there is a primary source of all things that gives them their very being, then God is the Creator of all things, and the notion of creation, while being of Biblical origin and therefore something *revealed* by God, is also something of philosophical provenance, *accessible* to the native powers of human intelligence.[29]

The argument also provides us with an initial philosophical approach to the notion of divine providence. When we speak of divine providence, we denote the idea that God is himself a wisdom and goodness that not only gives being to the world but also governs the world harmoniously in view of the good of creatures. This idea begins to emerge from the Second Way as a properly natural and rational idea. The natural, chronological causes of things we find in the

28. See on this Aquinas in *ST* I, q. 13, a. 11. Note that this conclusion is very similar to that of the argument we considered above, from the real distinction of *esse* and *essentia*, which is absent in God.

29. In *ST* I, q. 44, a. 2 Aquinas discusses the gradual development in ancient philosophy of an engagement with the study of created being, or of the primary cause of existence in things. His attribution of it to Plato and Aristotle suggests he thinks they approached it implicitly but still in some way "formally" and that the philosophical examination of "creation" is brought to light more perfectly by divine revelation. See *De pot.*, q. 3, a. 5, and Mark Johnson, "Did St. Thomas Attribute a Doctrine of Creation to Aristotle?" *New Scholasticism* 63, no. 2 (1989): 129–55, and Lawrence Dewan, "Thomas Aquinas, Creation and Two Historians," *Laval théologique et philosophique*, 50 (1994): 363–87.

world are themselves dependent upon God who gives them being. Consequently, they are in some sense his "instruments" in an analogical sense of this term. The vast order of interdependent entities and efficient causes in the world is in fact an expression of God's wisdom and goodness, presumably indicative of his intentions and designs for his creatures.[30] This "merely philosophical" idea of providence is incomplete, enigmatic, and even vexing, especially if we consider it in light of the problem of evils that human beings experience, but it is also one that leaves us open, philosophically speaking, to the possibility of a deeper mystery of God's providence, which may be understood only in light of divine revelation.

THE THIRD WAY FROM CONTINGENCY

The Third Way is about contingency and necessity. What is it that must be, and what is it that can be? The argument begins from the observation that all material things are subject to generation and corruption. They come into being and go out of being and thus are transient. The world we live in is a world of impermanence, of transitory material things that can exist but need not exist and that eventually cease to be. Contingency understood in this sense denotes the possibility of a thing to be or to not be based on the fact that each thing is subject to material corruption. It is in this sense that we can call contingent beings transient and impermanent. The argument that follows from this has its ancient origins in *Metaphysics* XII, 6 of Aristotle, where the philosopher argues that any given material thing that comes into being is not explainable without there being something "necessary." Necessary things are understood here in a particular sense, not as "logically necessary to any possible world we can conceive of" (as some contemporary analytic philosophers tend to mean).[31] Rather, it means something onto-

---

30. See on this, *ST* I, 104, a. 1.

31. See the influential background texts of Rudolf Carnap, *Meaning and Necessity: A Study in Semantics and Modal Logic* (Chicago: The University of Chicago Press, 1947), and Saul Kripke, *Naming and Necessity* (Cambridge, MA: Harvard University Press, 1972).

logically permanent and not subject to corruption, something that always is. In fact, Aristotle (and Aquinas after him) thinks there are "levels" of necessity in the world. There are necessary beings that do not come and go but that are in turn caused to be (perpetually, without end) by other necessary beings. For example, Aristotle famously thought that only beings in the sub-lunar sphere are subject to generation and corruption. The stars and the sun meanwhile persist forever and are necessary material beings. Behind them, however, there are separated substances that maintain the stars in existence and that themselves always exist. They in turn depend upon God for their existence. Medieval Muslim, Jewish, and Christian commentators on Aristotle sometimes considered angels as separated substances that are "necessary" in this sense, as existing incorruptibly while also being caused by God to exist. The angels exist perennially but as caused beings.

Once we consider this original context for the terms "contingency" and "necessity," it is much easier to understand the argument in question. It starts from the observational fact that the contingent things we experience in the world can possibly be or not be and argues that there must exist something more foundational that is necessary or always is.[32] Of course our modern cosmological vision is very different from that of Aristotle or the medieval monotheists who developed this argument from reading his texts. However, the reality of contingency in our physical world is undeniable, even as our understanding of the physical world becomes increasingly sophisticated and far-reaching due to the discoveries of modern physics.

Here then is how the argument proceeds. All things we experience are subject to material corruption. They have the capacity of being or not being. The most obvious example of this occurs in generation and corruption, the coming into being and going out of

32. *ST* I, q. 2, a. 3: "The third way is taken from possibility and necessity, and runs thus. We find in nature things that are possible to be and not to be, since they are found to be generated, and to corrupt, and consequently, they are possible to be and not to be."

being of individual material things. The tree comes into being by the seed of the parent plant, but it eventually dies and decomposes in the earth or is consumed by fire. The stone is forged over millions of years of pressure beneath the earth's surface, but eventually it is exposed to rain and undergoes dissolution and washes away. The living animal is born from its parents but eventually dies. The star comes from an initial energy burst and lasts billions of years, but eventually it burns out. Can there exist only a world of such transient and impermanent beings, or must there exist something that is permanent?

Contingent things come into being and go out of being due to their own material "potency" or susceptibility of undergoing corruption. No such being is ontologically necessary in the sense mentioned above (perpetually and permanently in existence), precisely because it is subject to material "redefinition" and corruption. However, every contingent being has come into being due to the causation of another or others, since it has not always existed. Furthermore, due to the kind of thing it is, no contingent thing can maintain itself in existence indefinitely, and so each material thing will eventually cease to exist. It is not a necessary being.

At this juncture we can argue in two different ways, one that is non-chronological, which Aquinas presents in *Summa contra Gentiles* I, c. 15, and one that is chronological, which he presents as the Third Way in the *Summa theologiae*.

In the *Summa contra Gentiles*, Aquinas simply notes that if every contingent being must depend for its coming into being upon another, then there cannot exist merely an actual infinity of such beings, since each one in turn requires explanation, due to the principle of causality, by recourse to another. Therefore, to explain a universe of contingent, impermanent beings, all subject to corruption and dissolution, it is necessary to have recourse to something that is necessary, immaterial, and eternal.[33]

---

33. *SCG* I, c. 15:

We find in the world, furthermore, certain beings, those namely that are subject to generation and corruption, which can be and not-be. But what can be has a

Aquinas's argument in the *Summa theologiae* is more complex. There he notes that if there are only ever material contingent beings, it is possible that at some point all things cease to exist. He means by this not that each of them ceases to exist at some point independently of one another, which is not controversial, but that at some point all of them should cease to exist in their totality. This would constitute a kind of cosmic system failure, in which things ceased to act by sequential causality so as to sustain other things in being, and so all things would eventually give out. As a metaphor, we might think of a symphony of musicians who cannot play indefinitely without losing the melody as an ensemble and eventually cease to play, falling into complete silence.[34] If this ever occurred in the order of generation and corruption, then at some point all things would have ceased to function to engender and sustain others in existence, and consequently, all new natural forms would have ceased to come into being.

So, let us presuppose that there are only material contingent beings and that they have always existed (since if they did not always exist, they would need a cause of their existence that is not contingent but necessary). Furthermore, let us presume that all of them are truly contingent, in which case there is no necessity that they exist. But if there were only contingent things in existence for a perpetual duration of time, then at some point in the past, what is possible for each of them singularly would have to have become true for all of them collectively. Each of them would cease to exist simultaneously.

---

cause because, since it is equally related to two contraries, namely, being and non-being, it must be owing to some cause that being accrues to it. Now, as we have proved by the reasoning of Aristotle, one cannot proceed to infinity among causes. We must therefore posit something that is a necessary being. Every necessary being, however, either has the cause of its necessity in an outside source or, if it does not, it is necessary through itself. But one cannot proceed to infinity among necessary beings the cause of whose necessity lies in an outside source. We must therefore posit a first necessary being, which is necessary through itself. This is God, since, as we have shown, He is the first cause. God, therefore, is eternal, since whatever is necessary through itself is eternal.

34. My musical analogy here is inspired in part by Bonino, *Dieu, "Celui Qui Est"*, 192–93.

However, nothing cannot give rise to something. Non-being cannot give rise to being. So, if all things had ceased to exist due to the possibility of radical corruption present in them all, the world of generation and corruption we live in now would not exist. But this world does exist. Consequently, there cannot be merely contingent being, but there must be something necessary and permanent. If this being that is necessary is itself caused, then it can only be caused by something that is itself necessary and uncaused. There cannot be an infinite series of necessary but dependent realities that explains its own existence adequately, so there must be a necessary reality that exists eternally, is uncaused, and causes the universe of contingent things to be. This is the reality we call God.[35]

Here we should note a few important features of this second version of the argument. First, Aquinas's argument is not based on the premise that it is impossible for there to exist an eternal world of generation and corruption. In fact, Aquinas himself affirms (against Bonaventure) that, philosophically speaking, it is possible to hypothesize that the world of material things has always existed, even though we cannot prove it to be the case one way or the other. Furthermore, Aquinas clearly thinks that even if the world of contingent things has always existed, one can still demonstrate philosophically the necessity of the existence of God based on the kind of world we experience actually. What is being argued here, then, is not that there cannot exist an "eternal" or perennial world of merely contingent things but that such a world can only exist if and because God exists, who is himself necessary and immaterial, not contingent and material.

35. Porro, *Thomas Aquinas*, 227:

It might be objected that perhaps it is not inevitable that all possible things not exist at the same time. We could think of a kind of continual succession of possible things. One would permit another to come into being and then go out of being, etc. However, even in this case we would have to come to a first possible thing that would have had to come into being from nothing. If it had always existed, it would not be possible but necessary and would go on existing always, which is precisely what Thomas intends to demonstrate.

Second, one may wonder whether the "necessary" causes of contingent things in our world need to be God. Might these causes not simply be the material potency in things and the diverse physical forces that give rise to generation and corruption? In other words, if we are trying to explain the coming and going of stars, planets, bacteria, plants, trees, rocks, and mammals in our world, why can we not simply refer to the substrate of matter and physical forces that undergirds all things? Perhaps all generation and corruption is caused at base by the continual rearrangement of matter due to the forces of physics that govern the interaction of material agents.

The problem with this objection is that even if it were true that things were eternally subject to physical forces rearranging material potencies in physical bodies, this situation would still leave us in need of further explanations and in turn would seem to confirm the tenor of Aquinas's argument. Why so? In effect, Aquinas is noting that all we see around us are material forms (with natures, instantiated in material parts) that come and go. We can of course argue that there is something more ultimate that remains "beneath" and "in and through" the change and transience of the various forms that come and go, such as the physical forces of the universe and its material substrate. But if that is the case, then we have arrived at precisely what Aristotle and Aquinas denote as a "caused necessity": things that have to be always but that are themselves in turn caused. If physical forces and material substrates have in fact always been and are in fact necessary, they themselves are something like Aquinas's "necessary beings." But in this case, they still require explanation. They are necessary causes that are themselves caused. Why? If there is always a material residue or potency present in all things eternally, it is a necessary feature of the world, but it is also never the cause of its own being, because it also always only exists concretely in diverse individual kinds of things that are subject to coming into being and going out of being. Matter is the *matter of* a set of distinct, caused, dependent things, and it has no independent existence. (If it did have an independent being, it would be a natural form itself or determinate kind of reality, subject to generation and corruption. Instead, it is a principle found within all physical things, a metaphysical constituent of physically generated beings.)[36]

Meanwhile, if physical forces always exist necessarily, they only exist in and between the kinds of aforementioned realities subject to corruption and change. Physical forces do not cause things to come into being and go out of being on their own, but they are forces that act between and within things, governing the conditions of existence of things that cause one another to come into and go out of being. The material contingency that things are subject to presupposes the truth of the "laws of physics," then, but the physical forces themselves do not provide a sufficient condition for the adequate explanation of contingency. If they did, we would not need to explain things according to their material parts that are subject to the forces in question, which of course we do. But if neither matter nor physical forces provides adequate final explanations of contingent physical forms, then they are not the most fundamental causes of contingent

---

36. Opposed to this view is the problematic theory of metaphysical atomism (not to be confused with the scientific knowledge of atomic structures). Atomism posits that there are no substantial changes among the realities we experience. The baby that is born, the tree that dies and decays into the earth: these are not substantial changes. Instead, there is a group of irreducible atomic elements that remain unchanged and simply undergo perpetual rearrangement of accidental configurations. "Substances" are mere aggregates of atoms in relation to one another. The problems with this view are numerous. First, even atomic elements studied by the modern sciences are subject to substantial change and come and go, and they too have material parts. So, the idea of atoms as merely given properly basic entities that are not subject to fundamental alteration or combination is erroneous. Second, there is a unity in substances (for example living things) that is evident. A living being is not explicable uniquely as a collection of organs, nor the organs as mere collections of cells, nor the cells as mere collections of chemicals, etc. The larger system of the whole (the formal nature of the animal) has its own proper unity and substantial integrity that is not reducible to the parts, and in fact, the behavior of the parts is only fully explicable if one understands it in relation to the ordered pursuits of the whole (the functions and aims of animal life, for example). Appeal to form/matter composition remains the best and most realistic way of understanding realities we encounter in the physical world, and this implies that there is a material potentiality in things that allows them to be subject to change at the instigation of and under the influence of others. Atomism is a kind of anti-materialism in this respect and thus an unrealistic theory of the ontology of material natures.

beings, even if they exist necessarily, and therefore they are caused necessities, themselves only explicable in the light of another cause that is distinct from them and must therefore be immaterial. Something exists, then, that is necessary and immaterial, and that is the transcendent and primary cause of contingent realities.

THE FOURTH WAY FROM DEGREES OF PERFECTION

The Fourth Way takes its point of departure from degrees of perfection we find in things. We make measures of perfection all the time, such as, for example, when we evaluate work assessments or academic exams that seek to measure competency or intelligence. We speak of people's virtues, like their degrees of kindness and character, and sometimes we also note the lack of these in ourselves and others. Items that are assessed for commercial purchase are spoken of in terms of their various perfections or limitations. We may also speak of an animal or plant as having a greater degree of perfection than another, as an excellent specimen of its kind, or as more naturally capable or more beautiful than others. Degrees of perfection or imperfection are a part of our world.

Degrees of perfection exist in a more fundamental way in the *diversity of kinds* of things and their various distinct, *hierarchically arranged* perfections. The universe of non-living things with its great perfection in longevity has a kind of endurance not found in living things. Presuming that endurance in being is a kind of perfection, the sun and the stars, for example, are more perfectly perpetual in being than all living things we know of. However, the world of living things can reproduce and survive from age to age through growth, nutrition, and reproduction, something non-living things are incapable of. Sensate animals have perfections that plants lack, since they can acquire sense knowledge of their environment, and the more sophisticated ones can learn by way of animal memory through various senses. In this respect, the clam or the oyster has a very basic perfection not found in non-living things, namely, the sense of touch. But the dog, the chimpanzee, or the dolphin is more perfect than the clam or the oyster in the realm of sensate knowledge, since these animals can learn and remember and form flexible new patterns of behavior based on previous experience. Human beings have yet more perfect features of knowledge and love than other sensate animals, due to their capacity for intellectual reasoning and free decision-making about the goods they love and wish to pursue. Intellect and free will are signs of a higher nobility and perfection in nature.

That being said, when Aquinas considers the argument from degrees of perfection, he is interested particularly in dimensions of reality that are denoted by the transcendentals, common features of all that exists, which we considered in chapter 1.[37] Being, unity, truth, goodness, and beauty exist in all things in some way. They also do so, for Aquinas, according to a diversity of perfections. Some things exist more perfectly than others and cause those others to be. Some things are more enduringly or fundamentally true than others. Some are better or higher in their degree of goodness, and some are more beautiful and splendid than others. In short, there are degrees of nobility in things according to these transcendental properties.

The reason the transcendental perfections are significant in this respect is that they are "pure perfections" which can in theory exist

---

37. *ST* I, q. 2, a. 3:

Among beings there are some more and some less good, true, noble and the like. But "more" and "less" are predicated of different things, according as they resemble in their different ways something which is the maximum; so that there is something which is truest, something best, something noblest and, consequently, something which is uttermost being; for those things that are greatest in truth are greatest in being, as it is written in *Metaph.* II. 1 (993b30).

Aquinas presents a slightly different version of the Fourth Way in his commentary on this text of Aristotle *In Meta.* II, lec. 2, §§ 294–96, where he makes this idea clear:

Now the term truth is not proper to one class of beings only, but is applied universally to all beings. Therefore, since the cause of truth is one having the same name and intelligible structure as its effect, it follows that whatever causes subsequent things to be true is itself most true.... [E]verything that is composite in nature and participates in being must ultimately have as its causes those things which have existence by their very essence.

to the infinite degree. We cannot think of an infinite degree of white or black, musical or comedic, or of an infinite species of man, unicorn, phoenix, or blue whale. However, the idea of infinite being, truth, goodness, and beauty implies no inherent contradiction, and it is intelligible as a potential measure of finite forms of these same perfections. But does such a reality exist?

Where things exist within a given order, they are intelligible according to a more profound grounding or explanatory root, a principle or cause of this order. This is a general truth, so that we can say that if the organs of the human body exist in such a way as to always interrelate to one another within one organism, then we have to understand them in relation to their larger context: human activity and the various organic systems of the human body. However, this principle is true for the transcendental features of being as well. If all that exists is in some way existent, one, true, good, and beautiful, then there must be a larger order of these features of reality in which all things fall according to diverse degrees of perfection.

Once we have acknowledged this more basic metaphysical idea, we can also note that everything in a given order of degrees refers to something first that is the reference for measuring all the others. That primary reality possesses the perfection at a maximum by which the others are in turn measured. Why must this be the case? Because in each order of degree, we can only assess the perfection of a given thing or feature of reality if we are able to identify the property, the scale of the property, and the term of the scale. Thus, we can only think about orders of goodness, for example, if the diverse degrees of goodness we find in all things exist in a scale, in which they are inserted, so to speak, according to measure. A real ontological scale of being implies, however, something first that is the measure of what is secondary or less.

Now what is first in the order of the scale of perfections must also in some real sense be the cause of the scale of perfections. It is not enough to claim that what is first in the order of perfections falls within a range of finite perfections and is itself one within a larger order of perfections, since in this case, we would still not understand why there is such an order in which all things exist, of which they form a part, but which none of them causes to exist. Against the backdrop of any scale of measure in the order of being, then, there must be some source to the order denoted by that scale. It is that which gives the perfections to all the others and in which they "participate" by receiving their perfection from what is first. And this is what we call "God," who gives being, unity, truth, goodness, and beauty to all things. If God did not cause all things to be and were merely a member of the scale of perfections (the most eminent to be sure), then God would be embedded within the order and would himself be grounded within a deeper scale or system. He would not explain it as a fundamental cause of its being. But the scale of perfections noted above requires an explanation that accounts for why there is or why there exists a degree of perfection in reality in the first place. No single member of any scale of relatively perfect beings can itself explain why the whole scale of perfection into which each single member is inserted exists. The scale cannot explain itself if it is composed of all the ordered members that compose it and give rise to it. Consequently, we cannot explain such an order of varied perfections unless there is something that causes all of them to be and possesses certain pure perfections in the most perfect and infinite of ways.[38]

We noted in chapter 1 that the transcendentals are convertible with one another; whatever has being is in some way unified, true, good, and beautiful. So what is most real or first in the order of being, which gives being to all others, will also be causally first in the order of the one and the many, the true and the real, the good and

38. *ST* I, q. 2, a. 3: "Now the maximum in any genus is the cause of all in that genus.... Therefore there must also be something which is to all beings the cause of their being, goodness, and every other perfection; and this we call God." Aquinas does not attribute these perfections to God in a "generic" way. As we have seen above, Aquinas thinks that being, unity, truth, goodness, and beauty are not in any genus but are common to all genera. But just as we can think of a scale of perfections in persons who are generically "musical" according to degrees, so we can think of a scale of perfections of beings that have existence, goodness, beauty, or truth according to degrees as well, even as these perfections are common to every genus and species of beings.

the noble, and the beautiful. God must be what is morally best and most beautiful, even as he transcends all our categories of comprehension. We know of him only from his effects of being, goodness, and beauty in the world, and we infer from these that he is infinitely perfect, transcending all created limitations. Indeed, were God limited in his nobility and perfection, he would not be the measure of the perfection of all being but would himself still be subject to measure by a yet higher standard and therefore also by a higher causal reality. But this is absurd, based on the principle of causality. Therefore, just because such a measure of all perfection must exist and is real, God must be infinitely perfect in being, beyond all finite measure and comprehension.

THE FIFTH WAY FROM TELEOLOGY

The final of the Five Ways is taken from the teleological order of things we observe in the world around us and in ourselves. Aquinas states it briefly in this way:

> The fifth way is taken from the governance of the world. We see that things which lack intelligence, such as natural bodies, act for an end, and this is evident from their acting always, or nearly always, in the same way, so as to obtain the best result. Hence it is plain that not fortuitously, but designedly, do they achieve their end. Now whatever lacks intelligence cannot move towards an end, unless it be directed by some being endowed with knowledge and intelligence; as the arrow is shot to its mark by the archer. Therefore some intelligent being exists by whom all natural things are directed to their end; and this being we call God.[39]

This form of argument begins with observations of the kind we considered in the first chapter of this book. The basic claim is that all the realities we observe, including material elements uncovered only by the modern sciences, are in some way characterized by ontological tendencies, or teleological inclinations. How is this the case? Let us restate some examples briefly.

39. ST I, q. 2, a. 3.

Non-living things are characterized by recognizable patterns of behavior, a set of efficient causes they produce that happen always or for the most part, based on the kinds of things that they are. Uranium has nuclear properties that make it fissionable, so that it may produce large amounts of energy. Crystals grow by accretion in assimilating atoms and molecules to themselves in consistently new geometrical patterns. Fire heats water. Ice typically renders cold the things it touches. These are basic types of natural outcome characteristic of the natural entities in question, indicative of their properties. They are teleological insofar as they are effects or outcomes that follow necessarily (always or for the most part) from the natures of the beings in question.

In living things, we find other, more manifest forms of activity that are characteristically tendential or teleological. All living things exist through genetic recombination and cellular reproduction. Plants are characterized by growth, nutrition, and reproduction but not by sensate knowledge. Animals are characterized by sense knowledge of various kinds and according to seeming degrees of perfection, as the dolphin is more perfect in sense knowledge than the oyster, for example. Human beings are oriented teleologically not only toward activities of nutrition, growth, reproduction, and sense knowledge but also toward activities of intellectual understanding and volition. All human beings seek the truth by nature— one clear sign of which is that no one likes to err intellectually or to be lied to—and all human beings seek happiness by nature (in however varied or psychologically convoluted ways). Human beings are ordered as rational animals toward the pursuit of knowledge and love of happiness.

If there are, in fact, teleological inclinations in things around us, the second part of the argument follows. Teleological acts or effects that are natural flow from the various things around us based on their respective properties, and these acts occur always or for the most part, since they are expressive of the very natures of things. In fact, we can only study and predict outcomes of natural activities in the modern natural sciences because we presume that there are normative effects that flow from causes in the things themselves, indicative of their properties and natures.

Third, then, such regular activity in the things around us makes evident to us that there is an intelligible order in things, one that the human mind does not invent for itself but discovers in the things themselves. Indeed, even the teleological order in our interior lives as rational beings is not chosen but discovered. There is an internal order to any authentic act of human reasoning—characterized by the laws of sound and valid logic—that is not the result of human free choice but is a determinate part of our intellectual nature as truth-seeking persons. Likewise with free will, there is an internal order to our deliberate acts by which we intend a thing, deliberate on the means to obtain it, choose the means reflectively, and decide to move to action effectively (as opposed to being compelled by coercion). These teleological structures of knowledge and love are indicative of our interior spiritual nature, not the result of our desire to possess such a nature. Our very subjectivity as persons, therefore, has an objective structure.

But where there is an intellectual order found in things that they themselves are not the source of but which characterizes them in their very being, it is necessary to ask why there is such a world of ordered things and activities. After all, none of the realities in question is the primary causal source of the order they each manifest and partake in. What is the sufficient reason for the existence of this order? The ultimate cause of it cannot itself be subject to an ordered teleological development that depends upon another, since if this were the case, appeal to it would not explain the order of the world in an ultimate way but would itself call forth the need for a further explanation, since the reality in question would itself merely be part of the larger order that is real all around us. We would then need to have recourse to yet another source so as to explain the intelligibility and order in things, and this cannot go on indefinitely by appeal to an actual infinity of caused causes, because then we would never adequately explain the real world that exists around us as it actually stands. Therefore, there must be something primary that is the cause of all ordered beings in the world. This primary reality that we call God is in some way intellectual or personal, since it is the source of order, and the order it produces can only come about from an intellect.[40]

At this juncture we might consider a classic objection to the teleological argument that is presented by Immanuel Kant in the *Critique of Pure Reason*.[41] Kant essentially argues that any form of the teleological argument allows one at most to arrive at the existence of an immaterial source of order in the world, a first world-orderer. However, he argues that this source need not be the Creator of the realities we see around us. Kant leaves open the possibility here of deism rather than the demonstration of monotheism. From a consideration of the order of the world, then, we might posit at most only a demiurge or a living source of order outside or within the physical world, the properties of which remain largely unclear or enigmatic.

How ought we to answer this objection? First, we should note that when Aquinas appeals to this argument within the context of the *Summa theologiae*, he is only arguing at this stage for something

40. Why an intellect? The order of the world cannot be produced by chance, because as we noted in chapter 1, chance always is preceded by and presupposes ontologically some form of order. Two friends meet by chance at the store because each is intentionally going to the store in an ordered way. The same is true of the chance interaction of isotopes, atoms, or DNA molecules. The order of the world cannot come from matter, because matter considered at its most basic level is pure potency for form, not formal determination. The order cannot come about ultimately from form-matter composites (such as vast aggregates of atomic matter coagulated according to the normative patterns created by the laws of physics). The reason is that these form-matter composites are always subject to inclinations based on the kinds of things they are and therefore undergo teleological realizations by which order is composed or expressed. They are not the source of this intrinsic tendential activity in themselves. It is precisely such tendential order that requires explanation. Therefore, the first cause of order cannot be chance or matter or even material form but must be immaterial and a source of order, which are properties of spiritual intellect.

41. *Critique of Pure Reason*, Transcendental Dialectic, ch. III, sec. 6: "The Impossibility of the Physical-theological Proof," [A621/B649–A630/B658].

ontologically primary that is the source of order in the world. That source is intellectual in some analogous sense of the term. But this does not mean that the argument must terminate in the conclusion that the cause of all order in the world is also the Creator who gives being to all things. Aquinas seeks to show by other arguments especially later in the *Summa theologiae* that he who is the source of all order is also the Creator, the source of all being.[42]

However, we can also note that the argumentative effect of the various Thomistic arguments is cumulative. The Fifth Way is distinct in point of departure, structure, and conclusion from the other four ways that precede it and Aquinas's other arguments for the existence of God. But some of its conclusions combine in significant ways with the conclusions of previous arguments we have examined, so that a collective logical outcome is achieved.

Consider for example the first argument presented in this chapter, taken from the real distinction of essence and existence in all things that we experience. We might consider that the order in things expressed in their teleological actions is in fact grounded in their respective essences or natures, since a thing behaves in a given way due to the nature it has. (I have provided various examples.) But we noted in the very first argument for the existence of God considered above that there is a cause of all things whose essence is not identical with their existence and that they are not the cause of their own essence. We concluded with the affirmation that God gives existence to all natures that are not God. If the Fifth Way argues effectively that there is a first cause and author of the ordered activity found in all things, and if this activity flows from the natures or essences of these things, then this primary reality is the cause of order in things *insofar as he is the cause of their essences or natures*. But one who is the source of order in all things is also the author of their very existence as created beings. In short, we can infer rightly that the intellectual cause of the teleological order manifest in all the realities

42. See in particular *ST* I, qq. 44 and 47.

we experience is also the transcendent Creator of their being, since they have not only their intelligible natures from God but also their very existence.

UNITY OF THE FIVE WAYS

There are unified ways of thinking of the Five Ways.[43] The first argument is from change, the second from the causality of being (much like the real distinction argument), the third from ontological contingency in material beings and the need for something necessary, the fourth from degrees of perfection, and the fifth from the existence of order and teleology in the creation. It is possible, though not essential, to categorize these five ways according to five causes, respectively: the material, efficient, formal, exemplary, and final. The First Way could be said to be concerned with material causality insofar as all things that have potency are subject to change and continually depend on other causal agents for aspects of their being. The Second Way is concerned with efficient causality considered in a broad and fundamental sense with respect to the very causes of existence in things that do not cause themselves to be. The Third Way touches upon formal causality insofar as it considers the contingency and non-necessity of forms in this world and the way that merely possible forms point us toward something that is truly necessary, not contingent. The Fourth Way considers the degrees of perfection and therefore the exemplarity that emerges within the ontology of things. It argues that because a unifying scale of perfections characterizes the very being of things, there must be some transcendent source of their perfections that does not fall within

43. See on this topic, Lawrence Dewan, "The Number and Order of St. Thomas's Five Ways," *Downside Review* 92 (1974): 1–18; Leo Elders, "Les cinq voies et leur place dans la philosophie de saint Thomas," in *Quinque sunt viae. Actes du premier Symposium sur les cinq voies de la Somme théologique*, ed. L. J. Elders (Città del Vaticano: Studi tomistici 9, 1980), 133–46; Daniel DeHaan, "Why the Five Ways? Aquinas's Avicennian Insight into the Problem of Unity in the Aristotelian Metaphysics and *Sacra Doctrina*," *American Catholic Philosophical Association* 86 (2012): 141–58.

the scale of finite perfections. The Fifth Way notes that teleological order in things that are not the cause of their own ordered developments implies intelligibility and therefore immaterial intelligence, which cannot be accounted for merely by recourse to an infinite series of created, dependent causes. Consequently, by beginning respectively from basic experiences of change, causal efficiency, formal contingency, exemplary degrees of perfection, and teleological order, the Five Ways provide distinct but convergent forms of argumentation for monotheism as the rational, demonstrative explanation for the world as we experience it. They also prepare us for a reasonable reflection on God's attributes, or the "divine names," such as the consideration of God's transcendent simplicity, perfection, goodness, infinity, eternity, omnipresence, truth, and love.

ARGUMENTS FROM SPIRITUAL OPERATIONS IN THE HUMAN PERSON

In our final and seventh section of this chapter, we can consider arguments for the existence of God based on the consideration of the spiritual faculties of intellect and will found in the human person. These faculties indicate the presence of a spiritual soul in the human person that cannot be derived from merely material or corporeal processes of the human body.[44]

44. Aquinas develops arguments of this sort in *ST* I, q. 75, aa. 2, 5, and 6; *SCG* II, cc. 49–51, 66–67, 78–81; and in a variety of other instances. There is a great deal of literature on the subject of Aquinas's arguments for the immateriality of the human intellect and the spiritual subsistence of the human soul after death. The arguments I will treat in this chapter give rise to controversies regarding both their substance and soundness. It is not possible for me to treat them exhaustively. However, one can find helpful discussion of Aquinas's notion of the human intellect and his arguments regarding immateriality in works such as the following: David Ruel Foster, "Aquinas on the Immateriality of Intellect," *The Thomist* 55, no. 3 (1991): 415–38 and "Aquinas's Arguments for Spirit," *American Catholic Philosophical Association* 65 (1991): 235-52; John Haldane, "The Metaphysics of Intellect(ion)," *American Catholic Philosophical Association* 80 (2007): 39–55; Therese S. Cory, *Aquinas on Human Self-Knowledge* (Cambridge: Cambridge University Press, 2013); James Madden, *Mind, Matter and Nature: A Thomistic Proposal for the Philosophy of Mind* (Washington, DC: The Catholic University of America Press, 2013); John O'Callaghan, "The Immaterial Soul and Its Discontents," *Acta Philosophica* 24, no. 1, (2015):

All the arguments work in this basic way:

(1) The human intellect (or will) is characterized by immaterial features and operations that cannot be explained by recourse to sensate or materially individuated bodily processes. Only an immaterial power can attain specifically immaterial operations. Therefore, the human intellect (or will) as a power is immaterial in its essential operational power and activity.

(2) But an immaterial power can only reside in the human soul if that soul (as the principle of life and form of the human body that gives the latter determination and organizes it from within) is in turn itself immaterial. Otherwise, a material soul would be the substantial source of an immaterial property, and this is absurd, since the faculty of the intellect (or will) depends upon the soul, but the lesser (in the order of corruptibility) cannot cause the greater (an incorruptible immaterial faculty). So a material soul cannot cause an immaterial faculty.[45]

(3) But even if the immaterial soul of the human person is incorruptible, and continues to exist after death, it still is not the cause of its own being, and indeed it only comes to be in and for a human body. Consequently, it is caused by another.[46]

(4) But an immaterial being (the soul) cannot be caused by merely material realities and must have an immaterial cause that gives it being. Furthermore, the soul is caused without intermediaries, since it has an autonomy in the order of being—that is, it is not dependent for its existence on either material things or other human persons. Therefore, whatever causes the soul is immaterial in nature and produces it as its Creator, sustaining it in being.[47] This is the case even as the immaterial soul is the form of the material body.[48]

(5) Furthermore, if the soul has faculties of intellect and will that

45–66; Adam Wood, *Thomas Aquinas on the Immateriality of the Human Intellect* (Washington, DC: The Catholic University of America Press, 2020).

45. *SCG* II, c. 79; *ST* I, q. 75, a. 2.

46. *SCG* II, cc. 83–89.

47. *SCG* II, c. 87.

48. *SCG* II, c. 90; *ST* I, q. 76, a. 1.

qualify it as a distinctively "personal" entity capable of knowledge and love, then the immaterial transcendent source of these qualities must also be in some analogous sense "personal." That is to say, the author of the spiritual souls of human persons must be both intelligent and loving, both in himself and toward creatures.

The most difficult claim in this chain of sequential reasoning is the first one, the idea that the human intellect (or will) is characterized by immaterial features and operations that cannot be explained by recourse to sensate or materially individuated bodily processes. The other four successive claims that may follow from this first are not simply obvious, but they are more intuitive than the first claim, so we will leave them to the philosophical consideration of the reader and concentrate only on the first claim in what follows. Let us consider, then, four brief arguments in favor of this first claim, three with regard to the intellect and one with regard to the will. These are in turn the argument from the universal, the argument from the formal content of intellectual knowledge, the argument from self-reflexivity, and the argument from the co-extension of the will with the intellect in its concrete exercise.

Immateriality of Human Intellection: Argument from Abstract Conceptual Universality[49]

Conceptual knowledge is universal. When we think about objects we know, we think in accord with a universal mode of reflection. So, for instance, our idea of a "human being" never applies to only one human individual. Instead, it can apply to all singulars of a like kind, such as Thomas or Catherine or any other human being in history, just as our idea of a house can apply to all domiciles. We only ever think in such abstract, conceptual modes. There are no purely singular-in-mode ideas the way there are singular-in-mode phantasms—the visual memory I have of an individual person or house.

---

49. Versions of this argument are found in Aquinas in such texts as *ST* I, q. 75, a. 5; *SCG* II, cc. 49–50; *De ver.*, q. 10, a. 8; *Quest. disp. de anima*, q. 6. See the discussion of it by Feser in *Aquinas*, 155–59.

When we think or speak conceptually, we designate the singular entity by universal forms of indicative language: *This* human person or *that* house or *this* rose. The notion of "this" is itself a universal concept that we employ to indicate a singular with intentionality. Every language has a word for singular indications, and people everywhere gesture at "this" to indicate their wish to designate an abstract kind in a singular instance.

Furthermore, we have universal concepts of a host of things, like natural kinds such as persons or mountains but also features of things (accidents) such as qualities or quantities, relations or places. It is important to note that such concepts of the natures of things grasp what they are, freed from their individuating material conditions. Consider two clear examples: the triangle and the human being.[50] A triangle is essentially a plane figure with three straight sides and three angles, in which the measure of the three angles always adds up to 180 degrees. However, that essential definition applies in equally and identically valid ways to triangles that are irreducibly different in sensible representation. All singular concrete triangles are *either* equilateral (three sides of the same length) *or* isosceles (two sides with the same length) *or* scalene (three sides of different lengths). Our concept of "triangularity" applies to all of them equally and identically as triangles, even though our sensate representations of them by visual sight and imagination must always necessarily be diverse. We imagine only one of the three kinds above in sensible figure. We grasp conceptually, however, that a triangle is "a plane figure with three straight sides and three angles" in any of these phantasmal configurations but never in strict dependence on a repeated sensate representation of the same kind. Likewise, a human being is human independently of various individuating characteristic features, such as whether the human being is black or white, male or female, young or elderly, sick or healthy. Indeed this universal truth is the basis of universal moral norms. No two individual

50. The example of the triangle is taken from Edward Feser in his book *Aquinas*, 153–57.

human beings are materially identical nor do they have identical individual features, but they do all possess a common human nature, as rational animals, and they do so across a scale of degrees of perfection (for example, as children grow into perfect maturity) and across a diversity of accidental features (such as skin color, height, and hair color).

How do we come to know the forms or natures of things in a universal mode? That is to say, how do we form concepts by and in which the mind penetrates the core of realities we experience and comes to know them in themselves in a universal way, freed from material conditions particular to this or that individual? This is the problem of abstraction. Plotinus and Descartes both posit that conceptual knowledge is not formed in and through sense experiences as such; it is provided from a higher source or is recollected as something simply innate in the soul.[51] On these views, we do not learn from external realities directly. Rather, the experience of them is only the occasion to recall what we already know. Materialists like Hume, meanwhile, posit that our "concepts" of reality are really only sense impressions and imagination.[52] This however does not allow us to account for the universal and abstract mode of our knowledge. Aristotle and Aquinas posit on the one hand that our knowledge is derived through the senses and from sense experiences of realities around us (against Plato's theory of forms) but that, on the other hand, our conceptual knowledge is formally immaterial in kind, not sensible or imaginative, against materialists like Hume.[53]

How does this process of abstraction work? Abstract concepts are not found in sensible realities but in our minds, and yet they correspond to the natures and properties of the realities around us.

51. See Plato *Phaedrus*, 247c–249c; Plotinus, *Enneads*, trans. S. MacKenna (London: Penguin, 1991) V, 1, 6, 4, 10–13, and 19–22; René Descartes, *Meditations*, from *The Philosophical Writings of Descartes vol. I-III*, vol. II, trans. J. Cottingham, R. Stoothoff, D. Murdoch, and A. Kenny (Cambridge: Cambridge University Press, 1991), 26.

52. David Hume, *A Treatise of Human Nature* (Oxford: Clarendon Press, 1975), Book I, sec. 1, "On Ideas."

53. Aristotle, *De Anima*, III, 5; Aquinas, *In III De Anima*, lec. 10.

What we know through our abstract universal concept of the human being is the nature of individual human beings around us. We have to presume that the individual sensible realities we experience (the human beings themselves) cannot produce the universal concepts in our minds that we derive from them, as if they were themselves the primary agents acting within our minds. Individual physical realities and even sense experiences and the phantasms to which they give rise in our imagination cannot themselves produce non-physical, non-sensible, abstract universal thought. The phantasms only pertain to aspects of the reality, like the color or shape of a human being or triangle, not the essential notion. Thus we can conclude that the concepts come from us, from our intellects that produce them. And yet our concepts illuminate or pierce into the very natures of things we experience sensibly. When we think about what a tree is as distinct from a human being, we think about what these respective things really are in themselves. Therefore, we need to posit an intellectual source of our concepts (one that is in us) that illumines our sense experiences or acts upon them to derive from the things we experience through our senses the conceptual knowledge we have of the things in themselves. This is what is called the "agent intellect."[54] It is a power of the human intellect that is active in and through our sense experiences that extracts a conceptual knowledge of essences and properties from the concrete individual forms we encounter in ordinary experience.[55] It does so in an abstract, universal mode.

54. Aquinas, *Quest. Disp. De Anima*, q. 4; SCG II, cc. 76–78.
55. Aquinas, *Quest. Disp. De Anima*, q. 4:

We must admit that an agent intellect exists. To make this evident we must observe that, since the possible intellect is in potency to intelligibles, the intelligibles themselves must move [i.e., actuate] the possible intellect. But that which is non-existent cannot move anything. Moreover, the intelligible as such, that which the possible intellect understands, does not exist in reality; for our possible intellect understands something as though it were a one-in-many and common to many [that is, universal]. However, such an entity is not found subsisting in reality, as Aristotle proves in the *Metaphysics* (VII, 13, 1039a 15). Therefore, if the possible intellect has to be moved by an intelligible, this intelligible must be produced by an intellective power. And since it is impossible for anything in potency, in a certain respect, to actuate itself, we must admit that

We may conclude, then, that the agent intellect exists in the human knower, but that it collects knowledge of realities around us through the external senses. The argument was made by a kind of a posteriori demonstration that passes from effects to a necessary cause of those effects, a cause we cannot perceive directly but which we can determine to exist necessarily because it alone can explain the effects.[56] We derive conceptual universal knowledge from prior experience of singular sensible realities. These realities themselves cannot produce such immaterial knowledge as it arises from within our intellects. The knowledge in question is universal and abstract, not singular and concrete, so it cannot come from the senses as such, which obtain to sensible properties in individual conditions but do not obtain to the formal knowledge of essences or properties perceived in their universal intelligibility as separable from individual material conditions. Our concepts correspond realistically

---

an agent intellect exists, in addition to the possible intellect, and that this agent intellect causes the actual intelligibles which actuate the possible intellect. Moreover, it produces these intelligibles by abstracting them from matter and from material conditions which are the principles of individuation. And since the nature as such of the species does not possess these principles by which the nature is given a multiple existence among different things, because individuating principles of this sort are distinct from the nature itself, the intellect will be able to receive this nature apart from all material conditions, and consequently will receive it as a unity [that is, as a one-in-many]. For the same reason the intellect receives the nature of a genus by abstracting from specific differences, so that it is a one-in-many and common to many species. However, if universals subsisted in reality in virtue of themselves, as the Platonists maintained, it would not be necessary to admit that an agent intellect exists; because things which are intelligible in virtue of their own nature move the possible intellect. Therefore it appears that Aristotle was led by this necessity to posit an agent intellect, because he did not agree with the opinion of Plato on the question of Ideas. Nevertheless there are some subsistent things in the real order which are actual intelligibles in virtue of themselves; the immaterial substances, for instance, are of this nature. However, the possible intellect cannot attain a knowledge of these immediately, but acquires its knowledge of them through what it abstracts from material and sensible things. [Trans. J. Rowan, *The Soul* (London: Herder, 1949).]

56. In other words, the form of demonstration of the agent intellect is not *proper quid* but, like the arguments for the existence of God, *quia* in nature.

to the essences and properties of the things we experience, grasped in an abstract mode. Therefore, there is something within our intellect that can produce universal, abstract knowledge that allows us to grasp the inner essences and properties of things we experience through the senses in an abstract mode. According to Aquinas, this occurs due to the work of the agent intellect.

How then does the agent intellect work? Evidently, this active process by which the intellect forms universal concepts must work initially upon the phantasms we experience in our senses—the sensibly derived impressed species of realities we encounter through the five senses. In other words, the agent intellect is present in and through our ordinary sense experiences of ourselves and realities around us. In and through these experiences, the agent intellect selects phantasms from our sense experiences of distinct realities and derives in them, through them, and from them a universal concept of the reality and its nature. This is actually a very simple idea. As we experience human beings, cats, trees, stars, and so forth, our intellect begins to form basic abstract concepts of these realities, and it gradually enriches its initial understanding through further study and consideration of the realities in question.[57] Obviously this process is aided significantly through cultures of shared language use and learning that stimulate us to pay attention to features of things around us and help induce or stimulate understanding in us through conversation with others.

When the agent intellect abstracts a universal concept from a sensate reality, it strips or divests the sense phantasms of their individuating features (such as, for example, the appearance of this man here in his particularity, qualities of character, size and weight, complexion, skin, and hair color) and grasps intellectually in and through the experiences something of the nature of this reality as

---

57. This means (a) we reach the very realities in question themselves through our sense experiences from which the intellect gathers some real knowledge of them and (b) we experience properties of a given reality first and only gradually come to fathom what is more essential to it.

such, its essence or its properties. For example, we may grasp that a given reality is a human being, which is a truth more profound than that of its particular individuating features.

Aquinas calls this universal concept (such as, human being, triangle, or tree) the "intelligible species" and says that it is received into what he calls the "possible intellect," that is, the intellect capable of being informed by new information or reception of new knowledge of forms.[58] By the work of the agent intellect, the possible intellect is thus "newly" informed by the intelligible species. But Aquinas also notes that purely passive knowledge of the reality is not sufficient to give our intellect an active understanding of the realities around us. After being informed by the intelligible species, the possible intellect must also now employ the species actively. For example, we typically make use of our conceptual knowledge of things around us (such as human beings, triangles, and plants) to navigate the world, making intellectual judgments about what things are and their properties and causes. The concepts we employ actively are products of the human mind, and they derive or proceed from the possible intellect, which has itself been previously qualified by abstract knowledge that was produced from the agent intellect.

We use our conceptual universal knowledge, then, to move back into reality, back into the singular sensible beings we experience in a newly qualified way with new conceptual information, so as to make intellectually qualified judgments. We pass from many experiences of human beings to the passive reception of the abstracted essential species of "human nature" to the active judgment about a concrete singular: "this is a human being." This is what Aquinas calls the "return to the phantasm."[59] Human beings make concrete judgments about the world using abstract concepts that allow them to see more deeply into the world around them. "This reality is a living animal endowed with a power for intellectual reasoning and deliberative choice-making." "All human beings can smile, because they possess

58. Aquinas, *Quest. Disp. De Anima*, qq. 1–3; SCG II, cc. 75–76.
59. See *ST* I, q. 84, a. 7, "conversio ad phantasmata."

both animality and abstract reasoning, and they alone can appreciate ironical ideas in an imaginative way." "This capacity to smile is not possible either for angels or non-rational animals." In judgments such as these, we are not merely experiencing sensible realities under the guise of mere animal prudence or instinct. Rather, we come to know the singular reality we are actively sensing in a specifically intellectual way in what it is essentially—in this case, a human being. In doing so, we make use of a concept of human nature that allows us to grasp the essence of what we are experiencing. Other animals engage with realities around them through the use of sense memories and animal instincts, but human beings do so aided by abstract, conceptual, and universal knowledge that allows them to explain the world analytically, to mold their environment by use of the arts, and to express themselves linguistically.

To summarize:

(1) The agent intellect derives an abstract species from sensate realities.

(2) This abstract species qualifies the passive intellect.

(3) The intellect then makes use of the abstract species actively to turn back to realities experienced to make judgments about those realities (that is, "This is a human being.")

This active use of our universal abstract understanding that occurs in judgment is what we call the concept. We actively judge by making use of our concepts.

Here, then, we arrive at the question of the immateriality of the human intellectual process of abstraction. To say that something is immaterial as such merely means that it is "not limited to a purely passive reception of forms" from other realities. The marble stone is passive in the face of movement. It is a material object sculpted by the sculptor. But the faculty of sight is not merely passive in receiving the impression of a red object. We actively see things around us, even as our seeing is receptive of the colors and light we perceive. Our capacity to see is active in seeing the form of red in the external reality, and it is also receptive of the quality of redness in question. It has an interiority and intentionality that is "immaterial" in the broad sense. We see red objects without ourselves becoming red in color. However, the actions of our senses, while having a kind of immateriality, still depend entirely upon physical organs and are corruptible. The senses only assimilate information from the external world around us by dependence on physical organs, which can function well or poorly. If we lose the organ of the eyes, or if the physical matter of the organ degenerates, we lose our capacity to see.

With thought and free will, however, we enter into a kind of immateriality that is spiritual, that is, intrinsically independent of matter in operation and existence. Does the operation of our intellect depend per se on a material organ? Is it the act of a physical organ? For example, do concepts depend upon the brain and the firing of neurons in the brain in the way that sight depends upon the physical activity of the eye? Can intellectual activity exist or subsist without the body, or is it in existence only so long as the body is in existence?

Here we can first distinguish between *intrinsic* or *essential* operational dependence upon a bodily organ versus *extrinsic* or *distinct* dependence upon a bodily organ. The first of these categories of operational dependence applies to the act of conceptual thinking if it is the act of a physical organ and is corrupted with death, as is seemingly the case with our sensations, which depend *intrinsically* upon the physical organs through which they operate. The second category applies if we know and think only in dependence upon sensations when they are present *but not specifically or essentially in and by the sensations as such.* This latter position accords with the view of Aquinas.[60] He follows Aristotle in positing that even though the intellect is immaterial in nature, it only makes judgments about things we actually experience sensibly as animals, and this process depends on sensations and physical experiences of reality, which in turn are rooted in a functioning organic body. The intellect therefore is only

60. See *ST* I, q. 84, a. 8, in which he comments on Aristotle's *On Sleep* III, 456b17–26. See also *ST* II-II, q. 154, a. 5, ad 3; *ST* III, q. 68, a. 12, corp. and ad 2 and ad 3.

active in and through sensate processes of the body, even if it is immaterial in nature. If this view is correct, then a person who is unconscious, whether from sleep, illness, or brain damage, retains an immaterial power of the intellect but cannot reflect actively on his experiences, because the sense powers are dormant. However, this does not mean that his or her intellect is merely physical or material, and indeed it is conceivable that the intellectual powers could subsist in the human soul after death, even if they are not currently active in the human person who is unconscious or physically disabled.

Why, however, should we say that the intellect is immaterial and spiritual in operation? In light of what we have said above regarding the formal object or specification of human knowledge, we can argue in the following way:

First, no organic potency that is intrinsically dependent upon matter can attain an object that is intrinsically free from matter. But the intellect can attain such objects. It can achieve knowledge of the following, for example:

(1) the universal notion of essence or property—that is, the essence or property abstracted from all individuated features of matter—such as, "house", "human nature", "quantity," "animal", and "action."

(2) The abstract in itself—existing not in reality but as a characteristic of universal thought: "humanity," or that by which man is man; "truth," or knowledge that corresponds to reality; "principles," or the origins or causes of explanation.

(3) The immaterial—for example, knowledge of God who is immaterial attained through arguments for the existence of God and consideration of the divine attributes.[61]

61. I am presuming here the validity and soundness of the six previous arguments, in order to suggest the soul is capable of knowledge of immaterial reality. The argument is not circular. This "way of argument" for the existence of God considers another mode of approach through the spiritual operations of man, which themselves indicate their spiritual character in part from the fact that they are capable of ascent to knowledge of God's immaterial existence by way of entirely distinct arguments with entirely distinct premises.

One could argue for the immateriality of the intellect from any of these three forms of conceptual thought, but the first is the most evident, and it can be considered alone at this stage of the argument. As we have noted, the universal concept is immaterial, because it transcends the limits of any particular time and place or material condition, which characterize all material things necessarily due to their individuating material conditions. A concept of triangularity or human nature is not reducible to the material elements that constitute this or that triangle or human being, with this shape or that gender, for example. But if the intellect knows essences and properties in their non-material features by means of the immaterial concept that is universal, then the intellect is itself immaterial. Why? Because otherwise a sense power, bound by physical conditions and concrete rootedness in time and place as to its material object, would be capable of attaining to an object that transcends the material conditions of individuality, that is, to an essence or property obtaining in many material individuals. But this is not possible. Individual material beings can only have contact with and attain to other individual material beings. They are physically congruent or contiguous to one another, like neurons firing in succession in the brain or physical bodies touching other physical bodies, individually. The essences of things known abstractly are not reducible to individual material conditions of these singular entities but pertain to the formal natures of the entities, those that determine all of the material individuating conditions. As such, these formal essences, when known by the intellect, allow one to understand all such entities of a given kind, including those that are not physically congruent or contiguous with one another. The lesser cannot attain the greater under these conditions, just as a material body cannot be immaterial and attain a nature or essence that transcends individual material conditions. The sense powers like sight and hearing always consider sensible singular entities, like this visual object here or that sound there, while the intellect attains to the universal as such, extracted from such conditions. The sense powers depend upon some form of spatial contact with their objects through the medium of physical organs, by which we see, hear, or feel, but the intellectual powers attain universal knowledge that is not dependent upon such quantitative, sensible context. Consequently, the sense powers cannot attain the universal as such while the intellect can and does.

Therefore, only an immaterial operation can attain knowledge of the formally immaterial and universal as such. But the intellect does know the immaterial, and indeed knowledge by means of universal concepts is precisely what characterizes the essential activity of the intellect. Therefore, the essential activity of the intellect is immaterial. If this is the case, however, then the rest of the arguments noted above flow from our conclusion fairly readily and organically. An immaterial power can only reside in the human soul if the soul is itself immaterial, since a corruptible material soul cannot cause or give expression to an immaterial faculty and immaterial processes. So the soul is immaterial.[62] But the immaterial soul of the human

62. We should note that the operation of the intellect is an operation of the human soul. A living human being who has vegetative and sensible processes and an organic living body also has intellectual operations that are his operations. They pertain to the very same and identical being as his digestion or growth or sensations or emotions. But this means that the operations of the intellect are rooted in the intellectual power and that this power pertains to the soul of the human being as such. Action follows upon being, and if a thing acts spiritually, then this action pertaining to it is rooted in some real way in the essence or being of that thing. The spiritual power and operation of human intellectual cognition is rooted in the powers of the human soul as such. These operations are immaterial. And therefore they cannot be rooted in something merely material. Otherwise, there would be substantial disunity: the operation of the intellect would be lodged accidentally or juxtapositionally in a purely material substance. Then our conceptual intellectual thought would not be our own thought, the thought of the thinking subject whose bodily actions and sensations we experience. But we are one living being, body and soul. Thus the intellectual, spiritual operations are rooted in a soul that is itself in some way immaterial. But what is immaterial (in this case the soul) cannot be eradicated merely by the corruption of the material body. The soul therefore being immaterial *subsists* or *is subsistent in itself* in distinction from the body, even if the body is corrupted (that is, at death).

This is not to say the following: (a) that a soul without a body is a complete person (The opposite is true. A soul without a body is not a complete person but a mere soul, the soul of a person.); or (b) that the soul subsistent without the body is simply subsistent per se, independently of any extrinsic cause. (This is not the case. The soul can only subsist because it is kept in being as an immaterial substance by a higher causality:

person is not the cause of its own being. It must have an immaterial cause that gives it being. So the soul is caused to be by a transcendent first cause of its being. But if the soul has qualities of intellect that qualify it as a distinctively "personal" entity capable of knowledge, then the immaterial transcendent cause of these qualities must also be in some incomprehensible but analogous sense "personal," and this is what we call "God," the author of the immaterial soul in the human person.

Immateriality of Human Intellection: Argument from the Formal Realism of Knowledge[63]

Another argument can be made from the realism of human knowledge, insofar as it grasps the very forms or essences of things without itself becoming these things. The intellect has the potency to assimilate the essence of a given external reality as such, abstracted from its individuality. Otherwise stated, by means of our conceptual knowledge of such realities, we are able to grasp what they *really* are in themselves—for example, a triangle, a human being, a tree and so forth—and in this way, by means of our conceptual knowledge, we really do come to know what things around us are essentially, including ourselves as rational animals. This potency is actuated, however, without the form of the intellect—the intellect in its very nature—becoming the reality that is known. The human intellect does not become a triangle or a man in knowing the real essence of the triangle or the man.

But if the mind were a *material* reality capable of truly receiving another form as such, it would have to receive it by way of being changed and assimilated into that natural entity or joined to it, as

---

God the Creator. However, this is a consideration outside the scope of our immediate inquiry.)

63. This argument is of Thomistic provenance (see *ST* I, q. 75, a. 2; *SCG* II, c. 49) and follows from many of the principles noted above but I am indebted to Edward Feser for the formulation of this version of it. See *Aquinas*, 153–55. See also Edward Feser, "Kripke, Ross, and the Immaterial Aspects of Thought," *American Catholic Philosophical Quarterly* 87, no. 1 (2013): 1–32, and James Ross, "Immaterial Aspects of Thought," *Journal of Philosophy* 89 (1992): 136–50.

when a block of wood is consumed by fire or joined to metal to make a chair. This just is the way that a material reality combines with the form of another or changes into it. Chlorine is dissolved into water. Plants assimilate water. Animals that die decompose in the soil. The forms of things undergo alteration through time, and they eventually change passively from one thing to another.

But since the intellect can know the very natures and forms of things without becoming those things, its form of knowledge and conceptual assimilation of essences is immaterial, not material.

Notice how this process contrasts with the assimilation of sensible qualities perceived by the human sense powers. In some respects, the process is similar. The physical sensations we have do allow us to assimilate specific qualities of the things around us without becoming those things. We feel hot or cold, we see red or white, or we hear sounds like birdsong or moving cars. In doing these things, we are physically affected in our sense organs, but we do not become the things we sense. Indeed, there is a kind of intentionality of sensible forms. Our sense organs do not become the external realities they sense or their real qualities, but they possess some phantasm within themselves that is received from the very qualities present in the external world. However, even in these cases, clearly the senses and their intentionality do not allow us to possess or grasp the formal determination of the other reality itself, such as the essence of the fire or water, the bird or the car. Rather, they allow us to grasp various qualities or quantitative properties of the reality in question in its material individuality and in a sensible mode but not in an abstract mode. We have no sensate or imaginative grasp of universal knowledge. Our tactile sensation of the cold is distinct from our intellectual concept of the cold. In fact we can only have sense knowledge of some specific qualities in the world by means of a given sensible organ because it has a certain connaturality to the reality in question under some sensible aspect. For example, there is an organic receptivity to color in the eye and sound in the ear. We cannot grasp sound sensibly with the eye or hear color visibly with the ear.

Furthermore, the sensible operation in question pertains to a connaturality based on the organic structure of the sense faculty in question, as we can feel heat and coldness by the sense of touch through the medium of our skin and its material organic properties, while we can hear sound through the medium of the ear and the subjacent biological systems that provide for animal listening.

In conceptual knowledge, however, we do not merely grasp a sensible property of the reality in a sensate way, limited to the specific scope denoted above. Rather, we grasp the essence of the very reality in itself and in its totality. Our conceptual knowledge is not limited to one area of experience, like the hearing of sounds or seeing of colors, but pertains to all forms and properties of things, to whatsoever exists.[64] It is not bound to one form of organic contact, through a sense organ, but learns through all the senses and sense organs from the totality of existence, so as to reflect on all the forms of things we encounter. Since we grasp the things in themselves and assimilate them in an immaterial mode, then the activity of the intellect must in turn be immaterial, and the process by which it operates to grasp things immaterially must be itself immaterial. The form of the thing is in the intellect in an immaterial mode, and a formally material reality such as a sensate organ could not of itself produce an immaterial operation. For this reason, we must say that the distinctively human intellectual operation of knowing is spiritually immaterial in nature. By our conceptual knowledge, we can assimilate the formal determination (nature) of things we experience and thus know other things in themselves in a purely immaterial way without becoming those things. Only the immaterial intellect can do this.

64. This is why human beings alone can come to understand colors or sounds abstractly and analyze their relations according to scales and harmonies, and thus produce arts like painting or music. The latter arts presuppose the capacity for spiritual abstraction.

Immateriality of Human Intellection:
Argument from Reflexivity[65]

A third argument is based on the self-reflexivity of the human intellect. The argument can be stated this way:

(1) Properly speaking, self-reflection implies that a cognitive faculty is capable of knowing its own acts and itself *formally*—that is, essentially—in itself.

(2) If the intellect is capable of such self-reflection, it is inorganic. That is to say, the intellect is not characterized by spatial exteriority to itself the way organs in the body exist in spatial relation to each other, exteriorly within an organic body.

(3) But the intellect is capable of knowing its own act and itself in a self-reflective way. The mind can reflect upon its own operation as it is occurring and on its own formal nature in a way that the sense powers cannot.

(4) Therefore it is immaterial.

What is the basis for the second premise: "If the intellect is capable of such proper reflection, it is inorganic?" If a cognitive faculty knows its own act in itself, then both the principle and origin of the act and the term or object of the act are identical. In self-reflexive knowledge, it is the intellect that is the source of the knowledge and the term or object of the knowledge. In short, the mind knows itself. However, an act of sense knowledge that is specified by an organic, biologically enrooted action cannot be both its own principle and object, since the quantitative juxtaposition and exteriority of the matter prohibits this from taking place, as one cannot both see and see one's act of seeing, or hear and hear one's act of hearing. But one can know something intellectually and know one's act of knowing. Consider this by way of a contrary illustration from the sensate

65. One can find intimations of this argument in Aquinas in *SCG* II, cc. 48–49, 66 and *SCG* IV, c. 11. My version of it here takes inspiration from that of Henry Koren, *An Introduction to the Philosophy of Animate Nature* (London: Herder, 1955), 163–65.

powers. Imagine, for example, that we human beings could see our own eyes and that we could see them even in the very act of seeing, even while seeing an exterior object, or that we could hear our ear and our act of hearing, even while hearing an exterior sound. It is clear that we are not able to do this, because the physical reality in question and the sensible operation embodied within the organ imply material composition and spatial juxtaposition. Thus, the sense powers are not capable of this kind of self-reflexivity. In cases like this, the principle of the act and the term of the act are not identical. We see with the eye (the principle), but what we see is something exterior (the term). We cannot both see and see our eye seeing at the same time.[66]

In fact, the identity of object and principle of the kind we are

66. Gyulia Klima has offered an analogous reflection of this kind regarding neural firing patterns in "Reply to Bob Pasnau on Aquinas's Proofs of the Immateriality of the Intellect," in *The Immateriality of the Human mind, the Semantics of Analogy, and the Conceivability of God*, ed. G. Klima and A. Clayton (Newcastle-upon-Tyne: Cambridge Scholars Press, 2011), 49–60. The argument is summarized nicely by Adam Wood in *The Immateriality of the Human Intellect*, 212–13:

> Klima ... offers an intriguing suggestion as to why the intellect could not cognize all sensible or corporeal forms by means of a subset of these forms, such as neural firing patterns. For the intellect to operate this way, he argues, would generate a version of Russell's paradox. Consider: if the intellect cognizes all corporeal forms by means of a subset of corporeal forms, such as neural firing patterns, then it would have to cognize its own forms (i.e., the firing patterns) as well. For that to be true, however, some of the intellect's forms would have to be capable of cognizing themselves. Otherwise for each neural firing pattern there would have to be another pattern cognizing it, and so on into infinity, exhausting all of the intellect's cognitive forms without ever cognizing anything other than itself. Supposing there are some self-cognizing forms, then, call the set of all and only the non-self-cognizing forms N. Surely we are able to form a concept of N; we are certainly able to discuss it intelligibility. The "Russellian question," Klima says, is whether our concept of N is itself self-cognizing. If it is, then it is not the concept of *only* non-self-cognizing forms, for it is not itself non-self-cognizing. If it is not, then it is not the concept of *all* non-self-cognizing forms, as it leaves itself out. To extricate ourselves from this contradiction, Klima thinks, we must reject the assumption that got it started, namely that we cognize all corporeal forms by means of a subset of those forms.

This is a good illustration of the irresolvable conundrums to which naïve materialism can give rise.

indicating excludes any physical external intermediary. We can see ourselves seeing not immediately but only by the medium of a mirror, but to directly see ourselves seeing would imply an immediacy. We cannot do this, because we only ever see anything through the intermediary of a physical organ, namely, the eye. By contrast, human beings can immediately know ourselves thinking and in doing so can know our own act of thinking. This is the immediacy of the intellect in its self-reflexivity. We do know through the intermediary of conceptual knowledge, but in the conceptual knowledge, we are able to grasp both the principle of the knowledge and the term. There is no spatial exteriority present, as there would be in a material process.

Again, in an organic potency of the human animal, like the sense power of sight, the object of sense knowledge is received through the organ so that the organ serves as a necessary condition and physical medium for the sense power of the object. We see through the medium of our eyes. We hear through the medium of our ears. So in an organic potency, the object cannot be identical with the potency itself. We can potentially see or hear something other than our act of seeing or hearing. The sense organ intermediates between the two. This is why a strong noise can deafen the ear, or a powerful light can blind the eye, by damaging the organ. Again, due to this organic mediation, we cannot see the organ that is itself seeing, because the act of the organ seeing depends upon it being specified by something else that it is juxtapositionally receptive to, as the eye can turn toward the light or the ear toward the sound. However, we can think immediately about ourselves as intellectual knowers and our act of thinking, which contrasts with these various experiences of sense knowledge that take place through the mediation of a physical organ.[67] This kind of wholly immanent activity is not possible for a

67. Aquinas, SCG II, c. 66:

Sense-cognition is limited to corporeal things. This is clear from the fact that sensible qualities, which are the proper objects of the senses, exist only in such things; and without them the senses know nothing. On the other hand, the intellect knows incorporeal things, such as wisdom, truth, and the relations of

process that depends upon the external juxtapositions of one thing to another that arise in organic, material processes.

Moreover, an organ is something material and extended, having parts outside of parts. In the case of sight, there is the cornea, the retina, and so on. So we cannot see all that is entailed in the act of seeing or sense immediately all that is present in the act of touching. The organic and material dimensions of our sense powers are opaque to us. My nerve endings might touch the surface of the table, but they do not touch the inside of the nervous system itself. The neurons firing in my brain may contact or touch one another, but in doing so, they do not by that same process attain contact with their own individual inner mechanisms. But the intellect can know both the object of knowledge in question (a house or a person, for example) *and* the act of knowing, *and* it can think about the whole of itself at once as a reality capable of knowing. As noted, once we see that this form of self-reflexivity cannot occur in an organic power, we understand that the intellect must in some way be immaterial in its essential activity.

Finally, it is important for this account to observe that the human intellect begins from sensations and operates in return to them. This implies that even if its intrinsic operations are intrinsically immaterial, they also operate in and through formally extrinsic but necessary dependence upon phantasms. In other words, we think only conceptually and immaterially, but it is impossible to think conceptually and immaterially without recourse to phantasms or inner images of some kind. The reason for this is that our intellect alights on what exists, and in our embodied state as spiritual animals, *we only have access to realities in existence through the medium of our sensations*, whether these are internal sensations (of ourselves) or external

---

things. Therefore, intellect and sense are not the same. Likewise, a sense knows neither itself nor its operation; for instance, sight neither sees itself nor sees that it sees. This self-reflexive power belongs to a higher faculty, as is proved in the *De anima* [III, 2]. But the intellect knows itself, and knows that it knows. Therefore, intellect and sense are not the same.

See also *SCG* IV, c. 11.

sensations (of ourselves and other realities). The intellect is actuated by contact with the real, but it only has such contact when the sense powers are active. This is why our intellect, while immaterial, is bound to the senses for its operations, and when those senses are impaired, then the act of the intellect is also affected or thwarted in some way, such as in sleep and dreams, brain damage, illness, or drunkenness or narcotics. This is also why the intellect can only develop conceptually and rationally once there is a sufficient development of the internal organs and sense powers, as in the case of the unborn human fetus or even the small child that is still "pre-rational," even though the spiritual faculties are part of the human being by virtue of the form of the body (the soul) prior to the manifestation of any rational activity.[68]

Immateriality of Human Free Will:
Argument from Intellectual Self-determination and Freedom to Choose Contraries Only Known Through Intellectual Means[69]

A final argument can be made based on the nature of the human will and its characteristic freedom. The will is a power of the soul that is distinct from the intellect and has its own proper object. Whereas the intellect seeks the truth and is oriented toward the knowledge of the truth, the will is an appetite for the good and is inclined toward happiness and the pursuit of union with the good. We can choose among various goods that we think will reasonably guarantee us happiness. Most of our human volitional decisions, then, entail a decision about how to arrange our various loves in order of priority and how to love various goods in relation to their priority and order to one another. We have by nature an innate capacity to love various goods, and so too in virtue of our intelligence and freedom, we can order our preferential loves and pursuits rationally. In

68. On the spiritual soul as the form of the body in the embryonic human being, see Feser, *Aquinas*, 138–42; John Haldane and Patrick Lee, "Aquinas on Human Ensoulment, Abortion and the Value of Life," *Philosophy* 78, no. 2 (2003): 255–78.

69. For a version of this argument in Aquinas, see *SCG* II, c. 47, as well as *ST* I, q. 83.

doing so, we strive for the complex enjoyment and happiness that arises from the reasonable possession of these various goods in an ordered way.[70] Since we can only love what we first come to know, however, the will depends upon the intellect and is an appetite that flows out of it, even as it has its own distinct acts, such as our voluntary intentions or choices, which are not acts of the intellect per se but acts of the will: love, desire, intention, decision, choice, and execution. Love depends upon knowledge and does not arise except from knowledge, but love is not merely reducible to knowledge, nor is knowledge reducible to love.

The immateriality of the will follows from a consideration of what was said above in two ways, both regarding the immateriality of the intellect's object and the self-reflexivity of the intellect. Regarding the first, we should note that the will can move the intellect from within to various potential objects of interest.[71] We only come to love what we have first come to know, but we also seek to know better that which we have come to love. This freedom to choose to study those truths we are most interested in is based on the loving desire of the human person for greater potential knowledge of a given reality. We may love to think about this or that person or subject matter. But if this is the case, then the will can act in a way that is interior to the intellect with regard to the *intellect's proper object.* That is to say, our volitional loves can act directly upon the truth known in a universal, immaterial mode. Voluntary love can affect the essential action of thinking from within, and it can orient from within without any violence to our knowledge precisely in its immaterial mode of functioning. This means that the will is itself able to desire the truths that the mind knows in an immaterial way and is itself therefore also immaterial in its operation. If it were not immaterial, it would not be able to act upon the immaterial objects of the intellect directly from within, nor would it be able to be specified and informed of the immaterial knowledge procured by the intellect.

70. *ST* I, q. 82, a. 1 and q. 83, a. 1.
71. See the analysis of Aquinas in *De Malo*, q. 6.

This truth is further clarified by the fact that if the will can exert or move the intellect from within, the intellect can also specify the will from within, granting it knowledge of what it loves. For example, the truths that the intellect comes to know in an immaterial mode *about the goodness of various realities* give specification to the will by awakening in it a love for the rational good. The will comes to love and in turn chooses goods that it apprehends by means of the intellect, since we only love what we first know and deliberate rationally about the things we choose intentionally.[72] This means that the intellect is also interior to the will, while remaining distinguishable from it, and gives specification to the will as a faculty. But an immaterial specification can only be given to the will from within in keeping with the will's own object—namely, the good known and desired—if the will is itself just as immaterial as the intellect. This is why the will cannot be determined from the senses alone, nor can it be determined from the passions, the external will of others, or physical coercion. It is a spiritual, immaterial power determined from within only through reasoning and free self-determination.[73] This is also why the will can choose rational contraries not subject to the senses, such as to eat or to fast, to avoid pain or to undergo surgery.[74] The will is not subject merely to sense appetite nor instinct

72. *De Malo*, q. 6:

If we should consider the objects of the will and the intellect, we find that the object of the intellect belongs first and chiefly to the genus of formal cause, since its object is being and truth. But the object of the will belongs first and chiefly to the genus of final cause, since its object is the good, in which all ends are included, just as all understood forms are included in the truth. And so good itself, insofar as it is a comprehensible form, is included in the truth as something true, and the true itself, insofar as it is the end of intellectual activity, is included in the good as something good. Therefore, if we should consider the movement of the soul's powers regarding the object specifying the act, the first source of movement comes from the intellect, since the understood good in this way moves even the will itself. And if we should consider the movement of the soul's powers regarding performance of the act, then the source of the movement comes from the will. For the power to which the chief end belongs always moves to action the power to which the means to the end belongs. [Trans. R. Regan, *On Evil* (Oxford: Oxford University Press, 2003).]

73. *SCG* II, c. 47.
74. *SCG* II, c. 48.

nor passions but is subject to decisions made in the light of deliberate reason. The will receives its direction in love through rational deliberation of the intellectual subject who acts according to the universal scope of reason.

Secondly and more briefly, what was said above about the intellect being capable of self-reflexivity is also true about the will in two ways. The intellect can reflect on all that happens to the will and can know the will from within, which it could not do if the will were a mere organic power like the power of sight or hearing. And the will can also love itself from within, by loving its own freedom and its own act of loving and the will can will its own act of willing and loving, just as the intellect can know itself knowing and know the act of knowing.

Conclusion

Let us conclude our discussion of the immaterial operations of the soul by returning to where we started. They indicate indirectly but really that there is an immaterial, transcendent cause of the existence of the soul. The reasoning may be stated succinctly if somewhat intuitively. If the intellect and the will are immaterial powers of the soul, then the soul itself as a principle of life must be immaterial and therefore not subject to material corruption. A material substrate could not give rise to immaterial operations, as the lesser cannot give rise to the greater. If there are immaterial operations in the soul, they must come from an immaterial substrate; indeed the soul must be immaterial by nature.

Second, the soul is not the cause of its own being, as indeed human persons have not always existed but come to be. If the soul is immaterial, however, it must be caused to be by something immaterial and transcendent, not something material and historically conditioned by immanent, material causes, such as the cosmic processes that affect the development of the universe and the gradual emergence and evolution of living things that are non-rational. If the transcendent cause of the soul is immaterial, it is not a material biological

creature or material non-living thing, but must have personal characteristics analogous to intellectual operation and spiritual love. After
all, the effects (spiritual souls) must in some way resemble the cause
(the Creator). God is not only "intellectual" but also "free and loving"
in a way that is utterly different from but also somehow like or analogous to the personal characteristics of the human being.

SCIENCE, CAUSALITY, AND ARGUMENTS FOR THE EXISTENCE OF GOD

As noted at the start of this chapter, none of these arguments depends essentially on the findings of the modern natural sciences or
the scientific methods of study developed in contemporary physics,
chemistry, or biology. However, insofar as these arguments make
appeal to a variety of basic metaphysical claims about natural kinds,
individual beings, and causality, they are based on a form of philosophical realism that any modern natural scientific discipline necessarily presupposes and that its methodology therefore cannot suppress. If this idea is correct, then the findings of the modern natural
sciences can never either *prove* or *disprove* the existence of God due
precisely to the formal object of study they engage with and are focused upon. These sciences, whether one speaks primarily of physics, chemistry, or biology, analyze the material composition of physical realities, their formal constitutions, and the relationships of
efficient and final causality that obtain between them, as well as
their accidental arrangements. As such, they can discover important
truths about either the constitution of material bodies, such as the
chemical elements and atomic composition of diverse substances,
or the biological composition and natural history of living things—
that is, the likely historical development of DNA and its mutations
through recombination in various ancestors of currently existing
species—or the laws of micro or macro physical development in
the world, for example, analysis of fundamental forces in physics or
of the history of the formation of cosmological systems.

However, in any of these cases, the study in question considers quantitative features of material beings under a particular aspect, which of necessity pertains to their quantitatively measurable material constitution. Such sciences, therefore, do *not* consider realities insofar as they exist or are caused to be, are contingent or orderly, are or are not good, are one or multiple in nature, are beautiful or ugly, exhibit gradations of perfection, are or are not self-organizing, are or are not intelligent, or free and ethically just or unjust. The study of these sciences thus cannot permit us formal entry into the sphere of the metaphysical as such, nor can it prevent such entry. We cannot prove the existence of God from the empirically-based study of modern cosmology, nor disprove it. To approach a deeper knowledge of reality, that which leads to knowledge of the mystery of God, properly philosophical and metaphysical reflection is required.

Of course, in our own era many people claim to reduce all questions of metaphysics, life, intelligence, and personal freedom to questions of modern physics (through the media of biology and chemistry). Ultimately, then, the sum of reality is to be explained by particles of matter and the forces of the physical world, which are unveiled gradually to us through the study of modern physics. But to advance this idea, one must rely upon the unfounded presumption that everything we experience may be reduced to the monochromatic or epistemologically simple explanations provided by contemporary physics and its ongoing discoveries. However, this viewpoint is untenable. It is not merely impossible hypothetically on the presupposition that our knowledge of the physical world is still limited. It is impossible theoretically, necessarily, and in principle. Knowledge of matter produced by the study of modern physics simply never can explain features of reality not reducible to the quantitative dimensions of reality, and these include such basic features of things as their substantial unity (at the macro or micro level), qualities, natural kinds, causality, order and intelligible regularity, teleological operations, existence and contingency, unity and multiplicity, goodness, beauty, and hierarchical coordination. Nor can the modern sciences explain the origin and nature of logical argumentation—which deals in relations of abstract, universal reasoning, not physical processes—or the origins of mathematical knowledge—which is possible only due to our spiritual capacity for abstract, universal knowledge of quantities. We could extend the list. Indeed, the study of physics cannot even explain why physicists desire to know the truths of physics and believe such discoveries to have necessary value. The point is that no amount of sophistic rhetoric or ideological demagoguery will allow atheistic polemicists to suppress the basic metaphysical questions about reality that inevitably always return when we consider these ordinary features of reality and that when treated with respect, conduct the intelligence to consider anew the reasonableness of belief in the existence of God.

One can even say that the very basis of our study of the natural sciences is our metaphysical knowledge, which pertains to more fundamental truths of reality, in both the ontological and the epistemological orders. Therefore, to the extent that one advocates for the advance of the study of the modern sciences (on the premise that they yield realistic knowledge of the world, which of course they do), then one likewise necessarily advocates at least implicitly for a genuine metaphysical knowledge of the world of just the sort that inevitably permits and invites demonstrative knowledge of the existence of God. In fact, the habitual exercise of modern scientific learning is parasitical upon the kind of metaphysical realism that can and should lead us progressively to the acknowledgement of the existence of God. To the extent that the modern sciences flourish, they also always inevitably promote the necessary conditions for philosophical realism, and this realism in turn makes it possible at least in principle to re-engage with metaphysics as a science of being, which has God as its principal source or transcendent cause.[75]

75. This is true, in fact, despite the prevailing atheistic ideologies that are often predominant in the academic culture of natural scientists. This is not a paradoxical or contradictory claim. People who know a great deal about modern science have had to spend a great deal of time studying these sciences nearly exclusively, and they are often philosophically under-informed and insufficiently metaphysically reflective, just as many

Consider briefly some examples. We noted in chapter 1 that there are pre-demonstrative principles that pertain to the very structure of reality that each person knows. Here, we mentioned the principles of non-contradiction, identity, causality, finality, and sufficient reason, noting how the awareness of these principles leads us to acknowledge as something properly basic that there are all around us various substances with characteristic properties. In the context of the natural sciences, how might we illustrate these principles? For one thing, all scientific learning takes its point of departure from a more fundamental experiential realism, in which we seek to understand the natures and behaviors of physical bodies around us, be they living or non-living. The scientist who seeks to explain the properties of the human gallbladder, uranium, or planet formation must be able to tell that the biological organ of the gallbladder, the chemical element of uranium, and the planet studied through data culled from telescopes are distinct realities (principle of non-contradiction), that they are really real and have distinct natures and properties (principle of identity), and that they have causal histories and repetitive, predictable patterns of behavior so that we can explain them (principles of causality and sufficient reason). These may seem like trivial metaphysical observations, but in fact they have far-reaching consequences. If there truly are distinct *things* that have properties (this human body, this uranium, this planet), then we can speak about natural substances and their features, such as their quantity and qualities, which are really distinguishable. The problem of their independent existences, contingency, order, and diverse perfections then comes into view almost surreptitiously as a presupposition to scientific study but not as its principal focus. Natural scientists are not so much metaphysicians in principle as they are metaphysicians in practice, since they must presume and make use of the core metaphysical realism that the human intellect both facilitates and requires as a source of their own study of the contours of reality.

philosophers and theologians (myself included) are under-informed regarding the natural sciences. But everyone depends upon metaphysical knowledge, whether they have studied it or not, since it is the most basic form of natural knowledge, underlying all others.

The Five Ways, for example, flow in a serene and linear fashion from a consideration of realities that the modern sciences themselves must presuppose and that they continually alert us to albeit only implicitly: change implies causal dependence; causal effects require prior ontological causes with determinate ontological content (that is, water dissolves chlorine because of what water is); contingency is not self-explanatory and points us toward something necessary; there are hierarchies of perfection in nature; there is both discernible order and teleological activity present in things we appeal to in giving explanation for why and how things operate as they do. The "story" we tell of the universe from age to age as we enrich our knowledge of the cosmos, of chemical and physical compounds, and of biological entities and their histories does not give us direct knowledge that God exists but is latent with and presupposes real metaphysical knowledge, so that it always invites us anew to the possibility of the philosophical ascent to God. It does so ineradicably. This is why there just never will be a scientific age that does away with basic metaphysical questions. To do away with the metaphysical realism the sciences presuppose, one must do away with metaphysics itself, and ultimately that means not only doing away with the sciences and with scientific explanation but also doing away with language itself insofar as it denotes ontological causation, an idea that Nietzsche preserved from Aristotle but to which he attached a different value judgment.[76]

---

76. Friedrich Nietzsche, *Writings from the Late Notebooks*, trans. K. Sturge (Cambridge: Cambridge University Press, 2006), 6[13] (pp. 125–26):

> The last thing in metaphysics we'll rid ourselves of is the oldest stock, assuming we *can* rid ourselves of it—that stock which has embodied itself in language and the grammatical categories and made itself so indispensable that it almost seems we could cease being able to think if we relinquished it. Philosophers, in particular, have the greatest difficulty in freeing themselves from the belief that the basic concepts and categories of reason belong without further ado to the realm of metaphysical certainties: from ancient times they have believed in reason as a piece of the metaphysical world itself—this oldest belief breaks out in them again and again like an overpowering recoil.

Consider likewise, *Late Notebooks*, 6[11] (p. 124):

In sum, the modern sciences are not able to do the work sufficient to "banish God from the universe." For that one must have recourse to something other, older, and more fundamental and elemen-
tal: the human will to power, or more accurately stated, the will to
ignore or eradicate all seeming evidence or vestiges of God and the
sacred, to burn all rational pathways to God, whether by despair or
through misguided courage or more likely a distinctive mixture of
both.[77] Human beings have this atheistic capacity not because they
are physical things but only because they themselves have immaterial
capacities for intellectual and voluntary autonomy by which they can
insulate themselves spiritually from within by a kind of rationalist immanentism, not aware of nor vulnerable to the reality of God in his
transcendence.[78] However sincerely intended, the autonomy and intellectual error that atheism represents is a *spiritual phenomenon* that
is distinctively human in kind, something that other animals are incapable of, due to the absence in them of any spiritual soul or immaterial faculties. In fact, atheism is the product of a spiritual immanentism
that only a rational being can produce, one who seeks autonomous
freedom in the face of religious claims through excessive attachment
to intellectual lies. This is why it is itself an indirect sign of the existence of God. It is something found uniquely within a spiritual animal possessing immaterial faculties created by God and thus capable
of this kind of noble delusion. Other animals lack the intelligence to
be capable of atheism. (Whereas angels, on a Thomistic account, have
too high and enlightened a form of intellect to be capable of atheism.)

The inventive force that thought up categories was working in the service of
needs—of security, of quick comprehensibility using signs and sounds, of
means of abbreviation—"substance," "subject," "object," "being," "becoming"
are not metaphysical truths.—It is the powerful who made the names of things
law; and among the powerful it is the greatest artists of abstraction who created
the categories.

See also *Late Notebooks*, 14[93] (p. 250).

77. See Henri de Lubac, *The Drama of Atheist Humanism*, trans. A. Nash, E. Riley, M.
Sebanc (San Francisco: Ignatius, 1995).

78. See the penetrating reflections of Cornelius Fabro in *God in Exile: Modern Atheism*, trans. A. Gibson (New York: Newman, 1968), 24–27; 882–907; 1061–85.

Seen in this light, it is not so mysterious that human beings should seek to reduce all forms of legitimate knowledge to that which is obtained by the empirical methods of the modern natural sciences. If one does opt for this form of thinking, it eventually facilitates a disposition of moral autonomy in which human beings can dispose of all lesser things by their own lights and a cosmology of metaphysical anthropocentricism in which human understanding is exalted as the final arbiter of purpose and meaning, one in which religious claims become increasingly improbable, impossible, or absurd. Inevitably for the atheist, the human being becomes the unique protagonist of self-awareness in an impersonal universe and just happens to have capacities for deciphering or fabricating meaning developed spontaneously out of the night of the world. Persons reach no terminus beyond themselves. In an atheist universe, then, personhood seems ephemeral, an epiphenomenon that will eventually fall into night and return to non-being. But in another sense, the quest for autonomy is the principal driving factor in the atheistic cast of mind. This is the case whether this drive stems from the desire to be free from the murky shadows of religion, or it is motivated by the mature psychological acceptance of having no "cosmic" help besides one's own, or it flows from alienation at the thought of God and transcendent morality, or from the simple desire for mono-methodological scientific clarity.[79] In any case, modern atheism tends by its emphasis on "authentic" intellectual autonomy to accentuate a sense of the primacy of the person, at least as a subject of intellectual, political, and liberal agency. And yet paradoxically, this only ever occurs in a diminished sense, as the person of the atheist himself, however noble, represses his or her own native aspiration to transcendence, which is the deepest and most vital inheritance of the intellect, apart from which the human being's true vocation as an intellectual remains indecipherable.

79. I'm referring obliquely here to David Hume, Sigmund Freud, Karl Marx, and Bertrand Russell, respectively.

CONCLUSION

In the first part of our consideration of rational credibility and religious belief we raised the question of the ultimate explanation of things. Is the universe subject to a religious interpretation? In this second chapter, I have argued that monotheism provides the rational explanation of the source and origin of all that exists. God is the primary source of intelligibility that stands behind all that exists, the transcendent author of a universe of contingent, orderly realities that point back indirectly but clearly toward their unknown author. Atheism taking up the mantle of modern science, on the other hand, can provide ever-more well-researched histories of the order and origin of things, but it becomes murky and ultimately silent on the metaphysical origins of being, change, and the natures of things. As such, the rational credibility of a theistic cosmos appears vibrant.

Furthermore, I have argued that the human person is a spiritual animal with immaterial faculties of intellect and will, which cannot be understood uniquely in light of the human body or human sensation. Instead, there is an immaterial principle (the spiritual soul) within each human being that is the deepest source and well-spring of his personal identity. Because the operations of this spiritual soul are well-known through experience to every human being, the immateriality of the intellect and will are perhaps even more widely appealing as a phenomenon in need of a transcendent explanation. Atheist materialists, on the other hand, make great appeal to images of the independence and autonomy of the human person, but in reality, they posit a cosmos in which genuine personhood, freedom, and love are impossible and these experiences are illusions. To the Christian theist, by contrast, there is something in the human person, spiritual knowledge and love, that is somehow like God (in his image, by similitude) but also unlike him, because it is merely created, derivative, and ontologically imperfect.

To argue in this way is to suggest that the ultimate ontological measures of the universe are personal in character. God, the source and origin of all things, is personal in some analogical sense, and God has given existence to human beings who are personal. In both these senses, we may speak of a "personal universe." But this personal character of the universe is also obscure or mysterious. On the one hand, God remains for us, naturally speaking, an unknown person. He is hidden by the veil of his own creation, which acts as a sort of natural iconostasis, one that makes it clear to our reason that God is real but that also conceals him from view. The personal God known to us philosophically is also a God we fail to know personally, if we know God merely by means of our natural reason. And yet the desire to know God in himself and to know who God is inter-personally—in what Eleanor Stump terms a "second-person" relationship of "I and thou"—is entirely natural and even philosophically warranted.[80] For as Aquinas notes, he who knows the effect desires also by nature to know the cause and to know the cause in itself. So it is natural that human reason should desire to know not only whether God exists, but if he does exist, to know God personally and if possible immediately.[81] In this sense, it is not irrational, as Aquinas argues at length in the *Summa contra Gentiles* III, to desire by nature to see the essence of God.[82] This is somewhat paradoxical. It is rational for human beings to desire to know what lies beyond the range of their own natural capacities but only because the desire to know the identity of God stems from our best rational aspirations for truth. It is natural to desire to see God. How can we know God personally, though, if he does not reveal himself to us?

Likewise, our own life as personal beings of knowledge and love (who seek truth and desire happiness), is opaque on a multitude of fronts. What should we live for? What goods will give us genuine happiness, and what can we reasonably hope for in life? How do we

---

80. See Eleonore Stump, *Wandering in Darkness: Narrative and the Problem of Suffering* (Oxford: Oxford University Press, 2012).

81. *ST* I, q. 12, a. 1.

82. Aquinas, *SCG* III, cc. 50–54. I will return to this point in chapter 4 at some length.

stand before God in this life subject to the constraints of time and faced with the inevitable horizon of human death? Who are we to become before God in this life and in the life to come? If God is truly infinitely good and wise, why are his creatures at times so deeply affected by privations of goodness, in the form of evil and suffering? Likewise, and perhaps even more importantly, is there any way for human beings to find deliverance from evil and suffering? Is any genuine "salvation" available to the human race? Here, too, natural reason asks "reasonable questions" of a philosophical sort, at least by the standards of ancient Greek philosophy. And yet these are questions natural reason itself cannot provide complete or exhaustive answers to. Here, too, our need for God and his divine revelation is exposed. The mystery of our own human personhood, its meaning and destiny, is something we cannot fully understand without some form of higher assistance from God.

We have identified two difficult areas of inquiry: the hidden identity of God and the ultimate vocation and meaning of human persons. In both of these domains, human philosophy asks valid questions it cannot procure answers to. And herein then, we see the rational fittingness of divine revelation. God can reveal to us his own identity, and God can also reveal to us our own human destiny. Who is God and what might we hope for in life? These are questions that the New Testament addresses decisively. In this sense, the Catholic intellectual tradition understands natural reason and divine revelation as deeply harmonious sources of truth.[83] The human being can decrypt the truth that God exists, but he or she cannot know God personally without divine revelation. The person who has received the divine revelation of Christ can in turn initiate the study of God by way of philosophical inquiry. The order of the two to one another is not diachronic in any fixed sense. Some come to God primarily by way of divine revelation first and philosophy second, while for others the order is the inverse. However, in either case there is

83. As noted in chapter 1 regarding the teaching of the First Vatican Council, in *Dei Filius*, ch. 2.

an order of perfection that is architectonic. Philosophy tells us that the universe is enigmatically personal. Divine revelation reveals to us the persons of the Holy Trinity (the inner identity of God as Father, Son, and Holy Spirit). Philosophy tells us that the human person has an immaterial soul, characterized by activities of knowledge and love. Divine revelation unveils to us the vocation to supernatural beatitude. The human being is made in the image of the Holy Trinity and is called to a higher form of supernatural knowledge and love of God in conformity to the eternal Word of God and the eternal spiration of the Holy Spirit. Life in time for human beings is characterized above all by the calling of human beings into a pilgrimage of grace, to find God by grace, and to live with God in friendship.

Therefore, it is the mystery of the Trinity that unveils to each human being who God is and what human beings might rightly hope for. This mystery of God as Trinity does not flow organically from the natural knowledge of God derived from metaphysics, but it complements it, since it suggests that God wishes us to know him not only through the medium of our own personal reflections but also by engagement with him in person. This complementarity of ways is fitting, since grace does not destroy nature but heals and elevates our nature. It is this form of cooperative knowledge by way of faith and philosophy, revelation and natural reason, that we will pursue in the third chapter on the historical and conceptual coherence of Christian revelation when reflecting on the mystery of the inner life of God as Holy Trinity.

3

Christian Revelation and Reasonable Mystery

The Conceptual Form and Historical Coherence of Trinitarian Monotheism[1]

The previous chapter presented what I take to be reasonable arguments for the existence of the one God and Creator of all that is. This idea builds on the previous argument in chapter 1, where I suggested that the appeal to God as the Creator (monotheism) provides the best explanation for reality and that there are grounds for taking seriously the claim that God could reveal himself to us. In this chapter, then, I aim to provide a basic sketch of Christian doctrine regarding the mystery of God, namely, that God is a Trinity of persons. What is the reason for this order of presentation? The overall argument of this third chapter seeks to present a protracted argument for the reasonableness of Trinitarian monotheism. Arguments for the existence of God can stand on their own in distinction from theological claims, since they have their own formal intelligibility. But it is also the case that human beings make decisions about the truth of reality by thinking about many subjects at once:

1. One section of this chapter was previous published as Thomas Joseph White, "One God in Two Testaments: On the Biblical Ontology of Trinitarian Monotheism," in *Engaging Catholic Doctrine: Essays in Honor of Matthew Levering*, ed. Robert Barron, Scott Hahn, and James R. A. Merrick (Steubenville, OH: Emmaus Academic, 2023), 191–208.

philosophical arguments, ethical beliefs, likely historical truths, and claims about divine revelation, to name a few. In this process, the claims of divine revelation and the activity of philosophical discernment are distinct, but they also remain closely interrelated and in a sense inseparable. Thinking about the Trinity as the supernatural mystery at the heart of reality is thus a consequent to thinking about the philosophical rationality of monotheism; the inverse is also true. If it is philosophically reasonable to think that God exists, then it is theoretically possible that God is Trinitarian and has revealed himself to us by becoming human. Likewise, grace does not destroy nature, and theology does not ignore the truths of philosophy. Belief in the Trinity requires philosophical accountability. Indeed even within Catholic theology, the use of philosophical reflection regarding God in his unity is integral to any rightly ordered reflection on God the Holy Trinity.

In this chapter, then, I offer a general sketch of Trinitarian doctrine, setting it out in a historical order. The aim is to show that the doctrine itself is grounded in the sources of Christian revelation and that it provides an intellectually coherent even if numinous reflection on the deepest mystery of faith. In this light, I argue first that New Testament doctrine presupposes and recapitulates Israelite monotheism, second that the teaching of Jesus of Nazareth is implicitly Trinitarian, third that the New Testament authors offer us basic analogical notions with which to think constructively about the mystery of the Trinity as the inner life of God, and finally that these analogies were analyzed and developed progressively into a clear doctrine by the early Church. The point of this reflection is not to reduce the mystery of the Holy Trinity to a product of human historical reasoning nor to claim that we fully comprehend the mystery but only to show that the Church's basic doctrine is founded in the New Testament, as interpreted reasonably by the early Church. In addition, as I will argue, even a basic understanding of the doctrine allows us to begin to understand how the mystery of the Holy Trinity illumines our human experience and permits us to understand creation and the human person more profoundly in the light of God. In all this, I am alluding to two of the criteria of rationality that I presented at the end of the first chapter when considering claims about revelation: the *internal coherence* of the revelation of God and the way it *illumines* or casts ultimate light upon reality as otherwise known. How is the doctrine of the Trinity understood in its internal coherence as a claim about the innermost mystery of God, and how is this claim meant to cast light on our experience and understanding of reality?

THE PRESUPPOSITION OF OLD
TESTAMENT MONOTHEISM

There is only one God, the Creator of all that is, who sustains all things in being. This is the basic claim of Biblical monotheism, present in both the Old and New Testaments.[2] God is present in all things because he is the Creator, the actual cause of all that exists, but God is also utterly distinct from all that is. He is mysteriously present to all that exists ("omnipresent") in a way that transcends

2. Use of the term "monotheism" sometimes gives rise to controversy. Some claim that it must denote a concept of philosophical theism derived from the Enlightenment era, alien to an earlier epoch of Christian revelation and traditional theological reflection. Erik Peterson argued that ancient non-Biblical religious traditions employed monotheistic ideas to legitimate hierarchical political authorities but that this notion of monotheism is absent from the New Testament. [*Der Monotheismus als politisches Problem. Ein Beitrag zur Geschichte der politischen Theologie im Imperium Romanum* (Leipzig: Hegner, 1935).] My view is that there are in fact many forms of monotheism, characterized by appeals to differing revelations and diverse philosophical ideas about the one God, which give rise to distinctive, often multilayered, religious traditions of reflection. In employing this term, I am presuming both the irreducible role of the biblical revelation in giving shape to the New Testament notion of the one God *and* the irreducible role of philosophical reflection, which also takes place within a longstanding Christian tradition of debate. In other words, I am presuming what I take to be the Catholic "both-and" view of revelation and philosophy. The general notion of monotheism is potentially broad and can incorporate problematic conceptions of God. The "biblical" qualifier suggests a clarification and correction of the human content of the idea of monotheism, one made possible initially by revelation but also by the human philosophical life of human beings thinking and debating within the tradition of Christian philosophy, as well as with those who contest against it.

our comprehensive understanding. As the creative source of all things he is more internal to us than we are to ourselves, because he is intimately present to all that he causes to exist.[3] But he is also non-material and therefore hidden from view, unknown, and yet we must say according to Biblical monotheism that God is in some way personal. God is wise, good, all-powerful, eternal, and merciful.[4]

The Trinitarian teaching of the New Testament is likewise fundamentally monotheistic. There is one God, who is Father, Son, and Holy Spirit.[5] Thus, the Church concludes in her doctrinal teaching that the Trinity *is* the one God, and the one God *is* the Holy Trinity. According to this logic, the revelation of the Trinity presupposes the truth of the Old Testament, that God is one, as a truth revealed to Israel. At the same time, this revelation of God's inner life as Trinity

3. Jer. 23:23–24: "Am I a God at hand, says the LORD, and not a God afar off?... Do I not fill heaven and earth? says the LORD." Ps. 139:7–8: "Whither shall I go from thy Spirit? Or whither shall I flee from thy presence? If I ascend to heaven, thou art there! If I make my bed in Sheol, thou art there." See likewise Isa. 66:1; Prov. 15:3; 1 Kings 8:7; Acts 17:34; Col. 1:17; Heb., 1:3, 4:12. I am alluding here to both Dionysius's idea that "God is [in] all things as the cause of all things," and Augustine's notion in the *Confessions* III, 6, 11 that God is closer to us than we are to ourselves. Dionysius, *The Divine Names* V, 4. My translation is based on Aquinas's Latin rendering of the phrase in *ST* I, q. 4, a. 2: "[O]mnia est, ut omnium causa." Augustine, *Confessions* III, 6, 11: "[I]nterior intimo meo et superior summo meo" (more interior to my innermost and higher than my highest self).

4. Biblical evidence includes God's personal name (Ex. 3:14–15; Deut. 18:5), his personal knowledge (Prov. 15:3; Isa. 48:17; Acts 15:18); intentional love (Jer. 31:3; Rom. 5:8); intentional choices (Isa. 48:10–11; Ps. 115:3); wisdom (Prov. 3:19; Wis. 7:22–30) and compassion (Deut. 30:3; Isa. 49:15). I am presuming that personal terms are attributed to God analogically, so that they signify God only imperfectly and imply that God is more dissimilar to created human persons that he is similar. The Fourth Lateran Council in 1215 makes this point in a succinct but poignant way: "For between Creator and creature no similitude can be expressed without implying greater dissimilitude [non potest tanta similitudo notari, quin inter eos maior sit dissimilitudo notanda]." Lateran IV, c. 2 (*Denzinger*, 803).

5. On Christological monotheism in the New Testament, see Larry W. Hurtado, *One God One Lord: Early Christian Devotion and Ancient Jewish Monotheism*, 3rd edition (Edinburgh: T & T Clark, 2015); *Lord Jesus Christ: Devotion to Jesus in Earliest Christianity* (Grand Rapids, MI: Eerdmans, 2005). On the divinity of the Holy Spirit in the New Testament within the context of Second Temple monotheism, see for example Marianne Meye Thompson, "The Gospel of John and Early Trinitarian Thought: The Unity of God in John, Irenaeus and Tertullian," in *The Bible and Early Trinitarian Theology*, ed. C. A. Beeley and W. E. Weedman (Washington, DC: The Catholic University of America Press, 2018, 109–17).

is meant to extend and perfect the revelation given to Israel, bringing it to completion.

It is this last idea that I will explore especially in the initial part of
this chapter. How does the New Testament revelation claim to bring
to completion and in fact perfect the revelation given in the Old Testament? I will not pretend here to offer a comprehensive analysis
of this seemingly immeasurable topic but will offer only a tentative
treatment of three internal tensions or paradoxes in the Old Testament meaningfully brought to resolution by the New Testament revelation of God.

The Question of Perfect Knowledge of God

In a sense, the basic claim of Old Testament revelation is rationalist in orientation: revelation enlightens human persons because it
provides the true metaphysical explanation of reality in accord with
reason's own best aspirations, acting as a lodestar of truth that offers human beings the saving knowledge of God they need in order
to free themselves from the shackles of religious ignorance.[6] On
this reading, which is traditional from the point of view of orthodox Catholic theology, the gift of revelation is beneficial, because
it allows us to address intellectually the natural enigmas raised in
the first chapter of this book. It is reasonable to explain the world
by recourse to a Biblical form of monotheism, the claim that there
is one principle alone, God, who gives being to all things, and that
God, while hidden, is in some sense personal, analogically speaking. If this is the case, then revelation *heals* errant human reason by
granting it perspective and orientation in the midst of its confusion

6. See for example Deut. 4:8; Ps. 119:105; Jer. 14:22; Is. 45:18–22; Prov. 6:23; Wis. 13:1–
19, 18:4, and in the New Testament, Rom. 1:21–23 and Acts 17:22–30. On this theme of
rational enlightenment stemming from biblical revelation, see Joseph Ratzinger, "Vérité
du Christianisme," lecture delivered Nov. 27, 1999 at the Sorbonne, Paris. Extract in *Le
Monde* (1999), full text in *Documentation catholique* (2000) n. 1: 29–35. The essay is republished in English in Joseph Ratzinger, "Christianity—The True Religion?," in *Truth
and Tolerance: Christian Belief and World Religions*, trans. H. Taylor (San Francisco: Ignatius, 2004), 162–83.

and potential lack of clarity.[7] This theme of rational healing effec-
tuated by prophetic revelation is prevalent in Biblical literature, and
it is no doubt significant that in the age of Hellenistic philosophers,
the Biblical authors underscored that the God of divine revelation
could also be known, however imperfectly, by way of the tools of
human reason and natural philosophical reflection.[8]

Nevertheless, the Old Testament revelation also promises a
higher form of knowledge of God, one that not only entails the healing of natural reason so that it can reach the summit and limits of its
own powers but also provides for its supernatural *elevation*, granting
the human person an intimacy with God and knowledge of God's
personal identity not hitherto available, now made possible in virtue
of divine revelation. God manifests his personal identity to Israel as
a people, initially with Abraham and the patriarchs, and in a foundational way in the Mosaic revelation and the Torah, epitomized sym-
bolically by the divine name given to Moses:

Then Moses said to God, "If I come to the people of Israel and say to them,
'The God of your fathers has sent me to you,' and they ask me, 'What is his
name?' what shall I say to them?" God said to Moses, "'I AM HE WHO
IS.'" And he said, "Say this to the people of Israel, 'I AM has sent me to
you.'" God also said to Moses, "Say this to the people of Israel, 'The LORD
[YHWH] ... has sent me to you': this is my name for ever" (Ex. 3:13–15).

Through the covenant erected at Mount Sinai, the promises and
prophetic teachings of God, the ceremonial precepts of the law, and
the sacrifices and the Temple—all elaborated through the course of
Israel's ancient history—God presents the people of Israel with a
privileged knowledge of himself. In this relationship of privileged
knowledge, Israel is subject to a new and more exacting judgment

7. On the necessity of grace to heal certain natural features of human nature, see *ST*
I-II, q. 109, aa. 2–3.

8. See on this theme, Martin Hengel, *Judaism and Hellenism: Studies in Their Encounter in Palestine During the Early Hellenistic Period*, 2 vols. (Eugene, OR: Wipf and
Stock Publishers, 1974), whose work stands as a thematic corrective to the thematic
"de-Hellenization" project of Adolf von Harnack, which pitted Hellenistic currents of
thought over against both biblical Judaic and early Christian thought.

by God but is also offered privileged forms of mercy and divine friendship. In the midst of this friendship, God also remains hidden, often depicted in darkness, as unknown or not wholly known, as a God who cannot be manipulated or fully comprehended but who is also close to Israel in prophetic revelation, in liturgical worship, in the lives of saintly figures, in signs and miracles, and in the historical events God directs to the good of Israel. God is truly manifest and yet concealed in his prophecies, manifest and yet concealed by his providential governance of Israel through sacred history.[9]

A tension exists then in the Old Testament revelation between kataphaticism (authentic "positive" knowledge of what and who God is) and apophaticism (the radical hiddenness of God in darkness and the "negative" human knowledge of God that this hiddenness implies). On the one hand, God is known by way of the healing of nature, the natural enlightenment that the monotheism of Israel brings to all humanity, philosophically we might even say, and he is known positively by way of the revelation of his identity as the Lord of Israel. On the other hand, God remains naturally unknown in large part, since the scriptures acknowledge that natural human reason has no *direct* access to God, and God is not known perfectly in his own inner identity as the hidden Lord of Israel, whose justice, mercy, and love at times remain eclipsed or opaque. He remains enigmatic, even to his friends the prophets and to the people of Israel.

The New Testament does not abolish the profound and mysterious tension between positive and negative knowledge of God present in the Old Testament. However, it does seek to recapitulate and clarify its inner meaning. The darkness of God in his transcendence purifies the human mind of idolatrous notions of God and prepares

9. "Moses drew near to the thick darkness where God was" (Ex. 20:21). "Clouds and darkness are round about him; righteousness and judgment are the foundation of his throne" (Ps. 97:2). Aquinas says that, "we attribute to God the darkness of intangibility and invisibility insofar as he is light inaccessible, exceeding all [natural] light that we see, whether by the senses or by the intellect." See *In div. nom.* VII, lec. 3. [*In Librum Beati Dionysii de Divinis Nominibus Expositio* (Rome and Turin: Marietti, 1950).] Translation by the author.

the human mind for the fullness of the revelation of God's light. The New Testament claims that the positive knowledge of God given initially to Israel (namely, God as the Lord of Israel) finds its resolution in the revelation of Christ as God made man (that is, Jesus Christ as Lord).[10] The God of Israel has become human so that we might come to know most perfectly who God is in himself, as a Trinitarian communion of persons, Father, Son, and Holy Spirit.

This revelation augments the distinction between natural knowledge of God and supernatural, revealed knowledge of God, since human reason can understand of itself that God is one, but it cannot by itself penetrate into the mystery of the Holy Trinity. This distinction of natural and revealed knowledge is not absent from the Old Testament, but it is cast in sharper relief by the revelation of the Trinity. Both the Old and New Testaments claim that in various ways it is naturally reasonable for human beings to believe that there is one God who is the Creator. To come to know that God is in fact truly the God of Israel and especially that God is Trinity (in God's own inner life) is uniquely the work of grace, the work of God's unilateral initiative.[11] This revelation of God does not place the supernatural knowledge of God as Trinity in contradiction to natural knowledge of God as one. It actually *intensifies* the integration of the two forms of knowledge, while maintaining and sharpening the distinction between knowledge by way of revelation and knowledge by way of natural reason. In other words, the revelation of the Trinity *makes more clear* the distinction between the two distinct forms of knowledge but also *their organic integration* in our concrete lives, as we think of God as Trinitarian, that is to say, as both Father, Son, and Holy Spirit *and* as the one God.

10. On Christ as the Lord (*Kyrios*) of Israel, see for example Phil. 2:6–11; 1 Cor. 1:2, 8:6, 12:3; Rom. 10:9; Acts 10:36. On the Trinitarian name of God, see Matt. 28:19; Col. 3:17; Eph. 5:20; John 16:23, 17:6.

11. This logic is presupposed by the discourse of Paul at Athens in Acts 17:22–31, which finds echoes in the themes of natural and revealed knowledge of God in Wis. 13:1–9 and 18:1–9. On the subject of the grace of Trinitarian revelation, see Aquinas, *ST* I, q. 32, a. 1.

On this view, the knowledge of the mystery of the Trinity does not abolish the distinction of kataphatic and apophatic knowledge of God. The knowledge of the Holy Trinity is "still" apophatic and in a way even more so, since the revelation of the mystery of God as a communion of persons is itself deeply numinous. In this life, we do not see God face to face or behold the essence of God immediately (1 Cor. 13:12). The Incarnation of God both reveals God and conceals him, just as the divinity of Christ is manifest in his human developmental life, preaching, miracles, suffering, death, and bodily resurrection, but his divinity is also in part concealed and hidden within these same features of his human nature. Nevertheless, whatever our apophatic qualifiers, we also must note that according to the internal logic of the New Testament, it is only in Christ that the final purpose of God's self-revelation is made most fully manifest for all of humanity in history. God has given us true knowledge already now *in this life* of who God is truly in himself *in view of* the vision of God that is to be inherited in the life to come, knowledge by immediate intellectual perception, the beatific vision.[12] In other words, where the Old Testament *intimates* that our imperfect knowledge of God is an adumbration of a yet-more-perfect knowledge that is to come, the New Testament clarifies who God is in himself and reveals the teleological orientation of this knowledge by faith toward the vision of God in eternal life. We are made by God in his image, and we are elevated by God in his grace, so that in the eschaton we may see God face to face, and indeed we already possess, in light of Christ, a genuine knowledge of who God is in himself as Trinity.

According to this Catholic interpretation of the two testaments, the enlightenment of the Old Testament heals the fallen human being in his knowledge of God and grants Israel a privileged personal knowledge of God as the Lord. The darkness of God recalls his transcendence. Furthermore, the revelation of God's personal identity given to Israel prepares the human race for a future eschatological encounter with God that is more perfect and that manifests the

12. See for example, 1 John 3:2; Rev. 22:5; John 17:24.

inner identity of God to all peoples. From the more ultimate perspective of the New Testament, then, this same rational monotheism prepares man to recognize the *gratuity* of the revelation of the Holy Trinity as something exceeding the capacities of natural human reason. The revelation of God to Israel as the Lord is the precursor to God's perfect manifestation of himself to the human race by means of the Incarnation, passion, and resurrection of Christ as the God of Israel among us. It is knowledge of the Trinity that brings to fulfillment the eschatological motif of the knowledge of God in ancient Israel, and inaugurates the perfect knowledge of the "kingdom of God," the vision of God in the eschatological state.

Universalism of the Old Testament Revelation

Closely related to the first point just mentioned is the question of universalism in the Old Testament revelation of God. Here, the internal tension or paradox of the covenant is evident even from the beginning. In Genesis, Abraham is called into a covenant by God, and through him, an exclusive people is chosen as the elect people of God, but simultaneously, in this very initial seed of the covenant, Abraham is also told that his descendants will become a blessing for "all the nations of the earth."[13] This inner connection between the particularism of Israel (the Torah as the ground of a covenant with one people) and the universal extension of its revelatory significance for all the nations stands at the heart of all Old Testament literature. For example, God the Creator is revealed to Israel in a privileged way, but the nations are also judged as culpable for the errors of their religious constructs and anthropomorphic projections regarding God. The Mosaic law contains universal moral precepts—implicitly but really indicated in the Ten Commandments in particular—that are understood to identify ethical norms for all

---

13. See Gen. 17:1-9, 18:17–18, and 22:18. The citation is from the last of these verses. On the theological consideration of the figure of Abraham and the patriarchs, see R. W. L. Moberly, *Old Testament Theology: Reading the Hebrew Bible as Christian Scripture* (Ada, MI: Baker Academic, 2013), ch. 2.

peoples.[14] One sees, for example, the prophet Amos's appeal to the universality of these principles in his judgment of the nations in Amos 1:1–23.[15] And yet the gentile nations are also said to wander in moral obscurity due in part to their lack of religious enlightenment.[16] The prophets of the monarchical and post-exilic period call the people of Israel to re-instantiate the inner form of the covenant faithfully in new ways, implying God's special historical favor for Israel (Jer. 32:40, 33:22; Ez. 16:60, 37:25–27), but they also promise a time of the universal revelation of God to all the nations, wherein the covenant will be opened to all (Jer. 4:2; Is. 49:6, 56:6; Hag. 2:7; Mal. 1:11).[17] The messianic figure who is denoted in various places in the Old Testament is depicted as the king or suffering priest of the people of Israel in particular, but he is also one in whom the God of Israel is revealed to all the nations (2 Sam. 7:11–16; Ps. 2:7–9, 110:1–4; Is. 53; Dan. 7).[18]

At the center of the covenant is the knowledge of God. The covenant cannot be universalized to all peoples unless the knowledge of God is as well. The people of Israel have received a privileged knowledge of who the Lord is, according to indications of the prophets. But simultaneously, precisely in virtue of the particularity of their covenant, the people of Israel are meant to be a channel of the saving knowledge of God to all peoples. Consequently, their own particular knowledge of God must eventually shine as "a light to the nations," (Is. 42:6) when the covenant made with Israel extends and is opened up to all, so that knowledge is shared with those who previously did

14. For the two canonical lists of the Ten Commandments, see Ex. 20:1–20 and Deut. 5:7–21.

15. See the study of John Barton, *Amos's Oracles Against the Nations* (Cambridge: Cambridge University Press, 2009).

16. Deut. 4:6–8.

17. On the election of Israel and the potential and eventual universality of the covenant, see the thematic historical and theological treatments of Walter Eichrodt, *Theology of the Old Testament*; Horst Dietrich Preuss, *Old Testament Theology*, Vols. I and II, trans. L. G. Perdue (Louisville: Westminster John Knox Press, 1995).

18. On the Old Testament roots of New Testament messianic scriptural interpretation, see Donald H. Juel, *Messianic Exegesis: Christological Interpretation of the Old Testament in Early Christianity* (Waco, TX: Baylor University Press, 2017).

not truly recognize God. This occurs, according to St. Paul, precisely in and through the events of the incarnation, life, death, and resurrection of the Son of God. It is in the historical mystery of Jesus that the knowledge of the God of Israel is made manifest to all the nations.[19] This knowledge is brought to perfection *for Israel* by the fact that the God of Israel has become human and manifested the love and power of God precisely in and through the crucifixion and resurrection of Jesus, who is one in being with God the Father and with the Holy Spirit.[20] In other words, the events of the life, death, and resurrection of Jesus of Nazareth are the occasion for the perfecting of the knowledge of God among the elect people, the Jews, since it is precisely in these conditions that God is manifest as Trinity. But these events are also the occasion for the universal extension of the covenant to all peoples, from Israel to the world, as the God who is the true author of creation is also now revealed definitively to all humanity in the redemptive death and resurrection of Christ, the unique and universal savior of all humanity. The universalism of the covenant present in seed is brought to fulfillment in Christ, but by this very measure, the fulfillment is grounded in the universalism of the revelation of the identity of God the Holy Trinity. Knowledge of the Trinity now appears as the foundation for the universal offer of salvation and is manifest as the deepest wellspring of the covenant of grace.[21] Friendship with the God of Israel is friendship with

19. Consider in this respect Phil. 2:6–12, which refers in 2:10 to Isa. 45:22–23 ("Turn to me and be saved, all the ends of the earth! For I am God, and there is no other.... 'To me every knee shall bow, every tongue shall swear.'"), a prophecy of universal knowledge of the Lord found even among the gentiles. Similarly, see Rom. 14:11.

20. Phil. 2:6–12 affirms that the Old Testament promise of the universal knowledge of God has been brought to fulfillment specifically through the becoming human, suffering, death, and bodily resurrection of Christ, who is the Lord and is one with the God of Israel. See on this Richard Bauckham, "God Crucified," in *Jesus and the God of Israel* (Grand Rapids, MI: Eerdmans, 2008), 1–59, esp. 41–45, which considers the conceptual implications of the evident references to Isa. 45 and 52–53 in Phil. 2:6–12.

21. On the gnoseological character of salvation in Judaism and Christianity, see Ratzinger, "Truth of Christianity?" in *Truth and Tolerance*, 138–61. Aquinas likewise elaborates on the practical and soteriological consequences of the knowledge of the Holy Trinity made available by faith in *ST* I, q. 1, aa. 1 and 6 (on sacred doctrine as both speculative and practical and as oriented toward the vision of God), and in II-II, q. 1–2 on the

the Holy Trinity, and that friendship is made available in Christ to all the nations.

The Question of Eschatological Salvation

Our previous point leads organically to a third. What is God's response to the many serious occasions of natural and moral evil with which history is riddled? How does the creation come to an end? In fire and ashes, futility and meaninglessness, or in divine justice and redemptive glory? The prophets and sacred authors of the Old Testament progressively recognized the need for an eschatological resolution to this question. That is to say, in the course of the history of Israelite prophecy, there is the gradual manifestation of a clear teaching about the fate of the human being after death and about the resurrection from the dead.[22] These teachings emerge in response to the problem of evil as experienced concretely by the people of Israel. The prophets tell us that God will not permit either moral evil or natural death to have the last word regarding the fate of Israel or humanity. Instead, there is a mystery of God's final judgment of the spiritual soul of each human person (the particular judgment) and of the collective community of humanity eschatologically (the general judgment).[23] This teaching is developed in concert with a clear affirmation of the general resurrection, that is, the hope that God will vindicate the martyrs and saints by refashioning their bodies in

---

nature of supernatural faith, which should be seen as the epistemological context for the right understanding of *ST* I-II, q. 1–3 on the orientation of man toward supernatural happiness.

22. See in this respect the historical contextual study of N. T. Wright, *The Resurrection of the Son of God*, 85–206.

23. For earlier views, which present partially contrasting, sometimes searching reflections, see 1 Sam. 28:3–25; Job 19:22–25; Ecc. 2:16–16; Ps. 16:9b–10, 11b–c. On bodily resurrection and universal judgment, see Isa. 26:19, 52–53; Ez. 37:1–4; Dan. 12; 2 Macc. 7. On the day of the Lord and judgment of the nations, see Isa. 2:2–5; Joel 3; Amos 9:11; Zech. 14. On the immortality and spiritual life of the soul and personal judgment after death, see Wis. 3:1–19, 2:3, and 16:13. On the Judaic roots of New Testament eschatology, see the considerations of Joseph Ratzinger, *Eschatology: Death and Eternal Life*, 2nd edition, trans. M. Waldstein (Washington, DC: The Catholic University of America Press, 1988), 80–100.

a glorified state at the end of the ages. This eschatological hope exists in the Old Testament in parallel with the hope for the vindication of Israel as a chosen people before all the rival nations and the glorification of the physical cosmos by God.[24] Beyond suffering, evil, and death, there is a horizon of hope found in God and God's re-creation of the universe, Israel, and the human community. The evident question such claims raise is this: how and when will this eschatological salvation transpire? This existential-historical question leaves the teaching of the Old Testament perched upon a ledge, as it were, awaiting a higher fulfillment or recapitulative resolution that has yet to arrive.

While the Old Testament culminates, historically speaking, with eschatological teaching, the New Testament begins with eschatology. The New Testament kerygma of the apostles and their disciples unfolds historically in the wake of a primal eschatological event, the resurrection of Christ. We might think of this novelty as analogous to that of God's first creation of the world through the historical medium of the Big Bang, from which the physical cosmos unfolds. According to the New Testament, the bodily resurrection of Christ inaugurates a new creation that is currently coming into being. What remains a hope for the final ages in late ancient Judaism becomes the first principle and foundation of the new Christian teaching: the belief that Jesus of Nazareth, who was crucified and truly died, is also truly risen bodily from the dead and elevated by God in both body and soul to a higher state of glorification in which he can die no more. Furthermore, by his grace, this new life of glory is being communicated to members of the Church, the extended mystical body of Christ and people of God.

Significantly, the New Testament teaches that Christ is "the firstborn from the dead," (Col. 1:18) and the "Last Adam" (1 Cor. 15:45)—literally the eschatological man.[25] These teachings suggest

24. See Wright, *The Resurrection of the Son of God*, 121–28 on the national element of many of the texts noted above.

25. See on this topic, Andre Feuillet, *Christologie paulinienne et tradition biblique* (Paris: Desclée, De Brouwer, 1973), 156–80.

that the unique event of the historical resurrection of Christ is pro-
leptic and exemplary. It points us toward the final state of the cosmos
and demonstrates concretely and effectively the promise by God of
his intention to raise the dead and refashion the human race after the
pattern established by Christ. "For if we have been united with him
in a death like his, we shall certainly be united with him in a resurrection like his" (Rom. 6:5). If God has raised Jesus from the dead and
glorified his human body and soul, then the eschatological prophecies of the Old Testament are true.[26] Furthermore, if Jesus is himself
God made man, then it is also the case that God has truly identified
with us in our suffering and death by making himself freely subject
to human evil. He did so not in order to enshrine these conditions
of suffering with moral legitimacy but, on the contrary, to employ
his power and mercy to bring good even out of the conditions of the
fallen human race, wherein we are subject to evil.[27] In so doing, he
reveals himself as the Savior of the human race, but he also reveals
his own inner mystery of Trinitarian life and his love and mercy for
human beings. Even from within the darkest hour of human suffering at the Cross, God can communicate eternal life and make manifest his own identity as God the Trinity.

If this is the case, then the mystery of the Holy Trinity is also an
eschatological mystery. It is a mystery about the end of the world and
the final truth of man and the cosmos. In the end times, the Trinity
will save and re-create the human race and even the physical world as
we know it. This message stands in fundamental continuity with the
monotheism of the Old Testament, because it is concerned with the
truth about the God of Israel, the Creator and Savior, in his response
to evil, suffering, and death. It is only God the Creator who can truly

26. See the Pauline logic to this effect in 1 Cor. 15:1–57, which references or alludes to
Isa. 22:13, 25:8, 53:1–2; Ps. 16:10, 8:6; Gen. 2:7; Hos. 13:14.

27. I am alluding here to the Augustinian idea that evil is an ontological privation of
the natural good, not a good in itself, but that God may make use of such evils even to
our benefit. See this idea in *City of God*, XI, c. 18, with reference to the fallen angels and
the sanctification of human beings. Augustine references in this regard 2 Cor. 6:7–10 and
Sir. 33:15.

effectuate a divine victory over evil by the all-powerful re-creation and glorification of his creation, a process that has been inaugurated already in the bodily resurrection of Jesus Christ. If Christ is truly raised from the dead, then there is an eschatological destiny of both the body and soul of each human person and of the cosmos more generally. But by the same measure, if Christ is raised from the dead, then God is also the one God of Israel, who is indeed the Holy Trinity, revealed to us in and through the resurrection of Christ.

NEW TESTAMENT TRINITARIAN FULFILLMENT OF FIRST TESTAMENT THEOLOGICAL ASPIRATIONS

Let us note how the three points of continuity-amidst-tension we noted above correspond to three fundamental mysteries of the life of Christ. The problem of the *intimate knowledge* of God in the Old Testament is resolved through the manifestation of the mystery of the Trinity. This manifestation correlates chiefly with the mystery of the Incarnation. It is because God the eternal Word of the Father has become human and lived a human life among us that we have come to know the Father, the Word, and the Holy Spirit. The Incarnation of God in history reveals the inner life of God as Trinity and in doing so brings the monotheism of the Old Testament into Trinitarian focus.

The problem of *universalism* from the Old Testament is resolved especially through Christ's redemptive atonement, because it is his suffering and death that open and extend the covenant of Israel to all. Christ freely accepts suffering and death out of love for the human race, and he does so animated by a grace and innocence proper to the New Adam. Consequently, if the true knowledge of God is given to all in virtue of the Incarnation, its communication is brought to perfection in and through the crucifixion of Christ as a perfect expression of Trinitarian revelation. It is from the Cross above all that Israel becomes a light to the nations and the Word of the Father "speaks" to all the world the message of mercy and reconciliation.

The problem of *eschatological hope* in the Old Testament is resolved by the bodily resurrection and glorification of Christ on Easter night, so that what was promised by prophecy in the first covenant comes to fulfilment and manifestation in the new era of Christ resurrected and glorified in body and soul. The evil of human history is overcome or transcended definitively in the new creation inaugurated by this mystery. Behind this novelty there stands the activity and love of the God of Israel who has the power to make all things new. The mystery of the resurrection of Jesus reveals the God of Israel as the Trinity, the Father of hidden and transcendent love, who acts in his Son and in his Spirit. It is the God of love alone who can save the human race and who has inaugurated the new creation in the resurrection of Christ. We might say that the resurrection of Christ *confirms and perfects* the knowledge of God made possible by the Incarnation and the crucifixion.

It is of central importance to note from the start, then, that Trinitarian theology is monotheistic above all for *ontological* reasons rather than soteriological or functional reasons. It is because of who Jesus is—the eternal Son of God made man—that he is the Savior of the human race and can reveal to us who God truly is.[28] The God who is revealed in the New Testament is Father, Son, and Holy Spirit and also the one God of Israel. Therefore, the persons of the Trinity are one in being.[29] Indeed, as we shall see, the basic logic of the

28. John 8:28: "When you *lift up* the Son of Man then you will know that *I am*." As C. H. Dodd argued, the author of the fourth Gospel systematically transfers the characteristics and functions assigned by the Synoptic authors to the glorified Son of Man from the exalted state of the resurrection to the crucifixion event itself. See C. H. Dodd, *The Fourth Gospel* (Cambridge: Cambridge University Press, 1963), 432–43. However, it is also clear that the one revealed at the Cross is the pre-existent *Logos* who also possesses the plenitude of existence as "He who is." See also John 6:41, 8:12, and 8:58. I take it that this Johannine perspective on the being of Christ remains normative for Christian theology.

29. So for example, Jesus states in John 10:30, "I and the Father are one," clearly an echo of Deut. 6:4: "Hear, O Israel: The Lord our God is one Lord." The being and unity of God the Father are the being and unity of the Son and *Logos*, who is God from God. The Spirit who proceeds from the Father and the Son (John 15:26–27) is also he who is able to give eternal life to those to whom he is sent (John 3:5–6) which implies that he also is one with the Father and the Son as God.

New Testament entails that God the Holy Trinity is the unique Creator of the world. All these truths are ontological truths about the very identity of God.

Second, however, it is also essential to note that the understanding of Trinitarian belief as monotheistic is of preeminent importance for *soteriological* reasons. The Trinitarian truth about God provides profound responses to fundamental questions posed by the advent of Old Testament monotheism, and it does so in ways that address the human need for salvation. Who truly is God? Do God's activity and his offer of salvation extend in some way to all? Is God able and willing to save us from evil, and can we resolve the enigmas that surround questions of eschatology and the life that comes after bodily death? The Trinitarian answers to these questions established in Christ are marked at their core by a monotheistic content of Israelite derivation, carried over integrally and recapitulated anew in New Testament teaching. Finally, then, we can also say the inverse: not only does Trinitarianism depend on monotheism, but the historical fate of monotheism is tied in integral ways to the revelation of the Trinity. According to the New Testament claims noted above, Trinitarian revelation perfects our understanding of monotheism, both ontologically and soteriologically. It is because of the Incarnation, crucifixion, and resurrection of Christ that we know intimately by grace who God is, of God's true intention to offer all human beings the possibility of salvation, and of God's capacity and willingness to overcome evil through the eschatological re-creation of the world.[30] The truth about the Trinity is also the ultimate truth about the one God of Israel. The Trinity is God in his unique being and agency, revealed definitively in Christ.

---

30. This theme of soteriological revelation of the truth about God is found in Paul in Phil. 2:9–11, where Paul refers to Isa. 45:23, teaching that the resurrection of Christ is seen to be the manifestation to all the gentile nations that the God of Israel, the one true God, has saved humanity through the Incarnation, death, and resurrection of Christ. See likewise Rom. 1:4, 14:11; 1 Cor. 1:23–24, 15:20–24.

The Implicit "Hebraic Trinitarianism"
of the Historical Jesus

What I have argued above clearly presupposes that the historical Jesus of Nazareth truly was and is both God and man, a teaching of
the New Testament. However, if this claim is true, then it follows
that the historical Jesus made his identity manifest in some way by
his actions and words, at least implicitly if not overtly. How then
was the mystery of the Trinity revealed, first by Christ himself and
subsequently in the teachings of the apostolic community in the
writings of the New Testament? Does the basic doctrine of the Trinity originate with Jesus of Nazareth himself, as he is portrayed by
the four canonical gospels? If so, what is the form of this embryonic
"Trinitarianism" of Jesus? In treating this subject I will presuppose
that the four canonical gospels contain historically reliable information about Jesus. I am not adopting this viewpoint uncritically and
am presupposing, on the contrary, that excellent historical-critical
arguments can be given for the historical reliability of the four canonical gospels.[31] Nevertheless, the aim of this chapter is to consider the internal logic and coherence of Trinitarian *revelation*, not
to prove by rational demonstration that the New Testament portraits of Christ must be accepted on historical-critical terms, nor
even that it is rationally permissible to believe in the historical Jesus
as the gospels portray him. The former demonstration, compelling

31. Although they do not agree on all points of methodology or content, and one
may reasonably dispute various claims of each, the following authors do present reasonable historical portraits of Jesus within his historical context, globally compatible
with Christian faith: Pierre Benoit, *Jesus and the Gospels*, vols. 1 and 2, trans. B. Weatherhead (London: Herder and Darton, Longman and Todd, 1973 and 1974); Ben Witherington III, *The Christology of Jesus* (Minneapolis: Augsburg Fortress Press, 1990); Rudolf
Schnackenburg, *Jesus in the Gospels: A Biblical Christology*, trans. O. C. Dean (Louisville,
KY: Westminster John Knox Press, 1995); N. T. Wright, *Jesus and the Victory of God*;
Martin Hengel and Anna Maria Schwemer, *Jesus und das Judentum (Geschichte des frühen
Christentums*, Band 1 (Tübingen: Mohr Siebeck, 2007); Dale C. Allison, *Constructing Je-
sus: Memory, Imagination and History* (Grand Rapids, MI: Baker Academic, 2010); Ger-
hard Lohfink, *Jesus of Nazareth: What He Wanted, Who He Was*, trans. L. M. Maloney
(Collegeville, MN: Michael Glazier, 2015).

rational proof of the divine identity of Jesus, is not possible, precisely because our knowledge of Christ's divine identity is supernatural in character and made possible only by the illumination of faith that comes from beyond the horizon of natural human reasoning. The latter form of argument (for the rational warrant of the New Testament teaching on Christ) is probabilistic in character, based on historical likelihoods, and cannot of itself procure the grace of faith.[32] When conducted well, it allows one to see that theological study of Christ in the gospels is fully compatible with modern historical-critical consideration of the historical Jesus.[33] However, that kind of project is not what is undertaken in this book. Here we should seek to consider then only the theological foundations for belief in the Trinity as conveyed by Jesus himself as he is depicted historically in the primal apostolic reports of the Church.

Imminent Eschatology of Jesus

Let us recapitulate the three themes mentioned above with regard to the dynamic fulfillment of the Old Testament by the New, but in inverse order: eschatology, universalism, and true knowledge of

32. I have developed this argument in *The Incarnate Lord: A Thomistic Study in Christology* (Washington, DC: The Catholic University of America Press, 2015), in the "prolegomena" of that book, based on the Catholic Church's insistence on the supernatural character of the grace of knowledge by faith and its application to modern historiography by the French Dominican theologian, Ambroise Gardeil in *La crédibilité et l'apologétique* (Paris: J. Gabalda et Fils, 1928) and *Le donné révélé et la théologie*, 2nd ed. (Paris: Cerf, 1932), esp. 196–223.

33. See Second Vatican Council, *Dei Verbum*, § 19:

Holy Mother Church has firmly and with absolute constancy held, and continues to hold, that the four Gospels just named, whose historical character the Church unhesitatingly asserts, faithfully hand on what Jesus Christ, while living among men, really did and taught for their eternal salvation until the day He was taken up into heaven (see Acts 1:1). [*Denzinger*, 4226.]

The Church affirms doctrinally as a truth of *supernatural faith* that the New Testament portraits of Christ are grounded in history. In addition, the majority of modern Catholic theologians also maintain that core events of Christ's life, including his miracles, death by crucifixion, and historical resurrection apparitions to the apostles, can be shown by natural reason to be events grounded in history. See on this last point Walberg, *Revelation as Testimony*.

the divine identity. The claims of the historical Jesus are, as depicted in the gospels, nothing else if not eschatological in tone and orientation. In what way they are eschatological is of course a famously controversial subject.[34] My presupposition here is that Jesus of
Nazareth considered himself to be in some way the final emissary
of God inaugurating a climatic and definitive age of eschatological
fulfillment.

Consider in this respect several key traits of Jesus' teaching. First,
Jesus of Nazareth, in all four canonical gospels, speaks frequently of
the "kingdom of God," referring to it in a variety of ways: in parables,

34. There is an influential and prominent tradition in modern exegesis that runs
from early figures like Samuel Reimarus and Franz Overbeck to Albert Schweitzer to E.
P. Sanders that, in spite of all its internal variations, depicts Jesus of Nazareth primarily as an apocalyptic prophet who confronted both Jewish and Roman authorities and
was subject to radical disappointment in regard to his imminent eschatological expecta-
tions. It seems to me that this interpretive stance is perennially afflicted by an artificially
anti-supernaturalist and historicist portrait of human consciousness in general (characteristic of Neo-Kantianism) and of Jesus in particular, such that Jesus is seen as virtually
incapable of thinking in universal terms that transcend his own particular historical moment or of addressing the meaning of his own existence to all men. However, the gospels
depict him as doing this regularly within his historical context. Moreover, the proponents
of this reductive apocalyptic stance typically practice a performative contradiction at the
level of methodology, since they typically ascribe universalist Christological and eschatological thinking to Paul and the first generation of Christians after Jesus, who wrote
the gospels with a universal message to all in mind, while they deny that Jesus himself,
who lived in the same epoch, could have held such universal views of himself. Why not?
Presumably if he did, this would provide the simplest rational and historical explanation
of the genesis of early Christian views about Jesus held by his earliest followers. Modern Christian thinkers like Wolfhart Pannenberg [see *Jesus God and Man*, 2nd ed., trans.
L. L. Wilkins, D. A. Priebe (Philadelphia: Westminster Press, 1968)] and Walter Kasper
[see *Jesus the Christ*, trans. V. Green (London: Burns & Oates, 1976)] have made use of
the "limited horizon" view of Jesus as a self-intending eschatological prophet even while
holding to his divinity and bodily resurrection after death (in vindication of his mission).
They interpret his limited horizon of understanding of his mission within the context of a
larger kenotic movement of Christology, in which God takes on the natural limits of human forms of understanding within history. While their general motives are commend-
able, this theological strategy seems to me to be unnecessary and ultimately unwarranted.
The four canonical gospels each depict the historical Jesus as having a "high" understanding of his identity, soteriological mission and its ecclesiological and eschatological horizons. See in this respect the helpful and balanced perspective of the 1985 International
Theological Commission document, "The Consciousness of Christ concerning Himself
and His Mission," available at www.vatican.va.

as made present by his miracles, as denoting the inner meaning of his own mission and aims, in exorcisms, and in prophetic utterances about its future advent.[35] There is a significant thematic correspondence in the New Testament between diverse textual and authorial sources, presenting us with various historical incidents in the life of Jesus, that suggests in coordinated ways that his self-understanding was eschatological in nature. His language in these contexts is frequently "kingdom-centered." By appeal to this principle of correspondence, then, it seems reasonable to admit that the idea of the kingdom is central to Jesus' self-understanding.[36] Furthermore, his words denote the realization of the very presence of the God of Israel in Jesus' ministry; in his life and mission Jesus seeks to announce and render present the kingdom of God. This idea seemingly implies that Jesus is in some real sense a king (messiah or Christ) since a kingdom implies a monarch, *and* that Jesus represents the God of Israel who is the one true King of Israel, by being his emissary.[37] It also implies that Jesus takes his own ministry to be one that inaugurates the kingdom, which is eschatological in nature. The kingdom is told in parables, in which Jesus frequently alludes to his own authority and plays a central role as the protagonist of the parable who ushers in the end times.[38] The kingdom is happening through the miracles, which fulfill in particular the Isaian prophecies of the end

35. For examples of parables of the kingdom, see Mark 4:1–20, 4:26–29; Matt. 13:24–52; Luke 13:18–19. For miracles denoting the kingdom, see Matt. 4:23, 9:35. For teachings on the kingdom as denoting Jesus' mission and identity, see Matt. 3:2, 5:1–10, 6:10; Luke 4:43, 8:1, 10:9, 17:21; John 3:5, 18:36. For exorcisms as signs of the kingdom, see Mark 3:22–27; Matt. 12:28; Luke 11:20. For future and eschatological prophecies linked to the kingdom, see Matt. 5:20, 8:11–12, 16:28, 21:43, 24:14, 25:31–46, 26:29; Luke 22:29–30; Acts 1:6.

36. See the historical and textual argument to this effect by John P. Meier in *A Marginal Jew: Rethinking the Historical Jesus, Volume II: Mentor, Message, and Miracles* (New Haven, CT: Yale University Press, 1994), 239–73.

37. See the suggestive argumentation of N. T. Wright in *Jesus and the Victory of God*, 477–653.

38. Aspects of C. H. Dodd, *The Parables of the Kingdom* (New York: Charles Scribner's Sons, 1961) remain entirely valid on this point. There is a kind of realized eschatology unfolding in the telling of the parables, which signify the reality coming into being in virtue of the presence and activity of Jesus Christ.

times.[39] The kingdom is denoted by the exorcisms of Christ, which signify publicly that he is able to cast out the angelic powers that assault humanity and oppose God.[40]

Second, and correspondingly, Jesus refers to himself as the "Son of Man" as a most typical form of self-designation.[41] This enigmatic title seems purposefully intended to conceal as well as reveal who Jesus of Nazareth is. It seemingly has a double designation. It refers to Adam: Jesus is a descendent of the original human being, a son of Adam, and is therefore "human." The term thus refers to the common humanity that Jesus shares with us. Presumably this is why St. Paul refers to Christ in his letters as the "new Adam," translating the term of Jesus into one that his Hellenistic audience can understand more readily. Jesus resurrected represents the re-creation of humanity. The title "Son of Man" also seemingly refers to a typology in Daniel 7, an eschatological messiah figure who ushers in the new and final era of Israel and of the new creation. In Matthew's Gospel, Jesus repeatedly speaks of the eschatological judgment that will be enacted as that of the "Son of Man" who partakes of the authority of

39. See the argument of N. T. Wright in *Jesus and the Victory of God*, 198–243.

40. E. P. Sanders articulates a historical argument for this view of Jesus in *Jesus and Judaism* (Philadelphia: Fortress Press, 1985), 133–36.

41. The Son of Man sayings are of various kinds. (1) Authority claims: Jesus claims that the Son of Man has authority over the Sabbath and the authority to forgive sins. (See, for example, Mark 2:1–9.) (2) Suffering and death predictions: Jesus prophesies the death of the Son of Man as the key to the divine economy. (See, for example, the three foretellings of the Passion of the Son of Man in Mark: 8:31, 9:30-32, and 10:32–34.) In Mark 10:45, Jesus depicts the Son of Man as the Suffering Servant from Isa. 53, as well as the exalted figure of Dan. 7, uniting the two images; the Son of man is exalted in and through the service of suffering on behalf of the many. (3) Eschatological judgment of the Son of Man: The Son of Man is he who will sit in judgment over the nations, who will return in the glory of his Father (Mark 13:26). How one reacts to the Son of Man will also affect how one is judged in light of God. (Mark 8:38: "For whoever is ashamed of me and of my words in this adulterous and sinful generation, of him will the Son of man also be ashamed, when he comes in the glory of *his Father* with the holy angels" [emphasis added].) In the face of his imminent execution, according to Mark, Jesus claimed to be this exalted figure actually (or soon to be) seated at the right hand of the Father (Mark 14:62). On these broad divisions of the sayings, see Ben Witherington III, *The Many Faces of Jesus: The Christologies of the New Testament and Beyond* (New York: Crossroad, 1995), 55.

205

---

his Father, the God of Israel, and in which he (the Son of Man) will judge the nations. In Mark's Gospel, prior to his judgment by the high priest and subsequent execution, Jesus refers to himself as the "Son of Man" who will be seated on high, in power (Mark 14:62), referring to himself by use of the messianic Psalm 110, suggesting that his own death and resurrection will bring about the fulfillment of the Danielic prophecy (Dan. 7:13–14). It is by his death and resurrection that the Son of Man will enter into his reign. This is similar to the idea we find presented in Mark and Luke as they depict successive prophecies by Jesus of the Son of Man's crucifixion.[42] So too we find in John's Gospel the characteristically Johannine claim that the Son of Man will be exalted already even on the Cross and that he will in turn be glorified subsequent to his own death.[43]

To this structure of predictions of the in-breaking of the eschatological kingdom, there correspond Christ's historical appearances after his bodily resurrection, confirming and definitively inaugurating the kingdom that he had foretold. This is the basic claim of the New Testament: Jesus Christ confirmed the inauguration of his kingdom to his apostles after his bodily resurrection.[44] Or rather, the bodily resurrection of Jesus from among the dead manifests to the disciples that the end times have already begun now, even in the midst of history. St. Paul in 1 Cor. 15:4–5 tells us that Christ appeared first to Peter and the twelve and then to five hundred men at one time, confirming the reality of his bodily resurrection. In Luke's Gospel, Christ is depicted on the road to Emmaus after his resurrection, appearing to two disciples to whom he explains that his crucifixion and death were part of the divine economy willed by God for the redemption of the human race, and he makes manifest his hidden identity to them "in the breaking of the bread," an apparition with evident Eucharistic denotations.[45] Jesus signals that the kingdom of

---

42. Mark 8:31, 9:30,10:32; Luke 9:22, 9:44, 18:31.

43. John 3:14, 8:28, 10:17–18, 12:23, 13:31.

44. Acts 1:3: "To them he presented himself alive after his passion by many proofs, appearing to them during forty days, and speaking of the kingdom of God."

45. Luke 24:13–35. The quotation is from v. 35.

God is already present in the midst of the Church, in the Eucharist that contains the mysterious presence of his true body and blood. In Acts, the resurrected Christ teaches the apostles to await the final era of the kingdom of his Father (Acts 1:6–8). Similarly, in John's Gospel, the resurrected Christ teaches the apostles on Easter night that he is alive and that they now have the power to absolve sins with his authority.[46] My point here is not to examine diachronically each apparition narrative nor even to defend critically the historicity of the bodily resurrection in the face of skeptical objections but merely to demonstrate the *internal logic* of the eschatology of the historical Jesus as it is ascribed to him by the New Testament authors, both before and after his death, since these two together form a coherent whole and claim to manifest a divine logic of redemption underlying the coherence of the revelation itself.[47] Behind this stands the monotheism of the Trinitarian faith, since Jesus claims as the Son of God to inaugurate the kingdom of his Father, in the Spirit, a point that I will return to shortly.

Implicit Universalism of the Covenant of Israel

As depicted in the New Testament, Jesus of Nazareth also claims to open the covenant of Israel to the inclusion of peoples from the gentile nations, thus universalizing the covenant in a radical way. This idea is related to the death of Jesus, which is foretold by him in

46. John 20:19–23:

On the evening of that day, the first day of the week, the doors being shut where the disciples were, for fear of the Jews, Jesus came and stood among them and said to them, "Peace be with you." When he had said this, he showed them his hands and his side. Then the disciples were glad when they saw the Lord. Jesus said to them again, "Peace be with you. As the Father has sent me, even so I send you." And when he had said this, he breathed on them, and said to them, "Receive the Holy Spirit. If you forgive the sins of any, they are forgiven; if you retain the sins of any, they are retained."

47. For a sound modern examination of the historicity of the bodily resurrection of Jesus, see N. T. Wright, *The Resurrection of the Son of God*. For theological considerations regarding the bodily resurrection of Jesus, see White, *The Incarnate Lord: A Study in Thomistic Christology*, ch. 10, "The Ontology of the Resurrection."

all four gospels as a redemptive or atoning event, one that will allow or facilitate universal inclusion into the covenant.[48]

We see this paradigmatically first in the ways Jesus is depicted as announcing or foretelling his death and by the significance he ascribes to the event. Mark 10:45, for example, depicts Jesus as affirming that "the Son of man also came not to be served but to serve, and to give his life as a ransom for many." The phrase recalls Isaiah 53:11–12, an image of the suffering servant who gives his life for "the many" (a Semitic literary meme denoting "the multitude" or "all"), and Jesus weds this image with that of the Son of Man in Daniel 7.[49] In other words, the exalted eschatological messianic figure of Daniel 7 whom "all the nations serve" has in fact come "not to be served" but to be the suffering servant and the redeemer of the nations. This royal figure of the kingdom will be "exalted," as Psalm 110 and Daniel 7 foretell of the messiah, but in a paradoxical way. His messianic exaltation will occur not by means of an earthly kingdom in this life and temporal rule over gentile nations but in the life of the resurrection. The death of Christ and his resurrection save the nations, and this is the privileged occasion for the extension of the covenant from Israel to all peoples.[50]

We see this idea exemplified in another way by the prediction Christ makes of his own death in the context of the Eucharistic institution. In the three narratives of the synoptic gospels, Christ speaks about his forthcoming death the night before he dies within the context of the Eucharist. According to St. Matthew (Matt. 26:26–29):

Now as they were eating, Jesus took bread, and blessed, and broke it, and gave it to the disciples and said, "Take, eat; this is my body." And he took a cup, and when he had given thanks he gave it to them, saying, "Drink of it, all of you; for this is my blood of the covenant, which is poured out for

48. See the historical and textual study of Martin Hengel, *Atonement: The Origins of the Doctrine of the New Testament*, trans. J. Bowden (Philadelphia: Fortress Press, 1981).

49. Some modern Protestant exegetes like Morna Hooker and C. K. Barrett have disputed this connection of the servant of Isa. 53 and the messiah of Dan. 7 in Mark 10:45, but I find their arguments textually implausible.

50. This is of course the theological argument of the Letter to the Hebrews.

many for the forgiveness of sins. I tell you I shall not drink again of this fruit of the vine until that day when I drink it new with you in my Father's kingdom."

Here Jesus compares his own death to the primordial sacrifice of Ex. 24:8. There Moses is depicted sprinkling the blood of sacrifice at Mount Sinai over the people, which he calls the "blood of the covenant," so as to ratify the original covenant of God with Israel. In claiming to recapitulate this original sacrifice, now with twelve apostles representing the original twelve tribes, Jesus of Nazareth seems clearly to be asserting that his death is the foundational sacrifice of the covenant. In addition, by instituting the sacraments of baptism and the Eucharist, he provides concrete means for incorporating gentiles into the covenant that do not depend on Hebraic descent, circumcision, or the ceremonial laws of the Torah. This is why his actions are indeed quite radical and inevitably relativize the Torah system of sacrifices that precedes him, arguably by fulfilling them in such a way as to sublimate and supersede them.

It is noteworthy in this respect that Jesus of Nazareth was especially controversial because of his cryptic prophetic claims that the Temple would be destroyed and that he would, in a mysterious sense, replace the Temple himself through his bodily death and resurrection.[51] This idea is profoundly coherent with those denoted above. The Temple was the epicenter of the practice of the Old Testament ceremonial law, which was grounded above all in the divinely instituted system of sacrifices depicted in Exodus and Leviticus and conducted in Christ's own time as the most essential religious practice of the life of the people of Israel. This system of sacrifices was of course restricted to the elect people who alone were permitted access to the Temple and who alone were obliged to perform the rituals of offering prescribed by the Mosaic law. Precisely by claiming to bring to fulfillment, sublimate, and supersede the use of these rites,

51. On Jesus' body and person in a sense replacing the Temple, see John 2:14–22; Mark 13:1–2, 14:58, 15:29, 38. See the developed argument on this point by N. T. Wright, *Jesus and the Victory of God*, 405–27, 510–18.

including the use of the temple itself as a locus of sacrifice, Jesus also claimed to open the covenant to all peoples. This seems to be the idea that is at the heart of his provocative prophetic gesture in the "pavilion to the gentiles," where the money-changers were present and where he overturned the tables that existed for the exchange of Roman coinage into Israelite coinage (Mark 11:15–17). His gesture suggests prophetically that with his death, the system of sacrifices is now being broken or interrupted, and those who formerly were not included in the covenant (that is, the gentiles) will now have a way of participating in the covenant of the people of God.[52]

Unsurprisingly we find the same idea in the early Christian community. St. Paul sees the death of Christ as the centerpiece of salvation history, the principle of atonement and reconciliation for the whole human race.[53] The author of the Letter to the Hebrews sees in the death of Christ a unique and definitive sacrifice, wherein the first covenant ceases to have its legal mandate and the second covenant in the blood of Christ is inaugurated for the Church and the whole human race.[54] The First Letter of Peter sees in Christ's death the fulfillment of Old Testament prophetic types and depicts Christ as the suffering servant, who is the final and definitive agent of redemption for the whole human race.[55] The First Letter of John notes that Christ is a "paraclete," or legal advocate, who may render all human beings just in virtue of the unique holiness and justice of his unique death.[56] The point of making these observations is to show that according to the logic of the New Testament, the death of

52. Consider here the argument of Bruce D. Chilton and Craig A. Evans in *Jesus in Context: Temple, Purity, and Restoration* (Leiden: Brill, 1997) and N. T. Wright, *Jesus and the Victory of God*, 413–27.

53. See, for example, 1 Thess. 5:10; 1 Cor. 8:11, 15:3; 2 Cor. 5:14; Gal. 1:4; Rom. 5:6–8.

54. Hebrews 5 and 9-10. See Albert Vanhoye, *La lettre aux Hébreux. Jésus-Christ, médiateur d'une nouvelle alliance* (Paris: Declée, 2002).

55. 1 Pet. 1:1–2 and 19, which echo Ex. 24:8, 12:5, Lev. 1:10, and 1 Pet. 2:24, which echoes Isa. 53:11–12.

56. 1 John 2:1–2: "My little children, I am writing this to you so that you may not sin; but if any one does sin, we have an advocate with the Father, Jesus Christ the righteous; and he is the expiation for our sins, and not for ours only but also for the sins of the whole world."

Christ is central to the universalization of the covenant. As we will note below, this feature of New Testament teaching is also grounded in the more fundamental affirmation of Trinitarian monotheism.

Divine Identity: Jesus' Self-Identification with the God of Israel

In the four canonical gospels, Jesus of Nazareth not only depicts himself as God's eschatological agent and as one who universalizes the covenant but also as a person who is fundamentally one in being with the God of Israel. This claim is manifest in a number of ways, some implicit and some more overt. We can consider several of them here briefly.

First, there is Christ's own use of the divine name from Exodus 3:14–15 to designate himself as being one with the God of Israel. This "divine name" theology is most apparent in the Gospel of John, where Jesus employs the name to denote himself as "I am he who is," that is to say as one who *is* God.[57] Likewise, Christ claims in this Gospel to be one with the Father and to pre-exist the elect people as one who was even before the time of Abraham in virtue of his

---

57. John 8:24: "I told you that you would die in your sins, for you will die in your sins unless you believe that I am he." John 8:28: "When you have lifted up the Son of man, then you will know that I am he." John 10:38: "[T]he Father is in me and I am in the Father." The *ego eimi* of the Greek text here echoes "I am he who is" of Ex. 3:14–15. On the divine name given to Jesus in the Gospel of John, see Hurtado, *Lord Jesus Christ*, 370–73. One may object that this Gospel differs from the synoptics and that the high claims Christ makes about himself in John cannot be historical in nature. We should recognize that the Gospel does have a stylistic originality and that the words of Christ are interpreted and presented there in a post-paschal context meant to instruct the early Church. Nevertheless, it seems to me entirely feasible to believe that the historical Jesus attributed to himself titles and images from the Hebrew scriptures, including not only Son of Man, suffering servant, Son of God, or Messiah, but also "I Am." In the course of doing so, he gave these terms new inflections and meanings based in his own life and activity. It is this significance that the apostolic authors were in turn inspired to identify and draw out in their teaching and writing. See on this point *Dei Verbum*, §§ 17–20. On the historicity of the portrait of Christ in the Gospel of John, see Marie-Joseph Lagrange, *Évangile selon saint Jean (Études bibliques)* (Paris, Gabalda, 1925); Paul N. Anderson, *The Fourth Gospel and the Quest for Jesus: Modern Foundations Reconsidered* (Edinburgh: T & T Clark, 2008); Richard Bauckham, *Gospel of Glory: Major Themes in Johannine Theology* (Grand Rapids, MI: Baker Academic, 2015), 185–202.

divine identity.[58] In a convergent sense, Jesus speaks in John 17:6 and 26 of the Son having made manifest "the name" of the Father, as if the traditional name of God from the Old Testament (YHWH) has been revealed in the person of the Son, in Jesus himself. (We find a similar theology of the divine name in Paul in Philippians 2:6, as we will return to below.) In Mark's Gospel, Jesus self-designates twice by reference to the phrase "I Am," (*ego eimi* in Mark's Greek phrase) each time in tandem with an assertion of his own identity, once in a storm on the Sea of Galilee and once during his trial before the high priest just prior to his death.[59] Matthew's Gospel shows the historical Jesus *after* the resurrection re-designating the divine name in Trinitarian terms: "Go therefore and make disciples of all nations, baptizing them in the name of the Father and of the Son and of the Holy Spirit" (Matt. 28:19).[60] Based on these Biblical typologies derived from Christ, the Catholic Church claims traditionally that the name of the Holy Trinity is itself the recapitulation of the Old Testament name for God.[61]

Second, Jesus of Nazareth ascribes to himself an authority that surpasses that of all the previous prophets and in doing so suggests that his mission brings their teachings to fulfillment. This claim suggests an authority akin to or identical with that of the God of Israel. This is evident in the so-called "sermon on the mountain" discourse in Matthew 5–7, where Jesus ascends a mountain

58. John 10:30: "I and the Father are one." John 8:58: "Truly, truly, I say to you, before Abraham was, I am."

59. Mark 6:50: "Take heart, I am; have no fear" (translation modified). Mark 14:62: "And Jesus said, 'I am; and you will see the Son of man seated at the right hand of Power, and coming with the clouds of heaven.'"

60. For a more extensive treatment of Matthew's divine name theology, see Michael Patrick Barber, *The Historical Jesus and the Temple: Memory, Methodology, and the Gospel of Matthew* (Cambridge: Cambridge University Press, 2023).

61. *Catechism of the Catholic Church*, § 233: "Christians are baptized in the *name* of the Father and of the Son and of the Holy Spirit: not in their *names*, for there is only one God, the almighty Father, his only Son and the Holy Spirit: the Most Holy Trinity." The Catechism cites in this regard the Profession of faith of Pope Vigilius I from AD 552 affirming this teaching regarding the divine name as a definitive expression of the Church's faith.

in Galilee, a typological representation of Sinai, and then offers a re-interpretation of the Torah in the form of the beatitudes, ascribing to himself the authority to stand above and perfect the law of Sinai, analogous to the lawgiver (YHWH), who originally addressed the twelve tribes at Sinai (Matt. 5:21–22): "You have heard that it was said to the men of old, 'You shall not kill; and whoever kills shall be liable to judgment.' But I say to you that every one who is angry with his brother shall be liable to judgment; whoever insults his brother shall be liable to the council, and whoever says, 'You fool!' shall be liable to the hell of fire." Similarly Jesus of Nazareth claims in Mark 2:2–12 and v. 28 to have authority as the Son of Man over the interpretation of the law. He likewise claims the authority to heal on the Sabbath by virtue of his Sonship and unity with the Father in John 5:10–21. In contrast to some of the pharisaic traditions of legal interpretation, he claims to have final and authoritative interpretations of the law, seemingly as one who fulfills and surpasses the prophets of the Old Testament.[62]

Third, and relatedly, Jesus ascribes to himself the title of "Son" and "the Son" in relation to God, whom he denotes as "my Father" and "the Father" (Mark 13:32; John 5:19). This title is at once ontological and functional.[63] That is to say, the Son is he who reveals the Father, because he has a pre-existent, ontological relationship with the Father. The Son is one in being with the Father (John 10:30). At the same time, the Son is the one sent to Israel (Matt. 15:24) or sent into the world (John 5:30, 10:36) to reveal God as the Father and to bring the economy of salvation to its final achievement. This latter idea is evident in Jesus' synoptic parable of the king and the landowners, in which the prophets of the Old Testament are depicted as emissaries of a king sent by the landowner to the tenants—the people of Israel—who in turn ignore or mistreat the servants. However, the king at last sends his Son, whom the tenants in turn kill in order to take the

---

62. See in this respect Matt. 12:40–42, 21:33–46.

63. See the study of Martin Hengel, *The Son of God: The Origin of Christology and the History of Jewish-Hellenistic Religion*, trans. J. Bowden (London: SCM Press, 2012).

land for themselves (Matt. 21:33–36). This parable is a poignant witness to Jesus' filial self-awareness and the unique status that he claims as Son, as well as the exclusive role that he claims to have in the divine economy. This unique identity of Jesus as the Son is likewise depicted by Matthew's Gospel in relational terms. Jesus has a unique knowledge of the Father, because he has a unique relation ontologically to the Father (Matt. 11:27): "No one knows the Son except the Father, and no one knows the Father except the Son and any one to whom the Son chooses to reveal him." Sonship and Fatherhood characterize the relation of Christ to the Father and of the Father to Christ. Along the same lines, Christ's Aramaic term for God as father, *abba* (Mark 14:36), was clearly transmitted to and employed by the early Christian community, who seemingly made use of the term in purposeful imitation of Christ. They did this in Aramaic even though the community spoke Greek (Rom. 8:15; Gal. 4:6), a testimony to their intentional material imitation of Christ and to the idea that Jesus is the unique, natural Son of God who communicated to them the gift of adoptive sonship by grace (Gal. 4:1–7).

Fourth, the miracles of Jesus are depicted in the gospels as something he can do because he wishes to, suggesting that there resides in him, in addition to his human free will, a divine power and volition, expressive of the will he shares with the Father and the Holy Spirit as God.[64] That is to say, Christ as man can heal human beings

---

64. *ST* III, q. 43, a. 1:

God enables man to work miracles for two reasons. First and principally, in confirmation of the doctrine that a man teaches. For since those things which are of faith surpass human reason, they cannot be proved by human arguments, but need to be proved by the argument of Divine power: so that when a man does works that God alone can do, we may believe that what he says is from God: just as when a man is the bearer of letters sealed with the king's ring, it is to be believed that what they contain expresses the king's will. Secondly, in order to make known God's presence in a man by the grace of the Holy Ghost: so that when a man does the works of God we may believe that God dwells in him by His grace. Wherefore it is written (Gal. 3:5): "He who gives to you the Spirit, and works miracles among you." Now both these things were to be made known to men concerning Christ—namely, that God dwelt in Him by grace, not of adoption, but of union: and that His supernatural doctrine was from

when he wishes, because he is not only human but also divine, and he possesses in himself the authority and power of the God of Israel, which he receives in virtue of his being one with the Father and the Holy Spirit.

Let us consider two narratives, in which this intentional decision of Jesus is depicted as the personal will of the Son of God who has the power to perform miracles by his own volition. First, Luke 5:12–13:

> While he was in one of the cities, there came a man full of leprosy; and when he saw Jesus, he fell on his face and besought him, "Lord, if you will, you can make me clean." And he stretched out his hand, and touched him, saying, "I will; be clean." And immediately the leprosy left him.

And second, John 5:6–9:

> When Jesus saw him and knew that he had been lying there a long time, he said to him, "Do you want to be healed?" The sick man answered him, "Sir, I have no man to put me into the pool when the water is troubled, and while I am going another steps down before me." Jesus said to him, "Rise, take up your pallet, and walk." And at once the man was healed, and he took up his pallet and walked.

Christ can will personally to heal by his own power. Otherwise stated, the Son is a divine person always related to the Father as a distinct person, even while being one in power and will with the Father as God.[65]

Finally, as I have alluded to, Jesus designates himself as being personally related to the Father, even while also distinct from him as Son. In addition, however, he also designates himself as being personally distinct from and related to the Holy Spirit. The Spirit is referred to by Jesus in unambiguously personal terms as one who has

---

God. And therefore it was most fitting that He should work miracles. Wherefore He Himself says, (John 10:38): "Though you will not believe Me, believe the works"; and (John 5:36): "The works which the Father has given Me to perfect . . . themselves . . . give testimony to Me.'"

65. See John 5:19–30 on this last point and Aquinas's commentary on the matter in his *In Ioan.* V, lec. 5, 796–97. I have offered an analysis of this point in "Dyotheletism and the Instrumental Human Consciousness of Jesus," *Pro Ecclesia* 17, no. 4 (2008): 396–422.

divine authority and power and is distinct from the Father and from Jesus.[66] The Holy Spirit can render human beings righteous by the power of grace, as for example, we see in the affirmation of John the Baptist in Luke 3:16. He has authority to teach divine truth (Matt. 10:20; John 16:13). He can cast out demonic powers (Matt. 12:28). These are capacities typically reserved to a divine "office," one reserved to God based on God's knowledge and power. Christ acts in concert, therefore, not only with the Father but also with the Holy Spirit as he who sends the Spirit upon the apostles and the Church (Luke 4:1, 14, 18; John 16:8). According to John's Gospel, the Spirit is "sent" into "the world" from the Father and the Son in light of Christ's own mission, following his death and resurrection (John 14:26, 15:26, and 16:7). It is the Son of God who communicates the Holy Spirit to the apostles on Easter night (John 20:22). In the Gospel of John, Jesus assigns eschatological tasks to the Holy Spirit, which are in effect tasks reserved to God: the Spirit will assist the Church in preaching the truth. He will convict the world of its need for redemption, and prepare humanity for entry into eternal life (John 16:7–13).[67] Here the Johannine text implies that the Holy Spirit is one in being with the Father and the Son, even as he is personally distinct from the Father and the Son.

Conclusion: The Christological Roots of Trinitarian Theology

The claims we made above about Jesus' divine identity should be seen as qualifying or coloring in their entirety the claims we made about Jesus of Nazareth as an eschatological emissary of God who universalizes the covenant initiated in the Old Testament. How can the atonement of Christ crucified open the covenant to all, and how can his bodily resurrection reveal the ultimate mystery of God to all the gentile nations? Jesus is the Lord (YHWH). That is to say, he

---

66. See, for example, Mark 1:10–12, 12:36, 13:11; Matt. 12:28, 32; Luke 4:17–21.

67. See on this point Yves Congar, *Je Crois en l'Esprit Saint* (Paris: Cerf, 1979), 1:82–86; C. K. Barrett, *The Gospel according to St. John* (Philadelphia: Westminster Press, 1978), 90.

is the God of Israel who has become human. By virtue of his life, suffering, death, and resurrection, he has revealed the inner identity and mystery of God as Father, Son, and Holy Spirit. In other words, at the heart of the atonement and resurrection, the saving mysteries of Christianity, there is the mystery of the Incarnation, which itself implies the mystery of the Holy Trinity. We can only come to understand the inner logic of Trinitarian monotheism within the framework of the mysteries of the life of Christ: his Incarnation, atonement, and resurrection. But the inverse is also true. The Incarnation, atonement, and resurrection are only ultimately intelligible in light of the mystery of the one God as the Father, Son, and Holy Spirit. The Trinity is the deepest mystery of Christian revelation,— indeed, the mystery behind the mysteries, and so the logic behind the logic. We come to understand who God is as Trinity in virtue of the soteriological mysteries of the Incarnation, atonement, and resurrection. But we also ultimately understand these mysteries only in light of the Trinity.

This brings us to our first major conclusion of this chapter. We have argued that the monotheism of the Old Testament is essential to the perspective of the New Testament, since the New Testament presupposes that it is the God of Israel who reveals himself fully to humanity *in Christ*, who universalizes the covenant *in Christ*, and who definitively overcomes the power of sin and death *in Christ*. On the other hand, we have argued that the mysteries of the New Testament in which Christ accomplishes these things presuppose that he is one in being with the God of Israel and is also personally distinct from the Father and the Holy Spirit, both of whom the New Testament also identifies as the God of Israel. If both these claims are true, it follows that the Father, Son, and Holy Spirit revealed in the New Testament are simply identical with the one God of Israel, and therefore, they are *one in being*, since the monotheism of the Old Testament is presupposed by the logic of New Testament claims about God and soteriology. The monotheism of the Old Testament is Trinitarian and the Trinitarianism of the New Testament is monotheistic. How then might we claim simultaneously that God is both one in being and that God is the Father, Son, and Holy Spirit, three distinct persons who are eternally interrelated? In fact, the New Testament itself points us toward the definitive answer to this question and supplies the conceptual seeds of the subsequent Trinitarian doctrine of the Catholic Church, as we can now show.

THE TRINITARIAN MONOTHEISM OF THE NEW TESTAMENT

The New Testament itself provides conditions for thinking about the tri-unity of God in ontological terms by presenting us with an analogy from the immanent life of spiritual cognition and volition in man. Below, I consider this line of thinking briefly as it exists within several facets of New Testament theology: the notion of pre-existent Sonship, analogies for the immaterial procession of the Son, the distinct character of the procession of the Spirit, and the manifestation of personal distinctions in God according to the psychological analogy of intellect and will. If God is Trinitarian, then knowledge of this mystery should cast a light on all human realities, since the human being appears in a particular way to be in the image of the Trinity, in virtue of his spiritual nature. I will return to this idea at the end of this chapter.

Pre-existent Sonship

From the earliest period of Christianity, Christians affirmed that Jesus is "Lord" (*Kyrios*), an affirmation that is found throughout the New Testament.[68] This term, employed thematically by Paul, implies that Jesus is God. He is identical with the God of Israel, whose divine name in the Old Testament was conveyed euphemistically in the Septuagint under the Greek title *Kyrios* ("Lord").

---

68. For a partial but indicative list, see Rom. 1:7, 5:1, 5:11, 10:9; 1 Cor. 1:3, 8:6, 12:3; 2 Cor. 1:2–3; Gal. 1:3, 6:14; Eph. 1:2–3; Phil. 2:23; Acts 7:59, 9:17, 15:11.

Consequently, it is accurate to speak of primitive New Testament Christology as a form of "Christological monotheism." Jesus is one with the God of Israel.[69] Furthermore, the apostolic authors speak of this mystery being revealed above all in the resurrection of Jesus of Nazareth. That is to say, what was known imperfectly during the historical life of Jesus prior to the crucifixion is made manifest to the Church in a more perfect way subsequent to his bodily resurrection: that this man was from the beginning the Lord. Romans 1:1–4 states the idea quite clearly: "Paul, a servant of Jesus Christ, called to be an apostle, set apart for the gospel of God ... concerning his Son, who was descended from David according to the flesh and designated Son of God in power according to the Spirit of holiness by his resurrection from the dead, Jesus Christ our Lord."[70] Similarly Colossians 1:15 and 18 speak of Christ as both "the image of the invisible God, the first-born of all creation" and the "first-born from the dead." This parallelism suggests that the one first resurrected from among men (the first-born of the eschaton) is also identified as the eternally pre-existent Son of God who is from before all ages (Col. 1:13). Consequently, the resurrection is something new for Christ in his *humanity* (his body and soul), but it also points us back to who Christ is and was "from the beginning" in his pre-existent *person*, that is to say, as the Lord, the Son of God, from before the foundation of the world.

Along logically parallel lines, the New Testament also presents the ontological identity of Christ as something that pertains to him prior to his Incarnation. The Son exists from all eternity as one with the Father and has become man for the sake of the human race. His identity is made manifest to the world especially through his

69. On Christological monotheism in the New Testament, see N. T. Wright, *The Climax of the Covenant: Christ and the Law in Pauline Theology* (Minneapolis: Fortress, 1993); Hurtado, *Lord Jesus Christ*; Bauckham, "God Crucified," in *Jesus and the God of Israel*.

70. The traditional Catholic interpretation of this passage affirms that the resurrection *manifests* who Jesus is as Son of God (his pre-existent identity) and that his resurrection event also communicates power to his human nature (now glorified). The resurrection does not constitute him as Son of God; it reveals his identity as Lord and conveys new properties of his Sonship as God *to* his glorified human nature as man.

glorious resurrection and exaltation. There exists, then, a structure of thinking that entails a first descent or kenosis, and then a subsequent exaltation and recognition. St. Paul's words in Philippians 2:6–11 exemplify this order of descent followed by exaltation, where he says of Christ:

[T]hough he was in the form of God, [he] did not count equality with God a thing to be grasped, but emptied himself, taking the form of a servant, being born in the likeness of men. And being found in human form he humbled himself and became obedient unto death, even death on a cross. Therefore God has highly exalted him and bestowed on him the name which is above every name, that at the name of Jesus every knee should bow, in heaven and on earth and under the earth, and every tongue confess that Jesus Christ is Lord, to the glory of God the Father.

The subject of this text exists as one who possesses the "form of God" eternally and prior to his state of being human. The pre-existent Son takes on a human nature freely, in humility and lowliness, making himself subject in human obedience to the mystery of the Cross. His subsequent exaltation in the resurrection is the occasion for the universal recognition among the nations that Jesus is Lord, that is to say, he is rightly ascribed the very name of the God of Israel.[71] We might say that there is a descent and ascent structure to the passage: the eternal Son descends into the human condition without ceasing to be God, and when his human nature is glorified in the resurrection, he is recognized as the pre-existent Lord of creation. The resurrection is constituted by the glorification of the humanity of Christ, but it simultaneously manifests his divinity. Similar structures of thought exist in Colossians 1:15–20, 1 Timothy 3:16, Hebrews 1:2b–4, and John 1:1–17. In each of these texts, it is suggested that Jesus is God from before all time, one with the Father, yet also truly distinct from the Father as the Son, and that God the Son becomes man, taking human form.

71. Phil. 2:10 contains a reference to Is. 45:23, in which the prophet refers to the God of Israel as the only true God and Creator, who will be recognized by all the nations. According to Phil. 2:6–11 this is now occurring through the death and exaltation of Christ who is the Lord, manifest to the nations in his human life, death, and resurrection.

In addition, the New Testament teaches that the Son is the principle through whom all things were made.[72] Ancient Israelites from the Second Temple Period are typically thought to have been committed monotheists who ascribed the power of creation only to the Lord God of Israel, the unique Creator of all things. This is true of the early Christian movement as well, since the earliest Christians were themselves Israelites, and so they too believed that the one God of Israel alone has created all things on earth and in heaven, visible and invisible. The New Testament qualifies traditional Israelite monotheism, however, by affirming that it is the eternal Son who is the principle *through* whom God creates and sustains all things in being, so that the Son is understood as a kind of exemplary cause, the pre-existent wisdom in light of whom God gives being to all things:

[T]here is one God, the Father, from whom are all things and for whom we exist, and one Lord, Jesus Christ, through whom are all things and through whom we exist (1 Cor. 8:6).

[F]or in him all things were created, in heaven and on earth, visible and invisible, whether thrones or dominions or principalities or authorities—all things were created through him and for him (Col. 1:16).

In the beginning was the Word [Logos], and the Word was with God, and the Word was God. He was in the beginning with God; all things were made through him, and without him was not anything made that was made (John 1:1–3).

We should note the coherence of these ideas. Jesus is recognized in light of his bodily resurrection to be the Lord, one with the God of Israel, who is God the Father. Therefore, the Son of God is also pre-existent, eternal, and one with the Father, even as he is personally distinct from the Father. The begetting of the Son by the Father is "pre-existent," something pertaining to the Son from all eternity prior to his Incarnation as man.[73] This also means that the Son is the

72. See Heb. 1:2; Rev. 3:14.

73. John Henry Newman, *The Arians of the Fourth Century*, 3rd edition (London: Longmans, Green and Co., 1908), 158–59:

Nothing can be plainer to the attentive student of Scripture, than that our Lord is there called the Son of God, not only in respect of His human nature, but

principle of creation, he through whom all things were made. This idea of the Son as an exemplary cause of creation in God is related to the idea of an immanent emanation in God as God's eternal "wisdom" and "word," as well as God's "spirit." These analogies of internal procession applied to God have precedents in the revelation of the Old Testament, where divine wisdom is sometimes personified (Prov. 8:30–31; Sir. 1:1–10, 24:1–34; Wis. 7:22–30).[74] However, the New Testament provides a novel development of this idea of an immanent procession in God since it presents the eternal emanation of the wisdom and word of God as the person of the eternal Son of God.

---

of His pre-existent state also. And if this be so, the very fact of the revelation of Him as such, implies that we are to gather something from it, and attach in consequence of it some ideas to our notion of Him, which otherwise we should not have attached; else would it not have been made. Taking then the word in its most vague sense, so as to admit as little risk as possible of forcing the analogy, we seem to gain the notion of derivation from God, and therefore, of the utter dissimilarity and distance existing between Him and all beings except God His Father, as if He partook of that unapproachable, incommunicable Divine Nature, which is increate and imperishable. But Scripture does not leave us here: in order to fix us in this view, lest we should be perplexed with another notion of the analogy, derived from that adopted sonship, which is ascribed therein to created beings, it attaches a characteristic epithet to His Name, as descriptive of the peculiar relation of Him who bears it to the Father. It designates Him as the *Only-begotten* or the *own* [John i. 1, 14, 18; iii. 16; v. 18; Rom. viii. 32; Heb. i. 1-14] Son of God, terms evidently referring, where they occur, to His heavenly nature, and thus becoming the inspired comment on the more general title. It is true that the term *generation* is also applied to certain events in our Lord's mediatorial history: to His resurrection from the dead and, according to the Fathers, to His original mission in the beginning of all things to create the world; and to His manifestation in the flesh. Still, granting this, the sense of the word "only-begotten" remains, defined by its context to relate to something higher than any event occurring in time, however great or beneficial to the human race. Being taken then, as it needs must be taken, to designate His original nature, it witnesses most forcibly and impressively to that which is peculiar in it, viz. His origination from God, and such as to exclude all resemblance to any being but Him, whom nothing created resembles. Thus, without irreverently and idly speculating upon the generation in itself, but considering the doctrine as given us as a practical direction for our worship and obedience, we may accept it in token, that whatever the Father is, such is the Son.

74. See Roland Murphy, "The Personification of Wisdom," in *Wisdom in Ancient Israel: Essays in Honor of J. A. Emerton* (Cambridge: Cambridge University Press, 1995), 222–33.

Immaterial Procession of the Son:
Word, Wisdom, Image

As noted, the idea of an immanent intellectual and spiritual life in God is thematic in Old Testament monotheism. Even though the God of the Torah is hidden and transcendent, God is also known by actions that can be ascribed to him as a person in a real, if analogous, sense. That is to say, God chooses to act in accord with his wisdom and freedom. The dark hiddenness of God and the mystery of God's person are not competing ideas but mutually corrective and harmonious ones. God is concealed and unknown but also partially manifest precisely as personal.

The wisdom literature of late Second Temple Judaism sought to understand this idea of manifestation and concealment by reflecting on Israel's ancient prophetic traditions in philosophical ways. To do so, the scribal authors of Sirach and Wisdom made use of the notion of "wisdom" precisely to speak of God's immanent intellectual life and hidden and mysterious identity.[75] Here we see a foundation for the later Christian patristic distinction of *theologia* and *economia*.[76] *Theologia* in this context refers to the immanent life of God, who

---

75. Wis. 7:22–26 is particularly suggestive in this respect, due to its identification of wisdom as a principle of creation emanating from God, possessing his glory, and being an image of his goodness:

> [W]isdom, the fashioner of all things, taught me.... For wisdom is more mobile than any motion; because of her pureness she pervades and penetrates all things. For she is a breath of the power of God, and a pure emanation of the glory of the Almighty; therefore nothing defiled gains entrance into her. For she is a reflection of eternal light, a spotless mirror of the working of God, and an image of his goodness.

76. See in this respect the suggestive arguments on the economy as a reflection of divine wisdom according to Sirach by Jordan Schmidt in his "Wisdom, Cosmos, and Cultus in the Book of Sirach," (PhD. Diss., The Catholic University of America, 2017). The traditional distinction between *theologia* and *oikonomia* was first articulated by Origen in the third century (*Homilies on Jeremiah*, n. 18), and subsequently employed by Church fathers such as Basil and Gregory of Nazianzus, Maximus the Confessor, and John Damascene. The distinction is meant to denote that which is proper to God in himself (*theologia*: the inner life of the Holy Trinity) as distinct from the divine economy in which God reveals himself and communicates his life.

God is in himself. *Economia* pertains to God's manifestation of his identity through his effects of creation and redemption. The *theologia* is manifest in the *economia*: God reveals in the divine economy of creation and redemption who he truly is in himself. The wisdom of God is a bridge concept in this respect. God's wisdom is manifest imperfectly in his works, since these works reveal God as the origin of being, order, and goodness in creation and as the savior of the human race. That is to say, the economy has its prior origin in God, in who God truly is in himself. At the same time, the creation is like God's iconostasis: it conceals him. God is eminently wise, but we know of his wisdom and inner life only imperfectly from his effects.[77]

The Pauline epistles make use of the Old Testament notion of wisdom precisely so as to think about the immanent emanation of the Son from the Father.[78] This emanation is neither material nor comprehensible. The eternal Son of God is the wisdom of the Father, the eternal splendor of the Father's self-understanding, in whom and through whom all things were made (Col. 1:15–19, 2:3). By manifesting itself in Jesus Christ, the wisdom of God reveals to us once and for all who God truly is in himself (1 Cor. 1:24, 30). The imperfect knowledge of the Old Testament has given way to a more perfect knowledge about the immanent life of God, now made manifest in the Son (1 Cor. 1:21–22; Eph. 1:9, 3:10). The economy of the Incarnation reveals the "theology" of the Trinity.

John's Gospel characterizes this idea of immaterial procession by making use of the Greek term "*Logos*": "In the beginning was the *Logos*, and the *Logos* was with God and was God; in him all things were made" (John 1:1–3). Here, the Old Testament notion of the "word"

---

77. See on this point *ST* I, q. 13, a. 5, an idea I will return to below.

78. Gordon D. Fee, *Pauline Christology: An Exegetical-Theological Study* (Grand Rapids, MI: Baker Academic, 2013), 594–630, is skeptical that Paul is appealing to Wisdom or Sirach overtly. Paul does write, however, against the backdrop of a thought world shared with these authors, coming out of a common semantic and historical framework. See the alternative reflections of James D. G. Dunn, *The Theology of Paul the Apostle* (Grand Rapids, MI: Eerdmans, 2006), 266–80.

of God (*dabar* in ancient Hebrew) is translated into and interpreted by a Greek term that is more conceptual and that denotes spiritual interiority. *Logos* refers primarily not to the spoken word but
to the internal mental concept or thought form, the inner notion or
active contemplative idea in which God expresses and manifests his
own wisdom and self-understanding.[79] This *Logos* is also the transcendent exemplar or model of all that is. When God creates, all that
comes from God's *Logos* is effectively realized in the light of God's
self-understanding. Consequently, the eternal Word is God's transcendent archetype or model for all that he does as Creator.[80] Similarly, the words of God spoken to the prophets of the Old Testament
are brought to culmination in the one Word of God made man: "And
the Word became flesh and dwelt among us, full of grace and truth"

79. See the study by Mark J. Edwards, "The Johannine Prologue before Origen," in
The Bible and Early Trinitarian Theology, 118–31. See also Aquinas's unsurpassed conceptual analysis of the content of the idea of Christ as pre-existent *Logos* in *In Joan.* I, lec. 1–2.

80. Athanasius, *Against the Arians* I, 4 (11–12), comments in this way, harmonizing
the teaching of John with Paul:

> For, "In the beginning was the Word, and the Word was with God, and the
> Word was God (John 1:1)." And in the Apocalypse he thus speaks: "Who is
> and who was and who is to come." Now who can rob "who is" and "who was"
> of eternity? This too in confutation of the Jews has Paul written in his Epistle to
> the Romans, "Of whom as concerning the flesh is Christ, who is over all, God
> blessed for ever (Rom. 9:5);" while silencing the Greeks, he has said, "The vis-
> ible things of Him from the creation of the world are clearly seen, being under-
> stood by the things that are made, even His eternal Power and Godhead," and
> what the Power of God is, he teaches us elsewhere himself, "Christ the Power
> of God and the Wisdom of God." Surely in these words he does not designate
> the Father, as you [Arians] often whisper one to another, affirming that the
> Father is "His eternal power." This is not so; for he says not, "God Himself is
> the power," but "His is the power." Very plain is it to all that "His" is not "He;"
> yet not something alien but rather proper to Him.... For after making mention
> of the creation, he naturally speaks of the Framer's Power as seen in it, which
> Power, I say, is the Word of God, by whom all things have been made. If indeed
> the creation is sufficient of itself alone, without the Son, to make God known,
> see that you fall not, from thinking that without the Son it has come to be. But
> if through the Son it has come to be, and "in Him all things consist (Col. 1:17),"
> it must follow that he who contemplates the creation rightly, is contemplating
> also the Word who framed it, and through Him begins to apprehend the Fa-
> ther. [Trans. J. H. Newman, *Nicene and Post-Nicene Fathers*, vol. 4, ed. P. Schaff
> and H. Wace (Buffalo, NY: Christian Literature Publishing Co., 1892).]

(John 1:14). Here, the prophetic revelation of God reaches its summit, as God himself becomes human and by grace (or "gift") reveals his true identity and shares his divine life with human beings.

At the same time, John's Prologue speaks of the *Logos* as the "only-begotten" of the Father and as the "Son" (John 1:18). The language of begetting and sonship refers to generation. Therefore, these terms designate a continuity of nature between the Father and the Son, since an analogy from sonship designates one who has the same nature as his Father. The *Logos*, then, is eternally begotten of the Father immaterially (as indicated by the analogy from interior spiritual thought) in such a way as to possess in himself the divine nature (as indicated by the analogy from sonship). The Son is generated immaterially from the Father as his Word and consequently has in himself all that is in the Father, as one who shares fully in the Father's divine being and nature. According to John, immaterial procession implies immanence within the being of God, since the Father is in the Son and the Son is in the Father.[81] The Word who comes forth from the Father is within the Father and is one with the Father. He possesses as Son the fullness of the being and nature of the deity of the Father and is he through whom all things are made.

If wisdom and word are scriptural analogies employed to speak about immaterial procession, the notion of "image" is employed to designate an identity of essence or of natural kind shared by the Father and the Son. The prologue to the Letter to the Hebrews employs the Greek term "*charakter*," or image, to refer to the pre-existent Son as the perfect representation of the Father: "He reflects the glory of God and bears the very image of his nature, upholding the universe by his word of power" (Heb. 1:3).[82] In a similar way, Colossians speaks of Christ as "the image (*eikon*) of the invisible God, the first-born of all creation" (1:15). And in Philippians 2:6–11, Paul speaks of Christ as being simultaneously in the "form" (*morphe*) of

---

81. See John 14:11, as reflective of John 1:1–3.
82. Translation altered by the author. Here I have used the RSV translation but altered the Greek word *charakter* to give it the KJV signification.

God and the "form" of a servant, the latter being in virtue of his humanity. The first of these usages suggests that Christ is Son of God who is perfectly representative of the Father prior to his Incarnation, eternally and ontologically, in a transcendent way *as* God. To paraphrase this teaching in terms given subsequently in the Nicene creed: the Son is God from God, light from light, and true God from true God. The notion here is one of a shared and unique nature. Just as the Father is Lord and God, so too the Son is Lord and God, from the Father, having in himself all that the Father has as God. In his very person he represents or images adequately all that is in the Father. The second of these usages of "image" in Colossians expresses a complex idea: the eternal Son made man is the visible image of God because he is both God and man, so that it is *in his humanity* that he reveals who God truly is. It is the visible Son as human who reveals the invisible Father.[83] The third usage in Philippians 2, which employs a quite different Greek term *morphe*, suggests a distinction of natural modes of being: the Son exists in one natural mode of being with the Father as God and in another natural mode of being with human beings as man. He was in the form of God from all eternity as Son, and he has become one who is in the form of man in virtue of his Incarnation. He reveals to us simultaneously, then, the truth about who God is or even, we might say, "what" God is essentially (God's form) as well as the truth about what human beings are essentially, that is, the human form, now revealed in Christ the servant.

If we think of these three notions in logical continuity with one another, we see that the New Testament affirms that there is immaterial emanation or procession in God. The Father eternally begets the Son as his immaterial *Logos* or Wisdom. This immaterial emanation of the Father is the principle through which he creates all things and sustains them in being. However, the *Logos* of God has also become manifest to us by God's becoming human in such a way that God has truly become one of us, having an individual human nature. This

83. I am reading Col. 1:18 in correlation with 1:15, and vice versa.

Incarnation of God does not entail a surrender or loss of his divine nature nor a mixture of the divine and human natures. They remain distinct. There are two natures in Christ. But the Son of God makes his personal identity manifest in and through his human nature and in his human actions, including his personal sufferings as man. The passion and resurrection of Christ reveal the uncreated love of God. The Incarnation, death, and resurrection of Christ occur precisely so as to reveal to us the true identity of God, the mystery of the Holy Trinity, and to communicate a participation in God's own Trinitarian life through the grace of Christ.

The Distinct Procession of the Spirit

The notion of the Spirit of God or the Spirit of the Lord (YHWH) is present thematically in the Old Testament. In Genesis 1:2, "the Spirit of God" moves over the face of the waters of the new creation. Prophetic behavior is associated with inspiration and thus with the Spirit of God (Gen. 41:38; 1 Sam. 10:6; 2 Kings 2:9–15). The Spirit grants people wisdom and insight, or practical understanding (Ex. 35:31; Ezek. 11:24, 37:1), and gives people the possibility of exerting leadership and making good political judgments (Num. 11:25; Deut. 34:9; Judg. 3:10). The Spirit of God anoints kings (1 Sam. 16:13), and will also anoint the messianic king who is to come (Isa. 11:2, 42:1, 61:1). The Spirit will inhabit God's people in the restored kingdom that is to come (Ezek. 37:14). In eschatological prophecies, prophetic authors claim that the end times will be those in which the Spirit of God writes directly upon all the human hearts of the elect (Ezek. 11:19, 36:26; Joel 2:28–32). In all these cases, the global work of God in Israel is personified by speaking of the Spirit of God. Read in light of the New Testament, these denotations serve as adumbrations or prefigurations of the plenary revelation of the person of the Holy Spirit.

Thus in the New Testament, the Spirit is designated as a personal protagonist who is distinct from the Father and from Jesus. The Spirit is sent by the Father and accompanies Jesus in his work.

The sending of the Son into the world and the sending of the Spirit into the world are deeply interrelated mysteries, which reveal the Father's identity. When Christ is conceived of the Virgin Mary in Luke and in Matthew, this occurs by the power of the Holy Spirit (Luke 1:35; Matt. 1:20). The Spirit designates Jesus as God's anointed one in his baptism (Matt. 3:16–4:1; Luke 3:22, 4:1) and confirms Jesus' mission as messiah and Son by signs and wonders of his public ministry (Luke 4:18; Acts 10:38). In his resurrection, Jesus promises the disciples that he will send the Holy Spirit upon them once he has ascended to the Father (Acts 1:8, 2:33).

Both the epistles of Paul and the Gospel of John speak of the Spirit in distinctly personal terms as well. Paul refers to the Holy Spirit as an active agent given to us by God the Father (1 Thess. 4:8; Rom. 8:11). The Spirit is the source of sanctification (2 Thess. 2:13; Gal. 5:22–25). He works miracles and justifies inwardly by grace those who are baptized into Christ (Gal. 3:3; 1 Cor. 6:11; Rom. 5:5, 14:17). He is the Spirit of Christ (Rom. 8:9) and the Spirit of the Son (Gal. 4:6). The Spirit searches all things, even the depths of God (1 Cor. 2:10). The Gospel of John presents us with complementary ideas. There, the night before he dies, Jesus promises to send the Holy Spirit upon the disciples, and he denotes him by the particular term, "the Advocate," or "Paraclete" (for example, John 14:25–26). This term seems to suggest that the Spirit is like a legal counselor who moves his clients inwardly toward reconciliation and justification, which are made possible in light of Christ's saving sacrifice. The Spirit-Paraclete is to be sent upon the apostles "from the Father," and Jesus mentions that he is the "Spirit of truth who proceeds from the Father" (John 14:26, 15:26). He is also sent from the Son (John 16:7). On the eve of his resurrection, Christ breathes the Holy Spirit upon his disciples, communicating to them the authority in the Spirit to forgive sins (John 20:22–23).

I have alluded to these notions briefly and incompletely in this context simply to underscore that the New Testament treats the Spirit as a person or subject distinct from the Father and the Son, who works with the Father and the Son. He is from the Father and is the Spirit of Christ, the Son. With the Father and the Son, he accomplishes works of salvation that are reserved to the activity of God alone: the communication of justification and sanctification by grace, the communication of prophetic understanding, the granting of enlightenment as to the reality and significance of the resurrection of Jesus, and the working of miracles.

From these brief reflections, we can draw three preliminary conclusions about the Holy Spirit. First, the notion of subjective agency attributed to the Spirit by the New Testament suggests that he is a person distinct from the Father and the Son. Second, the Spirit does things that God alone can do. Therefore, the Spirit is equally God along with the Father and the Son. Thirdly, the texts of Paul and John suggest that in his mission as one "sent" into the world, the Spirit proceeds from the Father and from or through the Son. This order of derivation suggests how the persons are eternally related to one another by way of fontal origination. The Son eternally proceeds from the Father as his generated Word. Therefore, he originates from the Father. The Spirit can be said to proceed eternally from the Father through the Son and also from the Son by way of spiration.[84] This order of eternal immanent procession in God (the *theologia*) is represented accurately or revealed truthfully by the temporal missions of the Son and the Spirit in the creation (the *economia*). The Son is sent into the world by the Father, while the Spirit is sent by the Father and the Son and is the Spirit of the Son. The missions of the Son and the Spirit in the world reveal who God is in his eternal immanent life of emanation and procession.

Given this interpretation, we can note that according to the New Testament, the Father, Son, and Holy Spirit are each equally and identically the one God of Israel. There is only one God who is Father, Son, and Holy Spirit. If there is a distinction of persons in God,

84. On the biblical foundations for the doctrine of the *filioque* (the notion that the Spirit proceeds from both the Father and the Son), see Jean-Miguel Garrigues, *Le Saint-Esprit sceau de la Trinité: Le Filioque de l'originalité trinitaire de l'Esprit dans sa personne et sa mission* (Cerf: Paris, 2011).

this is because there is an order of processions. These processions are not material or physical and can be conceptualized by an analogy drawn from the spiritual life of the human person. The Son is the generated Wisdom and *Logos* of the Father, which we can understand imperfectly but really by similitude to an intellectual procession within the human person, the concept by and through which the human agent actively knows the world. The Spirit, meanwhile, is a spiritual procession that proceeds from the Father and the Word, or through the Word of the Father. Consequently, he can be compared by similitude to human love, the movement of the will by which the human person loves what he has already come to know.[85] A human being can come to know something through a concept and this conceptual knowledge instigates an inward movement of love. We can think here of the images of light and heat. The light of the Word bears within it the living flame of Love. We only come to love what we first have come to know. Likewise, from what we have come first to know we can in turn love what we know as light begotten of the knower instigates a fire of love. Consequently, in a real sense, voluntary love stems from or proceeds from knowledge, and actions of the will are informed by or determined from within by conceptual understanding.[86] On this reading of the New Testament, one can suggest that there is a similitude or "psychological analogy" of this sort when we speak of the Holy Trinity. The Son is an eternal procession according to knowledge, as *Logos*, while the Spirit is an eternal procession according to love, as the luminous Love of the Father and

85. I am alluding here to Augustine's classic reading of the Spirit as the bond of love between the Father and the Son, which will be explored in further detail below. For a contemporary defense of Augustine's understanding of the New Testament as depicting the Holy Spirit as love, see Matthew Levering, *Engaging the Doctrine of the Holy Spirit: Love and Gift in the Trinity and the Church* (Grand Rapids, MI: Baker Academic, 2016), ch. 1, 51–70.

86. See on this point, Aquinas, *De Malo*, q. 6; *ST* I-II, q. 8, a. 1; q. 9, a. 1; q. 11, a. 1; q. 12, a. 1; q. 13, a. 1; q. 14, a. 1. On the intellect's role with respect to the exercise of the will see Michael Sherwin, *By Knowledge and by Love: Charity and Knowledge in the Moral Theology of St. Thomas Aquinas* (Washington, DC: The Catholic University of America Press, 2005), esp. 18–62.

the Son. The aim of our reflections at this juncture is only to suggest the possibility of drawing the psychological analogy from scripture. This is a point of Trinitarian theology we will return to below.

TRINITARIAN MONOTHEISM BEFORE
AND AFTER NICAEA

The Apologists and the Monological Analogy for God

The argument I have advanced so far suggests that the New Testament is not merely susceptible to being read as a Trinitarian document but is rightly read as such. On this view, the Catholic Church has correctly interpreted what the document teaches. The Church's Trinitarian doctrine has its seeds in the explicit teaching of the apostolic writings of primitive Christianity. However, it is also the case that the Church's elaboration of the doctrine unfolded during centuries and in distinct stages.

Christianity in the second and third centuries faced two principal intellectual challenges. One was the threat internal to the Christian movement of Gnosticism, a heresy that denied the goodness of the physical world, the reality of the Incarnation, and the redemption of the human body. The other was external to the Church, the threat of Graeco-Roman incomprehension and persecution. In regard to both these challenges, the Church's early theological writers developed a reflection on the Father, Jesus Christ, and the Holy Spirit that appealed to the monotheistic character of the Church's faith. In response to thinkers like Valentinus, Basilides, and Marcion—the latter having views resembling the Gnostics—Irenaeus and Tertullian underscored the continuity between the two testaments, arguing that the God of the New Testament is also the God of Israel.[87] Christ's revelation of God as his Father presupposes the knowledge of the God revealed in the Old Testament as Creator of all things

---

87. See Irenaeus, *Against Heresies*, Books I–V, where book IV is especially concerned with the unity between the two testaments, and Tertullian, *Against Marcion* Books I–V, where book III treats the reasons for the Old Testament dispensation.

both visible and invisible.[88] The monotheism of the Torah is preserved by the early Church, not dissolved.[89] This is significant for soteriological reasons. If the Father of Jesus Christ is also the Creator of the visible world, then we should also understand that Christ seeks to redeem the physical world that God has created, not remove us from it.[90]

While the early Church sought to emphasize the continuity of the two testaments in the midst of her internal disputes, she also had to face simultaneously the challenge of explaining Christianity

88. See, for example, Irenaeus, *Against Heresies*, IV, 5, 2:

He, then, who was adored by the prophets as the living God, He is the God of the living; and His Word is He who also spoke to Moses, who also put the Sadducees to silence, who also bestowed the gift of resurrection, thus revealing [both] truths to those who are blind, that is, the resurrection and God [in His true character].... But our Lord is Himself the resurrection, as He does Himself declare, 'I am the resurrection and the life.' (John 11:25) ... Christ Himself ... together with the Father, is the God of the living, who spoke to Moses, and who was also manifested to the fathers. [Trans. A. Roberts and W. Rambaut, *Ante-Nicene Fathers*, vol. 1, eds. A. Roberts, J. Donaldson, and A. C. Coxe (Buffalo, NY: Christian Literature Publishing Co., 1885).]

89. Irenaeus, *Against Heresies*, IV, 1 and 2.

90. See *Against Heresies*, V, 2, 2–3 where Irenaeus argues from the Eucharist: the elements taken from the earth of the Creator (bread and wine) are transformed into the body and blood of Christ resurrected, which in turn bestow life on our bodies as well as our souls, all of which presupposes that the Creator who is the author of our human flesh is also the redeemer of our whole personhood, in Christ:

But vain in every respect are they who despise the entire dispensation of God, and disallow the salvation of the flesh, and treat with contempt its regeneration, maintaining that it is not capable of incorruption. But if this indeed does not attain salvation, then neither did the Lord redeem us with His blood, nor is the cup of the Eucharist the communion of His blood, nor the bread which we break the communion of His body. (1 Cor. 10:16) For blood can only come from veins and flesh, and whatsoever else makes up the substance of man, such as the Word of God was actually made. By His own blood he redeemed us, as also His apostle declares, in whom we have redemption through His blood, even the remission of sins. (Col. 1:14) And as we are His members, we are also nourished by means of the creation (and He Himself grants the creation to us, for He causes His sun to rise, and sends rain when He wills (Matt. 5:45)). He has acknowledged the cup (which is a part of the creation) as His own blood, from which He bedews our blood; and the bread (also a part of the creation) He has established as His own body, from which He gives increase to our bodies.

to the external gentile culture. If Jesus Christ reveals the one true God of Israel, the Creator, how might one make this teaching intelligible to those who have no previous initiation to the Old Testament scriptures? An answer was formed by appeal to the New Testament notion of the Son as the *Logos* or Reason of the Father. This idea is multifaceted and has several aspects.

First, we should note that thinkers in the early Church regularly appealed to Hellenistic philosophy to argue against the rationality of Graeco-Roman polytheism and for the reasonableness of Christianity. A key dimension to this argument pertained to monotheism: philosophy suggests that there is one unique transcendent principle behind creation which is in some way intellectual and good, that is to say, personal. Paul alludes to a common natural knowledge of this reality in his discourse to the Athenians (Acts 17:22–31), referring to their awareness of an unknown God (v. 23). The ancient Greek philosophers had criticized the problematic religious conceptions of their culture from within, as it were, speaking derisively of the religious myths of the poets as anthropomorphisms that mislead human beings both intellectually and politically.[91] The early Christians, such as Justin, Tertullian, Clement, Athanasius, and Augustine, developed this line of thinking in order to argue for the rationality of Biblical monotheism and its moral teachings. By appealing to the divine *Logos*, the early apologists were arguing for the rational superiority of Christian monotheism in regard to Graeco-Roman polytheism.[92]

91. See, for example, Xenophanes, fr. 11 and 14, *The Presocratic Philosophers*, ed. and trans. G. S. Kirk and J. E. Raven (Cambridge: Cambridge University Press, 1957), 168; Heraclitus, fr. 5, *The Presocratic Philosophers*, 211; Plato, *Apology* 18c and *Republic* III.398a, in *Plato: Complete Works*, ed. John M. Cooper, trans. G. M. A. Grube (Indianapolis, Ind.: Hackett, 1997); Aristotle, *Metaphysics* XII.8.1074b1–14.

92. See the argument of Ratzinger from "Truth of Christianity," 165–76, with particular attention given to Augustine's discussion of Varro's divisions of theology in the *City of God*. See, for example, Justin Martyr, *First Apology*, chs. 6 and 13, on God as transcendent Rationality and Christianity as rational worship of the one God. Justin states (chs. 5–6):

For not only among the Greeks did reason [Logos] prevail to condemn these things through Socrates, but also among the Barbarians were they condemned

Second, this idea clearly was not proposed by early Church fathers in such a way as to imply a substitution of philosophy for revelation, nor can one rightly claim that it led to a falsification of divine revelation by way of syncretism. The very grounds for the appeal to philosophical resources itself emerged from the continuity between the New and Old Testaments. That is to say, this appeal to philosophical rationality is Biblical in origin. This is true in one way simply materially, since both Testaments contain texts that allude to the capacity of the human being to discern the existence of God rationally by natural intellectual resources common to all men.[93]

However, there is a deeper reason, which is theological as such. If the mystery of God revealed in Christ is itself a recapitulation of the revelation of He who is, of the God revealed in Exodus and Isaiah as the giver of being to all that exists, then that mystery inevitably addresses and interpolates our natural capacity to reason about God. Why? The Bible affirms that God is "He who is" and is also the cause of the "existence" of things. So scripture itself teaches us of an ontological relationship and likeness between the world of beings around us and the unknown giver of being to that world, who is himself (according to revelation) incomprehensively transcendent and perfect in his being, the one who is the source of all that exists, revealed imperfectly within it and simultaneously hidden by it. This teaching would be unintelligible unless we were able ourselves (at least after

---

by Reason [or the Word, the Logos] Himself, who took shape, and became man, and was called Jesus Christ; Hence are we called atheists. And we confess that we are atheists, so far as gods of this sort are concerned, but not with respect to the most true God, the Father of righteousness and temperance and the other virtues, who is free from all impurity. But both Him, and the Son... and the prophetic Spirit, we worship and adore, knowing them in reason and truth, and declaring without grudging to everyone who wishes to learn, as we have been taught. [Trans. M. Dods and G. Reith, *Ante-Nicene Fathers*, vol. 1.]

On Christianity as the "true philosophy," see Justin, *Dialogue with Trypho the Jew*, chs. 1–9.

93. On natural knowledge of God and of the natural or moral law, see for example, Amos 1:3–15; Ps. 14:1–4, 97:7; Wis. 13:5; Rom. 1:18–28; Acts 17:22–31. Condemnation of culpable idolatry presupposes partial and potential knowledge of God. See on this point, Aquinas, *ST* II-II, 92, a. 2; 94, a. 1.

revelation and in its light) to think of the world's created existence as derived from God and simultaneously to think naturally of the "existence" of God. The very notion of God as Creator implies a kind of philosophical rationality: all things point back to God as their transcendent origin. If this idea of God as the Creator of our being were naturally unintelligible to us, then revelation itself would be so alien to human reason as to be intrinsically unintelligible, even with the inward assistance of grace. The reception of the Biblical revelation of God as Creator implies, then, that the human person is naturally capable of conceiving of God as the cause of all that exists and of all that we experience, even apart from Biblical revelation. It follows that the Church's early philosophical engagement with culture stemmed from her confession of the theological intelligibility and rationality of belief in the Creator, and this dimension of Christian self-explanation implies no betrayal of revelation. On the contrary, it stems from profound fidelity to that revelation.

Third and most importantly, the Trinity was explained by the early apologists in terms of the pre-existent and eternal procession or emanation of the Son from the Father as *Logos*. It is by and through *Logos* that God has made all things (John 1:1–3). The Rationality of God is at the origin of all that is. This statement is ambiguous: it could be merely a philosophical claim or a genuinely Biblical statement that entails faith in divine revelation. Likewise, it could pertain either to the *Logos* understood as a person eternally distinct from the person of the Father or to the *Logos* as an essential property of God, like goodness or wisdom. These two ambiguities are both present in the influential writing of Justin Martyr.[94] However, they are not problematic so much as suggestive and pregnant with meaning. They are important precisely *as* ambiguities. Why is this? They suggest

94. See for example *First Apology*, chs. 5 and 44, and the *Second Apology*, ch. 8, where Justin speaks of seeds of the Word (*Logos*) implanted in all men since the dawn of time, present especially in the philosophers, which prefigure the teaching of Christ and the prophets and point toward the God of reason. Does knowledge of the eternal Word derive directly from philosophy, or does the revelation of the *Logos* draw all the fragments or seeds to itself? Seemingly the latter.

to the philosopher in each of us that if God truly is the explanatory source of reality and is himself intellectual or "rational," then there can also be a hidden explanation for the world that stands above but not contrary to our philosophical competence, and this explanation is only made available in light of God's self-understanding and freely-given revelation. In other words, if God is transcendent reason, then it is also possible that God could reveal to us his inner life of rationality, his *Logos*. And analogously, such arguments suggest both that there is a natural, philosophical purpose for human reason that can be identified in light of the knowledge of God—namely, to seek the truth about God and all things in light of God—*and* that when we fulfill this purpose, we act as human beings made *in the image* of the divine *Logos*. This latter teaching is, to speak in accord with a later idiom, a supernatural truth, but the supernatural truth of the *imago Dei* confirms the natural philosophical vocation of man to seek a "true philosophy," meaning a life in accord with wisdom and with authentic ultimate explanations. Therefore, the search for the truth in human culture is not conducted in vain, nor is it opposed to divine revelation but confirmed and encouraged by it.[95] Furthermore, the philosopher as philosopher cannot say whether in the one God and Creator there are real distinctions of Father, Word, and Spirit, but he can acknowledge that the revelation of the Trinity as presented in this way is superior to materialism or polytheism. Why? Because the New Testament teaches that there is a pre-existent *Logos*, which is the fundamental theological explanation of reality, in God who is one. This affirmation concords with philosophical reason. Consequently, Christianity as a school of wisdom, or "*philo-sophia*," depends upon appeal to divine revelation but this revelation is more philosophically reasonable or intellectually ex-

95. This idea appears as a theme in the writings of Joseph Ratzinger. See, for example, *Introduction to Christianity*, trans. J. R. Foster (San Francisco: Ignatius, 2000), 74–79, 137–61; and *"In the Beginning...": A Catholic Understanding of the Story of Creation and the Fall*, trans. B. Ramsey (Grand Rapids, MI: Eerdmans, 1998); Pope Benedict XVI, encyclical *Deus Caritas Est* (2005), §§ 10 and 13. See the very similar argument of Athanasius in *Against the Gentiles*, in *Nicene and Post-Nicene Fathers*, vol. 4.

planatory than other interpretations of the world present in ancient Graeco-Roman culture.[96] Consequently, it merits special consideration from the philosopher as a most plausible and ultimate explanation of reality, one that is both revealed and rational.

For this reason, we see in the centuries leading up to Nicaea the co-simultaneous development of the idea of Christianity as the true philosophy, against the cultic practices of the Graeco-Roman religious traditions, and the presentation of God the Trinity as a monological subject by analogy with human reason. The Trinitarian notion of the *Logos* of God is also the explanation of the ground of the world as rational, based on the transcendent reason of God over against the irrational polytheism of the non-Biblical religious traditions. This is presented in a rudimentary way in chapter 5 of Tatian's *Address to the Greeks*:

God was in the beginning; but the beginning, we have been taught, is the power of the Logos. For the Lord of the universe, who is Himself the necessary ground of all being, inasmuch as no creature was yet in existence, was alone; but inasmuch as He was all power, Himself the necessary ground of things visible and invisible, with Him were all things; with Him, by rational-power (*dia logikaes dunameos*), the Logos Himself also, who was in Him, subsists.... For just as from one torch many fires are lighted, but the light of the first torch is not lessened by the kindling of many torches, so the Logos, coming forth from the rational-power of the Father, has not divested of the rational-power Him who begot Him. I myself, for instance, talk, and you hear; yet, certainly, I who converse do not become destitute of speech (*logos*) by the transmission of speech.... And as the Logos, begotten in the beginning, begot in turn our world, having first created for Himself the necessary matter. [97]

96. See this argument conducted thematically by Justin, *First Apology*; Tatian, *Address to the Greeks*; Clement of Alexandria, *Stromata*, esp. Book I, chs. 13–20; Tertullian, *The Apology*; Origen, *Against Celsus*, Book 1, and subsequently by Lactantius, *The Divine Institutes*; Athanasius, *Against the Gentiles*; Gregory of Nazianzus, *Second Theological Oration* (on the natural knowledge of the one God, as a prelude to the *Third Theological Oration* on the knowledge of the *Logos*); Augustine, *City of God*, Books 6–10.

97. Trans. J. E. Ryland, *Ante-Nicene Fathers*, vol. 2, ed. A. Roberts, J. Donaldson, and A. C. Coxe (Buffalo, NY: Christian Literature Publishing Co., 1885). [Translation slightly altered by the author.]

So likewise in Tertullian we see the notion of the eternal Son as the reason of God:

We have already asserted that God made the world, and all which it contains, by His Word, and Reason, and Power. It is abundantly plain that your philosophers, too, regard the *Logos*—that is, the Word and Reason—as the Creator of the universe. For Zeno lays it down that he is the creator, having made all things according to a determinate plan; that his name is Fate, and God, and the soul of Jupiter, and the necessity of all things. Cleanthes ascribes all this to spirit, which he maintains pervades the universe. And we, in like manner, hold that the Word, and Reason, and Power, by which we have said God made all, have spirit as their proper and essential *substratum*, in which the Word has in being to give forth utterances, and reason abides to dispose and arrange, and power is over all to execute. We have been taught that He proceeds forth from God, and in that procession He is generated; so that He is the Son of God, and is called God from unity of substance with God. For God, too, is a Spirit. Even when the ray is shot from the sun, it is still part of the parent mass; the sun will still be in the ray, because it is a ray of the sun—there is no division of substance, but merely an extension. Thus Christ is Spirit of Spirit, and God of God, as light of light is kindled.[98]

Lactantius gives subsequent expression to the idea in an extremely clear way:

I will now say what wise religion, or religious wisdom, is. God, in the beginning, before He made the world, from the fountain of His own eternity, and from the divine and everlasting Spirit, begot for Himself a Son incorruptible, faithful, corresponding to His Father's excellence and majesty. He is virtue, He is reason, He is the word of God, He is wisdom. With this artificer, as Hermes says, and counsellor, as the Sibyl says, He contrived the excellent and wondrous fabric of this world. In fine, of all the angels, whom the same God formed from His own breath, He alone was admitted into a participation of His supreme power, He alone was called God. For all things were through Him, and nothing was without Him.[99]

98. Tertullian, *The Apology*, ch. 21. [Trans. S. Thelwall, *Ante-Nicene Fathers*, vol. 3, ed. A. Roberts, J. Donaldson, and A. C. Coxe (Buffalo, NY: Christian Literature Publishing Co., 1885).

99. Lactantius, *Epitome of the Divine Institutes*, ch. 42. [Trans. W. Fletcher, *Ante-Nicene Fathers*, vol. 7, ed. A. Roberts, J. Donaldson, and A. C. Coxe (Buffalo, NY: Christian Literature Publishing Co., 1886).]

Here we see that the argument for the truth of Christianity is grounded by the apologists in the simultaneous affirmation of the transcendent rationality of God (God's eternal *Logos*) and the rationality of the human person, oriented toward God by spiritual worship. Against what they took to be the irrational religious practices of ambient paganism, the early Christian authors emphasized Eucharistic worship in the Church as "rational worship" or "true worship" according to reason.[100] Understood in light of the eternal *Logos*, then, the human being made in the image of God is meant to be reasonable, including in his religious orientation toward the true and saving God.

Prior to the Council of Nicaea in AD 325, there was also a thematic reflection in various authors on the real distinction of persons in God. We find this in the second century in Irenaeus and later in a more conceptually clear and thematic way in Tertullian and Origen. Irenaeus and Tertullian clearly affirm both that the Son and the Holy Spirit are truly God and that they are persons distinct from the Father.[101] In this way, they each anticipate later Nicene orthodoxy. However, Origen is a more complex case. On the one hand, he rightly emphasizes against the second century gnostic thinker Valentinus that the eternal generation of the *Logos* from the Father is one of eternal *immaterial* procession, not physical begetting. Valentinus paradoxically denies the goodness of the material world while projecting images of material generation upon the mystery of God with his materialistic conception of the pleroma. Origen responds by appeal

100. See for example, Justin Martyr, *First Apology*, chs. 6, 9, 13, 24, 25, 67; Augustine, *City of God*, 10, 6.

101. See Irenaeus, *Against Heresies* III, 16–19; IV, 20; V, 1, 6 and 8 on the divinity of the Son and Holy Spirit and their personal distinction from the Father. Tertullian provided Western Christians with a normative vocabulary for theological reflection on the Holy Trinity, by reference to persons, relations, and nature. See in this regard for example, Tertullian's *Against Praxeas* and the study of Jean Daniélou, in *The Origins of Latin Christianity*, trans. J. A. Baker (London: Darton, Longman & Todd, 1977). Tertullian's contribution to the Trinitarian and Christological conceptualization and terminology of Latin Christianity is significant, despite his well-known dependence upon Stoic conceptions of God that imply a kind of natural materialism in God, an idea that is metaphysically ambiguous.

to the New Testament analogies of immaterial generation of the Word and Wisdom of God, emphasizing that the Son is a *hypostasis*, or subsistent person, distinct from the Father and the Spirit.[102] However, Origen also speculates problematically in various places that the Father, Son, and Spirit are not only distinct persons but also distinct substances, or beings, eternally subordinate to one another.[103] This suggests either some form of Tritheism or more likely a kind of emanating hierarchy of being within the one divinity, in which the Father possesses attributes as God that are not fully partaken of by the Son, as one who is distinct in essence from the Father, derived from and subordinate to him eternally, who is in turn distinct in essence from the Holy Spirit, a yet more derivative and subordinate entity than the Son.[104] It is not surprising that Origen's views led to an internal crisis in early fourth-century Christian theology, since theologians were obliged to clarify what it means to say that there is a real distinction of persons in the Holy Trinity, even while affirming that there is a unity and identity of divine essence and being. This elaboration did not come about without deep intellectual conflict. Nicene Trinitarian thought emerged against the backdrop of this question. However, fourth- and fifth-century Church fathers also had to contend with the alternative views of Arius and Sabellius, who both posited pre-Nicene "answers" to the conundrum that were deeply problematic, and that in turn stimulated a response, out of which Nicene orthodoxy developed as a mature doctrinal interpretation of the New Testament.

---

102. See Origen, *De Prin.* I, 2, 2 and I, 2, 11; *Comm. John* 10.6.24, 32.12.192; *Contra Celsum* 3.16 and 28.

103. See *De Prin.* I,2,9 and *Comm. John* 20, 157 on the Son as a being distinct from the Father; *Comm. John* 13.151–53 on the ontological subordination of the Son and *Comm. John* 2.75 on the Spirit as a creature.

104. This ontology seems similar in particular respects to that of Plotinus, a contemporary of Origen from the same region and general intellectual milieu.

Personal Distinction in God: Pro-Nicene
Theology against Arius and Sabellius

Arius and Sabellius held positions that are specifically opposed to one another but united by a common generic presupposition. The common presupposition maintained by each was that it is impossible to affirm simultaneously that there are three persons in God and that these three persons are each the one God of Biblical monotheism. Given this presupposition, they each interpreted the scriptures in opposed senses. Arius is arguably best understood as a theologian who reacted to Origen by seeking to affirm the uniqueness of God and the truth of Biblical monotheism.[105] To do so, however, he thought it necessary to affirm the divinity of the Father alone and to deny the divinity of the Son and the Holy Spirit. Monotheism is not compatible with the affirmation of a real distinction of persons in God. Consequently, in the era just before the Council of Nicaea, Arius infamously denied that Jesus Christ is truly God and in so doing was understood by his peers as directly contradicting the New Testament.[106] Sabellius, meanwhile, had previously affirmed in the third century that the Son and Spirit are truly God but are not persons truly distinct from the Father. Rather, the Father, Son, and Spirit are merely names by which we denote distinct modes of God's appearance or action in the divine economy.[107] This position is often termed "modalism": there is no real distinction of persons in God, but rather, God appears *to us* in distinct modes that *we for*

105. See the perspectives of Rowan Williams, *Arius, Heresy and Tradition* (London: DLT, 1987), and Lewis Ayres, *Nicaea and Its Legacy: An Approach to Fourth-Century Trinitarian Theology* (Oxford: Oxford University Press, 2004), 20–30, 97–98. See also Frances M. Young, *From Nicaea to Chalcedon: A Guide to the Literature and its Background* (London: SCM, 1983), 58–64.

106. Williams, *Arius*, 100 cites from fragments of Arius's *Thalia*, i-ii : "God was not eternally a father. There was [a time] when God was all alone, and was not yet a father; only later did he become a father."

107. Tertullian describes the position of Sabellius in writing against his disciple Praxeas. See Tertullian's *Against Praxeas*, chs. 1–3. See likewise Ambrose, *Exposition of the Catholic Faith*, I, 1, 6 and I, 8, 57.

our part denominate under the terms Father, Son, and Spirit.[108] God is in fact uni-personal or perhaps a mystery unknown to us, utterly transcending personal identity.

Both of these positions presuppose that a distinction of persons threatens monotheism. One maintains the real distinction of persons and jettisons the divinity of the Son and Spirit (Arianism), while the other maintains the divinity of each person but jettisons their real distinction (Sabellianism or Modalism). Both positions suffer from a lack of understanding of the New Testament idea of immaterial emanation and procession and with it the implicit notion of derived equality in the persons of the Holy Trinity. The Son and Spirit derive eternally from the Father by immaterial generation and spiration. They receive from the Father all that the Father is and has as God. Consequently, they are truly one in being with the Father and equal in divine power, wisdom, and goodness as God, even as they are distinct from him hypostatically, that is to say, personally. It is the mature synthesis of the fourth-century fathers that allowed the early Church to articulate this mystery with both greater profundity and clarity.

The Nicene Doctrine: Athanasius, the Cappadocians, and Augustine

The Council of Nicaea affirmed in AD 325 that Jesus Christ as the Son of God is "light from light, true God from true God, begotten not made, one in substance (*homoousios*) with the Father." This doctrine was formulated in response to Arianism. The word *homoousios*, which means "consubstantial," denotes both a sameness of essence

---

108. Ambrose, *Exposition of the Catholic Faith*, II, 10, 86:

There is, therefore, but one only God, for it is written: "You shall worship the Lord your God, and Him only shall you serve." (Deut. 6:13) One God, not in the sense that the Father and the Son are the same Person, as the ungodly Sabellius affirms—but forasmuch as there is one Godhead of the Father and of the Son and of the Holy Ghost. But where there is one Godhead, there is one will, one purpose [shared by the three persons]. [Trans. H. de Romestin, E. de Romestin, and H. T. F. Duckworth, *Nicene and Post-Nicene Fathers*, vol. 10, ed. P. Schaff and H. Wace (Buffalo, NY: Christian Literature Publishing Co., 1896.)]

and a unity of being. The Council thus clearly denotes (1) the personal distinction of the Son from the Father, (2) the equality of the Son with the Father as God, (3) the fact that the eternal begetting of the Son by the Father is not a making or a creation of the Son, that is, the Son is not a creature, and (4) the unity of being and essence of the Father and the Son. Evidently, this formula signifies that there is a distinction of persons in God but not a distinction of essence or being. The Father and the Son are eternally personally distinct, but they are each the one God. Indeed, there is only one God.

Although the teaching of the Council of Nicaea signaled a definitive rejection of Arian theology on the part of the Catholic Church, it remained necessary to develop a more mature reflection on the mystery of the Trinity. This necessity intensified in the generation after Nicaea, as controversy ensued among bishops in the early Church, some of whom continued to entertain semi-Arian or neo-Origenist positions involving the eternal subordination of the Son to the Father.[109]

It is within this historical setting that the thought of Athanasius of Alexandria proved especially seminal by providing the universal Church with an orthodox interpretation of the New Testament. Athanasius developed three central ideas that were to affect virtually all subsequent Trinitarian theology in both the eastern and western Church. First, he provided a soteriological reason as to why the divinity of Christ matters greatly. His argument for the fittingness of the Incarnation is based on the concept of salvation. Human beings are fragile creatures subject to gravely menacing forms of evil, such as moral ruin, death, and eternal separation from God. Their salvation ultimately depends, then, upon God, who alone can save them from these threats. Salvation must consist in union with God, the offer of eternal life by grace, and bodily resurrection. But only God can effectively unite us to himself and communicate to us the good of salvation in both body and soul. If Christ is truly to be the savior of the

---

109. See on this, Ayres, *Nicaea and Its Legacy*, 85–166, and Athanasius's influential and polemical work from the period, *Against the Arians*.

human race, then, he must do so by uniting us to the mystery of God, but Christ can only do this if he is himself both God and human. Otherwise stated, the human race cannot save itself, and indeed creation as a whole cannot save itself. It is precisely because Christ is both true God and true man that he can unite our human nature to God so as to effectively save us. Consequently, it matters greatly for the very salvation of the human race that Jesus Christ is God and not merely a creature, as Arius erroneously taught. For Christ can save us effectively only because he is both God and human.[110]

Second, Athanasius rightly noted that the analogy from human thought is of key importance for a right understanding of the mystery of the Trinity.[111] Arianism had posited that the generation of the Word from the Father must entail ontological diminution: if the Son is derived from the Father, then he is necessarily less than the Father. But there are no degrees of perfection in the Godhead. Consequently, according to the logic of Arianism, the Son cannot be God and one in being with the Father. This objection presented orthodox Christians with a conundrum: if the Son is in fact one in being with the Father, how then might his generation from the Father be conceived of in such a way as to entail unity of being and equality with the Father? Athanasius noted that the Johannine notion of the *Logos* and the Pauline notion of wisdom both imply a similitude of *immanent* immaterial procession. The eternal Son of the Father is compared by analogy to rational thought proceeding from a person. Rational thought proceeds from a human subject, and yet that thought is "one in being" with the subject. So analogously, the Son who is the eternally begotten wisdom and *Logos* of the Father is one in being with the Father. Consequently, the Biblical analogy for the immaterial generation of the Son presents us not with an idea of an extrinsic creation, as if the *Logos* were a creature made *ex nihilo* by God, but with a similitude based on the immanent spiritual

---

110. This is the thematic argument of Athanasius's early work, *On the Incarnation*. Aquinas develops his own version of the argument in *SCG* IV, c. 55, §§ 5–11 and 14.

111. See, for example, Athanasius, *Against the Arians* I, 24–29.

procession of the *Logos*. Just as the Father is eternally wise in himself, so the Son proceeds forth from him eternally as his Word and
Wisdom, his thought, so to speak, through which he accomplishes
all things. However, in this case, the Son is a subsistent subject eternally distinct from the Father, who contains in himself the plenitude
of the divine being. All that is in the Father as God is in the Son as
God. Thus, Athanasius:

As we said above, so now we repeat, that the divine generation must not
be compared to the nature of men, nor the Son considered to be part of
God, nor the generation to imply any passion whatever; God is not as
man; for men beget passibly, having a transitive nature, which waits for pe-
riods by reason of its weakness. But with God this cannot be; for He is not
composed of parts, but being impassible and simple, He is impassibly and
indivisibly Father of the Son. This again is strongly evidenced and proved
by divine scripture. For the Word of God is His Son, and the Son is the Father's Word and Wisdom; and Word and Wisdom is neither creature nor
part of Him whose Word He is, nor an offspring passibly begotten. Uniting
then the two titles, Scripture speaks of 'Son,' in order to herald the natural
and true offspring of His essence; and, on the other hand, that none may
think of the Offspring humanly, while signifying His essence, it also calls
Him Word, Wisdom, and Radiance; to teach us that the generation was
impassible, and eternal, and worthy of God.[112]

And furthermore:

For the Son is in the Father, as it is allowed us to know, because the whole
Being of the Son is proper to the Father's essence, as radiance from light,
and stream from fountain; so that whoso sees the Son, sees what is proper
to the Father, and knows that the Son's Being, because from the Father, is
therefore in the Father. For the Father is in the Son, since the Son is what
is from the Father and proper to Him, as in the radiance the sun, and in the
word the thought, and in the stream the fountain: for whoso thus contemplates the Son, contemplates what is proper to the Father's Essence, and
knows that the Father is in the Son. For whereas the Form and Godhead
of the Father is the Being of the Son, it follows that the Son is in the Father
and the Father in the Son."[113]

112. Athanasius, *Against the Arians*, I, 28.
113. Athansius, *Against the Arians*, III, 3.

We should observe that because the begetting of the *Logos* is *immaterial*, it need not imply passibility, divine change, or temporality. It is an eternal begetting of the eternal Son without prejudice to the *immutability* of the divine essence.[114]

Third, Athanasius noted that if the Son is truly one in being (*homoousios*) with the Father, then he has the same divine wisdom, will, and power as the Father. Consequently, there is a unity of action of the Father and the Son. They share in the same divine willing and activity as God.

If He has the power of will, and His will is effective, and suffices for the consistence of the things that come to be, and His Word is effective, and a Framer, that Word must surely be the living Will of the Father, and an essential energy, and a real Word, in whom all things both consist and are excellently governed. No one can even doubt, that He who disposes is prior to the disposition and the things disposed. And thus, as I said, God's creating is second to His begetting; for Son implies something proper to Him and truly from that blessed and everlasting Essence; but what is from His will, comes into consistence from without, and is framed through His proper Offspring who is from It.[115]

This idea has significant theological consequences. On Athanasius's view, the Father and the Son only ever act as one principle, in virtue of their common deity. This idea eventually gives rise in later Christian theology to the classical principle that all activity of the persons of the Trinity *ad extra*—that is, "outside" the inner life of the Trinity—are equally operations of all three persons. When God the Holy Trinity creates, it is all three persons who act as God to create the world. When God the Holy Trinity gives grace to the creature, it is all three persons who act as God to give grace to the creature. God always acts as Father, Son, and Holy Spirit. This common activity can be distinguished from personal acts within the immanent life of the Holy Trinity. Only the Father eternally begets the Son,

---

114. See, for example, Athanasius, *Against the Arians*, I, 10; II, 14, and Paul Gavrilyuk, *The Suffering of the Impassible God: The Dialectics of Patristic Thought* (Oxford: Oxford University Press, 2006), 101–34.

115. *Against the Arians*, II, 2.

and only the Father and the Son eternally spirate the Holy Spirit. But when the persons act to create or sanctify, they do so in unity, as the one God, who is Creator and sanctifier.

These principles were both received and developed in the subsequent generation of Christian thought by the Cappadocian fathers, Basil the Great, Gregory of Nazianzus, and Gregory of Nyssa.[116] Although the riches of their theological writings defy rapid summary, we can note three points of particular significance common to their Trinitarian writings. First, the Cappadocians in particular underscore that the persons of the Holy Trinity are distinguished from one another *according to relations of origin*.[117] The Son originates from the Father as his eternally begotten *Logos* and so relates to the Father in his very person. He is eternally relative to the Father, even in all that he is. The Holy Spirit proceeds from the Father by eternal spiration and so also is relative to the Father in his very person. The Father possesses in himself the plenitude of divinity that he communicates to the Son by generation and to the Spirit by spiration. This suggests in turn that the Father too is wholly relative to the Son and Spirit eternally in his very person, as their unbegotten principle from whom they each derive their origin eternally.[118]

116. See on this point Ayres, *Nicaea and Its Legacy*, 187–221, 244–72, 344–63; Basil the Great, *On the Holy Spirit*; Gregory of Nazianzus, "Five Theological Orations" (*Orat.* 27–31); Gregory of Nyssa, *Not Three Gods* and *Against Eunomius*.

117. See, for example, Basil, *Against Eunomius* 2, 9; Gregory of Nazianzus, *Orat.* 31, 9; Gregory of Nyssa, *Against Eunomius*, II, 3 and 9; III, 4 and 6–7.

118. On the Father's relative identity in Nazianzus, see Orat. 31, 9 and in Nyssa, *Against Eunomius*, II, 2:

> For the term Father would have no meaning apart by itself, if Son were not connoted by the utterance of the word Father. When, then, we learned the name Father we were taught at the same time, by the selfsame title, faith also in the Son. Now since Deity by its very nature is permanently and immutably the same in all that pertains to its essence, nor did it at any time fail to be anything that it now is, nor will it at any future time be anything that it now is not, and since He Who is the very Father was named Father by the Word, and since in the Father the Son is implied—since these things are so, we of necessity believe that He Who admits no change or alteration in His nature was always entirely what He is now, or, if there is anything which He was not, *that* He assuredly is not now. Since then He is named Father by the very Word, He assuredly always was Father, and is and will be even as He was. [Trans. H. C. Ogle and

According to this conception, personhood is relational in the Holy Trinity. Each of the persons is truly God and possesses in himself the plenitude of the divinity. But each of the persons is also relative to the others, since the Father is eternally "for" the generation of the *Logos* and spiration of the Spirit, and each of them is eternally "from" the Father.[119] This notion of relational personhood allows the Cappadocian fathers to attain a profound understanding of "derived equality" in God.[120] The Son and Spirit derive all that they are in their being and personhood from the Father, but they also each receive from him all that is in him in virtue of his divine nature as God. The Father communicates his eternal divine life to the Son and the Spirit so that they each possess the fullness of the deity. Consequently, they are also equal to the Father as God, one in being with him and truly divine.[121]

Second, as these reflections suggest, the Cappadocians underscore in an explicit way why one must hold that the Holy Spirit, as he is presented in the New Testament, must be truly God. The Holy Spirit *proceeds* eternally from the Father (John 15:26) even as the Son is generated eternally, and the Holy Spirit is in personal relation

---

H. A. Wilson, *Nicene and Post-Nicene Fathers*, vol. 5, ed. Philip Schaff and Henry Wace (Buffalo, NY: Christian Literature Publishing Co., 1893).]

119. See on this Ayres, *Nicaea and Its Legacy*, 201–202, 247.

120. See Gregory of Nazianzus, *Orat.* 30, chs. 11 and 20. The notion of "derived equality" is taken from E. L. Mascall, *The Triune God: An Ecumenical Study* (London: Pickwick Publications, 1986), 16, and *Via Media: An Essay in Theological Synthesis* (London: Longmans and Green, 1956), ch. 2.

121. Gregory of Nyssa, *Not Three Gods*:

The Father is God: the Son is God: and yet by the same proclamation God is One, because no difference either of nature or of operation is contemplated in the Godhead. For if (according to the idea of those who have been led astray) the nature of the Holy Trinity were diverse, the number would by consequence be extended to a plurality of Gods, being divided according to the diversity of essence in the subjects. But since the Divine, single, and unchanging nature, that it may be one, rejects all diversity in essence, it does not admit in its own case the signification of multitude; but as it is called one nature, so it is called in the singular by all its other names, God, Good, Holy, Saviour, Just, Judge, and every other Divine name conceivable: whether one says that the names refer to nature or to operation, we shall not dispute the point.

to the Father as the origin of the Spirit.[122] This procession differentiates him from the Son, who is differentiated by generation. The relation is eternal (the Father can only be understood as the Father of the Spirit, as well as the Son) and so it is something proper to the Godhead.[123] Otherwise stated, because the Father is eternally Father of the Spirit, so too then, the Spirit must be eternal and must be himself God from God.

Moreover, the Holy Spirit as presented in the New Testament works by and in the power of God and is the source of divinization in human beings. No one can sanctify human beings by the gift of divinization—that is, the communication of grace to the human person—who is not himself divine. But the Holy Spirit does so, working as one with the Father and Son in the economy of salvation:

The Godhead of the Holy Spirit can be proved thoroughly scriptural.... Christ is born, the Spirit is his forerunner; Christ is baptized, the Spirit bears him witness; Christ is tempted, the Spirit leads him up; Christ performs miracles, the Spirit accompanies him; Christ ascends, the Spirit fills his place. Is there any significant function belonging to God, which the Spirit does not perform? Is there any title belonging to God, which cannot apply to him, except "ingenerate" and "begotten"? ... The Spirit it is who created and creates anew through baptism and resurrection. The Spirit it is who knows all things, who teaches all things.... He makes us his temple, he deifies, he makes us complete.... All that God actively performs, he performs.[124]

This is why the Holy Spirit is rightly worshiped, honored, and glorified as God in the life of the Church. He communicates divine life to the Church, as only one can who is himself God and who possesses the fullness of the divine nature. Consequently, the Holy Spirit must be considered consubstantial (*homoousios*) with the Father and the Son.[125]

122. See Basil, *On the Holy Spirit*, ch. 16, sec. 38; Gregory of Nazianzus, *Orat.* 31, 8.
123. Basil, *On the Holy Spirit*, ch. 26, sec. 63.
124. Gregory of Nazianzus, *Orat.* 31, 29. [Trans. L. Wickham, *On God and Christ: Five Theological Orations and Two Letters to Cledonius* (New York: St. Vladimir's Seminary Press, 2002).]
125. The doctrine of the divinity of the Holy Spirit was in fact affirmed at the Council of Constantinople in 381, in part through the influence of Gregory of Nazianzus.

Third, the Cappadocian fathers enunciate a classical principle of Christian theology that applies equally in both Trinitarian and Christological theology. A person only ever acts in and through a nature. A nature is only ever the nature of a distinct person.[126] This is true in the case of human persons: each individual has a human nature, and each individual human nature is the nature of a singular person, not that of distinct persons. The idea applies analogously in the case of the persons of the Holy Trinity. The divine persons are truly distinct hypostatically, and each of them has a given nature, that is to say, each of them is truly God. Each only ever acts, then, in and by virtue of the divine nature that is common to the three persons. However, here the dissimilitude appears. Three human persons may share the same nature, but they all have distinct individual natures. They are not the same individual being. This is not the case in the mystery of the Holy Trinity. The Father, Son, and Holy Spirit are not only one in divine essence or nature but also one in being. Their nature is common not only in kind but also in singularity of existence. They are each the one God. Consequently, there is nothing in the Father that is not in the Son and in the Spirit, nothing in the Son that is not in the Father and in the Spirit, and nothing in the Spirit that is not in the Father and in the Son. And yet the Father, Son, and Holy Spirit are truly distinct as hypostatic persons. Therefore, their mystery is utterly unlike that of three human persons in this respect. Their interpersonal communion is infinitely superior to any merely human communion of persons, no matter how sublime. It transcends all of our conceptions.[127]

From this last principle a profound truth follows. We can and should affirm that the Trinitarian persons act together as the one God, in virtue of their shared essence or nature. However, even when the persons of the Holy Trinity act as one, they always act as

126. The distinction between the nature common to a plurality of persons and the particular personal subject in which this nature exists originates with Basil in his *Epistle to Terentius* (PG 32, 798 A). I am grateful to Brian Daley for pointing this out to me.

127. A point made often by each of the Cappadocian Fathers. See, for example, Gregory of Nazianzus, *Orat.* 28, 7; 29, 11; 30, 18.

distinct persons in accord with their relations of origin. Thus the actions of God the Holy Trinity only ever stem from the Father, through the Son, who is his Word, and in the Holy Spirit, who is the Father's Spirit of holiness. God the Father gives being to the world or sanctifies the world *through* his *Logos*, who is his wisdom, *in* the power of the Holy Spirit, source of all holiness and goodness.[128] The Father, Son, and Holy Spirit are one God and act in creation as one agent, but there are also personal modes of action in the united operation of the Holy Trinity. The divine mode of the Father is that of he who is unoriginated, the principle and font of all Trinitarian life. He acts in creation as the eternal source of the divine Word and Spirit, and he acts through his Word and Spirit. The divine mode of the Son is that of he who is immaterially begotten Wisdom. He acts in creation as the Word of the Father, through whom the Father creates and sanctifies all that exists. The divine mode of the Spirit is that of he who is eternally spirated. He acts in creation as the Spirit of holiness, immanent to the Father, in whom the Father creates and sanctifies all things.

A generation after the Cappadocian fathers, Augustine of Hippo developed key ideas of Trinitarian theology taken from eastern Christian authors and articulated them anew within the context of the western Latin-speaking world. In doing so he contributed significant insights of his own. In particular, he sought to develop reflection on the similitude between the Trinity and the human soul—the so-called psychological analogy—by comparing the generation of the eternal Word to the production of wisdom in a human agent and by comparing the eternal spiration of the Holy Spirit to the activity of spiritual love in the human agent. The Son is thus understood by comparison with wisdom and the Spirit by comparison with love.[129] Augustine presumes that God is essentially transcendent, incomprehensible, and spiritual in nature, rather than material. God is like-

---

128. Nyssa makes this point in *Not Three Gods*.

129. See, for example, Augustine, *The Trinity*, trans. Edmund Hill (Hyde Park, NY: New City Press, 1991), IX, 1–3. On the Nicene origins of Augustine's theology see Lewis Ayres, *Augustine and the Trinity* (Cambridge: Cambridge University Press, 2010), 42–93.

wise the creative source of what is spiritual in human persons who are created in his image in virtue of their rational operations of intellect and will. Can one identify, then, a similitude between the Trinity and the inner spiritual life of the human person in his or her soul? Clearly there is an eternal procession in God that bears a similitude to the life of the human mind, because the first chapter of the Gospel of John teaches that the eternally begotten Son of God is the *Logos* of God. Augustine advances arguments for a complementary notion of the Spirit as love or charity, which pertains by similitude in us to the immaterial activity of the will. The Holy Spirit is the transcendent, uncreated love of the Father and the Son. He is charity in all that he is.[130] On this model, the Son is the eternally begotten wisdom and Word of the Father, while the Spirit is the eternally spirated love of the Father and the Son.[131] The two processions in God correspond to two distinct similitudes of knowledge and love.

Augustine affirms the paternal primacy of the Father as the eternal first origin of the Word and the Spirit.[132] The Father is the font of Trinitarian life. However, Augustine also clearly thinks that we can begin to discern an order to the mystery of the eternal processions of the Word and the Spirit. In the human soul, spiritual love proceeds forth from knowledge, since we only love what we first come to know. So by similitude in the life of God, the Spirit who is love proceeds from divine understanding. He is the Spirit of both the Father and his Word—a love that proceeds eternally from wisdom. As Augustine puts it, "According to the holy scriptures this Holy Spirit is not just the Father's alone nor the Son's alone, but the Spirit of them both, and thus he suggests to us the common charity by which the Father and the Son love each other."[133] He continues:

[I]t is not without point that in this triad only the Son is called the Word of God, and only the Holy Spirit is called the gift of God [who is love], and only the Father is called the one from whom the Word is born and

---

130. Augustine, *The Trinity*, VI, 7; XV, 27–28, 31–32, 43.

131. Augustine, *The Trinity*, V, 12–13; VI, 7; XV, 27, 37.

132. Augustine, *The Trinity*, XV, 29, 47.

133. Augustine, *The Trinity*, XV, 27.

from whom the Holy Spirit principally proceeds. I added "principally,"
because we have found that the Holy Spirit also proceeds from the Son.
But this too was given the Son by the Father—not given to him when he
already existed and did not yet have it; but whatever the Father gave to
his only-begotten Word he gave by begetting him. He so begot him then
that their common gift would proceed from him too, and the Holy Spirit would be the Spirit of them both. This distinction then within the inseparable trinity must be diligently looked into and not casually taken for
granted. It is this that allows the word of God also to be called distinctively the wisdom of God, even though both Father and Holy Spirit are also
wisdom. If therefore any of these three can be distinctively named charity, which could it more suitably be than the Holy Spirit? What is meant is
that while in that supremely simple nature substance is not one thing and
charity another, but substance is charity and charity is substance, whether
in the Father or in the Son or in the Holy Spirit, yet all the same the Holy
Spirit is distinctively named charity.[134]

Clearly, then, as we have noted, Augustine develops the idea,
held by previous Latin Fathers, that the Holy Spirit proceeds eternally from the Father and the Son.[135] Indeed, he posits that the Spirit
proceeds from them both as from one principle.[136] The idea here, in
effect, is that the Father gives to the eternally begotten Word all that
he possesses, including the active power to spirate the Spirit. The
Son, who is eternally Word from the Father, spirates the Holy Spirit
with the Father as one principle or origin of the Spirit. In this way,
Augustine understands the Spirit as the eternally reciprocal love of
the Father and the Son, their mutual gift of immaterial love, a person who is charity.[137]

134. Augustine, *The Trinity*, XV, 29.
135. See Hilary, *On the Trinity* 2, 29; 8, 20; 12, 56; and Ambrose, *On the Holy Spirit*, 1, 11.
136. Augustine, *The Trinity*, V, 14–16.
137. Augustine, *The Trinity*, XV, 37:

As then holy scripture proclaims that charity is God, and as it is from God
and causes us to abide in God and him in us, and as we know this because
he has given us of his Spirit, this Spirit of his is God charity. Again, if there is
nothing greater than charity among God's gifts, and if there is no greater gift of
God's than the Holy Spirit, what must we conclude but that he is his charity
which is called both God and from God? And if the charity by which the Father loves the Son and the Son loves the Father inexpressibly shows forth the

Perhaps there is a fundamental conceptual problem present in Augustine's thought, since he employs terms that are proper to the divine essence, such as wisdom and love, to denote the three persons in a distinct way. After all, if the three persons are truly one in essence, as the ineffable God, then they are each identically ineffably wise and loving. Wisdom and love are perfections of the divine essence that are present equally, identically, and co-eternally in all three persons. What Augustine has claimed, however, is that a further distinction is possible. Yes, on the one hand, it is true: wisdom can be attributed to the Son or love can be attributed to the Holy Spirit as an essential term proper to the divine nature, that is, common to the Father, Son, and Spirit. However, on the other hand, these same notions can be attributed to the Son and Spirit in distinct ways as relational terms, denoting the reception of the divine essence from another.[138] The Father from all eternity possesses the divine life in himself, so as to be eternally wise and loving, and he communicates this divine life to the Son by generation and to the Spirit by spiration with the Son. The Son receives the divine life relationally, as the begotten Word, while the Spirit receives the divine life relationally, as the spirated Love of the Father and Son. The Father does not become wise because of the Son or loving because of the Spirit.[139] Rather the Father communicates to the Son the totality of his divine life of wisdom and love, and the Father and the Son communicate the totality of the divine life to the Holy Spirit. The distinctions arise among them from relations of origin. The Son eternally derives from the Father as his begotten wisdom, by a similitude according to the immaterial generation of knowledge *from* the plenitude of wisdom of the Father. The Spirit eternally derives from the Father and the Son as their spirated love, by a similitude according to immaterial spiration of love *from* the plenitude of the love that the Father has for himself as God in and with his Word and Son.

communion of them both, what more suitable than he who is the common Spirit of them both should be distinctively called charity?

138. Augustine, *The Trinity*, XV, 6–13.

139. Augustine, *The Trinity*, VII, 1–2; XV, 37.

Like the Cappadocian fathers before him, Augustine affirms that the distinction of persons in God is made intelligible by recourse to the notion of relations of origin. The persons are equal and identical essentially as God, and they are distinct in virtue of the mode in which they communicate or receive the divine life or essence of God: as paternal, filial, or spirated. Logically, then, Augustine draws a connection between this idea and the notion that the Spirit is the shared mutual love of the Father and the Son, who is derived eternally by a relation of origin from both the Father and the Son. The distinction of the Son and the Spirit is rendered most intelligible for us once we begin to consider the mystery of their distinction according to relations of origin. They do not merely both relate to the Father as their primal origin; they also relate to one another. Since they are each equally and identically God, one with the Father in all that pertains to the divine essence, they are only distinguishable from one another according to a relation of origin.[140] The eternal Son comes forth from the Father and not from the Spirit, while the Spirit originates not only from the Father but also from the Son, as the Love who is their mutual gift. Thus, he is eternally distinguishable from the Son who is the Word of the Father.[141] These relational distinctions of the Son and the Spirit do not annul or void the mystery of divine unity. The wisdom and love common to all three persons are in the unbegotten Father, the Son who is the begotten Word, and the Spirit who is Love. Augustine thus maintains a "Cappadocian" understanding of the distinctions of persons by recourse to the idea of relations of origin and arguably deepens this insight by his developed reflection on the Spirit as one proceeding from the Son. At the same time, this way of thinking leads to a profound appreciation of the monotheistic character of the Trinitarian faith. Because the persons are distinguished uniquely by recourse to relational terms, they must otherwise be denoted as identical in all things pertaining to essence, power, wisdom, goodness, and so on. It is a necessary condi-

---

140. Augustine, *The Trinity*, V, 6, 9, 11, 14; VII, 2.
141. Augustine, *The Trinity*, V, 13–15.

tion of authentic Trinitarian reflection, then, that one should affirm a singularity of essence in God in such a way as to maintain an utter and transparent monotheism. Even if the revelation of the New Testament unveils to us the inner life of God as Trinity, it also stands in fundamental conceptual continuity with the Old Testament revelation of God as one.

CONCLUSION: BASIC TRINITARIAN CLAIMS

The purpose of this last section of our reflection on credibility has been to show the internal *coherence* of Trinitarian monotheism as a historical revelation and as a conceptual form of belief. My aim has been only to identify the first principles of Trinitarian doctrine in scripture and tradition, not to explore the mystery of the Holy Trinity in its full depth. Nor have I made any attempt to demonstrate the truth of Christianity from mere philosophical argument. The mystery of the Trinity is only understood and embraced in virtue of the grace of faith working through hope and charity. Here in conclusion, however, we may note several principles that are intrinsic to Trinitarian theology.

One God. The revelation of the New Testament presupposes that of the Old, and it is monotheistic in form. It is grounded implicitly in the teaching of Jesus Christ, with respect to his own identity, his unity with the Father and with the Holy Spirit. This teaching is preserved and developed conceptually in the apostolic writings of the New Testament. The Trinitarian mystery is essentially the mystery of God's inner identity as Father, Son, and Holy Spirit, but the knowledge of this mystery has ecclesial and eschatological dimensions. The revelation of the Holy Trinity occurs through the life, death, and resurrection of the Son of God and in the sending of the Holy Spirit upon the early apostolic Church. As such, it occurs in tandem with the opening of the covenant to all human beings through the death of Christ. This is the beginning of the universal "gathering" (*ecclesia*) or Catholic Church. This revelation also occurs as a disclosure about the ultimate fate of all creation in the eschatological end times in virtue of Christ's resurrected, glorified humanity. In other words, the mystery of the Trinity is first and foremost a mystery about the identity of God in himself, but it is inseparable from the revelation of the mystery of the Church and that of the universal resurrection of the dead and the cosmic re-creation it implies. These mysteries—namely, the Church and the eschaton of the resurrection—are ultimately only intelligible for Christianity as mysteries that point to the Holy Trinity as the one true God of the Bible, the true mystery of who God is.

Unity of essence and real distinction of persons. In this life, God the Holy Trinity is known to us not in an immediate way by vision but through the medium of divine revelation under the veil of faith. Nevertheless, the Catholic Church claims that we can come to certitudes about the mystery of God in himself and can express these imperfectly but truly in human language. Based on the teaching of the New Testament, it is true and necessary to say that God is one in being and essence. There is only one God, who is ineffable and incomprehensible in nature. And at the same time, God is three hypostases, that is, three "subsistent persons" or "distinct personal modes of being": Father, Son, and Holy Spirit. The persons are truly distinct. The Father is not the Son or the Spirit, the Son is not the Father or the Spirit, and the Spirit is not the Father or the Son. However, each of the persons possesses the plenitude of the divine nature and thus is truly the one God. Therefore, all that is in the Father is in the Son and the Spirit, and all that is in the Son is in the Father and the Spirit, and all that is in the Spirit is in the Father and the Son. The divine persons mysteriously each possess the plenitude of the divine life and perfection and are truly one in being. From this it follows that they have one will and one activity. When God creates or sanctifies, it is the Holy Trinity that creates or sanctifies and never simply one of the persons acting alone. Each of the persons acts with and from the others, according to an order of procession, the Father acting through his Son, and in their common Spirit. Consequently, we may say that God has revealed in the New Testament that there is in his eternal life a communion of persons.

Immaterial processions. The distinction of persons in God is numinous but intelligible based on the distinction between immanent activity and transitive activity. Immanent activity terminates within the subject, as in the case of immaterial actions of knowledge and love in human persons. Transitive activity terminates in an outward activity, such as that of an artistic production like carpentry, speaking, writing, or painting, which each actively transform the external world in some modest way.[142] The New Testament depicts the eternal generation of the Son by recourse to an analogy from the immanent activity of human thinking, and this is in turn the foundation for the transitive activity of creation. The Son is the eternally begotten *Logos*, who comes forth from the Father from all eternity and is one with the Father. This begetting of the *Logos* is immanent to the life of God prior to any initiative of creation. Likewise, the Holy Spirit is said to proceed eternally from the Father and the Son as their mutual Love. For Augustine, this is analogous to the procession of spiritual love in the human will that proceeds from knowledge, as when we know someone and then begin to love that person.

Relations of origin. Each person of the Holy Trinity possesses the plenitude of the divine nature that is communicated to them by and in the processions of generation and spiration. The Father gives to the Son as his eternal wisdom to possess in himself all that is in the Father as God. The Father is not made wise in virtue of his generation of the Son, but he generates the Son as begotten wisdom out of his eternal plenitude of wisdom as Father. The Father and the Son give to the Holy Spirit as their mutual Love to possess in himself all that the Father and the Son possess as God. They do not become loving or good in virtue of the spiration of the Spirit, but they eternally spirate the Spirit out of the plenitude of love that they possess as Father and Son. This means that there is a unique equality and indeed identity of nature in the three persons who are each the

142. Aquinas, *De pot.*, q. 10, a. 1, corp. and ad 1.

one God, and yet each is distinguishable from the others due to his distinct mode of relating to the others eternally. Later Augustinian theologians will say that in God, personhood is subsistently relational and that Trinitarian persons are subsistent relations. We might say in a colloquial way that persons in God are relational "all the way down" and "always already."

Psychological analogy. The Trinity is a mystery known to us only by divine revelation, but even now this mystery does cast light on all our other knowledge about the world. The revelation of the Trinity manifests to us that there is in God a transcendent mystery of communion-in-love that is inexpressibly higher and more perfect than any human love. This divine love, or eternal communion of persons, is the fundamental ground of all things, such that the Holy Trinity creates and sustains the world in being in light of the eternal love that the Father has for the Son in the Holy Spirit. Created persons are made in the image of God, and they are meant to contemplate the wisdom of God and participate in the charity of God—the love that he has for us individually and collectively. For Christians, then, personhood is something primal to all reality. Before there was human personhood, there was divine personhood, and before there was any human communion of persons, there was and is the divine communion of persons. In the beginning, there was personhood. God is a trinity of persons, and he created the natural order in view of the communion of human persons with him, so that we might participate by grace in his Trinitarian life.

I have noted that in the pre-Nicene period, the apologists like Justin Martyr sometimes depicted God as a monological subject who created through his Word. The distinction of persons was more consistently emphasized in the post-Nicene period by thinkers responding to Arianism and Sabellianism. But the pre-Nicene analogies for God are harmonious with those that come after the Council. God is a communion of three persons who share the same nature, and this is analogous in some sense to three human persons who each possess the same nature or essence. However, such an analogy must be corrected or correlated with another by noting that the three persons in God are mysteriously one in being, utterly unlike human persons. In keeping with the psychological analogy from human knowledge and love, then, one may consider God according to the analogy of one person or monological subject who has a fullness of knowledge and love. The eternal Father is fully wise and loving in himself. But we must also correct this analogy by noting that in God, the Word that the Father begets in his act of knowing is a person distinct from the Father. Likewise, the Spirit who proceeds from the Father and the Word as love is a person distinct from the Father and the Son. The first analogy to a communion of persons "breaks down" due to unity: God is a unity of persons in a way that three human persons are not. The second analogy to the monological subject "breaks down" due to the real distinction of persons: in human beings, the inner life of knowledge and love is proper to one person alone, while in God, the inner life of knowledge and love consists of a distinction of persons in communion. Each analogy is a corrective to the other, because God is truly one in being, like a single activity of knowledge and love, and God is truly a communion of persons who are one in divine essence, in similitude to a communion of human persons, but of an ineffable and incomprehensively higher unity and singularity of being.

Knowledge of God by revelation and by reason. The Catholic theological tradition affirms that the God of scripture can be known in two distinct but harmonious ways, by mode of revelation and by mode of natural reason. The mystery of the Holy Trinity as such can be known only from divine revelation, as I have noted. However, the revelation of the Trinity is also a revelation of the Creator, the one God who is author of all that exists. This revelation therefore invites and welcomes the cooperation of natural reason, which can seek to discern in creatures a basis for authentic philosophical knowledge of God in his unity and divine perfections. Indeed, the Catholic Church maintains on the basis of scripture itself that God's existence and perfections can be known with certainty through sound philosophical reflection on the structure of creation. This form of knowledge can in turn be placed in the service of reflection on the mystery of the Holy Trinity.

Kataphatacism and apophaticism. The knowledge of God is both positive and negative, luminous and obscure. This is the case in distinct ways both at the natural and supernatural levels. The natural knowledge of God, which is dependent upon sound philosophical reasoning, can achieve some indirect but real knowledge of God, his existence, and his attributes. This knowledge is imperfect and in some ways opaque. God as thus known from his creatures remains hidden in darkness, obscured from view by the iconostasis of his creation that simultaneously renders him imperfectly manifest even as it conceals him from our vision.

The supernatural knowledge of God is that which derives from divine revelation of the Holy Trinity. God can be known in a higher and more perfect way by revelation than he can by mere natural means. In addition, this knowledge that is conveyed to us by means of grace is intimate and personal, implying spiritual contact with the persons of the Holy Trinity in the illuminative clarity and obscure darkness of supernatural faith. Communion with the Holy Trinity by faith is more perfect and luminous than any merely natural knowledge of God. At the same time, communion with the Trinity by faith is obscure and numinous, maintained in this life through supernatural hope and love, not by direct vision or immediate intellectual apperception. "For we walk by faith, not by sight" (2 Cor. 5:7). As I discuss in the final chapter on Trinitarian mysticism, this apophaticism of the supernatural kind is something other than the mere absence of understanding, an imperfection of knowledge, or a lack of presence. It is, on the contrary, something positive in its own way, an effect of divine grace, one that inaugurates the mystery of the soul's marriage with God, leading the soul by light toward perfect vision and by love toward perfect union.

4

The Natural Desire to See God

In this final chapter, I would like to consider briefly the rational motives of the credibility of the Catholic faith from the point of view of philosophical reason. We should be clear, once again, that this topic does not consist in any attempt to demonstrate philosophically the truth of the Catholic faith, nor am I affirming any form of natural access to the supernatural content of faith, the formal object of faith that is the revelation of the Holy Trinity. The aim, rather, is to consider *in light of divine revelation*, presuming that it is the truth about God, what can motivate the human person to accept the truth of that revelation, *just insofar as* it harmonizes with the aspirations of natural reason. The primary motivations of consent to the faith for any genuine Christian believer are supernatural in kind. We believe God because God reveals himself and inspires us inwardly to desire supernatural union with God himself, by hope and by love.[1] But supernatural motivation does not exclude various forms of natural motivation, just as grace does not reject what is innate to human nature and its inherent inclinations.

Reflection on this particular topic, then, has its place internal to faith for a believer who is considering the natural reasonableness of supernatural consent already given to the faith, which has already

1. See *ST* II-II, q. 2, aa. 1, 2, 9.

been initiated by grace and accomplished in grace. This is an appropriate form of reflection for the believer insofar as grace does not suppress natural reason, so that the believer may pose probing questions concerning the natural reasonableness of the acceptance of divine revelation. Or, distinctly and analogously, a person who is investigating Christianity sympathetically, perhaps inwardly moved by grace already, may investigate the rational grounds of belief insofar as they exist. To the extent that these are discovered, the person may dispel objections against religious belief in Christianity in order to remove obstacles to the faith, even if such a person cannot procure formal understanding of the object of faith merely from natural reasoning.[2] This logically antecedent process of ground clearing is necessary for some people as a prelude to, or as part of the process of, inward consent to the mystery of faith.

As we noted in chapter 1 in our treatment of reasonable belief in revelation, the Catholic Church teaches that revelation ought to be accompanied by rational signs of credibility. In addition, she teaches that divine revelation casts light on created reality in such a way as to provide more ultimate and intensive explanations of reality. How, then, does the mystery of the Trinity cast light on the mystery of what it is to be human, made in the image of God, if God is Trinity, and if the human image of God is Trinitarian? How does the revelation of the Trinity assist supernaturally in intellectual comprehension of both the life of individual human persons, and their collective life in political communion, within the larger setting of the physical cosmos?

In this chapter I will seek to treat both these questions in a related way by referring to the natural desire of the human being to see God. The fact that Christian revelation posits the vision of the essence of the Holy Trinity as a final end of the human person is a reason that revelation should be taken seriously, philosophically, as offering a completeness to human existence that human reason can

---

2. See the wider consideration of these themes in Ambroise Gardeil, *La crédibilité et l'apologétique.*

comprehend imperfectly in its own terms and find compelling, but which our human nature cannot procure by its own powers. The vision of the essence of God, if it is real, is the greatest good of the human person. To a certain extent, as I shall argue, this claim is perfectly intelligible even from a merely philosophical point of view. The philosopher can entertain on his or her own terms the idea that immediate knowledge of the essence of God constitutes the greatest possible good for the human soul. If this is the case, then the Christian saints who orient their lives toward this end and live for the vision of God in a coherent and virtuous way provide a kind of rational testimony to the warrant for the acceptance of Christianity as divine revelation. They do so especially when they manifest this form of life by tending toward beatitude in heroic acts of virtue and when this contemplative life is accompanied by miraculous or extraordinary signs of contemplation of God that anticipate the beatitude of heaven. The lives of the saints invite us to aspire with them to the spiritually ecstatic happiness of eternal beatitude in heaven.

Similarly, the revelation of God as Trinity casts light on the notion of the human person as a being made for the knowledge of the truth, and for the pursuit of happiness and love, especially through the most perfect knowledge possible of the highest cause of all things, that is, God. The idea that the knowledge of the Trinity completes the human person corresponds to the idea of the human person as made in the image of the Trinity, which is most manifest in the immanent spiritual activities of knowledge and love. These activities are perfected especially when the human person turns actively toward God as the final end of human happiness. One becomes most like the Trinity by knowledge and by love when the primary truth known and the ultimate good one finds happiness in is the life of God himself.

There are collective political and cosmic implications to this claim. The human being who is *capax Dei* is also capable of attaining to the knowledge and enjoyment of God in communion with others in a collective life of divine truth, charity, justice, and mercy, in which God is mutually enjoyed and possessed by the community of the Church. The human community seen in this light is also the achievement or crown of the visible creation, the locus or place where the material and animal world meets with the invisible and spiritual world. In the human community, then, the cosmos returns to God, through the mediation of the rational animal, who is friends with God by grace. These claims are all true in a particular way only if human beings are capable of Trinitarian life, such that human persons made in the image of God can hope reasonably one day to see the Trinity face to face. The consideration of the natural desire to see God as a core feature of human beings thus provides us with an illuminating way of thinking about the explanatory power of Christian revelation, as well as one of the core rational motives for Christian belief.

ON THE PHILOSOPHICAL INTELLIGIBILITY
OF THE NATURAL DESIRE TO SEE GOD

Catholic Christianity, basing itself on the mystery of divine revelation, teaches that the human being is called by God and by his grace to enter into the beatific vision, the immediate vision of the essence of God. The idea is already presented in overt ways in the New Testament, where Paul speaks of seeing God "face to face" (1 Cor. 12:13) and John speaks of eventually seeing God as he is in himself (1 John 3:2). The book of Revelation meanwhile speaks about the city of God in heaven as a place in which the whole people of God gaze upon God and see him directly in his eternal light (Rev. 22:4–5). Subsequent to various debates on the nature of this vision, the magisterium of the Catholic Church came to the discernment that the vision in question pertains to God in himself.[3] The souls of the blessed

---

3. See the 1992 *Catechism of the Catholic Church*, 1023–1024, which in turn cites Benedict XII, *Benedictus Deus* from the year 1336:

> By virtue of our apostolic authority, we define the following: According to the general disposition of God, the souls of all the saints ... and other faithful who

truly see God in himself. This is true even though the human soul that enjoys the vision of God by grace only grasps what God is imperfectly, not comprehensively. In other words, the human being by the grace of the beatific vision may truly see God in himself, but he or she does not know God in the way that God knows and contemplates himself divinely and eternally.[4] The divine essence is intuitively known by the beatified saint but not comprehended.

Furthermore, medieval theologians debated about what kind of specific grace is given by God to those who die in a state of grace such that they can effectively see God intelletually and thus participate actively in the life of God. Though various positions emerged, most theologians posited a distinct form of grace conventionally termed the *lumen gloriae*, a grace formally created in itself, not equivalent with God as such but that has as its final end or effect in the human soul to elevate the soul into the immediate vision of God by grace. This occurs in such a way that the intellect intuitively perceives by vision what and who God is, as Trinity and Lord, and in such a way that the human heart, guided by knowledge, possesses a union by love with the transcendent goodness of God that is most intensive and immutably perfect in its plenitude, life, and duration. Formally speaking, the grace of the beatific vision is something created by God in the souls of the blessed, but it has as its terminus or final cause the realization of perfect union, so that the souls of the blessed see God intuitively and possess him in perfect love.[5]

---

died after receiving Christ's holy Baptism (provided they were not in need of purification when they died ... or, if they then did need or will need some purification, when they have been purified after death ...) already before they take up their bodies again and before the general judgment—and this since the Ascension of our Lord and Savior Jesus Christ into heaven—have been, are and will be in heaven, in the heavenly Kingdom and celestial paradise with Christ, joined to the company of the holy angels. Since the Passion and death of our Lord Jesus Christ, these souls have seen and do see the divine essence with an intuitive vision, and even face to face, without the mediation of any creature.

4. See Aquinas, *ST* I, q. 12, aa. 6–7.

5. On the *lumen gloriae*, see Aquinas, *ST* I, q. 12, a. 5. It is a created grace infused into the intellect that elevates the natural created mind so that it is able to perceive God in himself by grace.

At the same time, theologians have traditionally been at pains to demonstrate that this theological revelation of the final end of the human person, in which the human person is perfected by the vision of God, is not something diametrically opposed to the natural flourishing of the person as best we can understand human beings by recourse to philosophical reason. If God reveals that he is our destiny and that we are called by grace to see him face to face, is this revelation something wholly alien and violent to human nature, or does it correspond to something native to us, namely, to our natural desire to know God and even to a natural desire to see God in himself? Thus, one can pose the question philosophically in relation to the mystery of theological revelation: does the human being have a natural desire to see God?

It is interesting to note the way that Thomas Aquinas treats the topic of the natural human desire to see the essence of God in his great apologetic work, *Summa contra Gentiles*, especially in Book III. The *Summa contra Gentiles* in general presupposes the truths of the Christian faith as given by divine revelation, but it seeks to employ philosophical argumentation to demonstrate the truths taught by revelation *insofar* as these are accessible to human reason. In this sense, the work constitutes an extensive meditation on the *praeambula fidei*, truths of revelation otherwise accessible to human reason. Aquinas there also treats the doctrines of the faith derived from divine revelation themselves insofar as these can be defended from the charge of irrationality or incoherence. The former methodology prevails in Book I on naturally known attributes of God, in Book II on the creation, angels, and human persons, and in Book III, on the philosophical intelligibility of divine providence and on the final end of man. In Book IV, he treats the mysteries of the faith and defends them from the charges of irrationality and incoherence. This all being said, there is an interesting point of transition in Book III after Aquinas has argued for a philosophically defensible notion of divine providence and for the rational defense of man's natural desire to see God, where he introduces the notion of grace as a theological topic, illustrating its fitting metaphysical harmony with and logical compatibility with the philosophical notion of the natural desire to see God.[6]

What is significant to observe in this context is that when Aquinas transitions from truths naturally known that are compatible with Christian revelation to the motives for belief in the mysteries of Christianity and the reasons of fittingness for theological affirmation of the existence of divine grace, he appeals specifically to the unique Christian notion of the final end of man. In effect, Catholic Christianity teaches that the human person is ordained by God's providence and grace to see God face to face, to behold the essence of God the Holy Trinity, and to find therein perfect beatitude. Aquinas seems to think that this is the strongest or most motivating form of warrant for taking seriously the claims of Christianity from the point of view of philosophical reason and human anthropology. If God can be seen face to face, by the grace of Christ, then the beatitude that Christianity promises corresponds deeply to man's natural structure and highest philosophical aspirations. The human being is intrinsically orientated to the desire for perfect noetic union with the first truth, and only the perfect possession of what is utterly transcendent can give final rest and perfect fulfillment to the human spirit in its quest for ultimate happiness.

But is this vision of the human person true? Aquinas addresses this challenge head on, since he has a clear philosophical alternative position in mind.[7] Averroes had presented Latin Aristotelians like Aquinas with an interpretation of Aristotle in which the human being is most perfectly fulfilled *not* by the vision of God but by philosophical contemplation of the truth about God insofar as it can be obtained in this life. On this view, the human intellect can know

6. See in this respect the transition in *SCG* III from the treatment of the natural desire to see God, which is defended *philosophically* from principles of natural reason in cc. 25–50, to the consideration of the grace of the beatific vision in cc. 51–63. Later in *SCG* III, Aquinas will consider explicitly the notion of divine grace as an assistance given to the human person in view of eternal life (cc. 147–63).

7. See *SCG* III, cc. 39, 43, 49, 50.

something of God through his effects and thereby achieve a philosophical contemplation of God that procures a natural beatitude proper to man, and this beatitude represents the best and most ultimate instantiation of human felicity.[8]

In response to these ideas, Aquinas wishes to argue that the human being can indeed attain natural knowledge of God and his attributes, such as that indicated in chapter 2 of this book. In addition, one can reach a kind of natural beatitude or philosophical happiness that is distinctly human by contemplating God in this way, whereby one knows the nature of God indirectly through his effects. (Aquinas frequently refers to this as the "imperfect beatitude" of the philosophers.[9]) However, Aquinas also wants to argue from philosophical premises and by appeal to Aristotelian principles that even the philosopher who has natural knowledge of God from his effects can and should reasonably desire something more perfect, that is, immediate knowledge of God in himself. In other words, based upon the premise that we can attain real, if indirect, knowledge of God that makes us uniquely happy in some profound way, Aquinas wishes to argue that there is a philosophically grounded warrant to desire naturally a yet more perfect, immediate form of knowledge of God. That the human being has no natural access to this form of knowledge is evident, but if such a desire is natural, then one should not dismiss for philosophical reasons a claimant to revelation that affirms the grace of God provided in Jesus Christ makes possible an immediate intellectual vision of God, an eternal beatitude that stems from the plenary possession of eternal life. In this case, revelation and natural reason provide distinct but mutually compatible depictions of the ultimate human good, and the grace of Christ is

8. See the study by Jörn Müller, "Duplex beatitude: Aristotle's Legacy and Aquinas's Conception of Human Happiness," in *Aquinas and the Nicomachean Ethics*, ed. T. Hoffmann, J. Müller, and M. Perkhams (Cambridge: Cambridge University Press, 2013), 52–71.

9. Numerous evidences are amassed by Adriano Oliva in "La contemplation des philosophes selon Thomas d'Aquin," *Revue des sciences philosophiques et théologiques*, 96 (2012): 585–662. See for a clear example *ST* I-II, q. 3, a. 5. See also *SCG* III, c. 48.

given in keeping with the natural inclination and desire to reach the perfect truth about God, even as it is also given over and above that line of natural inclination to the truth and in superabundant fulfillment of it.

My aim here is not to reproduce Aquinas's extensive argumentation in this domain but merely to note some of its features that are readily intelligible and particularly pertinent to our theological considerations.[10]

First, we should note that Aquinas's general orientation to human knowledge presupposes that human beings seek to understand the various causes of things that they experience, a point I have discussed at some length in chapter 1. Human beings wish to understand what things are, their specific properties and components, their origins, and final purposes or ends.[11] Furthermore, study of the causes of the existence of things, as well as their perfections in the order of unity and multiplicity, truth, goodness, and beauty can lead us to an indirect but real understanding of the mystery of God. God is the transcendent efficient, exemplary, and final cause of creatures. We examined various pathways for reasoning demonstratively toward the affirmation of the existence of God in chapter 2, in keeping with this line of thought.

In the *Summa contra Gentiles*, Aquinas makes several significant claims about this natural understanding of God. Most notably, he argues that the knowledge of God we attain in this life pertains to our final end, our ultimate spiritual perfection. (This follows from the fact that God is infinitely good, and is thus the greatest good the human person can know and desire in this life, however imperfect our knowledge of God is.) He observes that the natural knowledge

10. I have presented more sustained arguments on the nature of the natural desire to see God in "Imperfect Happiness and the Final End of Man: Thomas Aquinas and the Paradigm of Nature-Grace Orthodoxy," *The Thomist* 78, no. 2 (2014): 247–89, which is contained in Book 4 of this collection.

11. Aquinas explicitly adverts to this philosophical principle as a starting point in *SCG* III, c. 39, paragraphs 3 and 5, and *SCG* III, c. 50, § 4, as well as *ST* I, q. 12, a. 1, in regard to the natural desire to see God.

of God we can attain in this life is indirect, since it begins from creatures we know more proximately and leads by inference to consideration of God in himself, whom we know by means of his creatures. However, even if it is indirect, such reflection on the nature and attributes of the transcendent God does permit us to consider God in himself, such that we can contemplate philosophically what God is eternally.[12] One can argue rightly that this natural, philosophical knowledge of God provides the highest form of understanding available to us in this life with respect to all other forms of study.[13] This is the case for two reasons. First, it provides us with knowledge of the highest and most perfect of realities. God possesses the perfect and infinite plenitude of being, goodness, and intellectual life. Thus, no matter how transcendent and incomprehensible God remains in regard to our limited understanding, he is also the most intrinsically intelligible of all realities and the one who alone possesses the greatest goodness from which all others mysteriously receive their existence.[14] Second, the reality in question is also that which is most ultimately explanatory of all others, since God is the creative cause of all that is. So our knowledge of his transcendent reality, however imperfect and indirect, still provides us with an understanding of what explains all else that possesses being.[15] In sum, then, the philosophical contemplation of God and of all things in light of God is a source of beatitude that is natural and philosophical in kind.

However, this "philosophical beatitude" obtained through the philosophical contemplation of God indirectly through the consideration of his creatures is also imperfect for a variety of reasons. One can even say that the beatitude we attain by the indirect natural contemplation of God as known through the medium of his effects is intrinsically dissatisfying. Why is this the case, especially if God is, as we have just noted, the most perfect of all beings we can know? Here, Aquinas appeals to a classical Aristotelian principle

12. *SCG* III, c. 39.
13. *SCG* III, c. 37.
14. *SCG* III, c. 25.
15. This is one way of interpreting *SCG* III, c. 37, § 8.

pertaining to the natural desire for knowledge of metaphysical caus-es.[16] When we know of a given reality only through its effects, we naturally desire to know it more perfectly, that is to say, to know it not only through its effects but also in its essence. When smoke aris-es from the forest, we naturally desire to know what source it origi-nates from. If a public miracle seems to occur, we wish to know if it truly comes from God or is a tale invented by religious enthusiasm or popular legend. If there is a medical symptom, clinicians seek to uncover the causes. When an artist creates great works, we seek to understand the unity of the artistic genius behind the works. Con-sequently, when we come to know of God only through his effects, through the metaphysical consideration of creatures, which is the only kind of natural knowledge of God we are capable of in this life, we also inevitably come to desire knowledge of God in his essence, that is to say, we naturally desire to know what and who God is, im-mediately in himself.

An important set of claims follows from this line of argument.[17] First, if what we are saying is true, then the positive and genuine character of our *natural* capacity for spiritual happiness should be acknowledged; our philosophical understanding of God by way of nature is a source of genuine beatitude. Second, however, this hap-piness leads organically or naturally to the desire to see God, and it does so *due to its imperfection*. Knowledge of God through the me-dium of his effects invites us naturally to desire to see God in him-self. Third, then, our achievement of indirect, imperfect knowledge of God, when understood in light of our natural desire to see God, is the source and sign of an innate desire for a yet greater and more perfect beatitude, one that can be achieved only if we are able to know God immediately in his own essence. However, as we have already established prior to the consideration of this argument, the only natural knowledge we have of God is indirect and imperfect,

---

16. See *SCG* III, c. 48, § 1; c. 50, § 3; and *ST* I, q. 12, a. 1.

17. See the argumentation in *SCG* III, c. 48 which advances arguments of the kind presented in this paragraph.

not immediate and perfect. Consequently, we can conclude and know simultaneously by natural reason that we have a natural desire to see God in himself and that we do not have the natural power in and from ourselves to achieve this aim.[18]

A non-trivial conclusion arises from this form of reasoning. One should affirm, based on St. Thomas's arguments, that it is humanly reasonable, philosophically speaking, to be open to some kind of assistance that would allow us to see God face to face, as a gift or a grace, if such a form of assistance truly exists. Furthermore, it is not reasonable either to presume or to conclude a priori that such an assistance or grace would be contrary to the innate aspirations of natural reason, which desires to know the plenary truth about God. One can even go so far as to make the logically connected claim that despite whatever motivations a person might have for refusing the mere possibility of grace that leads to the vision of God, such a stance is intrinsically unreasonable and fails to correspond to our true human inclinations and desires in their depths.

At this junction, it is appropriate to note two adjacent truths that should color our consideration of these Thomistic arguments. Both stem from the Augustinian, theological side of Aquinas's reflection on human nature. The first stipulates that even if our philosophical consideration of the human being as a rational animal is one that can lead us to acknowledge the natural desire to see God, it is still the case that human beings in the fallen state are marked by conflicting desires and inclinations due to the effects of original sin, personal sin, and the social structures of sin.[19] Human beings are not so simple as to merely desire the truth about the ultimate causes of reality. They also desire happiness through an acquisition of their own array of created goods, and they can often pursue such happiness without any overt reference to God. Indeed, in a fallen world, the latter disposition of a purely non-religious striving for self-perfection often

---

18. As Aquinas argues in *SCG* III, c. 50.
19. See *ST* I-II, q. 85, a. 1; q. 109, a. 3 and on the four wounds of sin that mark human existence after the fall, *ST* I-II, q. 85, a. 3.

predominates in human beings. Consequently, it is not clear that in concrete history, fallen human beings marked by the effects of sin can readily embrace the pathway of philosophical reflection delineated by an author like Aquinas. Even if it is natural to seek philosophical knowledge of God and to find real if imperfect happiness in doing so, it is unlikely in concrete human history that persons affected by sin should deeply embrace such aspirations unless their nature is addressed and healed inwardly by the work of grace, so that the supernatural orientation toward God who is revealed in Christ takes on a primacy in their lives and stimulates a recovery of the natural intellectual orientation toward God.[20] On this reading, the infusion of the life of grace into the human soul serves as the ordinary condition of possibility for the reemergence and rediscovery of the philosophically warranted, natural desire to see God.

Second and relatedly, the human being, even in its highest and most adept natural aspirations, such as that which inclines us to seek and desire perfect knowledge of God, *cannot* in virtue of this same natural inclination attain the supernatural object of Christian faith, hope, and charity as such, namely, the knowledge of, hope for union with, and love for the Holy Trinity. This latter inclination is supernatural and arises in the human soul uniquely as a gift of grace. In fact, Aquinas rightly insists that the natural inclination to beatitude by way of natural knowledge of God, which can lead to the natural desire to see God, cannot of itself procure any intrinsic inclination to the formally supernatural object of faith, the mystery of the Holy Trinity.[21] For this, a higher form of knowledge and a higher

---

20. Aquinas affirms this more or less explicitly in *ST* I-II, q. 109, a. 3.
21. *ST* I-II, q. 62, a. 1:

Man is perfected by virtue, for those actions whereby he is directed to happiness, as was explained above (I-II, q. 5, a. 7). Now man's happiness is two-fold, as was also stated above (I-II, q. 5, a. 5). One is proportionate to human nature, a happiness to wit, which man can obtain by means of his natural principles. The other is a happiness surpassing man's nature, and which man can obtain by the power of God alone, by a kind of participation of the Godhead, about which it is written (2 Peter 1:4) that by Christ we are made "partakers of the Divine nature." And because such happiness surpasses the capacity of human

inclination must be introduced into the human person by way of the theological virtues.[22]

Consequently, we can speak, as Aquinas indeed does, of two inclinations, one natural and one supernatural. The first arises from our natural activities of knowledge and love and develops in proportion to the capabilities and limitations of our rational nature. Among these capabilities is power to know of the existence of God and to enjoy imperfect beatitude through the philosophical consideration of God's nature. Human beings can and should naturally desire to see God in himself, even if they cannot procure this effect by their own power.[23]

The second inclination is an effect of the Holy Spirit's infusion of supernatural, habitual grace into the faculties of intellect and will, elevating them so that the human subject comes to know, aspire to, and love the mystery of God in himself, as he is manifest in divine revelation as Father, Son, and Holy Spirit. This inclination is

---

nature, man's natural principles which enable him to act well according to his capacity, do not suffice to direct man to this same happiness. Hence it is necessary for man to receive from God some additional principles, whereby he may be directed to supernatural happiness, even as he is directed to his connatural end, by means of his natural principles, albeit not without Divine assistance. Such like principles are called "theological virtues": first, because their object is God, inasmuch as they direct us aright to God: secondly, because they are infused in us by God alone: thirdly, because these virtues are not made known to us, save by Divine revelation, contained in Holy Writ.

22. *ST* I-II, q. 62, a. 3. Here Aquinas denies quite explicitly that there is any natural inclination of the human person to the supernatural beatitude of the beatific vision of the Holy Trinity.

23. Accordingly Aquinas does speak of an innate appetite to see God, proper to our nature, even though he does not think that this constitutes an inclination to the formally supernatural object of faith as such:

But just as man acquires his first perfection, that is, his soul, by the action of God, so too he has his ultimate perfection, which is his perfect happiness, immediately from God, and rests in it. Indeed this is obvious from the fact that man's natural desire cannot rest in anything save in God alone. For it is innate in man that he be moved by a desire to go on from what has been caused and inquire into causes, nor does this desire rest until it arrives at the first cause, which is God." *De Virtutibus*, q. 1, a. 10. [Trans., Ralph McInerny, *Disputed Questions on Virtue* [South Bend, IN: St. Augustine's Press, 1999).]

supernatural, since it has its origin and final end in God's initiatives of grace. God gives the inclination by grace and directs the soul by grace beyond its natural capacities into participation in the life of God.[24]

Nevertheless, the second of these inclinations is not "extrinsic" to the former in the line of final causality. The supernatural knowledge of God as Trinity is neither identical with nor equivalent to the imperfect natural knowledge of God that stems from philosophical consideration of God's created effects. But the supernatural inclination to knowledge and love of God as Trinity is one that presupposes the innate natural inclination to knowledge and love of God. Indeed, we must say that the supernatural inclination that is infused into us by grace enters into the depths of our natural inclinations toward God, healing and strengthening them in themselves and elevating them beyond themselves. When this occurs, the dormant natural desire to see God that is part of us and lies within our natural horizon of desire is awakened and strengthened, but it is also now specified by a higher order of graced yearning for the vision of the Trinity as such. The supernatural inclinations of infused faith, hope, and love reawaken and newly specify our natural desire to see God so that it becomes an effective hope in the vision of God, the Most Holy Trinity.

---

24. *ST* I-II, q. 62, a. 3:

[T]he theological virtues direct man to supernatural happiness in the same way as by the natural inclination man is directed to his connatural end. Now the latter happens in respect of two things. First, in respect of the reason or intellect, in so far as it contains the first universal principles which are known to us by the natural light of the intellect, and which are reason's starting-point, both in speculative and in practical matters. Secondly, through the rectitude of the will which tends naturally to the good as defined by reason.... Consequently in respect of both the above things man needed to receive in addition something supernatural to direct him to a supernatural end. First, as regards the intellect, man receives certain supernatural principles, which are held by means of a Divine light: these are the articles of faith, about which is faith. Secondly, the will is directed to this end, both as to that end as something attainable—and this pertains to hope—and as to a certain spiritual union, whereby the will is, so to speak, transformed into that end—and this belongs to charity. For the appetite of a thing is moved and tends towards its connatural end naturally; and this movement is due to a certain conformity of the thing with its end.

We should note that, on this view, grace transforms our human volition, and yet this transformation occurs in such a way that the novelty of Christian hope is not something wholly extrinsic to our natural desire to see God. Rather, the Christian faith provides our natural desire with a new formal specification and moves us from within by hope and love to tend more effectively toward the fulfillment of that natural desire with a vibrancy that transcends mere human philosophical whim or velleity. In this sense, the discovery of God by grace allows the fallen human being to know himself much more perfectly, as one who in his depths naturally desires to see God, even as this desire is supernaturally fulfilled in a superabundant way that exceeds anything our philosophical reasoning could anticipate or procure.

If this view of the matter is correct, what should we say about the natural potency for the desire to see God? Does the human being have an innate power to see God immediately, face to face? Can our natural appetite for the fullness of the truth about God lead to genuine perfect beatitude? Here, we can introduce a helpful distinction between an active natural power and a passive natural power. Active powers pertain to perfections we have achieved and may make use of, even if we do not do so at every moment. In a mature rational animal, there is the active power of human sight or mathematical reflection. These activities are proportionate to our nature. Natural passive powers or potencies, meanwhile, pertain to these same activities insofar as we do not yet possess them, even as we are naturally capable of developing them. The newly conceived human being in the womb does not yet have the active power to see or to reason mathematically, but there is a passive power in the new human individual that will develop such that he or she can eventually one day see and reason mathematically. In this respect, this human individual already differs naturally from many other newly conceived living beings that will not have such powers, even though the nautral powers in question have not yet emerged. They will do so eventually due to the nature of the individual in question.

We can return at this point to our questions from above. Does the human being have an innate power to see God immediately? Can our natural appetite for the fullness of the truth lead and direct us by its own inclination into supernatural beatitude? Seen from the perspective of our natural inclinations and their proportionate active powers, the answer to our questions above is clearly negative. We have no natural inclination toward or active power by which we can attain of ourselves to the immediate vision of God. Consequently we have no natural potency or passive power for the beatific vision of God, since passive powers develop eventually into active powers.[25] If we did have such a passive power for supernatural beatitude, we would be innately driven *by our nature* toward the formal object of faith as such—the awareness and knowledge of the Trinity—and even toward the eternal vision of the Trinity. In this case, we would not need the grace of faith to incline us to supernatural union with God. In fact, however, we do need something new in order to incline ourselves toward God in this higher mode, toward effective union with the Trinitarian life of God. The mystery of grace, which is manifest especially in the theological virtues, inclines the human person toward God in himself, who is known by supernatural faith in this life and by vision in the next.

Here, then, we can introduce a further distinction between the passive natural power of the human being—for eyesight or mathematical ability, for example—and what Thomists call the obediential potency of the human being as a rational animal.[26] Human beings,

25. See the particularly pertinent *ST* III, q. 10 a. 4 ad 2: "The vision of the Divine Essence exceeds the natural power of any creature, as was said in the first part [*ST* q. 12, a. 4]. And hence the degrees thereof depend rather on the order of grace in which Christ is supreme, than on the order of nature, in which the angelic nature is placed before the human." The Latin text is clarifying in this regard: "Ad secundum dicendum quod *visio divinae essentiae excedit naturalem potentiam cuiuslibet creaturae*, ut in prima parte dictum est. Et ideo gradus in ipso attenduntur magis secundum *ordinem gratiae*, in quo Christus est excellentissimus, quam secundum *ordinem naturae*, secundum quem natura angelica praefertur humanae." [Emphasis added.] Another Christological text of interest is *ST* III, q. 13 a. 2 c. and ad 2. See also, on nature and grace more generally, *ST* I, q. 112 a. 2.

26. See, for example, Thomas de Vio Cajetan in his commentary on *ST* I-II, q. 113, a. 10, n. IV–VI [Leonine edition of the *ST*, vol. VII (Rome, 1892), 343]; Domingo Báñez

unlike all other animals, are capable of being elevated into the life of God by grace, since they have spiritual powers capable of desiring perfect knowledge and love of God. Human beings are thus naturally capable of being elevated supernaturally into the life of God. The grace of God that acts upon and elevates this obediential potency within the human being can act in the human person without violence precisely because of the perfection and innate tendencies of human nature, which are oriented to fulfillment through understanding the truth about God and finding happiness in God. The offer of the beatific vision of the Holy Trinity does no extrinsicist violence to human nature, because human beings have a natural desire for the vision of God. We can see in light of Christian revelation, then, that there is something distinctive about the human person: it alone in all the visible creation possesses a radical capacity, or potency, for elevation into Trinitarian life. In fact, the human being has an innate natural desire to see God that arises from within its *philosophical* nature. Therefore, by that same measure, the human being has a capacity proper to rational nature that makes it potentially subject to the initiatives of grace. One can argue merely philosophically or from premises of natural reason that it is not impossible for God to

---

on *ST* I-II, q. 112, a. 1 [*Comentarios Inéditos A La Prima Secundae de Santo Tomás*, ed. V. B. de Heredia (Salamanca, 1948), 240]; F. C. R. Billuart on *ST* I-II, q. 112, a. 1 [*Summa Sancti Thomae*, tome III (Paris: Letouzey et Ané, 1880), d. 6, a. 2]: "Utrum gratia creetur vel educatur de potentia obedientiali animae"; Santiago Ramirez on *ST* I-II, q. 113, a. 10 [*Opera Omnia*, Tome IX, (Salamanca: Editorial San Esteban, 1992), 938–45]. The notion of obediential potency is not alien to the thought of Aquinas. See Thomas Aquinas, *Super Sent.*, III, d. 2 q. 1 a. 1 qc. 1 c.:

> Similiter non signatur etiam potentia passiva naturalis creaturae, quia *nulla potentia passiva naturalis est in natura cui non respondeat potentia activa alicujus naturalis agentis*. Unde relinquitur quod dicat in creatura solam *potentiam obedientiae*, secundum quam de creatura potest fieri quidquid Deus vult, sicut de ligno potest fieri vitulus, Deo operante. Haec autem potentia obedientiae correspondet divinae potentiae, secundum quod dicitur, quod ex creatura potest fieri quod ex ea Deus facere potest. [Emphasis added.]

Aquinas here is speaking about the absence of a natural potency in the human nature for elevation to union with the incarnate Word. See the commentary on this text by Lawrence Feingold, *The Natural Desire to See God according to St. Thomas Aquinas and His Interpreters* (Naples, FL: Sapientia Press, 2010), 106–8.

elevate human beings beyond the range of their natural inclinations and active capacities, insofar as we see in human beings the capacity to desire to see God in himself.[27] However, we can only know that this capacity is truly actuated and that we are genuinely capable of participation in divine life by way of the beatific vision due to the revelation of God and by his grace.

We should note that on this reading it is true to say that there is a natural desire to see God but not true to say that there is either a natural desire for or a natural inclination toward the supernatural object of faith, the divine life of the Holy Trinity. The latter is the object of supernatural faith, hope, and charity. The mystery of Trinitarian life can only be known to us, and can only perfect and elevate our natural inclination toward God and our natural desire for God, by newly specifying our knowledge and love in light of supernatural revelation.[28]

On this reading of Aquinas, ought we not to say that all persons, when they philosophize, should naturally come to the conclusion that they wish to see God, even apart from Christian revelation? This conclusion does not necessarily follow. In fact, one could argue for a contrary position, to wit, that non-Christian human beings outside the Church typically fail to come to a perfect understanding of the natural philosophical desire to see God apart from the concrete exercise of the supernatural life of grace and apart from divine revelation. The natural inclination to see God can remain a feature of our common human nature and still remain dormant, suppressed mostly or in part, or awakened but deeply confused in most fallen human beings. Nevertheless, the natural inclination of the human being to seek the fullness of the truth about God and to desire to see God is, on this view, also inalienable to our human nature and is specified through natural formal objects, not those that are divinely revealed. The Christian revelation can thus awaken the human being not only

27. Aquinas makes this argument from reason, for example, in *ST* I, q. 12, a. 1.

28. This is the affirmation we find, as noted, in *ST* I-II, q. 62, aa. 1 and 3, and I take it that it marks out a position distinct from that articulated by Henri de Lubac, in his reading of Aquinas.

to the ultimate supernatural end of man and his or her genuine perfect happiness—the beatific vision of the Trinity—but also to the natural orientation and inclination that he or she has toward the ultimate truth about God, which itself is open by obediential potency to a higher specification from within, to faith in and hope for eternal life. In a fallen world of human weakness, apart from divine revelation and apart from the inner working of grace, it is difficult for the human person to attain even the habitual practice of philosophical study and contemplation of God, let alone the natural desire to see God in himself. In concrete history, then, it is the revelation of the beatific vision of God made available by grace that alerts or recalls human beings back to their own deepest natural dignity, as human beings that are *capax Dei*, capable of God. In Christ alone can they come to recognize the deepest meaning of their own best natural aspirations, inclinations, and conflicted, restless desires.

THE TESTIMONY OF THE SAINTS

The notion we have defended in the first part of this chapter is somewhat paradoxical. There is a philosophically intelligible, rationally warranted desire to see God in himself, but the natural awareness of this is accompanied by a corresponding understanding that we cannot procure the effective vision of God by our own powers. At the same time, the fallen human being tends to ignore this deeper dimension of his or her human personhood, and it is only by grace that a person is typically reawakened to it or put in touch with it. In the life of grace, this natural desire is not only addressed and reclaimed but is also newly specified by a higher supernatural form of life. Human participation in the life of the Trinity by grace both exceeds and fulfills in a superabundant fashion the natural aspirations of the human mind and heart.

If this is the case, then the Christian saints, who in this life best exemplify the contemplation and love of God, should also teach us something about what is most characteristically human in us. It is precisely in this sense that they present us with a particular form of the argument for the rational credibility of Christianity. The saints, by their testimony to a life of contemplation of God and of virtuous charity that springs from that contemplation, suggest to us that there is a possibility of coming to terms with our deepest self, that dimension of ourselves that is capable of desiring perfect knowledge of God and perfect union with God as the highest and best realization of the human person. If this is possible only or especially on Christian soil, due to the sacramental life of the Church and the life of holiness embodied in the saints and their religious forms of life, then it is the Christian religion, in a sense, that enables human beings to discover and recover their own deepest aspirations and the true resolution of their most important interior natural desires. In this respect, the great saints are in their own way the most human of us all, since they indicate to us a plenary realization of our human nature, one that we may recognize even philosophically in some real sense, even if this truth is opaque to many.

At this point, it would be perfectly appropriate to illustrate these ideas with a suitably modern, historical-critical presentation of cases of hagiography, so as to manifest the virtues of persons like Anthony of Egypt, Ambrose of Milan, Benedict of Norcia, Bernard of Clairvaux, Francis of Assisi, Catherine of Siena, Teresa of Avila, Philip Neri, Vincent de Paul, John Bosco, or Theresa of Calcutta. These and a host of others would serve as noteworthy examples of great contemplative spirits who were not philosophers but whose contemplative lives, centered on the Trinitarian mystery and the person of Jesus, seemed to inform the totality of their thoughts and actions, often even in the midst of very complex political and ethical circumstances. Some led more active lives, while some were more monastic or eremitic. Here, I will only note four basic traits that I take to be common to all the greatest Catholic saints when they manifest and integrally live the primacy of the contemplative life, ordered by hope in the beatific vision and a very thorough-going or radical contemplative love of God and neighbor.

The first characteristic to mention is *the primacy of the contemplative life*. The saints by their lives of prayer and intellectual contemplation of God manifest their intention to treat the knowledge and love of God as the final end of the human person and to preserve and safeguard this end jealously, especially by loving God above all things unerringly, in view of eternal life.

Second, this knowledge and love of God in the greatest saints seems in their concrete, historical lives *to inform all that they have and do in the order of virtue*. Stated in technical terms, the saints assimilate the exercise of the various intellectual, artistic, and moral virtues comprehensively into their concrete lives of faith, hope, and charity toward God, so that all that they do intellectually, practically, and ethically is accomplished in view of their friendship with God.[29] Far from making them indifferent to others and inactive in practice, this tendency seems to move them outside of themselves by way of superabundance, as they pass from the inner life of contemplation to the external life of action in the service of God and others, motivated by faith, hope, and charity. Practically speaking, their contemplative lives then inform or habitually affect all they do and how they conduct their day-to-day lives.

Third, this integrated contemplative life that has God as its primary aim is stable and enduring, as well as dynamic. *It is characterized by fortitude and developmental growth*. One of the most remarkable things about the greatest of saints is the inner strength and perseverance they exhibit in living lives of contemplative love of God and of moral virtue, even under arduous circumstances. Their virtue is exhibited not merely according to the just mean or the norm of natural goodness but is frequently characterized by heroism, often in repeated instances.[30] This observation suggests that the contemplative lives of the saints are not only robustly intensive (according

29. See in this regard the reflections of Aquinas on charity as the form of the virtues, and its role in maintaining a contemplative friendship with God in faith, in *ST* II-II, q. 23, aa. 1, 7 and 8.

30. On heroic virtue, see *ST* I-II, q. 61, a. 4.

to degree of perfection) and humanly extensive (that is, affecting all aspects of life) but that they are also marked by persistence and growth. These are traits of mind that philosophically-minded persons can naturally admire or desire, since, as Aristotle notes in the *Nicomachean Ethics*, our natural capacity to contemplate the highest things is fragile and depends upon a host of positive external and internal circumstances that often do not obtain.[31] Our natural capacity for virtue is thus vulnerable, often compromised by external circumstances or internal weaknesses, and our time for contemplation of higher truths is limited. The saints seem to have a stability and depth of contemplation, by supernatural grace, that makes them more successfully human in this respect, as they experience the fruits of a robust interiority given over to knowledge and love of God and of the world as seen in the light of God. This fortitude is manifest not only in their prayer and volitional devotion to God but in their zealous love of other people, exhibited in works of charity and spiritual and corporal works of mercy.

Fourth and finally, we can note that the saints are sometimes *subject to particular elevations of ecstasy in both non-miraculous and miraculous modes*. By ecstasy, I mean to indicate those moments of deep inner possession of God by the human spirit through particularly intensive activities and movements of knowledge and love. This can happen by sanctifying grace and the gifts of the Holy Spirit in an internal and discreet way, so that the saints grow progressively in contemplative ecstasy and love of God, quietly, through a life of prayer. This inner life can be more experiential or prolonged, when the supernatural grace in question is more extraordinary. All this can occur without any external miracles, such as external manifest states of spiritual ecstasy that affect the physical body. Indeed, even in the absence of such, this interior contemplative life is still something extraordinary when considered in view of our nature and its inherent tendencies. Many of the great saints spent hours each day in prayer and expressed great peacefulness, heroic virtue, and active

31. See *Nic. Ethics* X, 7 (esp. 1177a18).

consolation toward others as a result of their lives of personal union with God, which is of course extraordinary.

This life of prayer and ecstatic possession of God can also be accompanied by miracles that indicate the grace and favor of God's special presence in the soul of the saint and the reality of his or her contemplative life as something exemplary. One can think here of the famous modern example of the inner elocutions that Mother Teresa of Calcutta received during her train ride to Darjeeling, in which Jesus Christ commanded her: "Come be my light," drawing her out into the ghettos of the poorest of the poor.[32] This grace was coordinated, presumably, with the intensive and extraordinary prayer experiences of that epoch of her life, in which she was seeking to intensify her friendship with God. It was complemented by the manifest fruit of her works of charity among people in poverty, and by the miracles accomplished during the course of her life, in conjunction with her prayers. Other examples could be indicated readily, such as the physical elevations of Teresa of Avila when she was in prayer, the stigmata of Francis of Assisi, or the public prayer in ecstasy of Philip Neri or Catherine of Siena. Historical examples abound. Presumably, God accompanies the inner life of the saints by such signs, whether publicly manifest or private and subsequently retold, so as to make evident that the saint's life is exemplary and that his or her model of life can be aspired to and imitated by others, albeit often in a less perfect mode.

Of course, the philosopher qua philosopher, Christian or otherwise, cannot say whether such phenomena are truly indicative of the grace of God and whether they signify outwardly the inward presence of a person's participation in supernatural life. My argument, however, is that the philosopher who adverts to the principles of natural reason as such, at least as we have indicated them, can say with Aquinas that the testimony of the saints to a vivid and integral contemplative life of knowledge and love of God, *if it is something*

32. See Mother Teresa, *Come Be My Light: The Private Writings of the Saint of Calcutta* (New York: Image Books, 2009).

genuine that is initiated by God's grace, is rationally desirable and philosophically defensible. If the human being naturally desires to know God as perfectly as possible in this life, and if it is possible with the assistance of God to know God intimately in this life by contemplative faith and in the life to come by immediate vision, then the lives of the saints who seem to know and love God in a higher way in this life and who aspire to perfect union with him in the next seem to possess in a higher way and at a more perfect register what the nature of the human being inevitably strives for but cannot procure for itself. The saints in this regard serve as a *philosophical* invitation to the Christian life and as a witness to the rational credibility of Christianity in light of the human being's native struggle for happiness. Of course, the embrace of the Christian life occurs by grace and is not procured by natural powers of the human person alone, but such an embrace of the Christian life, if it is facilitated by grace, clearly is not irrational or contrary to reason. In fact it advances the human being in keeping with the deepest inclinations of nature yet in view of elevated ends that the person cannot achieve without God's supernatural help.

Naturally the philosopher may contest that only a few become the greatest saints within the living Christian tradition, and so consequently, their example is of limited relevance and applicability. But this is like saying that only a few people become the greatest of philosophers, so it is not reasonable to embrace a life of philosophical reflection, since the perfect realization of this life is restricted to so limited a group of unique persons. In truth, philosophy and sanctity both admit of degrees, and each human person is capable in principle of a genuinely philosophical lifestyle, just as each is also capable of setting out toward perfect beatitude, aided by the supernatural virtues of faith, hope, and charity. In fact, the Catholic Church specifies that this way of life is more accessible than the philosophical lifestyle, since it depends less on external circumstances of education or social status and is made available to each simply by way of baptism and the other sacraments. Thus, the means of sanctification and of a contemplative life with the Holy Trinity are much more obtainable than the relative perfection of learning required if one is to embark on a consistent and profound philosophical way of life. Therefore, the Christian contemplative life is not only higher and more perfect in its final end and its mode of possession of God by way of knowledge and love in grace. It is also more extensively available to all, independently of cultural erudition or formation, by way of the sacraments as signs and instruments of grace, which engender and sustain the Christian contemplative life for whomsoever should desire to undertake it, with the help of God.

THE ILLUMINATION OF THE HUMAN CONDITION
BY WAY OF TRINITARIAN REVELATION

In the final part of this chapter, I would like to consider various ways that the mystery of the Trinity, if true, illumines the human condition. How does a consideration of the human person made in the image of God who is Trinity help one to understand better and more profoundly the human desire to see God? Because the human being is characterized internally by an immaterial life of knowledge and love, there is a likeness in human beings to the processional life of God as eternal Word and Spirit. This human life of processional knowledge and love, which emerges internally within the human subject, finds its most perfect fulfillment in the knowledge and love of God in himself, as well as in interpersonal communion with other human beings. In effect, there are two similitudes, the first based on the interior life of the human person tending toward truth and love as an image of the eternal processions of the Word and Spirit, and the second based on the interpersonal, mutual knowledge and love shared between human persons. Both are illumined by our understanding of the Trinitarian God revealed in faith and by our consideration of the grace of the Trinity, which elevates and transforms both of these aspectual forms of the *Imago Dei*. This is an idea I will seek to sketch out in four basic ideas.

Being Human unto God: Knowledge and Love
Illumined by Trinitarian Revelation

As we have noted, the human being has a natural capacity to desire knowledge of God that is immediate in kind. A human person can naturally desire to see God or know God in himself. If it is also true, however, that we can effectively know God in himself only by grace, then there is a divine light cast upon the human condition by theological revelation that we could not otherwise achieve by our own power. It is one that helps us better understand the obscurities of our human condition in a way we could not if we made use merely of our limited philosophical knowledge of God and of human persons.

The idea here can be stated simply in two parts. First, as we have already explored, philosophical reflection can lead in principle to the recognition that there are immaterial faculties of knowledge and love in the human person, and it can lead one to the affirmation that the transcendent principle of reality, God, is characterized by eternal knowledge and love. However, it cannot permit one to attain understanding of who God is in himself, nor can it lead to an effective pathway toward the eternal possession of the immediate knowledge of the essence and mystery of God. In this sense, philosophical reflection about God provides no reasonably defensible hope of perfect human beatitude. The revelation of the possibility of the Trinitarian knowledge of God, however, suggests that the human being taken in its nature as such is incomplete without the addendum of grace, and that it is merely in potentiality to a higher and more fulfilling elevation that it is capable of receiving but cannot procure from its own innate principles. Without the higher understanding of God as Trinity and the hope of and love for God in himself that grace procures, the human being remains something of a puzzle as regards his or her perfect final end, a puzzle that is illumined by the revelation of God as Trinity. In light of the Christian revelation, we can understand the situation of the human being as that of a spiritual being open to deification, and capable of transformation, by the communication of divine life. The obscurities of the human search for truth and happiness are thus illumined without being dissolved, and the deepest aspirations of the human mind and heart are confirmed even while also being elevated and fulfilled in a superabundant, supernatural fashion.

Second, the philosophical knowledge we have of God can neither confirm nor deny that the one God is Trinitarian, characterized by a life of eternal immanent processions of the Word and of the Spirit of Love. The revelation that this is the case, however, fully enlightens our understanding of the human person as made in the image of God, and characterized by internal processions of knowledge and love, in the dual faculties of the intellect and the will. This inner sanctum of human dignity at the heart of human personality, animating the thoughts and choices of each person, is now understood as a Trinitarian sanctum. The human being is a little Trinity. Each person is like the eternal Father, a person from whom spiritual operations emerge, who is an agent of truth and a being of love. The *imago* is perfected by grace, especially in relation to the Holy Trinity, as the human person begins to reflect or image the Father, the Son, and the Spirit, through true knowledge of the Trinity, in contemplation and loving possession of God. The human person thus knows the Father personally, the truth of the Father in his Word, and the love of the Father in his Spirit. This illumined image teaches us what our desire for truth, happiness, and love are ultimately for. They aim at the plenary possession of the knowledge and love of God. These desires are rendered perfect in the personal knowledge and love of the Trinity—Father, Word, Spirit of Love.

If this vision of our common human destiny is true, then it follows that the human being cannot and should not be instrumentalized in view of any final end less than God—such as the end of human politics, the aims of a false religion, or the collective common good of the cosmos. The person is a being of transcendence, and the right understanding of persons in the cosmos and in political community must take account of the God-oriented nature that each person possesses, a nature that is capable of being elevated into divinizing union with God by grace. The human being is not only made in the image of the Trinity but is also able to become a child of God by virtue of grace (Gal. 4:1–7). The metaphor of a "child" here is of one who participates in the same nature, as a human being by grace may begin to participate in the divine nature, in the Trinitarian life of God.

Persons in Communion

Although each individual person is a little Trinity from whom originate both knowledge and love, it is also the case that the world is composed of many such persons, who can commune in common truth and in a collective appreciation of the goods of creation. Persons live in natural bonds, or cells, of communion: the family, the workplace, the academy, the city, the nation-state, the international order, the Church. Each of these constitutes a form of common life in which the person can potentially flourish and find opportunities for encounter with others in shared forms of truth-seeking and happiness-seeking. Mutual love and mutual bonds of friendship exist in these forums between individuals, and between collectives such as friendships between families, institutions, or nations.

Understood in light of the revelation of the Trinity, one can perceive an analogy between the eternal inner life of God and the created interpersonal life of human beings. In God, there is a life of three persons, who are one in essence in such a way that each person possesses the plenitude of the deity, the fullness of the godhead. Thus, each person is the one God, and each person possesses fully within himself all of what is present as God in each of the others. They are each distinct in virtue of their respective relations of origin, and they are each identical in virtue of their shared divine essence and life. Human beings are, of course, quite different in form from the Holy Trinity. Three human persons are one in nature or essence insofar as each is fully human, but they are not one individual essence who are one in being. Nor are they transcendent, simple, eternal, infinite, and incomprehensible, as God is, but are instead created, finite, metaphysically composite, temporal, and quantitative.

Yet, there is an analogy between created persons and the uncreated life of the Trinitarian persons. Insofar as human beings share a common life of knowledge and love, they can come to know and love one another in all that they are essentially, and they can commune with one another interpersonally through activities of knowledge and love. In the Holy Trinity, this is true in a higher, substantial way, as God simply *is* his eternal life of self-knowledge and love. So too, the divine persons are all in all, perfectly within one another in virtue of their perfect unity of essence. Yet, human persons are *made from* this uncreated communion of knowledge and love, are *made in its likeness*, and are *made for* union with it. Moreover, *they are made to participate in this mystery of God collectively, with one another*. The human communion of persons can be elevated by grace to participate in *common* knowledge and love of God and in so doing can achieve a *common life* of human persons bound together by participation in the very life of the Trinity.

If such a mystery is real, then the revelation of the Trinity makes ultimate sense of our human familial and political life, our life in common together. We are called to find common meaning and shared mutual life not only in ourselves, in the pure immanence of our political, educational, and artistic projects as a human community, but in a higher life that elevates and unites us, in the life of the Church, in which we seek union together with the uncreated mystery of God. Mysticism is political, and politics is mystical, but the order of things is important. The mystery of the Trinity and our participation in it, by the mystical life of grace, opens up the political life of the human race from within, drawing that life upwards into God. This opening of the human person and the communion of human persons up into God rectifies the internal life of the political community of human civilizations, and when rightly lived and understood, it protects human beings from politically instrumentalizing one another through governmental life and from divinizing the political community artificially as a surrogate principle of absolute ontology.

Hierarchy and Personhood in the Cosmos

I have noted above that the human person is made for supernatural communion with God and thus cannot be subordinated metaphysically or instrumentalized politically in view of a lesser end than God, such as that of the nation-state, the international political order, or the natural cosmos. Indeed, this is also true of the Church: the human being cannot exist merely for functionary or subservient roles in the life of the Church, as if the outward political life of the Church—rather than the supernatural life of union with God, which in fact constitutes the inner essence of the Church's life— were the final end of man.

How, then, should one understand the hierarchy of being that is found in the cosmos and the role of the human person within that hierarchy? Let us consider three ideas in this regard. First, it is true that there is a kind of ontological hierarchy that passes from below to above—from the vast world of non-living beings, to living, vegetative realities capable of self-movement in view of ends of nutrition, growth, self-repair, and reproduction, to sensate animals that can sense, feel, and sometimes imagine, learn, and understand in an animal fashion, in view of the ends aforementioned, of nutrition, growth, and reproduction. Above the merely sensate animals, there are rational animals, human persons characterized by internal operations of immaterial knowledge and love. Christian revelation teaches that above human beings, there are angelic beings, which are purely spiritual in kind, creatures characterized uniquely by interior operations of immaterial knowledge and love. This entire chain of being is created by and subject to the transcendent and incomprehensible mystery of the Trinitarian God.

Second, because each person is capable of communion with God, he or she cannot be subject to any of the other beings within the hierarchical chain of being as a mere means to their flourishing or even *merely* as a part of a larger cosmic whole. The human being can live directly for God, as can the angels, and so even when a human person does not do this intentionally, due to religious obliviousness or error, it is still the kind of being by nature that can and must find *ultimate or perfect* happiness only in God. Thus, the human person has a dignity that cannot be effaced or altered, simply because it is an inalienably spiritual being that is made for ultimate truth and the enjoyment of perfect happiness in the possession of the greatest good. Consequently, even when the creature ignores God and makes itself or some other constellation of creatures a supreme end, the spiritual hollowness and isolation it faces is inevitable, even if this fact is only perceived gradually in some cases. If the creature perseveres in this alienation throughout its life, even into the world to come, the state it attains to in hell retains something residually natural, insofar as the creature maintains its spiritual identity and the effects of its own free self-determination for a rationally chosen end. However, this state is also profoundly unnatural, if one considers the creature in light of its perfection and happiness insofar as the creature remains self-alienated from its best and only true form of ultimate flourishing. Grace liberates the human person already in this life from false forms of enslavement to the primacy of the love of self or of other created realities, however noble, and turns the human self inwardly upwards into God, restoring an order of harmony between the human person and God, within the human person itself, between human persons, and between human persons and other creatures in the cosmos.

Third, the spiritual person within this order of hierarchy must respect the other non-humans that each also reflect God in his or her own way. Non-human creatures do not exist principally for human beings, though some of them are ordered in part toward human flourishing. They exist primarily for God and have an ontological integrity, nobility, goodness, and beauty that should be acknowledged and respected in this light. The physical cosmos in its vastness is an iconostasis of the omnipotence, eternity, and infinite perfection of God, who expresses himself outwardly in the physically vast, temporally extensive, and intelligibly intricate universe. The world of living things, of microbes, plants, and animals, that precedes human beings in time and that human beings depend upon for life and sustenance is also one that reflects the eternal life of God, an eternal life that gives temporal life to an innumerable number of species and individuals within each species, in a vast tapestry of evolving things, which reflects through time imperfectly but really the perfect liveliness of God. Human beings take up their form of life within this vast physical cosmos, teeming with life, and live within a larger collective good as physical, living beings among other physical beings, both non-living and living. As such, human beings are metaphysically bound to live in the common good of the cosmos, and we should seek to do so respectfully and responsibly, not only to protect the future of the human species by preserving natural resources for the generations to come, but also so as to respect nature in itself and to honor the transcendent and ineffable source of that nature, who is reflected obliquely within it.

Cosmic Ecclesiology

These ideas lead us to a fourth and final idea, that of an ecclesial ecology of human life and of the cosmos as a common good of participation in Trinitarian life. Human beings in particular, among all visible creatures, are made in the image of God. Correspondingly, in the order of grace, the twin spiritual faculties of intellect and will can come to resemble or reflect God in a more perfect and distinctive way by participation in the life of the Holy Trinity. Faith conforms the intellect to the eternal Word of God, while hope and love conform the will to the eternal Love of the Holy Spirit. These virtues turn the human being back to the uncreated mystery of the Father, in his Word and Spirit, and prepare the soul for deifying union with the uncreated ground of all being, who is God the Holy Trinity. The human community enjoys participation in this mystery of

transforming deification, not only individually but also collectively, in the social and corporate life of the Catholic Church, her sacramental life and liturgy, and in her common activities, including her
spiritual and corporal works of charity and mercy.

Here, then, the cosmos as a whole reaches a kind of hierarchical
summit and attains its highest aims or purposes as a collective common good. The whole human community lives directly from God,
in God, and for God in the order of grace, and it does so in a collective life of mutual friendship and common enjoyment of God, who
is known and loved for his own sake. Needless to say, this vision of
the human being in the cosmos is eschatological in orientation. The
ecclesial communion of all human persons who live in God can only
come to perfect fruition in light of the progressive work of purification and deification, which includes the purgatory of the life to
come and the final beatification and glorification of all the saints. But
if heaven is already "real" and a vast multitude of souls already collectively enjoy the beatific vision, then there is a collective common
good already in act, toward which this whole universe is directed and
in which the visible creation already participates initially, especially
in virtue of the inner life of grace that is present in the Church.

The bodily resurrection and glorification of Jesus Christ and the
Virgin Mary in their humanity anticipate a more final and complete
perfection and transfiguration of the physical cosmos that has yet
to take place. This transfiguration is supernatural, stemming from
principles other than those currently governing the physical universe in its natural developmental unfolding. In this regard, the final transfiguration of the physical cosmos is in many respects unfathomable and can be affirmed principally based upon the reality
of the historical resurrection of Jesus Christ and upon the certitude
the Church has in his abiding real presence in the Eucharist, which
gives testament down through the ages to the reality of his glorified
bodily state. Nevertheless, even with this imperfect form of information regarding the final state of the cosmos, enough light is cast,
and enough understanding is given, that we can see in the cosmos a

vast unfolding mystery of nature which is progressively transformed from within by grace, and of mysterious divine-human cooperation, that is to say, a spiritual marriage taking place in human nature, wherein God is gradually elevating human existence into a final participation in Trinitarian life. This elevation process is marked by tremendous setbacks, failures, revolts, and refusals, but the destiny of the human race remains inalienably stable in virtue of its metaphysical principles of nature and grace and in virtue of the living reality and glorious activity of the resurrected Christ, who remains with the Father and the Holy Spirit, the final end of all things. These principles of nature and grace can become obscure to our understanding, individually and collectively, and may even seem entirely unreal to many. However, because being precedes thought and is deeper than it, what is truly real is always at hand and can surface anew for consideration as we pass through the shadows of confusion into the light of reality. Whatever else may seem to be the case, when the world is rightly understood one can see that God endures eternally within and above all things, and that God will always remain the one true horizon and ultimate end of the human race.

CODA

On Thomism and
Postmodern Perspectivalism
Aquinas and Nietzsche on Truth
and Moral Agency

Any comparison of Thomas Aquinas and Friedrich Nietzsche appears initially to be a formidable task due to the multiple points of radical contrast in their respective philosophies. However, Nietzsche is rightly appealed to by many as the founder of the modern aspiration to post-metaphysical thinking or at least to an anti-traditional "revaluation of values" that has its basis in a radical critique of classical western metaphysics. (Both Martin Heidegger and Michel Foucault understand Nietzsche this way.[1]) Consequently, one can ask whether Nietzsche's very original understandings of truth and moral freedom evade (and perhaps overcome) the limitations of Aquinas's theories of truth and moral freedom, or whether, by contrast, Aquinas offers us insightful principles into metaphysics and ethics that allow us helpfully to explain the legitimate aspirations and

---

1. For precedents in Thomistic interpretations of Nietzsche that have influenced this essay, see Alasdair C. MacIntyre, *Three Rival Versions of Moral Enquiry: Encyclopedia, Genealogy, and Tradition* (Notre Dame: Notre Dame University Press, 1990), ch. 9, and Walter J. Thompson, "Perspectivism: Aquinas and Nietzsche on Intellect and Will," *American Catholic Philosophical Quarterly* 68, no. 4 (1995): 451–73.

limitations of the positions of Nietzsche. In this coda to my reflections on the reasonableness of Christianity, I will compare the two
thinkers on two points: first, the relation of truth to the language
of being; second, moral action and the philosophical estimation of
Christ's way of life. One might argue from such a comparison that
Aquinas's work is pertinent to us today for a proper understanding
of principles latent in philosophical postmodernism.

TRUTH IN AQUINAS AND NIETZSCHE

Aquinas on Truth

While Aquinas considers the subject of truth in many texts, the *locus classicus* is found in *De veritate* q. 1, a. 1.[2] There, he situates the
definition of the truth within the context of a consideration of our
knowledge of being. Aquinas begins by following Avicenna in noting that the basic object of the intellect is being (*ens*).[3] Before all
else, the human search for truth considers that which is real, or that
which truly exists. "The first thing that enters the intellect is being."[4] Aquinas then refers to the distinction between categorial

2. On truth as a transcendental in Aquinas, see Jan Aertsen, *Medieval Philosophy and
the Transcendentals: The Case of Thomas Aquinas* (Leiden: Brill, 1996), 71–112, 243–89;
*Medieval Philosophy as Transcendental Thought: From Philip the Chancellor (ca. 1225) to
Francisco Suárez* (Leiden: Brill, 2012), 209–72.

3. Aquinas, *De ver.*, q. 1, a. 1:

Now, as Avicenna says, that which the intellect first conceives as, in a way, the
most evident, and to which it reduces all its concepts, is being. Consequently, all the other conceptions of the intellect are had by additions to being. But
nothing can be added to being as though it were something not included in
being—in the way that a difference is added to a genus or an accident to a subject—for every reality is essentially a being.

4. Aquinas, *In Meta.* IV, lec. 5, 605 [Marietti]:

Now for the purpose of making this evident it must be noted that, since the
intellect has two operations [i.e., apprehension and judgment], one by which
it knows quiddities, which is called the understanding of indivisibles [by ap-
prehension], and another by which it combines and separates [by judgment,
in affirmations or negations], there is something first in both operations. In the
first operation the first thing that the intellect conceives is *being* [primum quod
cadit in conceptione intellectus ... [est] ens], and in this operation nothing else

modes of being, which are the most fundamentally distinct genera or kinds of being, and those modes of being that "transcend" the distinct categorial modes because they are proper to all the categories (and thus not in any one genus). These latter are the "transcendental" modes of being: *ens, unum, res, aliquid, verum,* and *bonum.* How might we better understand this distinction of categorial and transcendental modes of being?

The categorial modes of being are those initially employed by Aristotle to give a taxonomy of the basic structures of reality. The world consists of substances having distinct natures, which possess in turn diverse "accidents": quantities, qualities, relations, actions, passions, habits, time, place, and position.[5] In his commentary on Aristotle's *Metaphysics,* Aquinas makes it clear that he thinks there is a real distinction between each of these fundamental modes of being in realities themselves that we experience. The quantity of a given human being is not identical with his or her qualities, nor is either simply identical with his or her relations or location. In fact, each of the categories denotes something irreducible in the ontological order:

For it should be noted that a predicate can be referred to a subject in three ways.

(1) This occurs in one way when the predicate states what the subject is, as when I say that Socrates is an animal; for Socrates is the thing which is an animal. And this predicate is said to signify first *substance,* i.e., a particular substance, of which all attributes are predicated.

(2) A predicate is referred to a subject in a second way when the predicate is taken as being in the subject, and this predicate is in the sub-

---

can be conceived unless being is understood. And because this principle—it is impossible for a thing both to be and not be at the same time—depends on the understanding of being ... then this principle is by nature also the first in the second operation of the intellect, i.e., in the act of combining and separating. And no one can understand anything by this intellectual operation [of judgment] unless this principle is understood.

5. On Aristotle's categories, see Jonathan J. Sanford, "Categories and Metaphysics: Aristotle's Science of Being," in *Categories: Historical and Systematic Essays,* ed. M. Gorman and J. J. Sanford (Washington, DC: The Catholic University of America Press, 2004), 3–20.

ject either (a) essentially and absolutely and (i) as something flowing from its matter, and then it is *quantity*; or (ii) as something flowing from its form, and then it is *quality*; or (b) it is not present in the subject absolutely but with reference to something else, and then it is *relation*.

(3) A predicate is referred to a subject in a third way when the predicate is taken from something extrinsic to the subject, and this occurs in two ways. (a) In one way, that from which the predicate is taken is totally extrinsic to the subject; and (i) if this is not a measure of the subject, it is predicated after the manner of *attire* [habit], as when it is said that Socrates is shod or clothed. (ii) But if it is a measure of the subject, then, since an extrinsic measure is either time or place, (aa) the predicament is taken either in reference to time, and so it will be *when*; or (bb) if it is taken in reference to place and the order of parts in place is not considered, it will be *where*; but if this order is considered, it will be *position*. (b) In another way, that from which the predicate is taken, though outside the subject, is nevertheless from a certain point of view in the subject of which it is predicated. (i) And if it is from the viewpoint of the principle, then it is predicated as an *action*; for the principle of action is in the subject. (ii) But if it is from the viewpoint of its terminus, then it will be predicated as a *passion*; for a passion is terminated in the subject which is being acted upon.[6]

There are diverse "folds" of being present in each reality we experience, and every reality we encounter has this basic structure to it. These genera of being are properly basic so that what we know directly are only ever singular substances of given kinds, having diverse properties such as a given quantity, qualities, relations, and habits.

At the same time, there are deeper transcendental modes of being common to all reality. Everything that is, insofar as it is, has being (*ens*) and exists (*esse*). Insofar as a thing is, it is unified (*unum*) and distinct from others (*aliquid*). It has a certain essential intelligibility (*res*).[7] So, for example, a given quality (the capacity to play the piano) is distinct from a given quantity (weighs 80 kilograms). However, each of these traits of a given substance truly does exist, and each has its own intrinsic unity and intelligibility.

6. *In Meta.* VII, lec. 9, 891–92.
7. On the notion of *aliquid* as a transcendental, see Aertsen, *Medieval Philosophy as Transcendental Thought*, 218–20.

It is at this point that Aquinas defines "truth" and "goodness" as transcendental notions. All that exists—whether a substance, a given nature, or a property such as a quality—is in some way true and good. These two transcendental notions in particular are understood "relationally," because they each concern being insofar as it is related to another. Whatever has being is said to be "true" insofar as it is intelligible to another. Whatever has being is said to be "good" insofar as it is loved or desired by another.

Understood in this way, truth can be ascribed to everything that has being insofar as it is known or is capable of being known.[8] There is truth in the world insofar as the world has existence that is ontologically dense and intricately rich with intelligibility. Furthermore, such truth is ascribed to being analogically. That is to say, we do not ascribe truth only to one generic category of being or to one particular nature. We cannot say, for example, that all truth is reducible to that which is quantitative and empirically measurable or merely to that which is relational, because reality does not consist uniquely of quantity or of relations but also of unified substances with particular natures and a whole range of accidental properties, all of which have being and are intelligible to the human mind. So truth, like being and goodness, is said in many ways.[9] The goodness of a quality (such as British humor) is different from the goodness of quantity (a sufficient quantity of Burgundy for four people). The intelligible truth of a substance ("that famous French author") is distinct from the truth of a given time and place (midnight in Omaha). Truth does not exist only in human nature or in the human being, because the whole of common being (*ens commune*) is in some way "truthful," that is to say, characterized ontologically by intelligibility.[10]

Aquinas treats the categorial and transcendental modes of being as first principles of speculative reason, that is to say, as initial "givens" of human apprehension in ordinary experience. He does

---

8. See the interpretation of Lawrence Dewan, "Is Truth a Transcendental for St. Thomas Aquinas?," *Nova et Vetera* (English edition) 2, no. 1 (2004): 1–19.

9. Aristotle, *Metaphysics* IX, 10 (1051a34–1051b4); Aquinas, *In Meta.* IX, lec. 11, 1895.

10. *In Meta.*, proem.

not mean by this that each person arrives at a theoretically analytic understanding of any of these notions but simply that what they connote in reality is something known by each human being in a pre-critical, pre-reflective way.[11] Children apprehend themselves to be in a world of ordinary substances, having diverse quantitative dimensions, qualities, and so on. This does not mean that they are philosophical metaphysicians but only that they have an initial grasp of reality prior to and as a condition for their future mature reasoning and analytical reflection.

From such starting points, it follows, as Jan Aertsen notes, that Aquinas can speak of two kinds of philosophical resolution (*resolutio*) to first principles.[12] The first form of resolution can be characterized as epistemological and consists of a reflexive exercise in the face of skeptics who question whether the intellect has any true apprehension of the ontological structures of reality. It seeks to identify the first principles of speculative reason that are present in each person prior to analytic question-asking. This is the kind of knowledge without which any form of analysis, including metaphysical skepticism or arguments in favor of postmodern perspectivalism, would become impossible. Aquinas follows Aristotle's *Metaphysics* IV (3 (1005b19–20); 3 (1005b24); 6 (1011b13–20)) in locating the first principle of speculative reason in the principle of non-contradiction. One cannot rightly know or claim that a given facet of reality both *is* and *is not* the same under the same aspect at the same time.[13] The positive inversion of this principle is sometimes termed the principle of identity. The intellect does not fail to attain knowledge of some of the "folds" of reality we have noted above, both categorial and transcendental.[14] Everyone has at least some vague sense of the difference between a quantity and a quality, some capacity to differentiate different natural

11. *In Post. Anal.*, proem. and I, lec. 1; *ST* I, q. 79, a. 8.
12. Aertsen, *Medieval Philosophy and the Transcendentals*, 133–35, 156–57, 167–68, 393–94, 433–34.
13. *In Meta.* IV, lec. 6, 596–610.
14. See the argument to this effect, by Lawrence Dewan, "St. Thomas and the Principle of Causality," *Form and Being*, 61–80, which engages David Hume on the topic of our pre-reflective apprehensions of essence and causality.

kinds (such as the difference between a tree and a human being), as well as the distinction of beings around them (Paul as distinct from Peter). Likewise, each human person has some basic capacity to discern what is good from what is not and what is true from what is false. Even the skeptic must make use of this embryonic knowledge in some way to articulate and seek to problematize the grasp of reality that he or she already shares with others. There is no such thing as a purely naïve metaphysical or moral skepticism.

The second form of resolution is metaphysical as such. It goes forward from consideration of the categorial modes of being to metaphysical analysis of the primary causes and principles of reality. Aquinas differentiates different kinds of substance: non-living beings, vegetative beings, animals, and human beings.[15] Many of the things we experience in the physical world are material non-living substances. We can differentiate these from living substances. Aquinas seems to distinguish vegetative substances (plants) from animals, because the latter have sensate faculties and local motion, which are ontologically specific characteristics.[16] It is not as clear, however, that he interprets characteristic differences among animals as requiring the affirmation of ontologically distinct "species" of animal in any strong, ontological sense.[17] Animals are all "living sensate beings" characterized by "accidental" differences. Furthermore, St. Thomas thinks that it is possible, at least in principle, for living things to arise historically from non-living material bodies, even if life represents a principle not merely reducible to material parts and their quantitative arrangement.[18] Consequently, Aquinas is able to situate a differentiated hierarchy of being—from non-living beings to plants to animals—within a gradated ontological spectrum that allows for the progressive emergence of higher forms from lower ones.[19]

---

15. *SCG* II, cc. 65–66, 87; III, c. 22; *ST* I, q. 75, aa. 2–3.

16. *In de Anima* II, lec. 3, 255–61 [Marietti].

17. See, in particular, *De ente*, chs. 4–5.

18. *ST* I, q. 69, a. 2; q. 71, a. 1, ad 1; q. 73, a. 1, ad 3; q. 118, a. 1, sed contra.

19. See on this topic with regards to evolution, Dewan, "The Importance of Substance," *Form and Being*, 96–130.

The human being, meanwhile, marks out a distinct kind of being within the spectrum of animal life, because the human being has rational characteristics of abstractive intelligence and deliberative free-will.[20] Both of these necessarily imply immaterial features, which thereby give indirect but real philosophical evidence of the immateriality of the human soul.[21] The human being is a bridge, then, between the material and immaterial worlds.

Resolution to the highest cause of being is possible due to the ontological compositions, limitations, and interdependencies present in all the realities we experience directly, which in turn point us indirectly but necessarily toward the transcendent author of our being. From the basic metaphysical understanding we have of the ordinary world around us, we can raise the question of God. This happens as we eventually discern in the truth of the world the latent truth of its ontological givenness. All material things that exist are characterized by the flux of constant alteration due to the causal action of others. They exist in ongoing change and inevitable dependency, such that no material things, however vast their quantity, can in themselves serve as a sufficient ontological explanation for their own being, either individually or in the sum total. They point then to the existence of a transcendent immaterial author of material being.[22]

In all the things we experience that exist, the act of being is not caused by any of them essentially, in the sense that nothing is the cause of its own being. Thus, there is a givenness to the being of all things, collectively, in that each of them fundamentally can be or not be. Consequently the being of the world raises the question of why the world exists and points us toward the reality of One in whom there is no possibility of non-existence, whose nature it is to exist, He who is.[23]

There are gradations of perfection present in diverse realities, such as degrees of goodness, degrees of persistence in being, and

20. SCG II, cc. 447–48.
21. SCG II, cc. 49–51, 63–65.
22. See the first argument in Aquinas's "five ways," in ST I, q. 2, a. 3.
23. See the argument for the existence of God in De ente, ch. 4; SCG I, c. 22.

degrees of quality. Such hierarchical gradation points us toward the transcendent author of all perfections, in whom goodness is not participated or limited, persistence in being is not impermanent, and qualitative perfections are not limited.[24] Of course such a reality is incomprehensible. We can come to know from the world around us that God exists, but we do not know "what" God is.[25]

What I have offered here is of course only a very broad and partial indication of Aquinas's metaphysical aspirations.[26] The main point for our purposes, however, is that the immediate speculative knowledge that each person has of being leads inevitably to two basic capacities. One is the capacity to interpret our instinctive realism and ordinary ways of speaking about reality by recourse to a set of critical reflections regarding the first principles of knowledge that are present in each person necessarily, even in the skeptic. Thus, when we engage with theoretical skepticism properly, signs of realism in the mind of the skeptic himself can potentially lead us back to the philosophical recognition of the methodological inevitability of metaphysical realism. The other capacity is to think about the inherent diversity of beings in reality and to ask the fundamental question of the primary cause of all that exists. A realistic grasp of the truth about the structures we find in reality leads us to the philosophical question of the existence of God.

Nietzsche on Truth

One might ask what any of this has to do with Nietzsche. In one sense, the answer might simply be that Nietzsche starts from different premises and develops his thinking apart from or in opposition to all that a thinker like Aquinas affirms. However, the answer is more sub-

---

24. See the fourth argument in Aquinas's "five ways," in *ST* I, q. 2, a. 3.
25. *ST* I, q. 3, proem.
26. I have only alluded here briefly to the complex topics surrounding Aquinas's arguments for the existence of God. For a helpful exposition of Aquinas's arguments in this regard, see John Wippel, *The Metaphysics of St. Thomas Aquinas* (Washington, DC: The Catholic University of America Press, 2000), 400–500. On Thomistic responses to post-Kantian characterizations of philosophical theology as "onto-theology," see Thomas Joseph White, *Wisdom in the Face of Modernity*.

tle and significant. Nietzsche does not simply disagree with virtually all of what one finds in Aquinas on truth; he also seems to *agree* with Aquinas on the *interconnectedness* of many facets of truth-claiming. A certain kind of truth is dangerous and delusional for Nietzsche, because it leads to the kind of thinking that Aquinas espouses, and the attempt to avoid this kind of aspiration toward metaphysical truth requires a radical revision of the western metaphysical tradition, one that goes to extraordinary lengths to rethink the very nature of human language, thought, and the project of philosophy itself.

Understanding what Nietzsche means by truth is complex and highly disputed. For the purposes of clarity, the argument here proceeds in stages, passing from what is more certain to what is highly plausible as an interpretation of Nietzsche's key intent. We can begin, then, by considering whether Nietzsche is a positivist or perhaps a naturalist, who values empirical knowledge of the sense world above all as that which yields true understanding of reality.[27] It is clear that Nietzsche favors the empirical discoveries of the modern sciences as the privileged and most trustworthy form of knowledge over against traditional forms of metaphysical reasoning about reality, especially those that are theistic. In some basic sense, this is thematic in a work like *Daybreak*, where modern scientific knowledge is said to dispel classical metaphysical views of the dignity of the human person, natural essences, or final causality in view of a privileging of the knowledge of the material constitution of realities. "Science ... compels us to abandon belief in simple causalities. ... The 'simplest' things are *very complicated*—a fact at which one can never cease to marvel!"[28] Moreover, "[S]cience has taught us that the earth

27. For Anglo-analytic interpretations that emphasize Nietzsche's naturalism, see Christoph Cox, *Nietzsche: Naturalism and Interpretation* (Berkeley: University of California Press, 1999); Christian J. Emden, *Nietzsche's Naturalism: Philosophy and the Life Sciences in the Nineteenth Century* (Cambridge: Cambridge University Press, 2014). I am especially in agreement with the characterizations of Nietzsche's thought found in A. W. Moore, *The Evolution of Modern Metaphysics: Making Sense of Things* (Cambridge: Cambridge University Press, 2012), ch. 15, pp. 369–405.

28. Nietzsche, *Daybreak*, trans. R. J. Hollingdale (Cambridge: Cambridge University Press, 2015), 6.

is small and the solar system itself no more than a point."[29] And furthermore:

> The impartial investigator who pursues the history of the eye and the forms it has assumed among the lowest creatures, who demonstrates the whole step-by-step evolution of the eye, must arrive at the great conclusion that vision was *not* the intention behind the creation of the eye, but that vision appeared, rather, after *chance* had put the apparatus together. A single instance of this kind—and "purposes" fall away like scales from the eyes![30]

Nietzsche seems in the same light to value measurable facts over metaphysical theories about the value inherent in things:

> [E]verything for which the world "knowledge" makes any sense refers to the realm where there can be counting, weighing, measuring, refers to quantity—while conversely our feelings of value ... adhere to qualities, that is to the perspectival "truths" that are ours and nothing more than ours.... Qualities are our real human idiosyncrasy: wanting our human interpretations and values to be universal and perhaps constitutive values is one of the hereditary insanities of human pride, which still has its safest seat in religion.[31]

Nevertheless, it would be a mistake to understand Nietzsche as a mere scientistic materialist. At times, he makes clear that he thinks that mathematical theories of reality and scientific explanations are above all mere mental constructions, seductive to the human being precisely because they give the false impression that the human mind can attain real cause-effect explanation of the world. Facts can be construed by science in such a way that the scientist assumes a stance of interpretive power over against both reality and other persons. In the text just cited, for example, Nietzsche continues in the next sentence:

> Need I add, conversely, that quantities "in themselves" do not occur in experience, that our world of experience is only a qualitative world, that

29. *Daybreak*, 7.
30. *Daybreak*, 122.
31. *Writings from the Late Notebooks*, trans. K. Sturge (Cambridge: Cambridge University Press, 2006), 6[14].

consequently logic and applied logic (such as mathematics) are among the artifices of the ordering, overwhelming, simplifying, abbreviating power called life, and are thus something practical and useful, because life-preserving, but for that very reason not in the least something "true"?[32]

Indeed, Nietzsche excoriates Auguste Comte for his desire to displace religion with an unwarranted exaltation of the value of the modern sciences.[33] He disdains the Darwinian notion of the survival of the fittest, not only for any potential socio-political applications that might stem from the problematic use of the theory, but for its applications to physical living things in their evolution.[34] He mocks scientists for their "will to the truth," which is based on an unhealthy mental and moral asceticism, one that anesthetizes them to the power of life and turns them away from the real burdens and promise of human existence.[35] Most importantly, perhaps, he claims that the metaphysical pretension to final explanation in scientism is itself based on a form of faith, one historically and genealogically derivative in western European culture from Christianity and based upon a lingering nostalgia for final explanation.[36]

Here, then, we see Nietzsche's basic stance toward the truth begin to emerge. In a certain sense, he is an atheist like David Hume,

32. *Writings from the Late Notebooks*, 6[14]. We might think of how this kind of idea serves as an anticipation of Michel Foucault's claims regarding the articulation of modern scientific evidence as the latent expression of a will to power, in which scientific knowledge is employed to facilitate a kind of power over others. Consider in this respect *The Birth of the Clinic: An Archaeology of Medical Perception*, trans. A. M. Sheridan Smith (New York: Vintage, 1973). Foucault makes clear his own perceived debt to Nietzsche's conception of truth in the interview "Truth and Power," in *Power/Knowledge; Selected Interviews and Other Writings 1972–1977*, trans. C. Gordon et al. (New York: Pantheon, 1980), 109–33.

33. See in particular *Beyond Good and Evil*, trans. J. Norman (Cambridge: Cambridge University Press, 2015), 48.

34. *Writings from the Late Notebooks*, 14[123].

35. *Writings from the Late Notebooks*, 35[32], 7[3]. This point is developed thematically by Martin Heidegger in his essay published in 1956, "The Question Concerning Technology," trans. W. Lovitt in *The Question Concerning Technology and Other Essays* (New York: Harper & Row, 1977), 3–35.

36. Nietzsche discusses this in many places, but see especially *The Gay Science*, trans. J. Nauckhoff (Cambridge: Cambridge University Press, 2015), 344.

someone who thinks that the pretension to explanation in classical metaphysics and in monotheistic Christianity is unnecessarily otherworldly and epistemologically unwarranted. Nietzsche shares Hume's skepticism regarding any attempted deployment of traditional metaphysical forms of causal explanation in regard to external realities.[37] However, unlike Hume, Nietzsche is deeply interested in the internal dynamism of the will, which he invests with an almost mystical significance and explanatory function in philosophy, and in this respect, he is much more closely aligned with an atheist like Arthur Schopenhauer than he is with a naturalist or an empiricist.[38] By "mystical," I mean this: that the philosopher's knowledge of the internal moral dynamics of the will yields the most profound explanation of the dynamics of reality itself. His project is in some very real sense focused on a destruction of the metaphysical project of the western tradition in order to make room for something genuinely new in the order of ethical self-realization.[39]

We see this theme emerge most poignantly in Nietzsche's idea (in various works) of the truth as "dangerous" and of the moral errors in human beings that stem from the "will to the truth." "Perhaps nobody has ever been truthful enough about what 'truthfulness' is."[40]

Consequently, "will to truth" does *not* mean "I do not want to let myself be deceived" but—there is no alternative—"I will not deceive, not even myself"; *and with that we stand on moral ground....* Thus the question "Why science?" leads back to the moral problem: *Why morality at all,* if life, nature and history are "immoral"? ... But you will have gathered what I am getting at, namely, that it is still a *metaphysical faith* upon which our faith in science rests—that even we knowers of today, we godless anti-metaphysicians, still take *our* fire, too, from the flame lit by the

37. *Writings from the Late Notebooks*, 2[83].
38. I do not mean by this that Nietzsche simply appropriates Schopenhauer's theories of the will as his own.
39. Consider the messianic tone of Nietzsche's claims about himself in the preface of *Ecce Homo*, trans. J. Norman, in *The Anti-Christ, Ecce Homo, Twilight of the Idols and Other Writings* (Cambridge: Cambridge University Press, 2015).
40. *Beyond Good and Evil*, 177.

thousand-year old faith, the Christian faith, which was also Plato's faith, that God is truth, that the truth is divine.... But what if this were to become more difficult to believe ... if God himself were to turn out to be our longest lie?[41]

The search for the truth is dangerous in the human being, precisely because the will to live in the truth motivates human beings to produce inflated metaphysical and moral constructions of reason that they take to be verities.[42] Nietzsche is particularly concerned about the dangers of adherence to transcendent truths of a Platonic or Christian origin. These are "life denying," because they seek to locate the importance of human existence in something otherworldly, necessarily disconnected from our real ethical concerns with this-worldly joy, life, and meaning. This is why the religious will to truth in particular leads to a kind of nihilism, the denial of inherent meaning to our life in this world and the freedom it brings, privileging instead the search for a world to come, an alternative metaphysical reality.[43]

We should note here that Nietzsche's critique of the "explanatory appeal" in monotheism seems to form a juncture in the transition from the Kantian theory of "onto-theology" to that of Heidegger. For Kant, the onto-theo-logical constructions of reason that posit the existence of God as a supreme cause of reality are not philosophically demonstrative, but they are heuristic. The idea of God serves as a useful speculative principle to bind all knowledge of the world together under one all-subsuming principle, even if we can never know philosophically by speculative reason whether God exists. For Heidegger, however, the onto-theo-logical pretension of human reason eclipses the mystery of being in this world (*seindes* and *Sein*), covering reality over with an artificial system of causality and explanation.[44] Like Nietzsche, Heidegger wishes to overcome

41. *The Gay Science*, 344.
42. *The Gay Science*, 110, 344; *On the Genealogy of Morals* III, 27, trans. W. Kaufmann (New York: Vintage, 1967).
43. *Writings from the Late Notebooks*, 5[71].
44. See in particular Heidegger, "The Onto-theo-logical Constitution of Metaphysics," in *Identity and Difference*, trans. J. Staumbaugh (New York: Harper and Row, 1969), 42–74.

the classical notion of metaphysics and causal explanation in order to allow a new ontology of being-in-the-world to become manifest. Here, the comparison of Aquinas and Nietzsche becomes particularly illuminating. There are non-trivial senses in which the two thinkers agree. Each of them would seem to accept the idea that medieval philosophical metaphysics is concerned with the project of thinking about the transcendent cause of being, God, as that which is most ultimately real or which perdures eternally. Furthermore, this knowledge, according to Aquinas, is developed from beings we know more immediately, from the truth of realities we encounter in ordinary experience. Consequently, the philosophical knowledge of God that can be attained in this life is a kind of perfecting knowledge, oriented aspirationally toward a horizon, made possible implicitly by our ordinary knowledge of created being. In turn, it gives perspective on all other realities. Knowledge of God allows us to understand everything secondary in light of what is primary so as to understand the world in a sapiential way, interpreting creatures in the light of what is most ultimate, the hidden Creator and author of being, who in his all-sustaining Goodness is immanent to all that is and utterly transcendent of all that is.

Nietzsche does not believe in God, of course, but he does believe that the (illusory) search for transcendent metaphysical explanations that pre-modern philosophy articulated sought to explain *features of reality* that most modern people still take to be real: the intelligibility (or truthfulness) of the world prior to our intellectual analysis of it, a deeper causal order inscribed in things, teleology, and the objective grounds of moral value in human agency prior to our construction of any system of values. Where theists might indicate such metaphysical features of reality so as to discern their transcendent origin in God, Nietzsche, *precisely so as to purify human thought of the dross of the illusion of God,* seeks to dispel in turn the notion that these "features of reality" truly exist. To think in post-Christian terms, one must also seek to think in post-metaphysical terms. Basic notions of causal realism, essences, finality, and objective moral qualities in human persons should all be subject to the "revaluation of values."

However, as Aquinas rightly notes, these features of reality are typically accessed even through our most primitive "pre-demonstrative" intellectual perceptions of reality. The intellect discerns the causal nature of reality in its grasp of the categorial and transcendental modes of being, which is in some sense inevitable. This apprehension of reality is in turn exhibited even in our most basic categories of language and in laws of thinking, such as the principle of non-contradiction and the principle of identity. Nietzsche seems to hold a parallel conviction. If we are going to eradicate the bad habits of metaphysical thinking that we have inherited from the theistic tradition, we need to go down to the roots of ordinary language itself and cast a skeptical light upon all of these supposedly most basic "principles" of human thought. Thus, Nietzsche famously writes:

The last thing in metaphysics we'll rid ourselves of is the oldest stock, assuming we *can* rid ourselves of it—that stock which has embodied itself in language and the grammatical categories and made itself so indispensable that it almost seems we could cease being able to think if we relinquished it. Philosophers, in particular, have the greatest difficulty in freeing themselves from the belief that the basic concepts and categories of reason belong without further ado to the realm of metaphysical certainties: from ancient times they have believed in reason as a piece of the metaphysical world itself—this oldest belief breaks out in them again and again like an overpowering recoil.[45]

Also:

The inventive force that thought up categories was working the service of needs—of security, of quick comprehensibility using signs and sounds, of means of abbreviation—"substance," "subject," "object," "being," "becoming" are not metaphysical truths.—It is the powerful who made the names of things law; and among the powerful it is the greatest artists of abstraction who created the categories.[46]

45. *Writings from the Late Notebooks*, 6[13] (pp. 125-26); see likewise 14[93] (p. 250).
46. *Writings from the Late Notebooks*, 6[11] (p. 125).

Nietzsche seems to be referring here primarily to Kantian categories, rather than those of Aristotle or Aquinas. Like Kant, he thinks that metaphysical categories are constructions of reason that need not correspond to any real "noumenon" of human experience, but unlike Kant, he does not think they are heuristic ways in which we order our sense-experiences and engagement in the world in intelligible ways. Instead, they are the aggressive and arbitrarily imposed results of the will to power or the will to knowledge. This is true even of the principle of non-contradiction, which has been willed into existence by a clever philosopher.[47] Consequently, Nietzsche's reference to artists is not incidental. Human beings, and metaphysicians above all, are artists who fabricate or construct webs of meaning and the moral valuation of human acts. The genealogist has a "vocation" to tear down the idols of human language, or more accurately, to expose the presuppositions of *willfulness* to power latent in the fabrications of meaning set in place by a given culture. Here, then, we can see emerge in Nietzsche's anti-metaphysical thinking the post-structuralist projects of both Michel Foucault and Jacques Derrida—each also greatly influenced by Heidegger—who appropriate the Nietzschean project in two distinct ways.[48]

---

47. *Writings from the Late Notebooks*, 9[97].

48. Michel Foucault, *The Archeology of Knowledge and A Discourse on Language*, trans. A. M. Sheridan Smith (New York: Pantheon, 1972), 125:

> To describe a group of statements not as the closed, plethoric totality of a meaning, but as an incomplete fragmented figure; to describe a group of statements not with reference to the interiority of an intention, a thought, or a subject, but in accordance with the dispersion of an exteriority; to describe a group of statements, in order to rediscover not the moment of the trace of their origin, but the specific forms of an accumulation, is certainly not to uncover an interpretation, to discover a foundation, or to free constituent acts; nor is it to decide on a rationality, or to embrace a teleology. It is to establish what I am quite willing to call a *positivity*.... If, by substituting ... the description of relations of exteriority for the theme of the transcendental foundation ... one is a positivist, then I am quite happy to be one.

Jacques Derrida, *Of Grammtology*, trans. G. C. Spivak (Baltimore: The Johns Hopkins University Press, 1976), 73:

> This reference to the meaning of a signified thinkable and possible outside all signifiers remains dependent upon the onto-theo-teleology that I have just

Nietzsche's skepticism about the "objectivity" of metaphysical truths and ethical values is not motivated by nihilism. On the contrary, he believes that in the wake of the collapse of Christianity in secular European culture, there is a tendency toward nihilism in modern culture precisely because of the absence of meaning left by the simultaneous loss of religion *and* the *only partial* abandonment of the structures of Christian thinking.[49] The destructive aspect of his project is meant to eradicate this remainder of Christian influence, a lingering incoherency in the modern European soul, in order to permit the emergence of a new project of this-worldly life re-valuation. His aim is to replace the search for metaphysical absolutes with the Dionysian life of the will to power.[50] It is to this topic that we can now turn in the second half of this essay.

AQUINAS AND NIETZSCHE ON MORAL ACTION AND
PHILOSOPHICAL EVALUATION OF CHRIST

The Life-Affirming Ethics of Nietzsche

For Nietzsche, philosophical categories of metaphysical reason and moral action theory both stem from a hidden, arbitrary will to moral power that we might characterize as a kind of "transcendental illusion." Nietzsche seems to be a type of neo-Kantian anti-Kantian. Like Kant, he thinks that the modern philosophical subject constructs metaphysical theories—Kant's heuristic conceptions of God, but also, for example, theories of human dignity and universal moral law—principally in support of the *practical* aim of moral engagement and decision making. However, against Kant, Nietzsche wishes to follow through on radical consequences entailed by the fact that there is no real transcendent principle (whether God,

---

evoked. It is thus the idea of the sign that must be deconstructed through a meditation upon writing which would merge, as it must, with the undoing of onto-theology, faithfully repeating it in its *totality* and *making* it *insecure* in its most assured evidences.

49. *Writings from the Late Notebooks*, 5 [71-107].

50. See in this respect *Ecce Homo*, "Why I Am a Destiny," 1–5.

human dignity, or objective human morality) against which to measure the standards of human moral action.[51] Kantian morality is in
fact a mere phantom of the Platonic-Christian corpse of European
intellectual life, one that should be expelled.[52] Nietzsche seeks to offer an alternative genealogy of the origins of morality and to provide an alternative remedy to the crisis of meaning in our age.

In the beginning of *On the Genealogy of Morals* Nietzsche famously articulates this program as a "revaluation of values."[53] Di-
agnostically, he posits the origins of conventional moral conviction
as stemming from the will-to-truth, itself a repressed expression of
the will to power. Simply stated, the construction of a sense of moral
absolutes permits us to have power over others in the form of moral knowledge. This power may be self-protective, in the sense that
we seek by moral enunciations to provide a bulwark for ourselves
against the dangers of an unbridled strength in others. It may also
be resentful. The drive for moral reasoning can be motivated in the
weak by a *ressentiment* of power others have over us. Nietzsche's diag-
nosis is meant to unmask the pretensions of the will-to-knowledge.
This unmasking will allow us in turn to understand that behind the
dissimulations of moralism, there is the dynamism of the will to
power as the fundamental reality, one that is not illusory and that
needs to be accepted and even exalted.

In his later notebooks, which were intended to be published as
The Will to Power,[54] Nietzsche offers a positive enunciation of this
drive by casting it in terms of artistic creativity. "In truth, *interpretation is the means of becoming master of something.*"[55] "Art is *worth
more* than truth."[56] "We possess *art* lest we *perish of the truth.*"[57]

---

51. *On the Genealogy of Morals*, III, 12. See likewise Foucault, *The Archeology of
Knowledge*, 203, on the "transcendental narcissism" of Kantianism that still remains to be
purified from European philosophy.

52. *The Anti-Christ*, 11.

53. *On the Genealogy of Morals*, preface, § 6.

54. See *On the Genealogy of Morals*, III, 27 for the stated intention.

55. *Writings from the Late Notebooks*, 2[148] (p. 90).

56. *The Will to Power*, trans. W. Kaufmann and R. J. Hollingdale (New York: Vintage,
1968), 853.

57. *The Will to Power*, 822.

Heidegger took these statements to be indicative of Nietzsche's deeper philosophical stance.[58] In seeking to deracinate principles of the western metaphysical tradition, Nietzsche is seeking to affirm the primacy of interpretation. "Inasmuch as the word 'knowledge' has any meaning at all, the world is knowable: but it is variously *interpretable*; it has no meaning behind it, but countless meanings. 'Perspectivalism.'"[59]

Nietzsche affirms a primacy of "perspectivalism" in matters of truth. One can reasonably interpret him to mean that before all else, there is the inevitability of heterogeneous interpretations of reality. "Our 'knowing' restricts itself to ascertaining quantities ... but we can't stop ourselves experiencing these quantitative distinctions as qualities. *Quality* is a *perspectival* truth for *us*; not an 'in-itself.'"[60] If we combine this idea with Nietzsche's radical voluntarism, which underscores the primacy of constructivism with regard to moral values, then a uniform vision begins to emerge. For Nietzsche, the "moral" project of the will to power is first and foremost a *creative and destructive project*. The human being lives authentically by acknowledging his or her capacity to destroy or construct canons of beauty, morality, ontology, science, and religion.[61] The realization of the *inevitability* of this freedom is the beginning of wisdom.

The constructive project Nietzsche attempts to provide in the wake of this realization is depicted above all in his portrait of Zarathustra and also in his many maxims regarding "Dionysian" ethics.[62] The human being who comes after the unmasking of the pretensions of the Platonic-Christian tradition must accept to live in the great eternal "now," to live in this world, with its eternal recurrence of creation and destruction, of coming to be and passing away. The ethical sage pursues knowledge of nature (and thus there is a certain

---

58. Heidegger, *Nietzsche*, vol. I: *The Will to Power as Art*, trans. D. F. Krell (New York: Harper & Row, 1979), particularly 67–76, 92–106, 138–61, 211–20.

59. *Writings from the Late Notebooks*, 7[60].

60. *Writings from the Late Notebooks*, 5[36].

61. *Writings from the Late Notebooks*, 7[3].

62. *Ecce Homo*, "Thus Spoke Zarathustra," 6.

kind of naturalism in Nietzsche), but it is a "nature" above all of human psychology. The greatness of the human being is in accepting
the individual struggle to produce one's own values, even in the face
of our own eventual nothingness. To find the meaning of our lives in
the present moment, we must learn to live according to the visions
of nobility we construct, not the ones we receive. Each human being
must learn to dance over the abyss, embracing his or her own will to
power, engaging with the forces of destruction and creativity that animate the human will from time immemorial.

It is within the context of this ethical stance that we can best
come to understand Nietzsche's attempt at a philosophical evaluation of the person of Jesus of Nazareth. He is concerned not only
with the ethical delusions of the Christianity of his own age but with
the genealogy of morality one finds in the New Testament, which
has its remote origins in the sacerdotal religion of ancient Judaism,
and its proximate origins in the life and teachings of the founder of
Christianity.

Nietzsche follows Samuel Reimarus and Franz Overbeck in interpreting Jesus first and foremost as a self-designated eschatological preacher, articulating an apocalyptic vision of divine judgment
in reaction to the political crisis of Roman occupation. This viewpoint was later to influence Christian theologians, such as Karl Barth
and Wolfhart Pannenberg, who understood apocalypticism as something essential to Jesus' salvific message and the universal meaning
of the New Testament.[63] Nietzsche's portrait of Jesus cuts the other
direction, seeking to understand the apocalyptic consciousness of
Jesus as an indication of his intellectual limitations within his own
peculiar historical-cultural background.[64] Jesus' apocalyptic preaching stems from his suppressed will to power, which emerges in the
form of a religion of "revolt" against the ethics of power, that is, the

63. On Franz Overbeck and his influence on modern German Christology, see
Bruce L. McCormack, *Karl Barth's Critically Realistic Dialectical Theology: Its Genesis and
Development, 1909–1936* (Oxford: Clarendon Press, 1995), esp. 226–34.
64. *The Anti-Christ*, 28–30.

reality of the will to power, in favor of an illusory ethics of "love."[65] The goal of Nietzsche's interpretive stance is to explain genealogically the historical genesis of the Christian ethics of charity that he considers so particularly misguided.[66]

Jesus' ethical teaching on love has its remote origins in the sacerdotal "revaluation of values" developed by the priest-scribes of ancient Judaism. The genius of these thinkers was to employ the arts they had at their disposal (religious absolutism) to devise a form of life that would make the powerful and noble subservient to the oppressed and weak, thus conceiving of Israel as a people in morally superior terms to the nations that surrounded her.

> All that has been done on earth against "the noble," "the powerful," "the masters," "the rulers," fades into nothing compared with what the *Jews* have done against them; the Jews, that priestly people, who in opposing their enemies and conquerors were ultimately satisfied with nothing less than a radical revaluation of their enemies' values, that is to say, an act of the *most spiritual vengeance*. For this alone was appropriate to a priestly people, the people embodying the most deeply repressed priestly vengefulness. It was the Jews who with awe-inspiring consistency dared to invert the aristocratic value equation (good = noble = powerful = beautiful = happy = beloved of God) ... saying "the wretched alone are the good; the poor, impotent, lowly alone are the good."... [W]ith the Jews there begins *the slave revolt in morality*: that revolt ... which we no longer see because it—has been victorious.[67]

Judaism springs at base from a suppression and redirection of the will to power into a religious ethics of misdirected mercy that privileges the weak with regard to the strong. In the face of the superior Roman forces that threatened this great national religious ideal of Judaism, both from within and without, Jesus sought to embody the ideal of a universal ethics of love without any measure of vengeance or *ressentiment* toward those who opposed him. In this way, he aimed to redefine religious behavior beyond the power dynamics

65. *The Anti-Christ*, 23, 40.
66. *The Anti-Christ*, 30, 61–62.
67. *On the Genealogy of Morals* I, 7; see likewise *The Anti-Christ*, 25–27.

based upon guilt and sin, promoting instead the ideal of a universally inclusive religious fraternity. In this way, that is, by suppress-
ing the will to power so exhaustively, Jesus became one of the most
life-denying figures in history.[68]

Christianity, meanwhile, was unable to follow Jesus in his errant
but thoroughly consistent form of world-denying absolutism. The
first Christians made him into the Son of God and God as a product of their own *ressentiment* of the death of the master, transforming the occasion of his death into "atonement" and "sin offering."[69]
In this way, they re-positioned his uniqueness within the context of
a new form of universal Judaism, a religion of the weak who might
eventually conquer the strong through the medium of the ethics of
Christian morality. Nietzsche's program is meant to initiate us into
a thorough-going skepticism as regards this entire construction that
has so deeply influenced western thought. He wishes to aid a European world of fading Christian culture to set out on a new course,
the course he himself has initiated and depicted in symbolic terms
with the figure of Zarathustra.[70]

Aquinas on Ethics

Much of this contrasts with what we find in Thomas Aquinas. We
might first compare the two authors by returning to the question
of the relationship between moral action theory and artistic creativity. Here, St. Thomas adopts some very basic distinctions from
Aristotelian philosophy. Broadly speaking, one can distinguish the
speculative intellect, which considers the nature or structure of reality for its own sake, from the practical intellect, which directs human agency rationally in view of particular outcomes or practical
realizations. Evidently here, we are speaking of the same *faculty* of
the intellect being employed in two distinct modes: in view of the
consideration of the nature of things themselves, and in view of

68. *The Anti-Christ*, 33, 40.
69. *The Anti-Christ*, 40; *On the Genealogy of Morals* I, 8; III, 11.
70. *The Anti-Christ*, 54.

the transformation of the world.[71] This most broad distinction comprises sub-distinctions, most notably that made within the practical intellect between ethical or moral activity on the one hand and artistic activity on the other.[72] Moral activity is not characterized first and foremost by the external transformation of the human environment but by the internal ordering of human action, in view of both virtuous conduct toward other human beings and the achievement of happiness. Its final end is friendship, or the stable pursuit of prudent, just, and affable relationships in civic society, which facilitate common happiness in a shared life between persons.[73] Artistic activity is oriented toward the alteration of the external world in view of works of tools, technology, domicile and industrial artifacts, artisanal objects, and works of fine art. Systems of language, logic, and human law are also forms of artifacts for Aquinas, ones that stem directly and necessarily from human nature and are inevitable to any human culture but that are also in some respects "fabricated" and thus in certain respects conventional and historically variable.[74]

This simple taxonomy is useful for understanding the diversity of "virtues"—qualifications of soul stably possessed in view of rightly ordered action—that one can find present in human beings. There are speculative "intellectual virtues," such as the stable capacity to

71. *ST* I, q. 79, a. 11:

The speculative and practical intellects are not distinct powers. The reason of which is that ... what is accidental to the nature of the object of a power, does not differentiate that power; for it is accidental to a thing colored to be man, or to be great or small; hence all such things are apprehended by the same power of sight. Now, to a thing apprehended by the intellect, it is accidental whether it be directed to operation or not, and according to this the speculative and practical intellects differ. For it is the speculative intellect which directs what it apprehends, not to operation, but to the consideration of truth; while the practical intellect is that which directs what it apprehends to operation. And this is what the Philosopher says (*De Anima* III, 10); that "the speculative differs from the practical in its end." Whence each is named from its end: the one speculative, the other practical—i.e. operative.

72. *In Nic. Ethic.* VI, lec. 1–4.
73. *In Nic. Ethic.* XI, lec. 11.
74. See *In Post. Analyt.*, proem., *ST* I-II, q. 97.

demonstrate subtle mathematical truths or the capacity to understand the biological structures of living things. There are practical virtues that are distinctively artistic, like the capacity to write profound, meaningful literature, or the capacity to perform open heart surgery. And there are practical virtues that are distinctively ethical, such as the intellectual virtue of prudence, which is concerned with living well in view of happiness and ethically noble pursuits, and the moral virtue of justice, which seeks to render to individuals what is due to them in a given situation.

Without seeking to give a comprehensive list of Aquinas's division of the virtues, we can identify some simple points of contrast with Nietzsche from the basic sketch already elaborated. First, it is clear that while Nietzsche clearly wishes to disavow the speculative ambitions of someone like Aquinas, Aquinas's philosophy would oblige us to disavow the *practical* ambitions of Nietzsche. Nietzsche seems to identify the practical drive of the will to power as a fundamental source of all theoretical speculations regarding the traditional Aristotelian metaphysical principles ascribed to reality. For Aquinas, by contrast, there is no real possibility of a *voluntary genesis* of metaphysical truth. Yes, human beings do fabricate world-views, constructing myriad explanations of reality. But their explanatory systems always have their measure of truthfulness in relation to the status of reality as such, which every human culture has theoretical access to, over and against its own pre-existent traditions of explanation. Moreover, human beings desire to know the truth for its own sake and not merely to employ it in view of a pre-existent voluntary end that is ethical or anti-ethical in kind.

The two thinkers differ then on the relationship between the will and the intellect. For Aquinas the intellect has its own prerogatives that are not directed by practical impulses and indeed the speculative knowledge of nature, including human nature, helps us direct our practical actions, both ethical and artistic. Contrastingly for Nietzsche the will in its practical orientation is decisive for all engagements of the speculative intellect. Once we understand the core dive of the will in its creative impulse, we can in turn understand the generative force behind systems of the speculative intellect.

Behind this difference, there lies a deeper difference. For Aquinas, both the ethical and artistic virtues develop only as second-order considerations or modes of knowledge, each presupposing a pre-existent contact with reality by way of speculative, metaphysical knowledge. The condition of possibility for any human act of willing, whether ethical or artistically creative, is *speculative, intellectual contact with the being, truth, and goodness of reality*, by which we begin to love or admire features of reality. We can only will in the light of truth and our knowledge of those "transcendental" features of experience that were underscored in the first part of this essay.[75]

This is the case in two distinct ways, depending upon the kind of practical activity in question. The production of artifacts—whether they be entirely utilitarian, like tools, or more sublime and contemplative in purpose, as we find in the fine arts—always takes its start from a more epistemologically primal knowledge of the features of nature. The producer of the hammer has to have knowledge of metals and their relative densities, just as the designer of the violin must know a great deal about the resonant qualities of diverse kinds of wood. Artifacts result not from the production of new kinds of natural substances, as if a violin were as "natural" a being as a tree, but from novel configurations of parts of natural substances placed into

---

75. The idea is stated simply in *ST* I, q. 5, a. 2:

In idea being is prior to goodness. For the meaning signified by the name of a thing is that which the mind conceives of the thing and intends by the word that stands for it. Therefore, that is prior in idea, which is first conceived by the intellect. Now the first thing conceived by the intellect is being; because everything is knowable only inasmuch as it is in actuality. Hence, being is the proper object of the intellect, and is primarily intelligible; as sound is that which is primarily audible. Therefore in idea being is prior to goodness.

The pursuit of any practical aim is *motivated* and thus tends toward some kind of good. Consequently, any practical activity has its epistemological root in an already prior grasp of the actuality of the being of reality. No pure primacy of practical reason is possible for Aquinas.

new sets of relation to one another.[76] Typically, the fine artist is the person who can perceive (by way of artistic inspiration) those ways that natural realities can be altered by creative skill so as to depict in symbolic fashion some profound facet of human experience. The "truth" of art is complex, then, because it can be evaluated from the point of view of both the external world—whether the work in question truly depicts the depths of human experience or speaks to it insightfully—and the representation—whether the artistic piece itself is beautiful.[77] To employ an illustration of this Thomist understanding of art from Nietzsche himself: the latter clearly thinks his portrait of Zarathustra is one of the great literary monuments of human history, akin to Odysseus, Buddha, Socrates, or Jesus.[78] One can ask, however, whether *Thus Spoke Zarathustra* truly depicts the nature of the human condition *and* whether it depicts it beautifully or well (in contrast, for example, to the Nietzschean-inspired figure of Stephen Daedalus at the end of James Joyce's *Portrait of the Artist as a Young Man*). Arguably, the answer is "no" on both counts.

Ethical activity refers to being in a very different way for Aquinas. For Aquinas, ethics is concerned above all with the prudent and humble pursuit of that which is authentically good in order to live a life of authentic human flourishing in contemplative knowledge and personal love. Central to any happy life is the practice of love-of-friendship. "Moral philosophy considers all things that are required for human living; and among these friendship is especially

---

76. On the ontology of artifacts as distinct from natural substances, see Eleonore Stump, *Aquinas* (London: Routledge, 2003), 5–44.

77. On Aquinas's understanding of beauty, see Aertsen, *Medieval Philosophy and the Transcendentals*, 335–59; Pasquale Porro, *Thomas Aquinas*, 203–5.

78. See *Ecce Homo*, "Thus Spoke Zarathustra," 6:

> The fact that a Goethe, a Shakespeare, would not know how to breathe for a second in this incredible passion and height, that compared to Zarathustra, Dante is just another one of the faithful and not one who first *creates* truth, a *world-governing* spirit, a destiny—, that the poets of the Veda are priests and do not deserve even to tie the shoelaces of a Zarathustra, all this is the least that can be said and does not give you any real idea of the distance, of the *azure* solitude this work lives in.

necessary, to such an extent that no one in his right mind would choose to live in the possession of great external goods without friends."[79] For Aquinas, the cardinal virtues of prudence, justice, fortitude, and temperance, while necessary, are not ends in themselves—internal Stoic sculptures to admire narcissistically. Nor are they Nietzschean tools by which to have surreptitious power over others. Rather, they are necessary means or conditions sine qua non for the right exercise of virtuous friendship and for the sustaining of the practices of charity and justice that constitute rightly ordered life in society. The human being can become good, virtuous, and happy only by living equitably and charitably in common life with others.

This is only possible, however, if the person is first able to *know* the truth about others, both in their human nature and their individuality and singularity of being. We can only love what we first know, because love follows upon and flows from authentic knowledge of the good.[80] And authentic human love according to virtue stems from delight in and care for the good of the other.[81] There is an alterity to the directedness of all human spiritual love; it tends outward toward the ontological good that the other possesses and wills the flourishing of that good. Consequently, the truth of our love for the good of other persons is measured by the reality of the persons themselves, their very being and their capacities for goodness, which contributes to *their* authentic flourishing. It is only when persons who love in the truth care for one another in authentic and realistic ways that communities of genuine, humane common life can emerge.

Evidently, we have now travelled far down the path that leads away from Nietzsche's ethics of the will to power. His affirmation of the nobility of the individual's struggle for artistic creativity would seem to bring with it the inevitability of conflict stemming from the heteronomy of conflicting interpretive perspectives. For Aquinas,

79. *In Nic. Ethics*, VIII, lec. 1, 1539.
80. *In Nic. Ethics*, VIII, lec. 8.
81. *In Ioan.* XV, lec. 4, 2036 [Marietti].

life in society is not structured by the eternal return of conflictual cycles of authorial destruction and creation, in which the individual must overcome the limitations of the herd mentality to assert his or her (usually his!) superior dominion as a noble source of creative freedom. On the contrary, life in society is animated by a commonly shared search for the truth about the world, particularly the truth about the human person.[82] The fact that the human person is itself capable of knowing the truth about reality and of practicing oblative love toward others allows human beings to live within a collective social order in a particularly noble and profound way. This characteristic of human beings as *speculative* truth seekers and agents of truth provides the foundation for a *practical* common life of justice and charity, as well as artistic creativity and political prudence.

How does the person of Jesus Christ fit into or compete with this philosophical portrait of ethics that we have drawn from Aquinas's writings? First, it must be said that for Aquinas, the search for ethical happiness through a shared life with others comes not at the expense of the religious search for knowledge of God, nor as excluded by the latter, but as deeply related to man's openness to a religious interpretation of reality. This should be evident from the first segment of our considerations above. To be capable of knowing and loving the goodness of others as they are in themselves, we must be open speculatively to the transcendental features of reality in its metaphysical depths, at least grasped in implicit, pre-analytic ways. But to be open to these facets of reality is itself to be open to the transcendent mystery that is at the origins of finite, created reality, the mystery that we call "God." In fact, to be intellectually receptive to reality in its objective contours which inform our analysis is to admit that there is a deep structure to being that is there "before" our apprehensions of it and that is not of our own making. This suggests that if there is an original "will to power" that "eternally returns" and is at the basis of all being, it is the transcendent, omnipotent will of God, which stems from his ever more primaeval wisdom and goodness, and not something of purely human derivation. Only God can act as an "artist" at the very level of the ontological substance and being (*esse*) of things. This is a level of causal activity we can fathom only in a highly qualified, analogical sense that largely evades our comprehension.[83]

This openness to God inscribed within the human search for the truth is also for Aquinas the residual sign that the human person is capable of something more than a mere metaphysical knowledge of the created world. The search for the truth about our human condition opens up from within, as it were, through philosophical questioning, leading us toward the mystery of God. Contemplative knowledge of the divine nature serves for Aquinas as the final lodestar of the intellect.[84] The human intellect tends naturally to wish to know God as perfectly as possible, even while remaining unable to perceive God directly. We can come to know that God exists, obliquely, through the medium of created things, and can reflect on his nature and its attributes, but God also remains "hidden," since we naturally gain what philosophical knowledge we have of God only from the consideration of him based upon his creatures.[85]

This is why, philosophically speaking, Aquinas follows Aristotle in stating that friendship with other human persons is a core dimension of human existence, but simultaneously, we have no "natural friendship" with God.[86] Our knowledge of God is too indirect and obscure, and our natural religious practices are marked too greatly by superstition, experimentation, and uncertainty for us to have any *merely natural* warrant for their practice.[87] Consequently, if there is any capacity for human intimacy or friendship of charity with God, this must stem from a new divine initiative, namely, the mystery of grace.[88] Such friendship cannot be produced by the powers of human nature or any form of ethical ingenuity on our part.

---

83. *ST* I, q. 44, a. 2; q. 45, aa. 1–5.
84. *SCG* III, c. 37.
85. *ST* I, q. 12, a. 12.
86. See Aristotle, *Nicomachean Ethics* VIII, 7, 1159a5–8; *In Nic. Ethics* VIII, lec. 7, 1635–37.
87. *ST* II-II, q. 92–94.
88. *ST* II-II, q. 23. aa. 1–2.

Second, then, the life of Jesus of Nazareth is understood by Aquinas primarily as a theological mystery, that is to say, a reality that evades the scope of merely natural comprehension but can be understood (to some extent) under the auspices of the supernatural grace of faith. Faith here is understood as a supernatural virtue infused into the intellect that casts a light of judgment or penetrating insight upon a reality revealed by God.[89] By the light of faith, the human being can come to understand that "God was in Christ reconciling the world to himself" (2 Cor. 5:19). That is to say, the man Jesus of Nazareth is God.[90] In Christ, God has entered human history and experienced our human life and death and also human resurrection.

At the same time, however, even if Christ is only fully intelligible in the light of faith, we can also speak of the "philosophical" intelligibility of the Incarnation, or more accurately stated, of its "fittingness" (*convenientia*) according to Aquinas.[91] To know that God became incarnate as an individual human being is itself a gift of grace, but in the light of revelation, one may perceive a fitting rationale that stands behind the mystery. We have noted that the speculative openness to being that is characteristic of the human intellect makes every human person naturally capable of human friendship and of a search for the truth that has religious horizons. For Aquinas, the mystery of Christ preserves but also elevates this "structure" of nature, bringing it into the sphere of grace.

Simply stated, God became human so that human beings might be capable of a radiant intellectual knowledge of and friendship with God. In the personal encounter with Christ (made possible by his grace and mercy), the human being comes to know God in a qualitatively superior way and is able to relate to God effectively in a love of friendship.[92] Simultaneously, this grace serves to heal and strengthen human relationships that thrive best under the conditions of

89. *ST* I-II, q. 62, aa. 1 and 3; II-II, q. 4.
90. *ST* II-II, q. 2, a. 7; *SCG* IV, cc. 39–41.
91. *SCG* IV, c. 42; *ST* III, q. 1.
92. *ST* III, q. 1, a. 2.

virtuous, altruistic love but are frequently marred by ethical disorientation, egoism, personal antipathies, and moral weakness.[93] The charity of Christ is, for Aquinas, the "form" of the virtues, such that the human life patterned after the example of Christ is a most eminently virtuous life. By his grace, our life can be transformed from within by an effective love for the goodness of others.[94]

Evidently, the features of Thomistic Christology and ethics I am sketching here serve to underscore the traditional principle that "grace does not destroy nature, but perfects it."[95] The key point of the argument for our purposes is that Aquinas sees the mystery of Christ not as something that stands in opposition to human flourishing or that is life-destroying but as something that is divinely life-giving. Philosophy, for Aquinas, cannot determine whether the mystery of grace is real, but one can argue from sound philosophical principles that *if the mystery of Christ is real,* and if it can have the effects in human persons that are noted above, then it effectuates human flourishing in a way that is salutary to human beings even in their best and deepest rational aspirations. Philosophical desire and Christological grace should not be seen as intrinsically opposed to one another; rather, if rightly understood, they are deeply harmonious and congruent in aspiration.

CONCLUSION

We may conclude briefly with three ideas. First, with John Henry Newman, it is reasonable to underscore that what a reflective person believes about the meaning of human existence is not typically the result of a single argument or observation but stems from a collage of life impressions, considered reasons, probable beliefs, and working hypotheses. Newman calls this complex manner of making decisions about the truth of things the "illative sense."[96] Whether

---

93. *ST* I-II, q. 85, a. 3.
94. *ST* II-II, q. 23, a. 8; III, q. 8.
95. *ST* I, q. 1, a. 8, ad 2.
96. John Henry Newman, *An Essay in Aid of a Grammar of Assent,* ch. 9.

one is drawn intellectually, then, to what Aquinas affirms about the world or to what Nietzsche affirms (or to neither in particular) is typically not the result of one single reflection but of a great gathering of reflections and intuitions of multifarious kinds. I have tried to suggest in this essay that what one thinks about the intelligibility of being and the nature of human love are deeply interconnected. Nietzsche and Aquinas both believe this in two deeply incompatible ways.

Nevertheless, it seems to me that Aquinas's vision better displays the distinctions and complexities found within reality, and in this case, it even allows one to understand Nietzsche's vision somewhat better than one can if one has only Nietzsche as a guide. For Aquinas acknowledges rightly and reasonably that the work of metaphysical reflection upon the nature of reality is not reducible to a mere handmaid tradition within Christianity or a mere set of footnotes to platonic intuitions but can have a scientific or explanatory horizon on its own both before and after Christianity. He distinguishes the work of observational science from that of metaphysics and metaphysics from the science of theology, which reflects upon divine revelation. This means that one can advocate for the virtues and rights of modern observational sciences and their progress without confusing them with the aspiration to truth in metaphysics, which is itself something in turn distinct from the theological embrace of supernatural faith. The latter may surpass the capacities of philosophical reasoning but it does not substitute for it, nor can it really supplant the prerogatives of genuine philosophical inquiry. Meanwhile, on the practical side, Aquinas distinguishes the ethical intelligence of the person who seeks happiness and wisdom of life from the artistic intelligence, which works through cycles of novel creation, destruction, and re-creation in the pursuit of a sincerity of conformity between whatever art is produced and the nobility of the inner ideal of the artist. Aquinas argues that friendship is key to happiness, as is contemplation of the truth, and that both these sources of happiness persist before and after the artistic process. No nobility of individual genius in artistic creation and "metaphysical" poetic reconstitution of the real can procure the kind of happiness that supplants the basic human need for profound friendship, a topic that receives almost no treatment from Nietzsche. How are we supposed to take seriously a philosophy that simply forbids one from contemplating the strangeness and wonderment of existence and that has nothing to say about friendship? Is the embrace of such a philosophy really so courageous?

Second, we may note that the Thomist tradition that stems from Aquinas and the genealogical tradition that stems from Nietzsche (elaborated in postmodern theory) do seem to have one major trait in common. They both seek to take "pure positions" of opposed sorts in regard to the question of the primacy of metaphysics as it relates to the fate of moral theory.[97] For one tradition, a metaphysical orientation to reality underlies our basic human knowledge and ethical action. For the other tradition, many of the basic claims of the metaphysical heritage of the west are fundamentally problematic in kind, and the radical overcoming of them serves as a kind of ground-clearing to make room for distinctively post-metaphysical thought. Both traditions typically associate this metaphysical form of thought closely (but not exclusively) with the advent and development of Christian culture. In each case, the stance one takes toward the classical metaphysical tradition has profound consequences for one's conception of ethics and for one's understanding of the person of Jesus of Nazareth.

Pure positions are not always attractive. They are frequently one-sided and can deceive us by magnifying a given point artificially, reducing our view of the whole. However, the argument about whether the intellect is capable of knowing the being of reality and the structure of nature is in some respects an unavoidable one for a reflective person, and it is a very basic question that inevitably is connected to everything else. Consequently, the "illative sense" of a

97. See on this point the helpful analysis of Alasdair MacIntyre, *Three Rival Versions of Moral Enquiry.*

given thinker may gravitate more predominantly toward one of these two thinkers depending upon whether he or she believes that the aspiration to metaphysical knowledge of the classical sort is *epistemically realistic or not.* The study of Aquinas is of great help to us in charting out a metaphysical analysis of reality. Nietzsche is helpful for pointing out in consistent ways what must follow if we seek to consistently reject such knowledge. The austerity of his radicalism helps one discern clearly all that may be entailed in a rejection of the insights of classical metaphysics. Nietzsche poses serious objections to Kant's moral theory that cannot be ignored or placed in a conventional fashion at the service of Rawlsian liberalism and the contemporary expansion of identity politics based on race, gender, and sexual desires. If Nietzsche is right about human action and the will to power in interpretation, the liberal political project of Kant and Rawls is also a kind of will to truth based on illusory moralism and *ressentiment* of an alternative kind. With Nietzsche, one must always question the metaphysical *grounds* for morality, and if there are none, then the thin theoretical and practical criteria for the ethical life provided by Kant and his inheritors is a façade that will not suffice.

Finally, we may note that Nietzsche has great psychological insights into human *ressentiment,* but he does not demonstrate great interest in or understanding of the dangers of human *vengeance.*[98] Nietzsche wants to unveil to us the nobility of a pre-Christian, "pagan" ethics of violence, creativity, boldness, joy, sensuality, and life-affirmation. He deplores the "weakness" of a crucified God used to manipulate others and make the strong weak. The Christian vision is deplored as a myth generated by repressed resentment. What Nietzsche fails to observe, however, is that resentment is in fact merely a petty bourgeoisie vice. It is one that he knows a great deal about. It clearly deeply affects him personally and pervades his

---

98. See on this, René Girard, "Dionysius versus the Crucified," *Modern Language Notes* 99 (1984): 816–35; republished in *The Girard Reader,* ed. J. G. Williams (New York: Crossroad, 2004), 243–61.

invective form of writing. He wants to understand and overcome it, or at least certain versions of it.

However, as pallid and dissatisfying as petty bourgeoisie nineteenth-century Christian *ressentiment* is, it still functions imperfectly as a cultural bulwark against something much worse. Once it is removed, what arises in its wake is not something more courageous and noble but something base, held at bay by the artificially prolonged afterlife of a once Christian culture. For what was present in pre-Christian religions of sacrifice, and what Nietzsche's own writings arguably helped to unleash anew in the modern period, is something very different and far more serious than *ressentiment*: not the existential mediocrity and malaise found in the suburbs of the bourgeois but a neo-pagan human vengeance that bombs the suburbs into oblivion. What pallid Christianity prohibited was a return to the unconstrained vengeance of pre-Christian humanity. This new religiosity is tribal, spiritually and politically violent, deeply opposed to Christian *caritas*, and inherently anti-catholic, that is, anti-universal. Vengeance creates not a culture of unity in communion but a division of cultures opposed by systemic rivalry. It is indicative of man's capacity for irrational religion, insofar it is based on the heteronomy of an inevitable plurality of man-made myths and gods, tribal rivalries, violent nationalisms, and the incessant clash of political wills to power that stem from these latter. It also can thus lead to ritualized violence and cyclical bouts of blood feud.

Indeed, in a world before and after Christ, including a world that takes itself to be "anti-Christ," we should not be surprised to discover that the mere gods of men return. They may wear various titles, such as that of Dionysius or the *Übermensch*, but one thing they typically have in common is that they eventually require the re-establishment of blood sacrifice in the name of philosophically unjustifiable tribal allegiances that pretend to have imperative and absolute value. In this way, they are contrasted with the Christian notion of God that is transcendent and universal, based on the name of God as "He who is." For it is the hidden God of Israel who is the true Creator of heaven and earth. This God is not one with the world but is present to all the world as the universal communicator of existence to all. This same God, who is the author of all humanity, is also the redeemer of all, the Lord who is discovered in the particular human life of Jesus of Nazareth, the Word made flesh, whose love for the world is catholic or universal. So understood, the God of Israel is the "Alpha and the Omega," (Rev. 22:13), the author of all things who alone is from the beginning and who alone can raise the dead and bring all nations to life.

This is a different sort of eternal return, a circular activity of unfathomable divine creation and re-creation, stemming from the hidden and transcendent God who circumscribes all things. The life and creative wisdom of the God of Israel breaks into our lives in the resurrection of Christ. It gives new and unforeseen re-valuation to all old human values, even in the face of human evil and in response to it. From the Cross of God crucified and resurrected, the radiant charity of Jesus Christ now shines forever forth over all the gentile nations, that they might turn away from their antiquated lives of rivalry and violence, and turn toward him to receive from a source that is immeasurably greater and more noble. His eternal life is ever ancient in its beauty and ever new in its youthful daylight. For it is the uncreated and incomprehensible life of the Trinity that lifts human beings up and liberates them from their morbid weaknesses, so that they might themselves live vibrantly with the genuine fortitude of the saints, made strong by the truth and charity of the gospel. What the world has yet to discover, the true prophecy that our present age has yet to recognize is that the life of God is the glory of man and that the glory of God is man alive.

Bibliography

WORKS BY THOMAS AQUINAS

Collationes super Credo in Deum. Paris: Nouvelles Editions Latines, 1969.
De ente et essentia. In *Opuscula Philosophica*, vol. 1. Edited by R. Spiazzi. Turin and Rome: Marietti, 1950.
De principiis naturae. In *Sancti Thomae de Aquino opera omnia*, vol. 43. Leonine Edition. Rome: Editori de San Tommaso, 1976.
De veritate. In *Sancti Thomae de Aquino opera omnia*, vol. 22. Leonine Edition. Rome: Editori di San Tommaso, 1975–76.
Expositio super librum Boethii de Trinitate. In *Sancti Thomae de Aquino opera omnia*, vol. 50. Leonine Edition. Rome: Editori di San Tommaso, 1992.
Quaestiones disputatae de anima. In *Sancti Thomae de Aquino opera omnia*, vol. 24.1. Leonine Edition. Rome and Paris: Editions du Cerf, 1996.
Quaestio disputata de spiritualibus creaturis. In *Sancti Thomae de Aquino opera omnia*, vol. 24.2. Leonine Edition. Rome: Editori di San Tommaso, 2000.
Summa contra Gentiles. In *Sancti Thomae Aquinatis opera omnia*, vols. 13–15. Leonine Edition. Rome: R. Garroni, 1918–30.
Summa theologiae. In *Sancti Thomae Aquinatis opera omnia*, vols. 4–12. Leonine Edition. Rome: 1888–1906.
Expositio libri Boetii de ebdomadibus. In *Sancti Thomae Aquinatis opera omnia*, vol. 50. Leonine Edition. Rome: Commissio Leonina, 1992.

TRANSLATIONS OF WORKS BY THOMAS AQUINAS

Commentary on Aristotle's Metaphysics. Translated by J. P. Rowan. Notre Dame, IN: Dumb Ox Books, 1995.
Disputed Questions on Virtue. Translated by Ralph McInerny. South Bend, IN: St. Augustine's Press, 1999.
On Being and Essence. In *Medieval Philosophy: Essential Readings with Commentary.* Edited by G. Klima, with F. Allhof and A. J. Vaidya. Malden, MA: Blackwell Publishers, 2007.

On Evil. Translated by Richard Regan. Oxford: Oxford University Press, 2003.

Summa contra Gentiles I. Translated by A. C. Pegis. Garden City, NY: Doubleday, 1952.

Summa contra Gentiles II. Translated by J. Anderson. Garden City, NY: Doubleday, 1956.

Summa contra Gentiles III. Translated by V. J. Burke. Garden City, NY: Doubleday, 1956.

Summa Theologica. Translated by the English Dominican Province. New York: Benziger Brothers, 1947.

Truth. Translated by R. W. Mulligan. Chicago: Henry Regnery Company, 1952.

CONCILIAR, MAGISTERIAL, AND PAPAL WORKS

Catechism of the Catholic Church. 2nd ed. Vatican City: Libreria Editrice Vaticana, 1997.

Denzinger, Heinrich. *Compendium of Creeds, Definitions, and Declarations on Matters of Faith and Morals*. 43rd ed. Edited by P. Hünermann, edited for English by R. Fastiggi and A. E. Nash. San Francisco: Ignatius Press, 2012.

John Paul II. *Fides et ratio*. Encyclical Letter. September 14, 1998.

Vatican Council I. *Dei Filius*. Dogmatic Constitution. April 24, 1870.

Vatican Council II. *Dei Verbum*. November 18, 1965.

Vatican Council II. *Gaudium et spes*. December 7, 1965.

CLASSICAL AND MODERN WORKS

Abanes, Richard. *One Nation Under Gods: A History of the Mormon Church*. New York: Basic Books, 2003.

Aertsen, Jan A. *Medieval Philosophy and the Transcendentals: The Case of Thomas Aquinas*. Leiden: Brill, 1996.

———. *Medieval Philosophy as Transcendental Thought: From Philip the Chancellor (c.a. 1225) to Franciso Suárez*. Leiden: Brill, 2012.

Al-Azami, Muhammad Mustafa. "The Islamic View of the Quran." In *The Study Quran: A New Translation and Commentary*. Edited by S. H. Nasr. New York: Harper Collins, 2015.

Anderson, Paul N. *The Fourth Gospel and the Quest for Jesus: Modern Foundations Reconsidered*. Edinburgh: T&T Clark, 2008.

Aristotle. *The Complete Works of Aristotle*. Edited by J. Barnes. Translated by W. D. Ross. 2 vols. Princeton, NJ: Princeton University Press, 1984.

Athanasius. *Against the Arians*. In *Nicene and Post-Nicene Fathers*. Vol. 4. Edited by P. Schaff and H. Wace. Translated by J. H. Newman. New York: Christian Literature Publishing, 1892.

Augustine. *Confessions*. Translated by H. Chadwick. Oxford: Oxford University Press, 1992.

———. *The Trinity*. Edited by J. E. Rotelle. Translated by E. Hill. Hyde Park, NY: New City Press, 1991.

Ayres, Lewis. *Augustine and the Trinity*. Cambridge: Cambridge University Press, 2010.

———. *Nicaea and Its Legacy: An approach to Fourth-Century Trinitarian Theology*. Oxford: Oxford University Press, 2004.

Báñez, Domingo. *Comentarios Inéditos a la Prima Secundae de Santo Tomás*. Edited by V. B. de Heredia. Salamanca, 1948.

Barrett, C. K. *The Gospel According to St. John*. Philadelphia: Westminster Press, 1978.

Barton, John. *Amos's Oracles Against the Nations*. Cambridge: Cambridge University Press, 2009.

Bauckham, Richard. *Gospel of Glory: Major Themes in Johannine Theology*. Grand Rapids, MI: Baker Academic, 2015.

———. *Jesus and the Eyewitnesses: The Gospels as Eyewitness Testimony*. Grand Rapids, MI: Eerdmans, 2008.

———. *Jesus and the God of Israel*. Grand Rapids, MI: Eerdmans, 2008.

Beeley, C. A. and W. E. Weedman, editors. *The Bible and Early Trinitarian Theology*. Washington, DC: The Catholic University of America Press, 2018.

Bellah, Robert N. *Religion in Human Evolution: From the Paleolithic to the Axial Age*. Cambridge, MA: Belknap Harvard Press, 2011.

Benoit, Pierre. *Jesus and the Gospels*. 2 vols. Translated by B. Weatherhead. London: Herder and Darton, Longman and Todd, 1973 and 1974.

Billuart, F. C. R. *Summa Sancti Thomae*, tome III. Paris: Letouzey et Ané, 1880.

Bonino, Serge-Thomas. *Dieu, "Celui Qui Est"; De Deo ut Uno*. Paris: Parole et Silence, 2016.

Boulnois, Olivier. *Etre et Representation*. Paris: Presses Universitaires de Frances, 2015.

Bright, John. *A History of Israel*. 4th ed. Louisville, KY: Westminster John Knox, 2000.

Carnap, Rudolf. *Meaning and Necessity: A Study in Semantics and Modal Logic*. Chicago: The University of Chicago Press, 1947.

Carpenter, Amber D. *Indian Buddhist Philosophy: Metaphysics as Ethics*. London and New York: Routledge, 2014.

Chenu, Marie-Dominique. "Vérité évangélique et métaphysique wolfienne à Vatican II." *Revue des Sciences Philosophiques et Théologiques* 57 (1973): 632–40.

Chilton, Bruce D. and Craig A. Evans. *Jesus in Context: Temple, Purity, and Restoration*. Leiden: Brill, 1997.

Congar, Yves. *Je Crois en l'Esprit Saint*. Paris: Cerf, 1979.

Cottier, Georges. *Le Désir de Dieu; Sur Les Traces de Saint Thomas*. Paris: Parole et Silence, 2002.

Cox, Christoph. *Nietzsche: Naturalism and Interpretation*. Berkeley: University of California Press, 1999.

Dawkins, Richard. *The Blind Watchmaker: Why the Evidence of Evolution Reveals a Universe Without Design.* New York: W. W. Norton & Co., 1996.

De Lubac, Henri. *The Drama of Atheist Humanism.* Translated by A. Nash, E. Riley, and M. Sebanc. San Francisco: Ignatius, 1995.

De Smet, Richard. *Brahman & Person: Essays by Richard De Smet.* Edited by Ivo Coelho. Delhi: Motilal Banarsidass, 2010.

De Vaux, Roland. *The Early History of Israel.* 2 vols. Translated by D. Smith. London: Darton, Longman & Todd, 1978.

DeHaan, Daniel. "Why the Five Ways? Aquinas's Avicennian Insight into the Problem of Unity in the Aristotelian Metaphysics and *Sacra Doctrina*." *American Catholic Philosophical Association* 86 (2012): 141–58.

Dennett, Daniel C. *Darwin's Dangerous Idea: Evolution and the Meanings of Life.* New York: Simon & Schuster, 1996.

Derrida, Jacques. *Of Grammtology.* Translated by G. C. Spivak. Baltimore: The Johns Hopkins University Press, 1976.

Descartes, René. *Meditations.* In *The Philosophical Writings of Descartes.* 3 vols. Translated by J. Cottingham, R. Stoothoff, D. Murdoch, and A. Kenny. Cambridge: Cambridge University Press, 1991.

Dewan, Lawrence. "Is Truth a Transcendental for St. Thomas Aquinas?" *Nova et Vetera* (English edition) 2, no. 1 (2004): 1–19.

———. "The Existence of God: Can It Be Demonstrated?" *Nova et Vetera* (English edition) 10, no. 3 (2012): 731–56.

———. *Form and Being; Studies in Thomistic Metaphysics.* Washington DC: The Catholic University of America Press, 2006.

———. "The Number and Order of St. Thomas's Five Ways." *Downside Review* 92 (1974): 1–18.

———. "Thomas Aquinas, Creation and Two Historians." *Laval théologique et philosophique,* 50 (1994): 363–87.

———. *Wisdom, Law, and Virtue: Essays in Thomistic Ethics.* New York: Fordham University Press, 2007.

Dodd, C. H. *The Fourth Gospel.* Cambridge: Cambridge University Press, 1963.

———. *The Parables of the Kingdom.* New York: Charles Scribner's Sons, 1961.

Dunn, James D. G. *The Theology of Paul the Apostle.* Grand Rapids, MI: Eerdmans, 2006.

Eichrodt, Walther. *Theology of the Old Testament.* 2 vols. Translated by J. A. Baker. London, SCM, 1961.

Elders, Leo. "Les cinq voies et leur place dans la philosophie de saint Thomas." In *Quinque sunt viae. Actes du premier Symposium sur les cinq voies de la Somme théologique.* Edited by L. J. Elders. Città del Vaticano: Studi tomistici 9, 1980.

Emden, Christian J. *Nietzsche's Naturalism: Philosophy and the Life Sciences in the Nineteenth Century.* Cambridge: Cambridge University Press, 2014.

Fabro, Cornelius. *God in Exile; Modern Atheism; A Study of the Internal Dynamic of Modern Atheism, from Its Roots in the Cartesian* Cogito *to the Present Day.* Translated by A. Gibson. New York: Newman, 1968.

Fee, Gordon D. *Pauline Christology: An Exegetical-Theological Study.* Grand Rapids, MI: Baker Academic, 2013.

Feingold, Lawrence. *The Natural Desire to See God according to St. Thomas Aquinas and His Interpreters.* Naples, FL: Sapientia Press, 2010.

Feser, Edward. *Aquinas.* Oxford: Oneworld, 2009.

———. "Kripke, Ross, and the Immaterial Aspects of Thought." *American Catholic Philosophical Quarterly* 87, no. 1 (2013): 1–32.

Feuillet, Andre. *Christologie paulinienne et tradition biblique.* Paris: Desclée, De Brouwer, 1973.

Foucault, Michel. *The Archeology of Knowledge and A Discourse on Language.* Translated by A. M. Sheridan Smith. New York: Pantheon, 1972.

———. *The Birth of the Clinic: An Archeology of Medical Perception.* Translated by A. M. Sheridan Smith. New York: Vintage, 1973.

———. *Power/Knowledge; Selected Interviews and Other Writings 1972-1977.* Translated by C. Gordon et al. New York: Pantheon, 1980.

Freud, Sigmund. *Civilization and Its Discontents.* Translated by J. Strachey. New York: W. W. Norton, 2010.

Ganeri, Martin. *Indian Thought and Western Theism: The Vedanta of Ramanuja.* New York: Routledge, 2015.

Gardeil, Ambroise. *La crédibilité et l'apologétique.* Paris: J. Gabalda et Fils, 1928.

———. *Le donné révélé et la théologie.* 2nd ed. Paris: Cerf, 1932.

Garrigou-Lagrange, Reginald. *De Revelatione: Per Ecclesiam Catholicam Proposita.* Paris: J. Gabalda, 1921.

———. *La Synthèse Thomiste.* Paris: Desclée de Brouwer, 1946.

Garrigues, Jean-Miguel. *Le Saint-Esprit sceau de la Trinité : Le Filioque de l'originalité trinitaire de l'Esprit dans sa personne et sa mission.* Paris: Cerf, 2011.

Girard, René. "Dionysius versus the Crucified." *Modern Language Notes* 99 (1984): 816–35. Republished in *The Girard Reader.* Edited by J. G. Williams. New York: Crossroad, 2004.

Godfrey-Smith, Peter. *Other Minds: The Octopus and the Evolution of Intelligent Life.* New York: Harper Collins, 2017.

Gregory of Nazianzus. *On God and Christ: The Five Theological Orations and Two Letters to Cledonius.* Translated by Frederick Williams and Lionel Wickham. Yonkers, NY: St. Vladimir's Seminary Press, 2002.

Guilbeau, Aquinas. *Charles De Koninck's Defense of the Primacy of the Common Good* (forthcoming).

Haldane, John and Patrick Lee, "Aquinas on Human Ensoulment, Abortion and the Value of Life." *Philosophy* 78, no. 2 (2003): 255–78.

Hawking, Stephen. *A Brief History of Time.* New York: Bantam, 1998.

Heidegger, Martin. "The Onto-theo-logical Constitution of Metaphysics." In *Identity and Difference.* Translated by J. Staumbaugh. New York: Harper and Row, 1969.

———. "The Question Concerning Technology." In *The Question Concerning Technology and Other Essays*. Translated by W. Lovitt. New York: Harper & Row, 1977.

———. Hengel, Martin. *Atonement: The Origins of the Doctrine of the New Testament*. Translated by J. Bowden. Philadelphia: Fortress Press, 1981.

———. *Judaism and Hellenism: Studies in Their Encounter in Palestine During the Early Hellenistic Period*. 2 vols. Eugene, OR: Wipf and Stock Publishers, 1974.

———. *The Son of God: The Origin of Christology and the History of Jewish-Hellenistic Religion*. Translated by J. Bowden. London: SCM Press, 2012.

Hengel, Martin and Anna Maria Schwemer, *Jesus und das Judentum (Geschichte des frühen Christentums)*, Band 1. Tübingen: Mohr Siebeck, 2007.

Hick, John. *An Interpretation of Religion: Human Responses to the Transcendent*. 2nd ed. New Haven, CT: Yale University Press, 2005.

Hume, David. *A Treatise of Human Nature*. Oxford: Clarendon Press, 1975.

———. *Enquiries Concerning Human Understanding and Concerning the Principles of Morals*. Oxford: Clarendon Press, 1975.

Hurtado, Larry. *Lord Jesus Christ: Devotion to Jesus in Earliest Christianity*. Grand Rapids, MI: Eerdmans, 2005.

———. *One God One Lord: Early Christian Devotion and Ancient Jewish Monotheism*. 3rd ed. Edinburgh: T&T Clark, 2015.

Hütter, Reinhard. *Dust Bound for Heaven; Explorations in the Theology of Thomas Aquinas*. Grand Rapids, MI: Eerdmans, 2012.

International Theological Commission. *The Consciousness of Christ Concerning Himself and His Mission*. Vatican City: Libreria Editrice Vaticana, 1985.

Irenaeus, *Against Heresies*. In *Ante-Nicene Fathers*. Vol. 1. Edited by A. Roberts, J. Donaldson, and A. C. Coxe. Translated by A. Roberts and W. Rambaut. Buffalo, NY: Christian Literature Publishing Co., 1885.

Isayeva, Natalia. *Shankara and Indian Philosophy*. Albany: SUNY Press, 1993.

Israel, Jonathan. *Radical Enlightenment: Philosophy and the Making of Modernity 1650-1750*. Oxford: Oxford University Press, 2002.

Johnson, Luke Timothy. *The Real Jesus*. New York: Harper Collins, 1996.

Johnson, Mark. "Did St. Thomas Attribute a Doctrine of Creation to Aristotle?" *New Scholasticism* 63 (1989): 129–55.

Juel, Donald H. *Messianic Exegesis: Christological Interpretation of the Old Testament in Early Christianity*. Waco, TX: Baylor University Press, 2017.

Justin the Martyr. *First Apology*. In *Ante-Nicene Fathers*. Vol. 1. Translated by M. Dods and G. Reith. Buffalo, NY: Christian Literature Publishing, 1885.

Kant, Immanuel. *The Critique of Pure Reason*. Translated by N. K. Smith. London: Macmillan, 1990.

———. *Prolegomena to Any Future Metaphysics*. Translated by P. Carus. Indianapolis, IN: Bobbs-Merrill, 1950.

———. *Religion within the Boundaries of Mere Reason*. Edited by A. Wood and G. di Giovanni. Cambridge: Cambridge University Press, 1998.

Kasper, Walter. *Jesus the Christ*. Translated by V. Green. London: Burns & Oates, 1976.

Kirk, G. S. and J. E. Raven, editors and translators. *The Presocratic Philosophers*. Cambridge: Cambridge University Press, 1957.

Klima, Gyula. "Aquinas's Real Distinction and Its Role in a Causal Proof of God's Existence," *Roczniki Filozoficzne* 67, no. 4, (2019): 7–26.

Knitter, Paul. *No Other Name? A Critical Survey of Christian Attitudes toward the World Religions*. Maryknoll, NY: Orbis, 1985.

Koren, Henry. *An Introduction to the Philosophy of Animate Nature*. London: Herder, 1955.

Krauss, Lawrence M. *A Universe from Nothing: Why There Is Something Rather than Nothing*. New York: Free Press, 2012.

Kretzmann, Norman. *The Metaphysics of Theism: Aquinas's Natural Theology in Summa Contra Gentiles I*. Oxford: Clarendon Press, 1997.

Kripke, Saul. *Naming and Necessity*. Cambridge, MA: Harvard University Press, 1972.

Lagrange, Marie-Joseph. *Évangile selon saint Jean (Études bibliques)*. Paris: Gabalda, 1925.

Le Guillou, Marie-Joseph. "Surnaturel," *Revue des sciences philosophiques et théologiques* 34 (1950): 226–43.

Leftow, Brian. *God and Necessity*. Oxford: Oxford University Press, 2012.

Levering, Matthew. *Engaging the Doctrine of the Holy Spirit: Love and Gift in the Trinity and the Church*. Grand Rapids, MI: Baker Academic, 2016.

Lipner, Julius J. *Hindu Images and their Worship with Special Reference to Vaisnavism: A Philosophical-Theological Inquiry*. New York: Routledge, 2017.

Locke, John. "The Reasonableness of Christianity." In *Writings on Religion*. Edited by V. Nuovo. Oxford: Oxford University Press, 2002.

Lohfink, Gerhard. *Jesus of Nazareth: What He Wanted, Who He Was*. Translated by L. M. Maloney. Collegeville, MN: Michael Glazier, 2015.

Lonergan, Bernard. *Insight: A Study in Human Understanding*. New York: Longmans, 1957.

Long, Steven. *Analogia Entis: On the Analogy of Being, Metaphysics, and the Act of Faith*. Notre Dame, IN: University of Notre Dame Press, 2011.

MacIntyre, Alasdair C. *Three Rival Versions of Moral Enquiry: Encyclopedia, Genealogy, and Tradition*. Notre Dame, IN: University of Notre Dame Press, 1990.

Mansini, Guy. *Fundamental Theology*. Washington, DC: The Catholic University of America Press, 2017.

Mayer, Ernst. *What Evolution Is*. New York: Basic Books, 2002.

McCormack, Bruce L. *Karl Barth's Critically Realistic Dialectical Theology: Its Genesis and Development, 1909–1936*. Oxford: Clarendon Press, 1995.

McInerny, Ralph. *Praeambula Fidei: Thomism and the God of the Philosophers*. Washington, DC: The Catholic University of America Press, 2006.

Meier, John P. *A Marginal Jew: Rethinking the Historical Jesus, Volume II: Mentor, Message, and Miracles*. New Haven, CT: Yale University Press, 1994.

Moberly, R. W. L. *Old Testament Theology: Reading the Hebrew Bible as Christian Scripture.* Ada, MI: Baker Academic, 2013.

Monod, Jacques. *Chance and Necessity: An Essay on the Natural Philosophy of Modern Biology.* Translated by A. Wainhouse. New York: Vintage, 1992.

Müller, Jörn. "Duplex Beatitude: Aristotle's Legacy and Aquinas's Conception of Human Happiness." In *Aquinas and the Nicomachean Ethics.* Edited by T. Hoffmann, J. Müller, and M. Perkhams. Cambridge: Cambridge University Press, 2013

Murphy, Roland. "The Personification of Wisdom." In *Wisdom in Ancient Israel: Essays in Honor of J. A. Emerton.* Cambridge: Cambridge University Press, 1995.

Newman, John Henry. *The Arians of the Fourth Century.* 3rd ed. London: Longmans, Green and Co., 1908.

———. *An Essay in Aid of a Grammar of Assent.* Notre Dame, IN: University of Notre Dame Press, 1992.

Nietzsche, Friedrich. *The Anti-Christ, Ecce Homo, Twilight of the Idols and Other Writings.* Translated by J. Norman. Cambridge: Cambridge University Press, 2015.

———. *Beyond Good and Evil.* Translated by J. Norman. Cambridge: Cambridge University Press, 2015.

———. *Daybreak.* Translated by R. J. Hollingdale. Cambridge: Cambridge University Press, 2015.

———. *The Gay Science.* Translated by J. Nauckhoff. Cambridge: Cambridge University Press, 2015.

———. *On the Genealogy of Morals.* Translated by W. Kaufmann. New York: Vintage, 1967.

———. *The Will to Power.* Translated by W. Kaufmann and R. J. Hollingdale. New York: Vintage, 1968.

———. *Writings from the Late Notebooks.* Translated by K. Sturge. Cambridge: Cambridge University Press, 2006.

Oderberg, David S. *Real Essentialism.* London and New York: Routledge, 2007.

Oliva, Adriano. "La contemplation des philosophes selon Thomas d'Aquin," *Revue des sciences philosophiques et théologiques,* 96 (2012): 585–662.

Pascal, Blaise. *Pensées.* Translated by R. Ariew. Indianapolis: Hackett, 2004.

Pannenberg, Wolfhart. *Jesus: God and Man.* 2nd ed. Translated by L. L. Wilkins and D. A. Priebe. Philadelphia: Westminster, 1968.

Peterson, Erik. *Der Monotheismus als politisches Problem. Ein Beitrag zur Geschichte der politischen Theologie im Imperium Romanum.* Leipzig: Hegner, 1935.

Plato. *Complete Works.* Translated by D. J. Zeyl. Edited by J. M. Cooper. Indianapolis, IN: Hackett, 1997.

Politis, Vasilis. *Aristotle and the Metaphysics.* London: Routledge, 2004.

Porro, Pasquale. *Thomas Aquinas: A Historical and Philosophical Profile.* Translated by J. Trabbic and R. Nutt. Washington, DC: The Catholic University of America Press, 2016.

Preuss, Horst Dietrich. *Old Testament Theology*. 2 vols. Translated by L. G. Perdue. Louisville: Westminster John Knox Press, 1995.

Ramirez, Santiago. *Opera Omnia, Tome IX*. Salamanca: Editorial San Esteban, 1992.

Ratzinger, Joseph. *Eschatology: Death and Eternal Life*. 2nd ed. Translated by M. Waldstein. Washington, DC: The Catholic University of America Press, 1988.

——. *"Vérité du Christianisme."* In *Documentation catholique* 1 (2000): 29–35. Republished in English as "Christianity – The True Religion?" In *Truth and Tolerance: Christian Belief and World Religions*. Translated by H. Taylor. San Francisco: Ignatius, 2004.

Reynolds, Gabriel Said. *The Emergence of Islam: Classical Traditions in Contemporary Perspective*. Minneapolis: Fortress, 2012.

——. *The Qur'an and Its Biblical Subtext*. New York: Routledge, 2010.

Ross, James. "Immaterial Aspects of Thought," *Journal of Philosophy* 89 (1992): 136–50.

Sanders, E. P. *Jesus and Judaism*. Philadelphia: Fortress, 1985.

Sanford, Jonathan J. "Categories and Metaphysics: Aristotle's Science of Being." In *Categories: Historical and Systematic Essays*. Edited by M. Gorman and J. J. Sanford. Washington, DC: The Catholic University of America Press, 2004.

Scheeben, Matthias Joseph. *The Mysteries of Christianity*. Translated by C. Vollert. New York: Crossroad, 2008.

Schmidt, Jordan. "Wisdom, Cosmos, and Cultus in the Book of Sirach." PhD. Diss., The Catholic University of America, 2017.

Schnackenburg, Rudolf. *Jesus in the Gospels, A Biblical Christology*. Translated by O. C. Dean. Louisville, KY: Westminster John Knox Press, 1995.

Sherwin, Michael. *By Knowledge and by Love: Charity and Knowledge in the Moral Theology of St. Thomas Aquinas*. Washington, DC: The Catholic University of America Press, 2005.

Siderits, Mark and Shoryu Katsura. *Nagarjuna's Middle Way: Mulamadhyamaka-karika*. Somerville, MA: Wisdom Publications, 2013.

Söhngen, Gottlieb. "The Analogy of Faith: Likeness to God from Faith Alone?" Translated by K. Oakes. *Pro Ecclesia* 21, no. 1 (2012): 56–76.

——. "The Analogy of Faith: Unity in the Science of Faith." Translated by K. Oakes. *Pro Ecclesia* 21, no. 2 (2012): 169–94.

Stump, Eleonore. *Aquinas*. London: Routledge, 2003.

——. *Wandering in Darkness: Narrative and the Problem of Suffering*. Oxford: Oxford University Press, 2012.

Tanner, Norman P., ed. *Decrees of the Ecumenical Councils*. London and Washington, DC: Sheed and Ward and Georgetown University Press, 1990.

Te Velde, Rudi. *Aquinas on God*. Aldershot: Ashgate, 2006.

Mother Teresa. *Come Be My Light: The Private Writings of the Saint of Calcutta*. New York: Image Books, 2009.

Thapar, Romila. *The Penguin History of Early India: From the Origins to AD 1300.* New York: Penguin, 2015.

Thompson, Walter J. "Perspectivism: Aquinas and Nietzsche on Intellect and Will." *American Catholic Philosophical Quarterly* 68, no. 4 (1995): 451–73.

Turner, Denys. *Faith, Reason and the Existence of God.* Cambridge: Cambridge University Press, 2004.

Van Steenberghen, Fernand. *La philosophie au XIIIe siècle.* 2nd ed. Leuven: Peeters Publishers, 1991.

Vanhoye, Albert. *La lettre aux Hébreux. Jésus-Christ, médiateur d'une nouvelle alliance.* Paris: Declée, 2002.

Walberg, Mats. *Revelation as Testimony: A Philosophical-Theological Study.* Grand Rapids, MI: Eerdmans, 2014.

Wallace, William A. *The Modeling of Nature: Philosophy of Science and Philosophy of Nature in Synthesis.* Washington, DC: The Catholic University of America Press, 1996.

White, Thomas Joseph. "The *analogia fidei* in Catholic Theology." *International Journal of Systematic Theology* 22, no. 4 (2020): 512–37.

———. "Dyotheletism and the Instrumental Human Consciousness of Jesus." *Pro Ecclesia* 17, no. 4 (2008): 396–422.

———. "Imperfect Happiness and the Final End of Man: Thomas Aquinas and the Paradigm of Nature-Grace Orthodoxy." *The Thomist* 78, no. 2 (2014): 247–89.

———. *The Incarnate Lord: A Thomistic Study in Christology.* Washington, DC: The Catholic University of America Press, 2015.

———. "The Right to Religious Freedom: Thomistic Principles of Nature and Grace." *Nova et Vetera* (English edition) 13, no. 4 (2015): 1149–84.

———. *Wisdom in the Face of Modernity: A Study in Thomistic Natural Theology.* 2nd ed. Naples, FL: Sapientia Press, 2016.

Williams, Rowan. *Arius, Heresy and Tradition.* London: Darton, Longman and Todd, 1987.

Wippel, John. *Metaphysical Themes in Thomas Aquinas II.* Washington, DC: The Catholic University of America Press, 2007.

———. *The Metaphysical Thought of Thomas Aquinas: From Finite Being to Uncreated Being.* Washington, DC: The Catholic University of America Press, 2000.

Witherington III, Ben. *The Christology of Jesus.* Minneapolis: Augsburg Fortress Press, 1990.

———. *The Many Faces of Jesus: The Christologies of the New Testament and Beyond.* New York: Crossroad, 1995.

Wright, N. T. *The Climax of the Covenant: Christ and the Law in Pauline Theology.* Minneapolis: Fortress, 1993.

———. *Jesus and the Victory of God.* Minneapolis: Fortress, 1997.

———. *The Resurrection of the Son of God.* Minneapolis: Fortress, 2003.

Person Index

Abanes, Richard, 90n116
Aertsen, Jan A., 45n42, 75n98, 298n2, 300n7, 302, 323n77
Allison, Dale C., 200n31
Ambrose of Milan, 241n107–8, 253n135, 282
Anderson, Paul N., 210n57
Anselm, 78
Anthony of Egypt, 282
Aristotle, 20, 22n7, 23n8, 46n44, 47, 48n47, 50, 52n56–57, 55n60, 56, 67n83, 112n13, 129–30, 131n33, 137n37, 150, 156, 175, 196n27, 233n91, 268, 284, 299, 301n9, 302, 313, 326
Arius, 240–41
Athanasius, 224n80, 233, 236n95, 237n96, 243–46
Augustine, 64n75, 70n88–89, 185n3, 230n85, 233, 237n96, 239n100, 251–55, 258
Averroes, 268,
Avicenna, 298n3
Ayres, Lewis, 241n105, 243n109, 247n116, 248n119, 251n129

Báñez, Domingo, 278n26
Barber, Patrick, 211n60
Barrett, C.K., 207n49, 215n67
Barth, Karl, 317
Barton, John, 192n15
Basil the Great, 222n75, 247, 249n122–23, 250n126
Basilides, 231

Bauckham, Richard, 90n115, 193n20, 210n57, 218n69
Bautain, Louis-Eugène, 43n40
Bellah, Robert N., 15n1
Benedict of Norcia, 282
Benedict XII, 265n3
Benoit, Pierre, 200n31
Bernard of Clairvaux, 282
Billuart, F.C., 278n26
Bonaventure, 78
Bonino, Serge-Thomas, 105n2, 108n8, 120n21, 124n26, 132n34
Bright, John, 90n115

Cajetan, Thomas de Vio, 278n26
Carnap, Rudolf, 129n31
Carpenter, Amber D, 30n11, 31n12
Carraud, Vincent, 52n55
Catherine of Siena, 282, 285
Chadwick, Henry, 70n88
Chenu, Marie-Dominique, 52n56
Chilton, Bruce D., 209n52
Clement of Alexandria, 237n96
Collins, Steven, 30n11
Comte, Auguste, 308
Congar, Yves, 215n67
Copernicus, 64
Cory, Therese S., 146n4
Cox, Christoph, 306n27

Daniélou, Jean, 239n101
Dawkins, Richard, 20n6
de Lubac, Henri, 176n77, 280n28

Subject Index